Implicit Bias and Philosophy

Volume 1: Metaphysics and Epistemology

Implicit Bias and Philosophy

VOLUME 1

Metaphysics and Epistemology

EDITED BY
Michael Brownstein
and Jennifer Saul

OXFORD
UNIVERSITY PRESS

Great Clarendon Street, Oxford, OX2 6DP,
United Kingdom

Oxford University Press is a department of the University of Oxford.
It furthers the University's objective of excellence in research, scholarship,
and education by publishing worldwide. Oxford is a registered trade mark of
Oxford University Press in the UK and in certain other countries

First Edition published in 2016
Impression: 1

Published in the United States of America by Oxford University Press
198 Madison Avenue, New York, NY 10016, United States of America

British Library Cataloguing in Publication Data
Data available

Library of Congress Control Number: 2015947707

ISBN (Vol I) 978–0–19–871324–1
ISBN (Vol II) 978–0–19–876617–9
ISBN (Set) 978–0–19–876618–6

Printed in Great Britain by
Clays Ltd, St Ives plc

Contents

Contributors   vii
Contents of Volume 2   ix

Introduction   1
Michael Brownstein and Jennifer Saul

Part 1. The Nature of Implicit Attitudes, Implicit Bias, and Stereotype Threat

1.1 Playing Double: Implicit Bias, Dual Levels, and Self-Control   23
    Keith Frankish

1.2 Implicit Bias, Reinforcement Learning, and Scaffolded
    Moral Cognition   47
    Bryce Huebner

1.3 The Heterogeneity of Implicit Bias   80
    Jules Holroyd and Joseph Sweetman

1.4 De-Freuding Implicit Attitudes   104
    Edouard Machery

1.5 Stereotype Threat and Persons   130
    Ron Mallon

Part 2. Skepticism, Social Knowledge, and Rationality

2.1 Bias: Friend or Foe? Reflections on Saulish Skepticism   157
    Louise M. Antony

2.2 Virtue, Social Knowledge, and Implicit Bias   191
    Alex Madva

2.3 Stereotype Threat, Epistemic Injustice, and Rationality   216
    Stacey Goguen

2.4 The Status Quo Fallacy: Implicit Bias and Fallacies of
    Argumentation   238
    Catherine E. Hundleby

2.5 Revisiting Current Causes of Women's Underrepresentation
     in Science   265
     Carole J. Lee

2.6 Philosophers Explicitly Associate Philosophy with Maleness:
     An Examination of Implicit and Explicit Gender Stereotypes
     in Philosophy   283
     Laura Di Bella, Eleanor Miles, and Jennifer Saul

Index of Names   309
Index of Subjects   313

Contributors

LOUISE M. ANTONY, University of Massachusetts, Amherst

MICHAEL BROWNSTEIN, John Jay College of Criminal Justice/CUNY

LAURA DI BELLA, University of Sheffield

KEITH FRANKISH, The Open University

STACEY GOGUEN, Boston University

JULES HOLROYD, University of Sheffield

BRYCE HUEBNER, Georgetown University

CATHERINE E. HUNDLEBY, University of Windsor

CAROLE J. LEE, University of Washington

EDOUARD MACHERY, University of Pittsburgh

ALEX MADVA, California State Polytechnic University, Pomona

RON MALLON, Washington University, St Louis

ELEANOR MILES, University of Sussex

JENNIFER SAUL, University of Sheffield

JOSEPH SWEETMAN, University of Exeter

Contents of Volume 2

Introduction
Michael Brownstein and Jennifer Saul

Part 1. Moral Responsibility for Implicit Bias

1.1 Who's Responsible for This? Moral Responsibility,
   Externalism, and Knowledge about Implicit Bias
   Natalia Washington and Daniel Kelly

1.2 Alienation and Responsibility
   Joshua Glasgow

1.3 Attributability, Accountability, and Implicit Bias
   Robin Zheng

1.4 Stereotypes and Prejudices: Whose Responsibility?
   Indirect Personal Responsibility for Implicit Biases
   Maureen Sie and Nicole van Voorst Vader-Bours

1.5 Revisionism and Moral Responsibility for Implicit Attitudes
   Luc Faucher

Part 2. Structural Injustice

2.1 The Too Minimal Political, Moral, and Civic Dimension
   of Claude Steele's "Stereotype Threat" Paradigm
   Lawrence Blum

2.2 Reducing Racial Bias: Attitudinal and Institutional Change
   Anne Jacobson

Part 3. The Ethics of Implicit Bias: Theory and Practice

3.1 A Virtue Ethics Response to Implicit Bias
   Clea F. Rees

3.2 Context and the Ethics of Implicit Bias
   Michael Brownstein

3.3 The Moral Status of Micro-Inequities: In Favor of Institutional
     Solutions
     Samantha Brennan

3.4 Discrimination Law, Equality Law, and Implicit Bias
     Katya Hosking and Roseanne Russell

Index of Names
Index of Subjects

Introduction

Michael Brownstein and Jennifer Saul

Persistent inequalities between social groups are a blight on modern, liberal democracies, which pride themselves on the idea of justice and fairness for all. For example, women earned 80 cents on the dollar compared to men in 2009 in the United States,[1] and in 2011 held just 16.8% of seats in the House of Representatives.[2] Also in 2009 in the United States, 22.7% of blacks and 22.7% of Hispanics fell below the poverty line, compared with 9.3% of whites,[3] and black children seen in emergency rooms between 2006 and 2009 were less likely to receive pain medication for abdominal pain and more likely to stay in the ER for longer than 6 hours compared with white children for whom the same tests were ordered.[4] Many factors play a role in sustaining these inequalities: historical legacies, cultural stereotypes, residential and occupational segregation, non-neutral laws and policies (such as sentencing disparities between crack and powder cocaine), and, of course, explicit prejudice. But until recently, most people who hold conscious, strong, and genuine egalitarian beliefs have not considered *themselves* to be part of the problem. Recent psychological research has made it clear that they are likely to be very wrong.

What is clear is that most people possess what are called "implicit biases" concerning members of social groups.[5] "Implicit bias" is a term of art referring to evaluations of social groups that are largely outside of conscious awareness or control. These evaluations are typically thought to involve associations between

---

[1] United States Bureau of Labor Statistics. <http://www.bls.gov/opub/ted/2011/ted_20110216.htm>.

[2] United Nations Development Program Gender Inequality Index. <http://hdr.undp.org/en/media/HDR_2011_EN_Table4.pdf>.

[3] United States Census Bureau. <http://www.census.gov/compendia/statab/cats/income_expenditures_poverty_wealth/poverty.html>.

[4] Johnson et al. (2012).

[5] The term "implicit bias" is sometimes used for all unconscious associations, but here we will be focused on the subset of these that target members of social groups.

social groups and concepts or roles such as "violent," "lazy," "nurturing," "assert-ive," "scientist," and so on.[6] Such associations result at least in part from common stereotypes found in contemporary liberal societies about members of these groups. Substantial empirical support has developed for the claim that most people, often in spite of their conscious beliefs, values, and attitudes, have implicit biases and that those biases impact social behavior in many unsettling ways. For example, implicit racial biases are thought to cause a majority of people to give more favorable evaluations of otherwise identical resumés if those resumés belong to applicants with stereotypically white names (e.g. Emily, Greg) than if they belong to applicants with stereotypically black names (e.g. Jamal, Lakisha).[7] Even more ominously, participants in "shooter bias" tasks are more likely to shoot an unarmed black man in a computer simulation than an unarmed white man, and are more likely to fail to shoot an armed white man than an armed black man.[8] There are *thousands* of related studies uncovering the pervasiveness of implicit biases against blacks, women, gay people, and other members of socially stigmatized groups. Further-more, tests of implicit biases—such as sequential priming (Fazio et al., 1995) and the Implicit Association Test (IAT; Greenwald et al., 1998)—may predict biased behaviors, in some cases perhaps even *better* than traditional self-report measures.[9] Perhaps most surprisingly, implicit biases are commonly found both in members of the groups "targeted" by the biases and in those who devote their lives to fighting prejudice.

The existence and pervasiveness of implicit biases raise a number of meta-physical, epistemological, and ethical questions. For example, what is the struc-ture of implicit biases, and how do they fit into the architecture of the mind? Are implicit biases belief-like mental states? Are they mental states at all? Epistemo-logical questions about implicit biases are no less pressing. Is the pervasiveness of implicit biases cause for skepticism about social and/or scientific knowledge? What role does implicit bias play in group decision-making and communities of inquiry (including the philosophical community)? Finally, implicit biases raise both theoretical and practical ethical questions. Are individuals morally respon-sible for their implicit biases and/or the effects of these biases on their behaviour? Can we develop a framework that accommodates both psychological and socio-logical perspectives on prejudice and how to combat it? What remedies for discrimination can be justified in light of implicit bias research?

---

[6] Exactly what implicit biases are, as well as whether they are truly outside of conscious awareness and/or control, is a key topic for Volume 1, so these characterizations are necessarily rough. See the discussion in Section 1.

[7] Bertrand and Mullainathan (2003).

[8] Correll et al. (2002). See also Payne (2001) and Payne et al. (2002).

[9] See Nosek et al. (2007) and Greenwald et al. (2009). See Oswald et al. (2013) for critique and Greenwald et al. (forthcoming) for reply.

Alongside these questions stands the persistence of inequality within the discipline of philosophy itself. In the United States, women currently represent 16.6% of full-time philosophy faculty (Norlock, 2011). Even more strikingly, of the approximately 11,000 members of the American Philosophical Association, fewer than 125 are black, and fewer than thirty are black women (Gines, 2011). There are many plausible hypotheses for the gender and racial gaps in philosophy. But given what we know about other fields, it seems likely that implicit bias significantly contributes to the underrepresentation of women and non-white students and faculty in philosophy.[10] If correct, this notion raises the stakes for coming to an adequate understanding of implicit bias, not only for the sake of fairness to those individuals from underrepresented groups who might become philosophers in the future, but also for the sake of the discipline itself, the health of which requires contributions from individuals with diverse experiences, views, and values.

At the University of Sheffield during 2011 and 2012, a leading group of philosophers, psychologists, and others gathered to explore these questions. The two volumes of *Implicit Bias and Philosophy* emerge from these workshops. This first volume is comprised of two parts: "The Nature of Implicit Attitudes, Implicit Bias, and Stereotype Threat," and "Skepticism, Social Knowledge, and Rationality." In what follows, we first offer a brief introduction to research on implicit biases—in particular, their measurement and conceptualization by researchers in psychology. We then outline the focus of each section of this volume and describe its chapters in more detail, several of which propose addenda to or revisions of the conceptualizations offered by psychologists.

1 Implicit Attitudes

Philosophers and psychologists alike have known for a long time that people often have thoughts and feelings that they do not report verbally, and of which they may be unaware.[11] What is profoundly new, therefore, is not the discovery of "hidden prejudices" per se, but rather the ability to measure them scientifically. Advancements in measurement techniques have shown implicit biases to affect many kinds of behavior—even the behavior of those who intend to be unprejudiced, to be pervasive across populations, and to have many damaging consequences. The measurement of implicit biases is part of a broader development in research psychology focusing on "implicit cognition." The central constructs of

---

[10] See Chapter 2.6 of this volume (Saul, Miles, and Di Bella).

[11] This section ("Implicit Attitudes"), and the footnotes included therein, are adapted from Brownstein (2015) and Brownstein (forthcoming).

this field are "implicit attitudes," which can target consumer products, self-esteem, food, alcohol, political values, and—as these volumes attest—members of social groups in virtue of their social group membership.[12]

The most well known and influential "indirect" measure of attitudes is the Implicit Association Test (IAT; Greenwald et al., 1998). The IAT is indirect in the sense that it measures people's attitudes without having to ask them directly, "what do you think about φ?"[13] In a standard IAT, the subject attempts to sort words or pictures into categories as fast as possible while making as few errors as possible. A person taking the most well known IAT—the black–white IAT—will be presented with variations of the four images shown here.

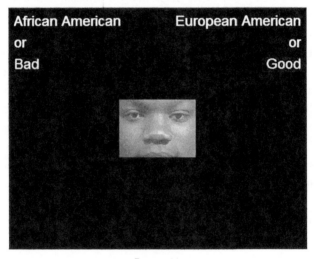

Image 1

---

[12] On implicit attitudes and consumer products, see Maison et al. (2004) and Perkins and Forehand (2012); on self-esteem, see Greenwald and Farnham (2000) and Zeigler-Hill and Jordan (2010); on food, see Friese et al. (2008) and Mai et al. (2011); on alcohol, see De Houwer et al. (2004) and Houben and Wiers (2008); and on implicit attitudes and political parties and values, see Galdi et al. (2008) and Nosek et al. (2010).

[13] We follow De Houwer et al.'s (2009) recommendation to use the terms "direct" and "indirect" to describe characteristics of measurement techniques and "implicit" and "explicit" to describe characteristics of the psychological constructs assessed by those techniques. "Direct" and "indirect" can also refer to different kinds of explicit measures, however. For example, a survey that asks "what do you think of black people" is explicit and direct, while one that asks "what do you think about Darnel" is explicit and indirect (because the judgment is explicit but the content of what is being judged (i.e., attitudes toward race) is inferred). Note also that the distinction between direct and indirect measures is relative rather than absolute. Even in some direct measures, such as personality inventories, subjects may not be completely aware of what is being studied. Finally, it is important to note that in indirect tests subjects *may* be aware of what is being measured. Indirect tests do not presuppose the introspective availability of one's attitudes; this is different from saying that those attitudes are introspectively unavailable (Payne and Gawronski, 2010).

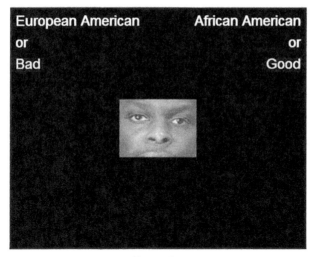

Image 2

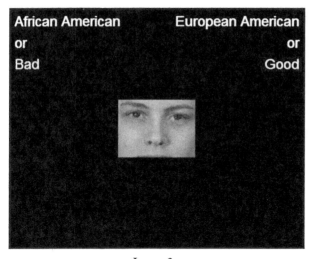

Image 3

The goal is to sort the pictures to the left or right. The correct response would be (in order from Image 1 to Image 4) left, right, right, left. Notice that the categories on the left and right pair a social group label with a positive or negative word. In Images 1 and 3, the pairing is "compatible" with widespread negative attitudes toward black people, while in Images 2 and 4 the pairing is "incompatible." Most white subjects (over 70%) will be faster and make fewer mistakes on compatible than on incompatible trials (Nosek et al., 2007).

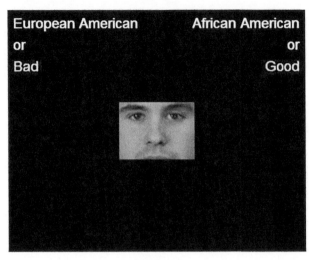

Image 4

Researchers consider this to represent an "implicit preference" for white faces over black faces. Remarkably, while roughly 40% of black participants demonstrate an implicit in-group preference for black faces over white faces, and 20% show no preference, roughly 40% of black participants demonstrate an implicit out-group preference for white faces over black faces (Nosek et al., 2002; Ashburn-Nardo et al., 2003; Dasgupta, 2004). This finding has upended the view that in-group favoritism is the primary driver of implicit bias. Rather, it appears that implicit bias is driven by a combination of in-group favoritism and sensitivity to the value society places on particular groups.

Although the IAT remains the most popular indirect measure of attitudes, it is far from the only one. Other prominent indirect measures, many of which are derivations of sequential priming, are semantic priming (Banaji and Hardin, 1996) and the Affect Misattribution Procedure (AMP; Payne et al., 2005). Also, a "second generation" of categorization-based measures has been developed in order to improve psychometric validity. For example, the Go/No-go Association Task (GNAT; Nosek and Banaji, 2001) presents subjects with one target object rather than two in order to determine whether preferences or aversions are primarily responsible for scores on the standard IAT (e.g. on a measure of racial attitudes whether one has an implicit preference for whites or an implicit aversion to blacks; Brewer, 1999). Multinomial (or formal process) models have also been developed in order to identify distinct processes contributing to performance on indirect measures. For example, elderly people tend to show greater bias on the standard race IAT compared with younger people, but this may be due to their having stronger implicit preferences for whites or having weaker control over their biased responding (Nosek et al., 2011). Multinomial models, such as the Quadruple Process Model (Conrey et al., 2005), are used to tease apart these possibilities.

While the emphasis in the empirical literature has been more on the measurement of implicit attitudes than on theorizing, researchers have also offered accounts of what implicit attitudes are. There are two questions here. First, what is an attitude? In psychology, attitudes are understood as likings or dislikings, or, more formally, as associations between a concept and an evaluation (Nosek and Banaji, 2009). This conceptualization of attitudes is importantly different from the typical usage in philosophy, which is much more expansive (including beliefs, desires, intentions, and so on).

Second, what makes an attitude implicit? We have defined implicit biases as largely outside of conscious awareness and control. This definition stems from the twin roots of research on implicit social cognition.[14] One stream of early research, spearheaded by Russ Fazio and colleagues, identified implicitness with automaticity. Fazio's work was influenced by the cognitive psychology of the 1970s, which distinguished between "controlled" and "automatic" information processing in memory (e.g. Shiffrin and Schneider, 1977). What Fazio showed was that attitudes can also be understood as activated by controlled or automatic processes. The "sequential priming" technique (Fazio et al., 1995) measures social attitudes by timing people's reactions (or "response latencies") to stereotypic words (e.g. "lazy" or "nurturing") after exposing them to social group labels (e.g. "black," "women," and so on). Most people are significantly faster to identify a word like "lazy" in a word-scramble after being exposed to the word "black" (compared with "white"). A faster reaction of this kind is thought to indicate a relatively automatic association between "lazy" and "black."

A second stream of research, spearheaded by Anthony Greenwald and Mahzarin Banaji, identified implicitness with unconsciousness. This stream of research interprets scores on questionnaire-style measures to represent the attitudes people know they have, while scores on indirect measures are thought to represent the introspectively unidentified "traces" of past experiences on one's feelings, thought, and behavior. This research was influenced by theories of implicit memory, which was understood generally as the influence of past

---

[14] Cogent histories of these twin roots are found in Dasgupta (2004), Payne and Gawronski (2010), and Amodio and Devine (2009). Another important precursor to contemporary research on implicit bias is Modern Racism Theory (McConahay et al., 1981; McConahay, 1982), which argues that "old fashioned" explicit racism has been channeled into more socially acceptable beliefs about public policy, such as affirmative action and desegregation programs.

experience on later behavior without conscious memory of the past experience (e.g. Jacoby and Dallas, 1981; Schacter, 1987). One can see the role of theories of implicit memory in Greenwald and Banaji's (1995) seminal definition of implicit attitudes as "introspectively unidentified (or inaccurately identified) traces of past experience that mediate favorable or unfavorable feeling, thought, or action toward social objects" (8). Here the emphasis is not on automaticity but on the introspective unavailability of implicit attitudes, or alternatively, the introspective unavailability of the past experiences that formed those attitudes.

These twin roots of the field have developed into more formal models of implicit attitudes, some of which can be understood as responses to findings that implicit attitudes *are* in some cases malleable and *do* sometimes emerge into consciousness.[15] *Single-process* models deny that implicit and explicit attitudes represent distinct kinds of mental states. For example, according to MODE (Motivation and Opportunity as Determinants; Fazio, 1990; Fazio and Towles-Schwen, 1999; Olson and Fazio, 2009) and the related MCM (Meta-Cognitive Model; Petty, 2006; Petty et al., 2007), attitudes are associations between objects and "evaluative knowledge" of those objects. MODE posits one singular representation underlying the behavioral effects measured by direct and indirect tests. The difference between direct and indirect measures, then, reflects a difference in the control that subjects have over the measured behavior. Control is understood in terms of motivation and opportunity to deliberate. When an agent has low motivation or opportunity to engage in deliberative thought, her automatic attitudes will guide her behavior and judgment. Indirect measures manufacture this situation (of low control due to low motivation and/or opportunity to deliberate).

Dual-process models, such as RIM (Reflective–Impulsive Model; Strack and Deutsch, 2004) and APE (Associative–Propositional Evaluation; Gawronski and Bodenhausen, 2006, 2011), define implicit and explicit attitudes in terms of distinct operating principles. The central distinction at the heart of both RIM and APE is between "associative" and "propositional" processes. Associative processes are said to underlie an impulsive system that functions according to classic associative principles of similarity and contiguity. Indirect measures are thought of as assessing the momentary accessibility of elements or nodes of a network of associations. Propositional processes, on the other hand, underlie a reflective system that represents the world in propositional format and assigns

---

[15] For a review of research on the malleability of implicit attitudes, see Dasgupta (2013). For awareness of implicit attitudes, see Gawronski et al. (2006) and Hahn and Gawronski (2014). See also Brownstein (2015, forthcoming) for discussion.

truth values to these representations. The reflective system is guided by agents' judgments of logical consistency, which are represented by scores on direct measures of attitudes. RIM and APE are similar, utilizing the same core distinction between associative and propositional processes. APE has been used in particular to explain the different conditions in which implicit and explicit attitudes change, as well as the interactions between and mutual influences of associative and propositional processes in judgment and behavior.

An alternative to both single- and dual-process models of implicit attitudes draws upon neuroscience. David Amodio and colleagues, for example, identify three distinct mechanisms underlying implicit social cognition in their Memory Systems Model (MSM; Amodio and Ratner, 2011). These mechanisms correspond to semantic memory, fear conditioning, and instrumental learning. Each is identified with a distinct neural region (the left PFC and temporal lobe for semantic memory, the amygdala for fear conditioning, and the basal ganglia for instrumental learning) as well as a distinct psychological construct (semantic memory = cognition, fear conditioning = affect, instrumental learning = behavior). While these mechanisms typically work in concert, MSM treats them as distinct constructs, the status or manipulation of which predicts distinct behaviors.

2 Part 1: The Nature of Implicit Attitudes, Implicit Bias, and Stereotype Threat

The first part of Volume 1 explores the ontology of implicit bias and stereotype threat. Stereotype threat occurs when members of a group that is stereotyped as poor at some particular activity are in a stereotype threat-provoking environment. That is, the stereotype is salient in a high-stakes situation, and they care about doing well. This can lead to both situational avoidance and reduced performance.[16] The exact mechanisms involved in stereotype threat are a matter of debate (see Chapters 1.5 and 2.3 in this volume, and Chapter 2.1 in Volume 2). Victims of stereotype threat are sometimes consciously thinking about their group membership and/or are aware of feeling anxious, but sometimes they are not. The stereotypes themselves involved in stereotype threat are usually widespread in the culture. However, victims of stereotype threat vary in the extent to which they implicitly hold the relevant stereotype, and those who hold implicit stereotypes more strongly tend to be less susceptible to the effects of interventions.[17]

---

[16] See e.g. Steele and Aronson (1995, 2002).   [17] Kiefer and Sekaquaptewa (2007).

Keith Frankish (Chapter 1.1) and Bryce Huebner (Chapter 1.2) both investigate the nature of the mechanisms involved in generating (and of combating) implicit biases. Frankish explores the potential of dual-process theories to make sense of these, while Huebner argues that we must incorporate a wider set of cognitive frameworks. Jules Holroyd and Joe Sweetman (Chapter 1.3) argue that it is a mistake to seek any sort of a unified understanding of implicit biases due to their heterogeneity. Edouard Machery's skepticism (Chapter 1.4) is equally strong but differently directed: he argues that implicit biases should not be understood as mental states. Finally, Ron Mallon (Chapter 1.5) argues for a revisionary understanding of stereotype threat as involving a rational response to problematic social circumstances. Each of these chapters is fairly revisionary, pointing to the need for further theorizing about the architecture of implicit social cognition and the processes underlying phenomena such as stereotype threat.

Dual-process theories claim that the mind is comprised of two streams for information-processing—one that is fast, automatic, nonconscious, associative, and equipped with a slow-learning memory system responsive to experience and social conditioning (Type 1 processes), and the other that is slow, controlled, conscious, and rule-governed, and whose memory system is capable of one-shot learning in response to explicit tuition (Type 2 processes). In Chapter 1.1, Frankish argues against a "strong" form of dual-process theory, according to which each system is unified, independent, and characterized by a long list of exclusive features. Instead he suggests that there are two broad types of cognitive processing, but that these are not wholly independent. On the basis of this more modest framework, he argues that implicit biases represent biased Type 1 judgments. He then considers the conditions under which unbiased Type 2 judgments can override biased Type 1 responses. For this to happen, "metacognitive motivation" is required: the agent must have a Type 1 desire to engage in, and act on, relevant Type 2 reasoning, and this desire must outweigh the bias itself. Failure to suppress biased implicit attitudes, Frankish concludes, is often due to the weakness of this implicit metacognitive desire. This conclusion has important consequences for the ethics of implicit bias (the topic of Volume 2).

Huebner (Chapter 1.2) rejects the notion that implicit biases are implemented exclusively by associative mechanisms. Instead, he develops a computational account of how associative and inferential systems collectively guide behavior in cases where implicit biases are at work. He argues for a tri-partite model of action-generation, involving the parallel operation of (1) Pavlovian systems that reflexively trigger approach/avoidance behavior, (2) associative "model-free" systems that assign values to actions on the basis of previous outcomes, and (3) "model-based" inferential systems that represent potential outcomes of future actions and assign values to action–outcome pairs. Huebner explains how the parallel operation of these action-generation systems is involved in the production and maintenance of implicit bias. Finally, he uses his framework to explain why some strategies for intervening on implicit biases are more likely than others to be successful. Drawing upon "Spinozoan" ethics, Huebner calls for simultaneous self-regulation of our reflexive reactions as well as activism aimed at reshaping the local environments to which our attitudes are attuned.

In Chapter 1.3, Holroyd and Sweetman consider whether "implicit bias" refers to a unified range of phenomena. Drawing upon a wide range of recent data, Holroyd and Sweetman argue that there are different kinds of implicit associations with importantly different characteristics. They consider and reject David Amodio and colleagues' view that there are essentially two kinds of implicit association: implicit semantic associations and implicit affective (or evaluative) associations. They argue instead that the heterogeneity of implicit bias is better expressed in terms of differences in content and behavioural predictions between different implicit associations, failures of correlation across implicit measures of attitudes (e.g. the IAT and "affective priming"), and variations in the relationship between implicit associations and explicit beliefs. Like Frankish and Huebner, Holroyd and Sweetman conclude by making specific normative recommendations on the basis of their metaphysical claims.

In Chapter 1.4, Machery proposes perhaps the most radical metaphysical claim in this volume. He argues that implicit attitudes are not unconscious and automatic mental states, and that this is because they are not mental states at all. Rather, he claims, implicit attitudes are traits—viz. multitrack dispositions to behave and cognize in particular ways. This characterization provides the best explanation of several puzzling properties of implicit attitudes, on Machery's view, including weak to null correlations between indirect measures of attitudes (as discussed by Holroyd and Sweetman in Chapter 1.3), large variation in the strength of one's measured implicit attitudes across contexts, and the low pre-dictive validity of measured implicit attitudes. Machery concludes by responding to six possible objections to his revisionist view.

In Chapter 1.5, Mallon argues that behaviors affected by stereotype threat should be understood as intentional, strategic responses to social circumstances. His view stands in opposition to more typical analyses that model such responses as resulting from hypervigilance triggered by automatic, Type 1, "subpersonal" processes. Although he does not seek to completely displace subpersonal processes in the explanation of stereotype threat, his broad aim is to make space for a non-alienating explanation of stereotype threat, i.e. an explanation that does not treat stereotype threat as something that completely bypasses our capacities as believing, desiring, and intending agents. On Mallon's view, we can make sense of stereotype threat in terms of our intuitive grasp of what rational actors do in socially threatening situations.

3 Part 2: Skepticism, Social Knowledge, and Rationality

The chapters in the second part of Volume 1 focus on a variety of epistemological questions related to implicit bias and stereotype threat. Some authors have recently argued for what might be considered tragic consequences of implicit bias: Jennifer Saul (2013) has argued that they give rise to a new and urgently worrying form of skepticism, and Tamar Gendler (2011) has argued that they give rise to a tragic dilemma which forces us to choose between being rational and being virtuous. Louise Antony (Chapter 2.1) and Alex Madva (Chapter 2.2) take more optimistic views. Antony suggests that we use naturalized methods to better understand the ways that we can turn biases to our epistemic benefit in order to find a way out of "Saulish skepticism." Madva argues that Gendler's claims of a tragic dilemma are wrong by showing us a way that we can be both virtuous and rational. Stacey Goguen's contribution (Chapter 2.3), on the other hand, can be seen as pointing out an underexplored tragic epistemic consequence of stereotype threat: epistemic injustice. Catherine Hundleby's and Carole Lee's contributions (Chapters 2.4 and 2.5) are explorations of ways that implicit bias can affect our scientific and ordinary reasoning endeavors. Hundleby focuses on status quo bias, suggesting that methods from argumentation theory can help us to both understand and combat this. Lee undertakes a detailed examination of recent research purporting to show a lack of gender bias in STEM subjects across various measures, pointing out alternative interpretations of the data. Finally, Jennifer Saul, Eleanor Miles, and Laura Di Bella (Chapter 2.6) explore ways that explicit and implicit bias may affect philosophy as a profession.

Saul (2013) argues that the demonstrated intrusion of implicit bias into our reasoning gives rise to a particularly pernicious form of skepticism. In Chapter 2.1, Antony describes two ways that this skepticism is different from, and worse than, traditional forms of skepticism (e.g. evil demon skepticism). First, "Saulish skepticism" is practical rather than speculative. It does not merely threaten the justification of some of our judgments; rather, it gives us positive grounds for believing that some of our judgments are unjustified. Second, Saulish skepticism threatens our normative conception of epistemic agency. If we cannot trust ourselves to (for example) evaluate the validity of an inference, how are we to govern our own epistemic lives? One possible response to Saulish skepticism is to aim to eliminate as much potentially biasing information as possible from decision situations where bias might be operating. But this is bad counsel, Antony argues, because it ignores the positive and essential role that biases play in epistemic life. The challenge of Saulish skepticism, then, is for us to see how to integrate a normative conception of *epistemic agency* (according to which we ought to deliberate strictly on the basis of evidential relevance) with a *naturalized* conception of ourselves (according to which we need epistemic shortcuts and tricks). Antony concludes with constructive suggestions for doing this.

Madva (Chapter 2.2) also seeks to defuse an apparent dilemma deriving from the pervasiveness of implicit bias. In recent work, Gendler (2011) and Egan (2011) have described an apparent tragic dilemma: because simply knowing what the prevalent stereotypes are seems to lead individuals to act in prejudiced ways, agents must choose between their normative aims to act in unprejudiced ways and their epistemic aims to know about statistical regularities, base rates, and so on. Madva argues, however, that we are not actually faced with a "tragic dilemma" between our normative and epistemic commitments. He argues that the obstacle to virtue is not knowledge of stereotypes as such, but rather the "accessibility" of such knowledge to the agent who has it. "Accessibility" refers to how easily knowledge comes to mind. Social agents can acquire the requisite knowledge of stereotypes, Madva argues, while resisting their pernicious influence, so long as that knowledge remains, in relevant contexts, relatively inaccessible.

In Chapter 2.3, Goguen argues that stereotype threat has significant consequences for epistemic aspects of our lives—consequences which have been underemphasized by both psychologists and philosophers. Goguen focuses on tracing out one such consequence: self-doubt. She argues that self-doubt can undermine epistemic self-trust, often by challenging a person's faith in their own rationality or humanity. The result is that stereotype threat can lead to a particular kind of epistemic injustice in that it can cause a person to question their own status as a rational and reliable knower, due to unfair and stigmatizing stereotypes about them. This effect is important because it helps flesh out two important claims—one made within stereotype threat research, and one within epistemic injustice scholarship. The first claim is that stereotype threat has a much wider range of effects than those on which researchers and scholars usually focus. The second claim is that epistemic injustice not only damages one's ability to produce and access knowledge, but also damages and distorts one's sense of oneself. Goguen's takeaway message is that stereotype threat has a much broader and deeper reach than we normally give it credit for.

In Chapter 2.4, Hundleby turns the focus to a less well recognized aspect of bias: "status quo bias," which motivates evaluations of people and social groups consistent with current social hierarchies. Status quo bias also affects the operations of scientific endeavors, as Hundleby shows through an analysis of androcentrism, understood as the treatment of men, males, or masculinity as a norm or standard for evaluation. She then considers the "fallacies" approach to combating status quo bias as a potential remedy. Using the current "presumptive inference scheme" account of fallacies developed by Walton (1995), Hundleby demonstrates the promise of the fallacies approach for addressing androcentrism and analogous forms of status quo presumptions in contemporary scientific endeavors and in ordinary reasoning.

In Chapter 2.5, Lee considers methodological issues in the study of implicit bias in higher education. She takes on a large correlational sociological study—Ceci and Williams (2011)—which suggests that gender bias is not found in publication, grant awarding, and hiring outcomes in STEM fields. Lee identifies two alternative interpretations of Ceci and Williams' data that are each consistent with the presence of implicit gender bias in these fields. First, sociological studies like Ceci and Williams' cannot rule out the possibility that the quality of application materials confounds findings about the putatively null effects of ongoing implicit gender bias in review/application outcomes; and second, the underrepresentation of women in manuscript submission, grant proposals, and job applications creates a sampling bias. Lee then argues that data emerging from experimental psychology—which demonstrates the existence of clear gender biases in STEM fields—ought to be given heavier evidential weighting than these large correlational studies. Lee concludes by identifying moderator variables present in STEM fields that may have contributed to Ceci and Williams' null results. The upshot of Lee's conclusion is that continued funding for resource-intensive gender-equity efforts—like the National Science Foundation's ADVANCE program—is crucial.

Finally, in Chapter 2.6, Di Bella, Miles, and Saul's paper constitutes the first-ever exploration of philosophers' explicit and implicit stereotypes and associations regarding gender and philosophy. They find that both male and female philosophers *explicitly* associate philosophers with maleness. Male philosophers also *implicitly* associate philosophy with maleness; but female philosophers *implicitly* associate philosophy with femaleness, to an increasing degree as they continue on in the subject. This collection of results has important implications for combating the underrepresentation of women in philosophy. First, the implicit association with maleness could well give rise to implicit bias against women in philosophy on the part of *male* philosophers, suggesting that measures such as anonymity will be important to put in place. (The importance of such measures is not undermined but is enhanced by the possibility that female philosophers implicitly associate philosophy with femaleness.) Second, the pattern of explicit and implicit biases found in women suggests that action to counteract stereotype threat is likely to be important and effective. Women in mathematics who explicitly associate mathematics with maleness but implicitly associate it with femaleness are the most susceptible to stereotype threat-reducing interventions.[18]

The chapters in this volume offer a mixture of challenges to existing approaches and promising ways forward in the metaphysics and epistemology of implicit attitudes. They have consequences for both psychological and philosophical models of the mind. And their import is far-reaching, extending beyond these areas to everyday and scientific reasoning, to our self-understanding, and to the efficacy of real-world interventions to combat prejudice and discrimination. Each chapter also represents a unique and productive exchange between the empirical sciences and philosophy. Our hope for this volume is therefore not only to show that understanding implicit bias is crucial for scholars working in philosophy of mind, philosophy of psychology, philosophy of science, and epistemology, but also to provide an example for how naturalistic philosophy can make progress in the years to come.

Acknowledgements

Michael Brownstein and Jennifer Saul are extremely grateful for each contribution to these volumes and to the valuable feedback provided by anonymous reviewers for Oxford University Press. Many thanks also to the OUP team: Peter Momtchiloff, Eleanor Collins, Manikandan Chandrasekaran, R.A. Marriot, and Hayley Buckley. We are also grateful to Keliy-Anderson Staley for providing the cover images, to Raymond Drainville for designing the covers, and to Lacey Davidson and Isabel Gois for creating the indexes. The Implicit Bias and Philosophy workshops at the University of Sheffield, from which these volumes emerged, would not have been possible without the generous support of the Leverhulme Trust and the expert organization of Angela Pepper. We would like to thank all the participants at these conferences for the fantastic discussions. Finally, we cannot thank our families enough. All our thanks to

---

[18] Kiefer and Sekaquaptewa (2007).

Reine Hewitt, Leda, Iggy, and Minerva Brownstein, and Raymond Drainville and Theo Drainville-Saul.

References

Amodio, D. and P. Devine (2009). "On the interpersonal functions of implicit stereotyping and evaluative race bias: Insights from social neuroscience." In Petty, R., Fazio, R. H., and Briñol, P. (eds.), *Attitudes: Insights from the New Implicit Measures*. New York, NY: Psychology Press: 193–226.

Amodio, D. and Ratner, K. (2011). "A memory systems model of implicit social cognition." *Current Directions in Psychological Science* 20(3): 143–8.

Ashburn-Nardo, L., Knowles, M. L., and Monteith, M. J. (2003). "Black Americans' implicit racial associations and their implications for intergroup judgment." *Social Cognition* 21(1): 61–87.

Banaji, M. R. and Hardin, C. (1996). "Automatic stereotyping." *Psychological Science* 7(3): 136–41.

Bertrand, M. and Mullainathan, S. (2003). "Are Emily and Greg more employable than Lakisha and Jamal? A field experiment on labor market discrimination." National Bureau of Economic Research, Working Paper No. 9873.

Brewer, M. (1999). "The psychology of prejudice: Ingroup love and outgroup hate?," *Journal of Social Issues* 55(3): 429–44.

Brownstein, M. (2015). "Implicit bias." *Stanford Encyclopedia of Philosophy*, Zalta, E. (ed.). <http:plato.stanford.edu/entries/implicit-bias/>.

Brownstein, M. (forthcoming). "Implicit bias and race." *Routledge Companion to the Philosophy of Race*.

Ceci, S. and Williams, W. (2011). "Understanding current causes of women's under-representation in science." *Proceedings of the National Academy of Sciences* 108: 3157–62.

Conrey, F., Sherman, J., Gawronski, B., Hugenberg, K., and Groom, C. (2005). "Separating multiple processes in implicit social cognition: The quad-model of implicit task performance." *Journal of Personality and Social Psychology* 89: 469–87.

Correll, J., Park, B., Judd, C. M., and Wittenbrink, B. (2002). "The police officer's dilemma: Using race to disambiguate potentially threatening individuals." *Journal of Personality and Social Psychology* 83: 1314–29.

Dasgupta, N. (2004). "Implicit ingroup favoritism, outgroup favoritism, and their behavioral manifestations." *Social Justice Research* 17(2): 143–68.

Dasgupta, N. (2013). "Implicit attitudes and beliefs adapt to situations: A decade of research on the malleability of implicit prejudice, stereotypes, and the self-concept." *Advances in Experimental Social Psychology* 47: 233–79.

De Houwer, J., Crombez, G., Koster, E., and Beul, N. (2004). "Implicit alcohol-related cognitions in a clinical sample of heavy drinkers." *Journal of Behavior Therapy and Experimental Psychiatry* 35(4): 275–86.

De Houwer, J., Teige-Mocigemba, S., Spruyt, A., and Moors, A. (2009). "Implicit measures: A normative analysis and review." *Psychological Bulletin* 135(3): 347.

Egan, A. (2011). "Comments on Gendler's 'The epistemic costs of implicit bias'." *Philosophical Studies* 156: 65–79.

Fazio, R. H. (1990). "Multiple processes by which attitudes guide behavior: The MODE model as an integrative framework." *Advances in Experimental Social Psychology* 23: 75–109.

Fazio, R. H., Jackson, J. R., Dunton, B. C., and Williams, C. J. (1995). "Variability in automatic activation as an unobtrusive measure of racial attitudes: A bona fide pipeline?" *Journal of Personality and Social Psychology* 69: 1013–27.

Fazio, R. H. and Towles-Schwen, T. (1999). "The MODE model of attitude-behavior processes." In Chaiken, S. and Trope, Y. (eds.), *Dual-Process Theories in Social Psychology*. New York, NY: Guilford Press: 97–116.

Friese, M., Hofmann, W., and Wänke M. (2008). "When impulses take over: Moderated predictive validity of explicit and implicit attitude measures in predicting food choice and consumption behavior." *British Journal of Social Psychology* 47(3): 397–419.

Galdi, S., Arcuri, L., and Gawronski, B. (2008). "Automatic mental associations predict future choices of undecided decision-makers." *Science* 321(5892): 1100–2.

Gawronski, B. and Bodenhausen G. (2006). "Associative and propositional processes in evaluation: an integrative review of implicit and explicit attitude change." *Psychological Bulletin* 132(5): 692–731.

Gawronski, B. and Bodenhausen G. (2011). "The associative–propositional evaluation model: Theory, evidence, and open questions." *Advances in Experimental Social Psychology* 44: 59–127.

Gawronski, B., Hofmann, W., and Wilbur, G. (2006). "Are "implicit attitudes unconscious?" *Consciousness and Cognition* 15: 485–99.

Gendler, T. S. (2011). "On the epistemic costs of implicit bias." *Philosophical Studies* 156: 33–63.

Gines, K. (2011). "Being a Black woman philosopher: Reflections on founding the collegium of Black women philosophers." *Hypatia* 26(2): 429–37.

Greenwald, A. G. and Banaji, M. R. (1995). "Implicit social cognition: attitudes, self-esteem, and stereotypes." *Psychological Review* 102(1): 4.

Greenwald, A. G., Banaji, M. R., and Nosek, B. (2015). "Statistically small effects of the Implicit Association Test can have societally large effects." *Journal of Personality and Social Psychology* 108(4): 553–61.

Greenwald, A. G. and Farnham, S. (2000). "Using the implicit association test to measure self-esteem and self-concept." *Journal of Personality and Social Psychology* 79(6): 1022–38.

Greenwald, A. G., McGhee, D. E., and Schwartz, J. L. K. (1998). "Measuring individual differences in implicit cognition: The implicit association test." *Journal of Personality and Social Psychology* 74: 1464–80.

Greenwald, A. G., Poehlman, T. A., Uhlmann, E. L., and Banaji, M. R. (2009). "Understanding and using the Implicit Association Test: III. Meta-analysis of predictive validity." *Journal of Personality and Social Psychology* 97:1: 17–41.

Hahn, A. and Gawronski, B. (2014). "Do implicit evaluations reflect unconscious attitudes? *Behavioral and Brain Sciences* 37(1): 28–9.

Houben, K. and Wiers, R. (2008). "Implicitly positive about alcohol? Implicit positive associations predict drinking behavior." *Addictive Behaviors* 33(8): 979–86.

Jacoby, L. and Dallas, M. (1981). "On the relationship between autobiographical memory and perceptual learning." *Journal of Experimental Psychology: General* 110(3): 306.

Johnson, T., Weaver, M., Borrero, S., Davis, E., Myaskovsky, L., Zuckerbraun, N., and Kraemer, K. (2012). "Racial and ethnic disparities in the management of pediatric abdominal pain." Public talk at the Pediatric Academic Society, Boston, Massachusetts.

Kiefer, A. K. and Sekaquaptewa, D. (2007). "Implicit stereotypes and women's math performance: How implicit gender–math stereotypes influence women's susceptibility to stereotype threat." *Journal of Experimental Social Psychology* 43: 825–32. doi:10.1016/j.jesp.2006.08.004.

Mai, R., Hoffmann, S., Helmert, J., Velichkovsky, B., Zahn, S., Jaros, D., and Rohm H. (2011). "Implicit food associations as obstacles to healthy nutrition: The need for further research." *The British Journal of Diabetes and Vascular Disease* 11(4): 182–6.

Maison, D., Greenwald, A., and Bruin, R. (2004). "Predictive validity of the Implicit Association Test in studies of brands, consumer attitudes, and behavior." *Journal of Consumer Psychology* 14(4): 405–15.

McConahay, J. (1982). "Self-interest versus racial attitudes as correlates of anti-busing attitudes in Louisville: Is it the buses or the Blacks?" *The Journal of Politics* 44(3): 692–720.

McConahay, J., Hardee, B., and Batts, V. (1981). "Has racism declined in America? It depends on who is asking and what is asked." *Journal of Conflict Resolution* 25(4): 563–79.

Norlock, K. (2011). "2011 update to 'Women in the Profession: A Report to the CSW'." <http://www.apaonlinecsw.org/workshops-and-summer-institutes>.

Nosek, B. A. and Banaji, M. R. (2001). "The go/no-go association task." *Social Cognition*, 19(6): 625–66.

Nosek, B. A. and Banaji, M. R. (2009). "Implicit attitude." In *The Oxford Companion to Consciousness*. Oxford: Oxford University Press: 84–5.

Nosek, B. A., Banaji, M. R., and Greenwald, A. G. (2002). "Harvesting intergroup implicit attitudes and beliefs from a demonstration website." *Group Dynamics* 6: 101–15.

Nosek, B. A., Graham, J., and Hawkins, C. (2010). "Implicit political cognition." In Gawronski B. and Payne B. (eds.), *Handbook of Implicit Social Cognition: Measurement, Theory, and Applications*. New York, NY: Guilford Press: 548–64.

Nosek, B. A., Greenwald, A. G., and Banaji, M. R. (2007). "The Implicit Association Test at age 7: A methodological and conceptual review." In Bargh, J. A. (ed.), *Automatic Processes in Social Thinking and Behavior*. Philadelphia, PA: Psychology Press.

Nosek, B. A., Hawkins, C., and Frazier, R. (2011). "Implicit social cognition: From measures to mechanisms." *Trends in Cognitive Sciences* 15(4): 152–9.

Olson, M. and Fazio R. H. (2009). "Implicit and explicit measures of attitudes: The perspective of the MODE model." In Petty, R. E., Fazio, R. H., and Briñol, P. (eds.), *Attitudes: Insights from the New Implicit Measures*. New York, NY: Psychology Press: 19–63.

Oswald, F. L., Mitchell, G., Blanton, H., Jaccard, J., and Tetlock, P. E. (2013). "Predicting ethnic and racial discrimination: A meta-analysis of IAT criterion studies." *Journal of Personality and Social Psychology* 105(2): 171–92. doi: 10.1037/a0032734.

Payne, B., Cheng, C. M., Govorun, O., and Stewart, B. (2005). "An inkblot for attitudes: Affect misattribution as implicit measurement." *Journal of Personality and Social Psychology* 89: 277–93.

Payne, B. and Gawronski, B. (2010). "A history of implicit social cognition: Where is it coming from? Where is it now? Where is it going?" In Gawronski, B. and Payne, B. (eds.), *Handbook of Implicit Social Cognition: Measurement, Theory, and Applications.* New York, NY: Guilford Press: 1–17.

Payne, B. K. (2001). "Prejudice and perception: The role of automatic and controlled processes in misperceiving a weapon." *Journal of Personality and Social Psychology* 81: 181–92.

Payne, B. K., Lambert, A. J., and Jacoby, L. L. (2002). "Best laid plans: Effects of goals on accessibility bias and cognitive control in race-based misperceptions of weapons." *Journal of Experimental Social Psychology* 38: 384–96.

Perkins, A. and Forehand, M. (2012). "Implicit self-referencing: The effect of nonvolitional self-association on brand and product attitude." *Journal of Consumer Research* 39(1): 142–56.

Petty, R. (2006). "A metacognitive model of attitudes." *Journal of Consumer Research* 33(1): 22–4.

Petty, R., Briñol, P., and DeMarree, K. (2007). "The meta-cognitive model (MCM) of attitudes: Implications for attitude measurement, change, and strength." *Social Cognition* 25(5): 657–86.

Saul, J. (2013). "Skepticism and implicit bias." *Disputatio* 5(37): 243–63.

Schacter, D. (1987). "Implicit memory: History and current status." *Journal of Experimental Psychology: Learning, Memory, and Cognition* 13: 501–18.

Shiffrin, R. and Schneider, W. (1977). "Controlled and automatic human information processing: Perceptual learning, automatic attending, and a general theory." *Psychological Review* 84: 127–90.

Steele, C. M. and Aronson, J. (1995). "Stereotype threat and the intellectual test performance of African-Americans." *Journal of Personality and Social Psychology* 69: 797–811.

Steele, J., James, J. B., and Barnett, R. (2002). "Learning in a man's world: Examining the perceptions of undergraduate women in male-dominated academic areas." *Psychology of Women Quarterly* 26: 46–50.

Strack, F. and Deutsch, R. (2004). "Reflective and impulsive determinants of social behaviour." *Personality and Social Psychology Review* 8: 220–47.

Walton, D. (1995). *A Pragmatic Approach to Fallacies.* Toronto: University of Toronto Press.

Zeigler-Hill, V. and Jordan, C. (2010). "Two faces of self-esteem." In Gawronski, B. and Payne, B. (eds.), *Handbook of Implicit Social Cognition: Measurement, Theory, and Applications.* New York, NY: Guilford Press: 392–407.

PART 1

The Nature of Implicit Attitudes, Implicit Bias, and Stereotype Threat

1.1

Playing Double
Implicit Bias, Dual Levels, and Self-Control

Keith Frankish

Implicit bias is sometimes thought of as a surprising discovery, uncovered by recent experimental work in social psychology. It is true that much important experimental work has been done recently, but there is a wider context to discussions about implicit bias, involving ideas about the duality of the human mind that have been around for a long time. The idea that some mental processes operate outside consciousness is—I shall argue—part of our everyday (or 'folk') conception of the mind, and implicit bias can be seen as involving a familiar phenomenon which I shall call 'playing double'. This chapter summarizes this context and draws on it to sketch a theoretical framework for thinking about implicit bias and how we can control it.

The chapter is in three parts. The first looks at implicit bias in everyday life. It begins by introducing an example of implicit bias and discussing how it contrasts with explicit bias. It then locates implicit bias within a pattern of everyday talk about implicit mentality and argues that systematic implicit bias is best thought of as manifesting a form of belief. The second part looks at the dissonance characteristic of many cases of implicit bias—cases where a person's implicit beliefs appear to conflict with their explicit ones. It asks whether such conflict is real, setting out a sceptical worry about the very existence of explicit belief, and goes on to sketch an account of explicit belief as a form of commitment. The upshot is a layered picture of the human mind, with a passive implicit level supporting an active explicit one, and this 'dual-level' view is fleshed out and compared briefly with other theories of mental duality. The third part of the chapter turns to the question of how we can overcome implicit bias. We tend to identify with our explicit mental states and processes and want them to control our behaviour. But how is such self-control possible? If we are systematically biased, how can we even form unbiased beliefs? And if we can, then how can we make them effective? The dual-level view has implications for these questions, assigning a crucial role to metacognitive mental states of certain kinds. This section discusses these issues and outlines the conditions for explicit control. The chapter concludes by identifying some predictions of the proposed account.

1 Implicit Bias

1.1 Implicit bias in real life

In the current context, a biased person is one who is disposed to judge others according to a stereotyped conception of their social group (ethnic, gender, class, and so on), rather than by their individual talents. Such a disposition displays bias since it involves a deviation from norms of fairness.[1] A person is *implicitly* biased if their behaviour manifests a stereotyped conception of this kind, even if they do not explicitly endorse the conception and perhaps explicitly reject it. The possibility of such implicit bias is a matter of ethical concern, since it means that bias may persist in an unacknowledged, 'underground' form, even when it has been explicitly repudiated.

There is now a large body of evidence for the existence of forms of implicit bias in various experimental settings (see the Introduction to this volume for references).[2] But the broad concern, I take it, is that implicit bias may affect our behaviour and judgements across a range of everyday situations, much as explicit bias might do. Eric Schwitzgebel gives a fictional example of such implicit bias. Juliet is a white American philosophy professor. She knows there is no scientific evidence for racial differences in intelligence, and she argues with sincerity for equality of intelligence—a view which also harmonizes with her liberal outlook on other matters. Yet Juliet's unreflective behaviour and judgements of individuals display systematic racial bias:

When she gazes out on class the first day of each term, she can't help but think that some students look brighter than others—and to her, the black students never look bright. When a black student makes an insightful comment or submits an excellent essay, she

---

[1] I take fairness to be a norm of rationality as well as a social norm. Some writers would not use the term 'bias' for deviations from merely social norms.

[2] It is still unclear what the experimental data tell us about bias in everyday life. There are many different measures of implicit attitudes, which do not correlate well with each other and may be measuring different things (for example, Bosson et al., 2000; Olson and Fazio, 2003). Moreover, recent meta-analyses suggest that the best-known measure of implicit bias, the Implicit Association Test (IAT), is a poor predictor of real-world ethnic and racial discrimination (Oswald et al., 2013, 2015).

feels more surprise than she would were a white or Asian student to do so, even though her black students make insightful comments and submit excellent essays at the same rate as do the others. This bias affects her grading and the way she guides class discussion.

(Schwitzgebel, 2010: 532)

Juliet's spontaneous interactions with non-students display a similar systematic bias. Schwitzgebel notes that there need be no self-deception involved in this. Juliet might be aware that she possesses this bias, and she might even take steps to counteract it, perhaps by trying to be especially generous in her assessment of black students—though, as Schwitzgebel observes, such condescension could itself be seen as indirectly manifesting the bias. Although this is a fictional example, it is, in my experience, one that people find readily comprehensible and recognizable, and the experimental data are worrying precisely because they suggest that cases like it may be common in real life.

Can we be more precise about what makes Juliet's bias implicit, and about how implicit bias contrasts with the explicit sort? We might say that Juliet's bias is nonconscious, or unconscious, whereas explicit bias is conscious. This needs qualifying, however. There are different things we might mean by 'conscious', and there are senses in which Juliet's racial bias *is* conscious. First, as noted, Juliet may be aware of its existence and may consciously think *that* she is racially prejudiced, though without consciously endorsing the prejudice. It might be better to say that Juliet's bias—or, rather, the mental state underpinning it—is not introspectable: she cannot report straight off that she possesses it, as she can report her explicit views, and she becomes aware of it only through observing, or being informed of, its effects on her behaviour. (Even this may be too strong, however; there is evidence that some aspects of implicit attitudes like Juliet's are introspectable; see, for example, Gawronski et al., 2006; Hahn et al., 2014). Second, though Juliet's bias is evident primarily in behaviour that is not consciously controlled (unreflective behaviour, as I shall call it), it may also reveal itself in behaviour that is consciously controlled (reflective behaviour).[3] It affects her conscious judgements, decisions, and feelings, and Juliet may consciously perform actions that display it—for example, consciously disciplining herself to do her grading. That is, implicitly biased actions may be consciously intended, although they are not consciously intended *to be biased*.

This suggests a better characterization of the way in which Juliet's bias is nonconscious: she does not endorse it in her conscious reasoning and decision making. Although Juliet may be conscious of behaving and judging as if there are

---

[3] I assume here that there is such a thing as reflective behaviour. I will defend this claim later in the chapter.

racial differences in intelligence, she does not consciously think *that* there are racial differences in intelligence. If that thought occurs to her, she rejects it. This is compatible with her having some introspective awareness of her bias, provided she does not endorse it. By contrast, explicit bias would be bias that *is* endorsed in conscious deliberation. Thus, whereas implicit bias affects both unreflective behaviour and (some) reflective behaviour, explicit bias manifests itself only in reflective behaviour.

1.2 Implicit bias as belief-based

The claim that we have implicit mental states runs against a philosophical tradition, often associated with Descartes, that the mind is completely transparent to itself. However, this tradition is not the only one. There is also a long history of theoretical speculation about nonconscious processes (see Frankish and Evans, 2009), and there is a firm commonsense basis to the notion of nonconscious mentality. It is obvious that much of our behaviour is controlled without conscious thought. Think of driving a car, playing sports, or conducting a casual conversation. When all is going well, the actions involved are spontaneous and unreflective. Indeed, giving thought to them tends to break the flow and harm performance. This unreflective mode is our default one, and nonconscious processes take care of the bulk of our behaviour.[4]

Yet this unreflective behaviour is intelligent, in the sense of being responsive to our beliefs and desires, and we would naturally explain it in belief-desire terms. For example, we would explain the way a driver manipulates the controls of their car by reference to their desires to follow a certain route and to obey the traffic laws, together with their beliefs about the workings of the controls, the rules of road, the behaviour of other road users, and so on. And we would expect their behaviour to change if these beliefs and desires changed. That is, unreflective behaviour (or much of it, at any rate) appears to be the product of practical reasoning, rationally responsive to the agent's beliefs and desires. From this perspective, the mental state underpinning Juliet's bias looks like a belief. As Schwitzgebel's description makes clear, the state affects her behaviour in a systematic way, prompting different behaviours in different contexts. Thus, we may suppose that if Juliet wanted to impress a visitor with the quality of discussion in her class, then she would avoid calling on black students to speak, but if she wanted to allow weaker students a chance to shine, then she would give

---

[4] Even Descartes allowed that much of our behaviour is the product of nonconscious processes, including such activities as walking and singing 'when these occur without the mind attending to them', though he did not regard these processes as mental (Descartes, 1642/1984: 161).

black students preference. A simple association between black people and low intelligence would not affect her behaviour in this way, interacting rationally with her desires and background beliefs. If Juliet behaves like this, then, it seems, she does not merely *associate* black people with lower intelligence; she *believes* that black people have lower intelligence. The biasing state is not a rogue influence which distorts her nonconscious practical reasoning but a standard input to that reasoning.[5]

It is true that not all Juliet's behaviour fits this pattern. Some of her *reflective* behaviour (in particular, what she says) manifests a different and contradictory belief. We might think that this undermines the belief attribution and conclude that there is no clear answer as to what Juliet believes (this is the moral Schwitzgebel, 2010, draws). However, there is another, and I think, more attractive, option. There are numerous dualities in folk psychology, which point to the existence of two distinct forms of belief: an implicit form, which guides thought and behaviour without being consciously recalled, and an explicit form, which requires conscious recall and affects reflective behaviour only (Frankish, 2004). I shall say more about this shortly, but, given this possibility, the conflicting evidence need not undermine the attribution of the biased belief. For the belief may be an implicit one, and the conflicting evidence, which comes from Juliet's reflective behaviour, may indicate the existence of a distinct explicit one.[6]

It may be objected that the state underpinning Juliet's bias is different from the implicit beliefs and desires manifested in unreflective behaviour. For those mental states are *available* to consciousness. If a driver were to give conscious thought to what they are doing, they would draw on the same beliefs and desires that guided their unreflective behaviour. And the biasing mental state is not available to consciousness in this way. When Juliet consciously reflects on the merits of different students, she does not take it as a premise that black people are less intelligent than white people. But this in itself does not make implicit bias special. Much of the knowledge that guides our unreflective behaviour is also unavailable to consciousness. A driver might find it impossible to articulate much of the knowledge that guides their unreflective driving—about the rules of the road, the precise route they need to take, the functions of the controls, and so on.

---

[5] The remarks here concern everyday implicit bias like that displayed by Juliet, but there is abundant evidence that implicitly biased responses exhibited under experimental conditions are also belief-based and can be modified by argument, evidence, and logical considerations; see Mandelbaum (2015).

[6] For present purposes I assume that implicit propositional attitudes are internal representational states that play a causal role in reasoning and decision making. The overall account could, however, be modified to accommodate other views, such as dispositional ones.

This is typical of unreflective behaviour. As William James noted, our inter-actions with the world are shaped by a wealth of background knowledge that we cannot articulate (using 'knowledge' in the loose sense for a body of beliefs). James cites routines such as dressing and opening cupboards: 'Our lower centres know the order of these movements, and show their knowledge by their 'surprise' if the objects are altered so as to oblige the movement to be made in a different way. But our higher thought-centres know hardly anything about the matter' (James, 1890: vol. 1, 115). Nor, I would add, is it plausible to think that all such background knowledge was consciously acquired in the first place. Much of it is simply picked up during our routine interactions with the world. The mental states that produce implicit bias, I suggest, are of a piece with such background knowledge.

1.3 Beliefs versus attitudes

In characterizing implicit biases as grounded in beliefs, I am departing from the usual practice, which treats them as manifesting *attitudes*, in the social psycho-logical sense, and I shall pause briefly to consider how the two characterizations differ. An attitude is an overall evaluation of something—a person, group, object, issue, and so on. Attitudes have a valence (positive or negative) and an intensity, and they are usually described as having cognitive, emotional, and behavioural aspects or components. Experimental work on attitude measurement suggests that we have two types of attitude: explicit attitudes, which are introspectable, and implicit attitudes, which are not (for surveys, see, for example, Crano and Prislin, 2008; Nosek et al., 2011). It is this work that has stimulated recent philosophical interest in implicit bias, which is usually seen as manifesting a negative implicit attitude towards a group.

Attitudes in this sense are thus different from *propositional* attitudes, such as beliefs and desires, which are directed to propositions and have a single dimen-sion (cognitive, volitional, and so on). The question of the relation between beliefs and attitudes is a complex one and turns on the precise conceptions of these states that are employed—for example, on whether attitudes are internal mental states or character traits (for the latter view, see Chapter 1.4 (Machery)). Here I shall confine myself to two general points that bear on my current strategy.

First, from a commonsense perspective at least, attitudes have beliefs as components (or as components of their bases): one's overall attitude to some-thing is determined in part by one's beliefs about it (Webber, 2013). If we take this view, then the belief account of implicit bias and the attitude account are compatible, with the former focusing on the cognitive component of the com-pound state that the latter focuses on. If, on the other hand, we employ a technical notion of attitude on which attitudes do not have beliefs as components—say, one on which they are associative states of some kind—then it is doubtful that implicit biases are attitudes, for the reasons discussed in the previous subsection. Associations do not guide practical reasoning in the way that Juliet's bias does. Of course, it may be that not all implicit biases have the profile that Juliet's has, and we may need a pluralistic picture of the phenomenon to account for this.[7] But if we want to allow that *some* implicit biases are like Juliet's, then a belief account should be part of that picture.[8]

Second, the belief account of implicit bias will not be crucial to the account of self-control to be developed later in the chapter. Responding to skepticism about conscious self-control, I shall sketch a dual-level account of the mind on which conscious thought processes can, in the right circumstances, override implicit biases. This account will not depend on the belief account of implicit bias (though it will assume that there are implicit propositional attitudes), and it may be adopted by those who treat implicit bias as arising from non-propositional attitudes.

2 Dual Levels

2.1 Playing double

I have argued that at least some implicit biases are the effect of implicit beliefs. However, the cases of implicit belief discussed so far did not display the dissonance that often goes with implicit bias. It is not just that Juliet does not explicitly believe that there are racial differences in intelligence, but that she explicitly believes that there are no such differences. This sort of conflict is present in many cases of implicit bias, and I shall consider it now.

There are in fact many mundane cases where a person's conscious beliefs seem to conflict with the beliefs that guide their unreflective behaviour. Consider absentmindedness (the following example is borrowed from Schwitzgebel, 2010). Ben has been informed that a local bridge is closed and realizes he will need to take a different route to work. However, over the following days he repeatedly fails to adjust his travel plans, though he recalls the closure immediately on arriving at the bridge. Somehow, Ben's newly acquired conscious belief remains inert, and the nonconscious processes that guide his driving behaviour

---

[7] On the 'heterogeneity' of implicit bias, see Holroyd and Sweetman (this volume).

[8] For other belief-based accounts of implicit attitudes, see De Houwer (forthcoming); Hughes et al. (2011); Mandelbaum (2015); Mitchell et al. (2009). For critical discussion, see Gendler (2008a, 2008b); Levy (2014); Madva (ms).

continue to rely on outdated information. Cases of akrasia can (perhaps surprisingly) be seen as manifesting a similar conflict. One forms the conscious intention to perform (or to refrain from) some action, but the intention remains inert and one's behaviour manifests a different intention, which has not been consciously adopted.

Of course, the dissonance in absentmindedness and akrasia is only temporary, whereas implicit bias like Juliet's is persistent. But there are everyday precedents for this too. We often accept a proposition yet fail to take it to heart and act upon it. Again, Schwitzgebel gives an example. Kaipeng is convinced by, and fully accepts, Stoic arguments for the view that death is not an evil, yet his actions and reactions are much the same as those of people who think the opposite (he fears death, regrets others' deaths, and so on). Another example comes from Mark Twain's *Huckleberry Finn*. Huck accepts the norms of his slave-owning society and believes it is wicked of him to help the escaped slave Jim. He tries to pray to change his ways, but in vain:

[T]he words wouldn't come. Why wouldn't they? It warn't no use to try and hide it from Him. Nor from *me*, neither. I knowed very well why they wouldn't come. It was because my heart warn't right; it was because I warn't square; it was because I was playing double. I was letting *on* to give up sin, but away inside of me I was holding on to the biggest one of all. I was trying to make my mouth *say* I would do the right thing and the clean thing, and go and write to that nigger's owner and tell where he was; but deep down in me I knowed it was a lie—and He knowed it. You can't pray a lie—I found that out. (Twain, 1885: 270)[9]

Although we would not say that Huck is implicitly *biased* (at least not if we think of bias as involving a deviation from rationality), this description of 'playing double' has strong similarities to Juliet's case. In both cases there is a conflict between the principles a person verbally endorses and what they hold on to 'deep down'—their gut instincts, manifested in their unreflective behaviour. Twain is being bitterly ironic, of course. Huck's heart is perfectly right; it is society's norms that are not. But he clearly expects his readers to find this kind of implicit/explicit conflict intelligible and recognizable.[10]

---

[9] I quote this passage since it vividly illustrates the phenomenon discussed. I considered censoring the offensive word contained within it but, after consultation, decided against doing so. Twain is clearly not endorsing the word, and Huck's casual use of it serves to emphasize his cognitive dissonance.

[10] For more discussion of this and other cases of 'inverse akrasia', see Arpaly (2003); Bennett (1974); Faraci and Shoemaker (2014). For discussion in the context of theorizing about implicit attitudes, see Brownstein and Madva (2012a, 2012b).

2.2 Skepticism about explicit belief

It might be suggested that the conflict in Huck's case is only apparent. Huck does not really believe that he ought to turn Jim in. He *says* that he should turn Jim in, and (we may suppose) *thinks* that he believes that he should do so. But his utterances reflect what he thinks he ought to say, and he is mistaken about his own beliefs. He has only one belief—the implicit belief that he should help Jim. Perhaps the same goes for Juliet too? She says she does not believe that there are racial differences in intelligence, but her behaviour shows that she is wrong about this. (The suggestion is not that she is lying about what she believes, just that she is mistaken; her self-knowledge is limited.) If we find this interpretation less plausible in Juliet's case than in Huck's, that may be simply because we regard her implicit belief, unlike his, as irrational; it is not clear that the two cases involve different types of mental state.[11] On this view, then, the dissonance in these cases is not between the subject's implicit and explicit beliefs, but between what they believe and what they think they believe.

There is in fact a strong theoretical case for endorsing this view and generalizing it. Peter Carruthers argues that (with limited exceptions) we have no direct introspective access to our own propositional attitudes—our beliefs, desires, intentions, and so on—and that our beliefs about them are the product of rapid nonconscious (and often unsound) inference from sensory evidence (Carruthers, 2011, 2014). For a mental state to be conscious, Carruthers argues, it must be globally broadcast to all cognitive systems (either because that is sufficient for consciousness or because it makes the state accessible to the mindreading system, which generates the higher-order representations required for consciousness). And the only states that are so broadcast are sensory ones. What we think of as conscious thoughts are simply sensory images in working memory, especially images of utterances (inner speech). When broadcast, these images may have important effects on our judgements, decisions, and other propositional attitudes, but they are not themselves propositional attitudes, since they do not have the right causal roles. A consequence of this is that (again with limited exceptions) there are no conscious propositional attitudes—no events of believing, desiring, judging, deciding, and so on.

On this view, then, implicit bias appears in a different light. If bias is grounded in propositional attitudes, then it is always implicit, and education and social disapproval have not driven it underground but rather changed our attitudes

---

[11] There is, however, evidence that people conceptualize cases like Huck's differently from ones like Juliet's, assigning praise and blame in an asymmetrical way; see Faraci and Shoemaker (2014); Pizarro et al. (2003).

towards it and fostered the false belief that we are free from it. (Doubtless they have also reduced bias itself, but not by reducing explicit bias, since there is no such thing.) This view also has consequences for the control of bias. If there are no conscious decisions, then our conscious minds cannot exert control over our actions and cannot override responses arising from nonconscious processes, including biasing ones. As Carruthers puts it, 'we need to get used to the idea that most of the conscious events that we identify ourselves with aren't [propositional] attitudes at all, while the decisions that determine our behavior are exclusively *un*conscious in character' (Carruthers, 2011: 380).

For present purposes, I shall grant that conscious mental events are wholly sensory in character. For I want to argue that this still leaves open a robust sense in which we can talk of having conscious beliefs and desires and making conscious judgements and decisions—and thus a sense in which we can consciously override implicit biases. In order to explain this, we need to turn to the other strand in folk psychology mentioned earlier.

2.3 Explicit belief as commitment

There are numerous dualities in folk psychology, which point to the existence of an explicit form of belief, distinct from the implicit form (see Frankish, 2004). Here I shall focus on just one, in the self-ascription of belief. We sometimes ascribe mental states to ourselves on the basis of inference from self-observation. This is common with character traits and unconscious mental states. Noticing that I place my feet oddly as I walk along the pavement, I speculate that I have a fear of treading on the cracks. Reflecting on her grading practice, Juliet infers that she has an implicit belief that there are racial differences in intelligence. Such self-ascriptions have the same status as ascriptions to other people, and we treat them as fallible. But we also self-ascribe mental states without thinking about ourselves at all. We can think simply about a state of affairs and declare an attitude towards it. Looking at photographs of Hawaii, I declare that I want to go there. Reviewing the evidence for racial differences in intelligence, Juliet declares that she believes there are none. This sort of mentalistic self-ascription—*avowal*—is treated as authoritative, and a challenge to it is taken as a challenge to the speaker's sincerity or integrity. If we were to doubt Juliet's declaration that she believes that there are no racial differences in intelligence, then she would probably be affronted.

Now it could be that avowal is not really outward-looking and authoritative in the way we suppose. Perhaps it involves rapid nonconscious introspection or self-interpretation. However, there is another explanation, which justifies our intuitions about it. This is that avowals are *performative* utterances—utterances that both state that the utterer performs an action and simultaneously perform that very action. A promise, for example, is a performative utterance; in sincerely saying that I promise to do something, I make it the case that I promise to do it. If avowals are performatives, this explains their authority: a sincere avowal brings about the state it describes, and a challenge to it is a challenge to the speaker's sincerity (Frankish, 2004, ch. 8; Heal, 1994, 2002).

More specifically, I suggest that avowals are commitments to certain deliberate policies of reasoning and action. A key notion here is that of *acceptance* (for example, Cohen, 1992; Engel, 2000; Frankish, 2004). To accept a proposition is to adopt a policy of *standing by* its truth—to asserting it, defending it, taking it as a premise, and acting in line with it. Acceptances can be pragmatic and context relative (lawyers accept what their clients tell them, scientists accept their hypotheses), but they can also be open-ended and serve general epistemic ends. Explicit beliefs, I suggest, are just such open-ended acceptances. Explicit desires and intentions can be thought of as conative analogues of acceptance—policies of taking the desired outcome as a goal or of performing the intended action. I shall use the term 'premising policies' as a general term for all these policies, cognitive and conative. If explicit propositional attitudes are premising policies, then we can actively form them by committing ourselves to appropriate policies, and avowals, I suggest, function to self-ascribe, and thereby make, such commitments. This explains not only the authority of avowals but also why they are outward-looking. In debating whether or not to commit to standing by a certain proposition or to adopting a certain goal, we focus not on ourselves, but on the proposition or goal itself.

I shall add two points to flesh out this suggestion. First, premising policies involve *reasoning* in certain ways. Explicitly believing that p involves taking p as a premise in one's conscious reasoning and decision making. We can commit ourselves to doing this because conscious reasoning is—or so I claim—action-based. Within cognitive science, reasoning processes are usually thought of as subpersonal ones. But reasoning can also be an intentional, personal-level activity. We can deliberately *work things out*, motivated by (usually implicit) desires to solve problems and beliefs about what strategies may work. Strategies we can use include constructing arguments in accordance with learned rules, running thought experiments, manipulating models, diagrams, and images, and interrogating ourselves (the last serving to stimulate memory, make connections, and generate hypotheses; Dennett, 1991). These actions can be performed both overtly, in dialogue, monologue, or writing, and covertly, using inner speech or other forms of actively generated sensory imagery (see Frankish, 2004, 2009; for defence of the claim that we can actively form and manipulate sensory imagery, see Carruthers, 2009). (For convenience, I shall focus on imaged utterances from now on; similar points apply to other imagery used in conscious reasoning.)

Second, the commitments also extend to acting upon the results of this conscious reasoning. To believe something is to be guided by it in both thought and action. So if I work out that my explicit beliefs entail a certain proposition, then I am committed to adopting that proposition as a further explicit belief (or to abandoning or revising one or more of the original beliefs). And if I work out that my explicit beliefs and desires dictate that I should perform a certain action, then I am committed to performing the action (or making revisions).

On this view, overt and imaged speech acts can function as judgements and decisions. An act of saying that I believe that p (or just that p) assumes the role of the judgement that p if I treat it as a commitment to a policy of standing by p and to reasoning and acting accordingly. An act of saying that I will perform action A assumes the role of a decision to perform A if I treat it as a commitment to performing A and to planning and acting accordingly. Similarly, episodes of inner speech assume the role of occurrent beliefs and desires if we treat them as expressing premises and goals in our conscious reasoning, in accordance with prior commitments. This, in essence, is my response to Carruthers: sensory images can assume the causal role of thoughts in virtue of being treated as such in active reasoning.

Now, treating a sensory image as a thought involves having certain propositional attitudes towards it. Treating an imaged utterance as a judgement involves (a) believing that the utterance expresses a commitment to a certain premising policy, (b) desiring to honour this commitment (or to honour such commitments generally), (c) believing that this commitment requires certain reasoning activities and overt actions (their precise nature varying with circumstances and one's other premising policies), and so on. These propositional attitudes confer the status of a judgement on the utterance and motivate the actions that are performed as a consequence of it. And these propositional attitudes will typically not themselves be explicit, conscious ones (and in the rare cases where they are, the propositional attitudes they themselves depend on will not be). Rather, they will be implicit, nonconscious states. Thus, on this view, implicit propositional attitudes partially *realize* explicit ones and make them effective in action.

What emerges, then, is a two-level picture of the human mind, with an explicit level of conscious, commitment-based states and active reasoning realized in and supported by an implicit level of nonconscious, passively formed states and involuntary processes. It is tempting to characterize these levels as *personal* and *subpersonal* (Frankish, 2009). This captures the idea that explicit reasoning is something we do, whereas implicit reasoning is done by our mental subsystems.

However, it is important to add the caveat that implicit mental *states*, like explicit ones, are properly ascribed to persons.

2.4 Dual levels and dual processes

This view just outlined can be regarded as a form of dual-process theory, and since implicit bias is often discussed in the context of such theories, I shall say a little about how it differs from other theories of the type. In broad outline, dual-process theories posit two different mental processes by which a response may be generated: one (type 1) that is fast, automatic, nonconscious, and undemanding of working memory, and another (type 2) that is slow, controlled, conscious, and demanding of working memory. Type 1 processes are also variously described as associative, parallel, heavily contextualized, heuristic, and biased, and type 2 processes as rule-based, serial, decontextualized, analytical, and normative. Dual-process theories have been proposed in several fields, including deductive reasoning, decision making, social judgement, and learning and memory (for surveys, see Frankish and Evans, 2009; Frankish, 2010).[12] There are many varieties of dual-process theory and many challenges for it, including that of identifying which features are essential to each type of process and which merely typical ones.

The view proposed here—*dual-level theory*, we might call it—can be regarded as a non-standard form of dual-process theory in which type 2 processes are identified with explicit, intentional reasoning activities involving the manipulation of sensory imagery, and type 1 processes with implicit, subpersonal reasoning processes. Many of the standard features follow from this. For example, explicit processes are slow, serial, and effortful because they involve performing sequences of actions, and they are conscious because these actions involve the manipulation of sensory imagery. Implicit processes do not involve intentional action or sensory imagery and are consequently faster, effortless, (possibly) parallel, and nonconscious. However, other standard contrasts do not carry through straightforwardly into dual-level theory. I shall mention three that are prominent in debates about implicit bias.

First, type 1 processes are typically described as automatic, and type 2 processes as controlled. Dual-level theory retains a version of this contrast: explicit processes are intentionally controlled whereas implicit ones are not. However, implicit processes are not automatic in the sense of being reflex-like, mandatory,

---

[12] Some theorists have described the processes as belonging to two separate mental *systems* (for example, Evans and Over, 1996; Stanovich, 2004). However, this description is ambiguous, and some who have used it now prefer to talk simply of two *types of processing* (Evans and Stanovich, 2013).

or inflexible. As stressed earlier, much unreflective behaviour is rationally responsive to the agent's beliefs and desires and is in that sense intelligently controlled.
Second, type 1 processes are often described as associative and type 2 ones as
computational or ruled-governed. This contrast is not present in dual-level theory.
There may be implicit associative processes of various kinds, but, as argued earlier,
a great deal of implicit propositional reasoning also takes place. And although
explicit thinking often involves constructing arguments in accordance with learned
rules of inference, it may also involve manipulating sensory imagery in associative
ways.[13] Third, type 1 processes are sometimes characterized as biased and type 2
ones as normative. On the proposed view this is only a weak contrast. It is likely
that the implicit mind is modularized to some degree, and implicit belief formation
and reasoning may employ a variety of heuristics and shortcuts that are adaptive
but not in accord with normative theory (see, for example, Carruthers, 2006).
Explicit processes by contrast, being intentional, can be responsive to learned
norms of evidence and reasoning. However, there is no general assumption that
implicit processes are biased and explicit ones normative. In some contexts implicit
processes may generate normative responses, and explicit reasoning and judgement may be influenced by many factors besides normative theory, including
culturally acquired biases and learned rules of thumb (Carruthers, 2013b).

3 Self-Control

3.1 Escaping bias

With this dual-level theory in place, I turn now to the question of how we can
control implicit bias. One immediate question is how we can even *want* to control
it. If we are systematically biased, how can we form unbiased judgements and
motivate ourselves to act upon them? This presents a special challenge for dual-
level theory, on which explicit belief formation is motivated by implicit propositional attitudes. How does a person such as Juliet, who implicitly believes that
there are racial differences in intelligence, get themselves to accept that there are
no such differences?

It is true that implicit bias may impede the formation of unbiased explicit
beliefs. If Juliet has an implicit belief (an intuition or gut feeling, we might say)
that black people are less intelligent than white people, then this will incline her
to form a corresponding explicit belief. However, she may have other implicit
beliefs and desires that prompt the formation of the belief that there are no racial

---

[13]   Compare Keith Stanovich's account of serial associative cognition (Stanovich, 2009).

differences in intelligence, and these may be stronger. In particular, she may have normative beliefs about how she should think—about what counts as good evidence, the relative weight that should be given to different considerations, the untrustworthiness of gut feelings, and so on, together with beliefs about the social norms governing attitudes on this topic. And these, in conjunction with strong implicit desires to adhere to the norms in question, may induce her to accept (form the policy of premising) that there are no racial differences in intelligence, even if she still implicitly believes that there are such differences. (If social considerations play a large role, we might classify the resulting attitude as a pragmatic acceptance rather than a belief proper, but in either case, the result will be that Juliet is committed to maintaining an unbiased propositional attitude that is in tension with her implicit one.)

The mechanisms of acceptance thus offer Juliet a route by which she can escape her bias. This points to the purpose and importance of explicit cognition. By engaging in explicit reasoning and by forming and maintaining premising policies we create for ourselves a distinctively personal level of mentality, whose states and processes are available to reflection and under intentional control. The activities involved afford us a new kind of self-control, allowing us to resist responses produced by subpersonal mechanisms and to create new strategies for regulating our behaviour. Of course, this freedom is not absolute; explicit reasoning and belief formation is itself driven by implicit mental states and processes. But the explicit mind forms a new level of complexity within the overall system, shaped by normative beliefs about how one should think, and modifiable in the light of tuition and reflection.

All this supposes, of course, that we can make our explicit beliefs and desires effective in action. I said that in adopting premises and goals we commit ourselves to acting upon them. But how can we do this—especially if they conflict with our implicit beliefs and desires? Suppose Juliet comes to believe that her unreflective behaviour is implicitly biased, as she might through observation of her own behaviour, the testimony of others, or inference from data about how widespread such bias is. How can she suppress her bias and ensure she is guided by her explicit belief? She might, of course, try to eradicate the implicit belief that produces the bias, but this may not be easy. Implicit beliefs cannot be formed and changed by decision. (When we talk of one-off changes of mind, we are referring to changes in our premising commitments; Frankish, 2004.) Juliet would have to employ indirect means, exposing herself to evidence and argument that undermines the implicit belief—a process which might not succeed at all. Can she exercise a more direct form of self-control, in which her explicit belief *overrides* her implicit one? I turn to this now.

3.2 Explicit belief and action

In order to explain how explicit beliefs can override implicit ones, I need to say more about how explicit thoughts influence action. On the dual-level view an explicit thought is a self-generated (imaged) utterance, and the way in which it guides behaviour is not fundamentally different from the way in which an externally generated utterance might. In each case the influence is mediated by certain (typically implicit) propositional attitudes towards the utterance. My saying to myself that I will go to the bank does not immediately move me to go to the bank, any more than your telling me to go to the bank does. In each case I need to interpret the utterance as prompting me to go to the bank (as a commitment to going in the first case, as an instruction to go in the second) and then be motivated to act upon this prompt (desiring to fulfil my commitments or to follow instructions).

It is a consequence of this that actions guided by explicit beliefs and desires (reflective actions) will also have explanations in terms of implicit beliefs and desires. Suppose I consciously judge that I need to talk to my bank manager and consciously decide to go to the bank in the morning. Then, these explicit mental states could be cited in explanation of my subsequently going to the bank. However, the conscious decision will have become effective in virtue of implicit mental states, including a belief that I am committed to going to the bank and a desire to execute my commitments, and these implicit states could also be cited in explanation of the action. Since these implicit beliefs and desires concern my premising commitments I shall refer to them as *metacognitive* states. (Note that 'metacognitive' here does not mean *higher-order*. The implicit beliefs and desires in question are not about other implicit beliefs and desires but about the premising policies that constitute explicit beliefs and desires.)

The action thus has two different intentional explanations. This may be counterintuitive (though not more so than the idea that there are no conscious thoughts at all), but it is not incoherent or unacceptable. The two explanations are not incompatible, but pitched at different levels. If asked why a person performed a certain reflective action, we highlight the explicit beliefs and desires that prompted it. But if asked how these thoughts guided the action, we turn to lower-level processes involving implicit beliefs and desires. This is a familiar move; we give an explanation at one level, but drop down a level in order to explain the mechanisms underlying it. It is widely assumed that explicit thought processes will be susceptible to such reductive explanation in some way; the novel suggestion here is simply that the underlying mechanisms are themselves intentional (albeit involving intentional states of a different type). Even this is not unprecedented. We often highlight a certain event in the explanation of human action without mentioning the implicit beliefs and desires that make it effective. For example, we might explain why a soldier performed a certain manoeuvre by citing an order from a commanding officer. But in asking *how* the order controlled the action, we give an explanation in terms of the soldier's implicit beliefs and desires relating to the order, his duty, the penalties for disobedience, and so on. Similarly, we might highlight the role of a promise, a warning, or a threat in the explanation of an action, and in each case, another explanation would be available that refers to largely implicit beliefs and desires about the event in question. The present proposal simply assimilates explanation in terms of conscious thoughts to this pattern.[14]

3.3 Conditions for override

With this machinery in place, we are now in a position to state conditions for the direct override of implicit bias and to understand different ways in which it may fail. Suppose subject S has an implicit belief that not-p and an explicit belief that p, in the senses outlined earlier. And suppose that in context C each of these beliefs would, in conjunction with S's other attitudes of the same type, dictate a different and incompatible action; call them A_1 and A_2 respectively. What determines whether the implicit or explicit belief guides action in C? We can highlight four necessary conditions for the explicit belief to override the implicit one.

(1) S must consciously recall p in C, representing it in inner speech or some other sensory medium. Recall is a necessary condition for override since the commitment involved in explicitly believing p is to using p as a premise *in conscious reasoning*, and conscious recall is a precondition for this. It may be asked why S could not commit simply to *acting* as if p were true, and leave the working out entirely to implicit processes. There are two points to make in reply. First, it is doubtful that the strategy would be psychologically feasible. Working out what actions the commitment requires would involve implicit *hypothetical* reasoning—bracketing one's actual implicit beliefs (which are incompatible

---

[14] Carruthers argues that if conscious mental events depend on subsequent reasoning for their efficacy, then they cannot count as decisions and judgements. A decision or judgement should settle what one will do or think, without the need for further reasoning about commitments and suchlike (Carruthers, 2011, ch. 4). Again, my response is to make a distinction of levels. A conscious decision or judgement settles the matter *at the explicit level*. The further reasoning that is required to make these events effective occurs at a lower level—the level of implementation (Frankish, 2012; Carruthers responds in Carruthers, 2013a).

with p) and calculating what one would do if one believed p. And there is a strong case for thinking that the capacity for hypothetical thinking depends precisely on explicit, type 2, processes (see, for example, Carruthers, 2006; Stanovich, 2004). Second, even if the strategy were feasible, such heavy reliance on implicit processing would defeat the object of explicit belief formation. The purpose of adopting premising policies is to enhance our self-control by taking active control of our reasoning and decision making, and conscious recall of relevant inputs is required for this.

(2) S must recognize that, given their other premises and goals, p dictates that they should perform A_2. This may involve explicit argument construction, but the process could be enthymematic, and the conclusion might occur to S spontaneously, courtesy of implicit processes. What is crucial is that S should realize, at least implicitly, that the conclusion is dictated by their premises and goals.

(3) S must form a commitment to performing A_2 (as opposed to revising their explicit beliefs and desires or living with inconsistency). This will often involve a conscious decision—the production of an imaged utterance that expresses a commitment to performing A_2 and is interpreted as such at an implicit level. This is not essential, however; S might implicitly realize that they are committed to performing A_2 immediately upon recalling p, without the mediation of a conscious decision. (This would be especially likely if it is obvious that A_2 is dictated and there is no temptation to do anything else.) Either way, S must form the implicit belief that they are committed to performing A_2. Assuming they also have a general desire to fulfil their commitments, they will now have implicit beliefs and desires that directly motivate A_2.

(4) S must have sufficient metacognitive motivation. Having implicit beliefs and desires that dictate A_2 does not ensure that S will perform A_2. For by hypothesis S also has implicit beliefs and desires that dictate A_1. They will perform A_2 only if their motive for doing so is stronger than their motive for performing A_1. If it is not, then S will not act on their commitment, falling into akrasia. So condition (4) is that S's desire to fulfil their premising commitments (or at least to fulfil this one) be stronger than the desire that motivates A_1 (and stronger than any other desire that motivates an incompatible action).

If these conditions are met, then, *ceteris paribus*, S's explicit belief will override their implicit one, and they will perform A_2 rather than A_1. If the conditions are not met, then override will fail. Note that these conditions do not require that S be *aware*, either consciously or nonconsciously, that they have an implicit belief that is currently prompting A_1, though they may suspect that they do and this may assist override by boosting their resolution to fulfil their premising commitments. Note, too, that the conditions can easily be modified to accommodate views on which implicit bias arises from associative attitudes rather than beliefs. We would simply revise (4) to stipulate that S's desire to fulfil their premising commitments must be strong enough to outweigh the biasing effects of the relevant implicit attitude. Thus, those who reject the belief-based account of implicit bias can still subscribe to the proposed account of self-control, provided they accept that we have implicit beliefs and desires *as well as* implicit associative attitudes.

Can we do anything to reduce the chances of override failure? We can distinguish two kinds of failure in executing a premising policy: failures of competence and failures of motivation. By failures of competence I mean failures due to lapses of memory, skill, or knowledge—for example, failure to recall a premise in a relevant context or failure to see that a group of premises dictates a certain conclusion or action (conditions (1) and (2) respectively). By failures of motivation I mean failures arising from the relative weakness of the agent's desire to execute their premising policies, or at least to execute this specific policy. The most obvious example of motivation failure is where condition (4) is not met: a subject fails to act on their decision to perform an action because their implicit desire to execute their decision (to fulfil the commitment they have made) is, in the context, outweighed by an implicit desire to do something else. In a slightly different case, a subject might realize that their premises dictate a certain action but not be sufficiently motivated to commit to performing it, leading to a failure of condition (3). Motivation failure might also affect conditions (1)–(2). If an agent's commitment to their premises is weak, they may fail to put sufficient effort into memory search and conscious reasoning, resulting in motivational parallels to the failures of competence. (Recall itself is not, of course, under intentional control and is heavily context-dependent, but it can be intentionally stimulated by, for example, self-interrogation.) In general, high metacognitive motivation will be an important factor in effective override.

We can illustrate this by returning to Juliet and her implicit belief in intelligence differences. In some circumstances the conditions for her explicit belief to override this belief will easily be met. Suppose Juliet is asked by an academic colleague whether she thinks there are racial differences in intelligence. The question will immediately remind her of her explicit belief on the matter, and it will be immediately obvious what response it dictates, so conditions (1) and (2) will be met. And since social norms dictate the same response as her explicit belief, Juliet will feel little temptation to give a different response, even if her metacognitive motivation is relatively weak. So conditions (3) and (4) will be met too, and Juliet will say that there are no racial differences in intelligence. Contrast this with a case where Juliet is alone in her study grading essays. Her implicit belief inclines her to give lower grades to her black students, though her explicit belief dictates that she take steps to resist this and grade impartially. Here the conditions for override are less likely to hold. Since grading places a heavy load on working memory, Juliet may not recall her explicit belief at all, and if she does she may not realize what it requires of her in each case. These failures of competence may be compounded by motivational failure. If Juliet's metacognitive motivation is relatively weak, she may not make the effort required to recall and consistently apply her explicit belief, and when she does she may not have the resolution required to overcome her gut feelings about what grades different students deserve.

To sum up, in order to suppress an implicit bias, it is not sufficient to have an explicit unbiased belief and an explicit desire to be fair; one also needs a strong *implicit* metacognitive desire to make those explicit propositional attitudes effective in reasoning and action—strength of will, we might say. Failure to suppress implicit biases, I suggest, is often due to the weakness of this implicit desire.

3.4 Some predictions

I shall conclude with some predictions of the proposed account, which might form the basis for experimental work or even practical techniques for combating implicit bias. I shall not attempt to describe specific protocols, but merely sketch some ideas which others may wish to take up.

The predictions concern agents who have a biased implicit belief and an unbiased explicit belief. The general prediction is that we should be able to manipulate the relative influence of a subject's biased and unbiased beliefs in a given context by manipulating the likelihood of conditions (1)–(4) being met. Raising the chances of their being met should tend to reduce the effects of the bias, and lowering the chances of their being met should tend to increase them. (Assuming explicit beliefs can override associations as well as beliefs, this prediction should also hold if the bias arises from an associative attitude rather than a belief.)

Thus, one specific prediction is that offering reminders of the unbiased belief and its implications should reduce bias by increasing the chances of conditions (1) and (2) being met, while placing demands on working memory should increase the effects of bias by reducing the chances of those conditions being met. These predictions are, however, unlikely to be unique to the present account (though their falsity would of course undermine it).

Other specific predictions focus on motivation. Since override is motivated, we should be able to manipulate it by manipulating the agent's motivational state.

Thus, boosting an agent's motivation to execute the premising policy that constitutes the unbiased belief should increase the chances of all four conditions being met and so reduce the effect of the bias, whereas reducing this motivation should have the opposite effect.[15] Boosting might be achieved by providing subjects with direct or indirect reminders of the importance of the issue and of the harmful effects of the bias, and reduction by offering contrary suggestions. Similar effects should be obtainable by manipulating the agent's motivation for acting on their implicit belief. For example, if a subject is told that their inter-locutor knows their 'gut feelings' and will reward them for acting on them, then this should boost their motivation for acting on their implicit belief, reducing the likelihood of override.[16] (An extreme version of this scenario is talking to God. As Huck says, you can't pray a lie.) Again, however, these predictions are unlikely to be specific to the present account; many theories will predict correlations between a subject's attitudes towards their bias and the likelihood of their acting on it.

Perhaps the most distinctive prediction of the account is that we can manipulate implicit bias by manipulating a subject's desire to honour their commitments *generally*. Boosting this general desire should have the knock-on effect of boosting their specific desire to execute their premising commitments and so reduce the effects of implicit bias. This might be achieved by priming subjects with suggestions of the importance of keeping promises and sticking to commitments, or presenting them with stimuli associated with integrity, consistency, self-discipline, and strength of will (controlling of course for possible confounding factors). Sugges-tions and stimuli that tend to weaken a subject's desire to keep their promises and honour their commitments should have the opposite effect and increase the effects of bias. These predictions arise from the role commitment plays in the dual-level account of implicit bias, and as far as I know they are unique to the account. Confirmation of them would therefore be strong support for it.

4 Conclusion

On the view I have sketched, implicit bias is more a part of us than we may like to think, and perhaps more natural to us too, reflecting the operations of subperso-nal belief-forming mechanisms that were designed to be adaptive not impartial. We all play double sometimes. But while bias may be natural, so is the capacity to

---

[15] For potentially relevant empirical findings, see studies on 'implicit motivation to control prejudice' (for example, Glaser and Knowles, 2008; Park et el., 2008; Park and Glaser, 2011).

[16] See 'bogus pipeline' manipulations (for example, Nier, 2005) in which subjects are told that the Implicit Association Test (used to measure implicit attitudes) is akin to a lie-detector test. The result is a closer correlation of subjects' implicit and explicit attitudes.

overcome it. Our ability to engage in explicit thought is one of our most distinctively human features, and with sufficient strength of will we can use it to reflectively control our actions, override our biases, and become better, fairer people.

Acknowledgements

Thanks for comments and advice are due to Michael Brownstein, Ward Jones, Maria Kasmirli, Jenny Saul, an anonymous referee, and the participants in the Implicit Bias and Philosophy project.

References

Arpaly, N. (2003). *Unprincipled Virtue: An Inquiry Into Moral Agency*. Oxford: Oxford University Press.

Bennett, J. (1974). 'The conscience of Huckleberry Finn'. *Philosophy* 49(188): 123–34.

Bosson, J. K., Swann, W. B. Jr, and Pennebaker, J. W. (2000). 'Stalking the perfect measure of implicit self-esteem: the blind men and the elephant revisited?' *Journal of Personality and Social Psychology* 79(4): 631–43.

Brownstein, M. and Madva, A. (2012a). 'Ethical automaticity'. *Philosophy of the Social Sciences* 42(1): 68–98.

Brownstein, M. and Madva, A. (2012b). 'The normativity of automaticity'. *Mind and Language* 27(4): 410–34.

Carruthers, P. (2006). *The Architecture of the Mind: Massive Modularity and the Flexibility of Thought*. Oxford: Oxford University Press.

Carruthers, P. (2009). 'An architecture for dual reasoning'. In Evans, J. St. B. T. and Frankish K. (eds.), *In Two Minds: Dual Processes and Beyond*. Oxford: Oxford University Press: 109–27.

Carruthers, P. (2011). *The Opacity of Mind: An Integrative Theory of Self-Knowledge*. New York, NY: Oxford University Press.

Carruthers, P. (2013a). 'On knowing your own beliefs: a representationalist account'. In Nottelmann, N. (ed.), *New Essays on Belief: Constitution, Content and Structure*. Basingstoke: Palgrave Macmillan: 145–65.

Carruthers, P. (2013b). 'The fragmentation of reasoning'. In Quintanilla, P. (ed.), *La Coevolución de Mente y Lenguaje: Ontogénesis y Filogénesis*. Lima: Fondo Editorial de la Pontificia Universidad Católica del Perú: 181–204.

Carruthers, P. (2014). 'On central cognition'. *Philosophical Studies* 170(1): 143–62.

Cohen, L. J. (1992). *An Essay on Belief and Acceptance*. Oxford: Oxford University Press.

Crano, W. D. and Prislin, R. (eds.) (2008). *Attitudes and Attitude Change*. New York, NY: Psychology Press.

De Houwer, J. (forthcoming). 'A propositional model of implicit evaluation'. *Social Psychology and Personality Compass*.

Dennett, D. C. (1991). *Consciousness Explained*. New York: Little, Brown and Co.

Descartes, R. (1642/1984). 'Objections and replies'. In Cottingham, J., Stoothoff, R., and Murdoch D. (eds.), *The Philosophical Writings of Descartes: Volume 2*. Cambridge: Cambridge University Press: 63–383.

Engel, P. (ed.) (2000). *Believing and Accepting*. Dordrecht: Kluwer.

Evans, J. St. B. T. and Over, D. E. (1996). *Rationality and Reasoning*. Hove: Psychology Press.

Evans, J. St. B. T. and Stanovich, K. E. (2013). 'Dual-process theories of higher cognition: advancing the debate'. *Perspectives on Psychological Science* 8(3): 223–41.

Faraci, D. and Shoemaker, D. (2014). 'Huck vs. JoJo: moral ignorance and the (a) symmetry of praise and blame'. In Knobe, J., Lombrozo, T., and Nichols, S. (eds.), *Oxford Studies in Experimental Philosophy: Volume 1*. Oxford: Oxford University Press: 7–27.

Frankish, K. (2004). *Mind and Supermind*. Cambridge: Cambridge University Press.

Frankish, K. (2009). 'Systems and levels: dual-system theories and the personal-subpersonal distinction'. In Evans, J. St. B. T. and Frankish, K. (eds.), *In Two Minds: Dual Processes and Beyond*. Oxford: Oxford University Press: 89–107.

Frankish, K. (2010). 'Dual-process and dual-system theories of reasoning'. *Philosophy Compass* 5(10): 914–26.

Frankish, K. (2012). 'Dual systems and dual attitudes'. *Mind and Society* 11(1): 41–51.

Frankish, K. and Evans, J. St. B. T. (2009). 'The duality of mind: an historical perspective'. In Evans, J. St. B. T. and Frankish, K. (eds.), *In Two Minds: Dual Processes and Beyond*. Oxford: Oxford University Press: 1–29.

Gawronski, B., Hofmann, W., and Wilbur, C. J. (2006). 'Are "implicit" attitudes unconscious?' *Consciousness and Cognition* 15: 485–99.

Gendler, T. S. (2008a). 'Alief and belief'. *The Journal of Philosophy* 105(10), 634–63.

Gendler, T. S. (2008b). 'Alief in action (and reaction)'. *Mind and Language* 23(5): 552–85.

Glaser, J. and Knowles, E. D. (2008). 'Implicit motivation to control prejudice'. *Journal of Experimental Social Psychology* 44(1): 164–72.

Hahn, A., Judd, C. M., Hirsh, H. K., and Blair, I. V. (2014). 'Awareness of implicit attitudes'. *Journal of Experimental Psychology: General* 143(3): 1369–92.

Heal, J. (1994). 'Moore's paradox: a Wittgensteinian approach'. *Mind* 103(409), 5–24.

Heal, J. (2002). 'On first-person authority'. *Proceedings of the Aristotelian Society* 102: 1–19.

Holroyd, J. and Sweetman, J. 'The Heterogeneity of Implicit Bias'. This volume.

Hughes, S., Barnes-Holmes, D., and De Houwer, J. (2011). 'The dominance of associative theorizing in implicit attitude research: propositional and behavioral alternatives'. *The Psychological Record* 61: 465–96.

James, W. (1890). *The Principles of Psychology*. New York, NY: Henry Holt and Co.

Levy, N. (2014). 'Neither fish nor fowl: implicit attitudes as patchy endorsements'. *Noûs*. doi: 10.1111/nous.12074.

Madva, A. (ms). 'Why implicit attitudes are (probably) not beliefs'.

Mandelbaum, E. (2015). 'Attitude, inference, association: on the propositional structure of implicit bias'. *Noûs*. doi: 10.1111/nous.12089.

Mitchell, C. J., De Houwer, J., and Lovibond, P. F. (2009). 'The propositional nature of human associative learning'. *Behavioral and Brain Sciences* 32: 183–246.

Nier, J. A. (2005). 'How dissociated are implicit and explicit racial attitudes? A bogus pipeline approach'. *Group Processes and Intergroup Relations* 8(1): 39–52.

Nosek, B. A., Hawkins, C. B., and Frazier, R. S. (2011). 'Implicit social cognition: from measures to mechanisms'. *Trends in Cognitive Sciences* 15(4): 152–9.

Olson, M. A. and Fazio, R. H. (2003). 'Relations between implicit measures of prejudice: what are we measuring?' *Psychological Science* 14(6): 636–9.

Oswald, F. L., Mitchell, G., Blanton, H., Jaccard, J., and Tetlock, P. E. (2013). 'Predicting ethnic and racial discrimination: a meta-analysis of IAT criterion studies'. *Journal of Personality and Social Psychology* 105(2): 171–92.

Oswald, F. L., Mitchell, G., Blanton, H., Jaccard, J., and Tetlock, P. E. (2015). 'Using the IAT to predict ethnic and racial discrimination: small effect sizes of unknown societal significance'. *Journal of Personality and Social Psychology* 108(4): 562–71.

Park, S. H. and Glaser, J. (2011). 'Implicit motivation to control prejudice and exposure to counterstereotypic instances reduce spontaneous discriminatory behavior'. *Korean Journal of Social and Personality Psychology* 25(4): 107–20.

Park, S. H., Glaser, J., and Knowles, E. D. (2008). 'Implicit motivation to control prejudice moderates the effect of cognitive depletion on unintended discrimination'. *Social Cognition* 26(4): 401–19.

Pizarro, D., Uhlmann, E., and Salovey, P. (2003). 'Asymmetry in judgments of moral blame and praise: the role of perceived metadesires'. *Psychological Science* 14(3): 267–72.

Schwitzgebel, E. (2010). 'Acting contrary to our professed beliefs, or the gulf between occurrent judgment and dispositional belief'. *Pacific Philosophical Quarterly* 91(4): 531–53.

Stanovich, K. E. (2004). *The Robot's Rebellion: Finding Meaning in the Age of Darwin*. Chicago, IL: University of Chicago Press.

Stanovich, K. E. (2009). 'Distinguishing the reflective, algorithmic, and autonomous minds: is it time for a tri-process theory?' In Evans, J. St. B. T. and Frankish, K. (eds.), In *Two Minds: Dual Processes and Beyond*. Oxford: Oxford University Press: 55–88.

Twain, M. (1885). *Adventures of Huckleberry Finn (Tom Sawyer's Comrade)*. New York, NY: C. L. Webster.

Webber, J. (2013). 'Character, attitude and disposition'. *European Journal of Philosophy*. doi: 10.1111/ejop.12028.

1.2

Implicit Bias, Reinforcement Learning, and Scaffolded Moral Cognition

Bryce Huebner

Recent data from the cognitive and behavioral sciences suggest that irrelevant features of our environment can often play a role in shaping our morally significant decisions. This is not always a bad thing. But our inability to suppress or moderate our reflexive reactions can lead us to behave in ways that diverge from our reflectively held ideals, and to pursue worse options while knowing there are better ones available (Spinoza, 2002: 320). Nowhere is this clearer than it is where racial biases persist in those who have adopted egalitarian ideals. My primary aim in this chapter is to sketch a computational framework of implicit biases, which can explain both their emergence and their stability in the face of egalitarian ideals. I then use this framework to explain why some strategies for intervening on implicit biases are likely to be more successful than others. I argue that there are plausible ways to adjust our goals and manipulate our local environments to moderate the expression of implicit bias in the short-run, but I also maintain that the dynamic nature of learning and valuation, as well as the impact of stress on cognitive processing, necessitate more comprehensive interventions designed to reshape the cognitive niche we inhabit. Expressed bluntly, the freedom to act on what we know to be best can only arise in a world where our reflexive and reflective attitudes are, by their very nature, already aligned. So if we wish to gain control over our implicit biases, we must intervene on the world to which our attitudes are attuned, and do so in a way that instills anti-racist attitudes.

1 The Dual-System Hypothesis

The phenomenon of implicit bias has become quite familiar.[1] White people often display *reflexive* signs of distrust and aversion, including increased blinking rates and decreased eye contact, when they interact with black people (Dovidio et al., 1997). People are more likely to misidentify someone walking along a dimly lit street as dangerous if he is black; and many white people routinely feel the urge to cross the street to avoid black people. Such behavior undoubtedly helps to sustain racialized hierarchies, perpetuates racist assumptions about social status, and affects the viability of multiracial interactions. More troublingly, the assumption that black men are likely to be dangerous can, and often does, have a significant impact on prosecution rates and sentencing decisions, and it can play a deeply tragic role when quick decisions are made about whether a person is carrying a gun (Correll et al., 2006). In any particular case, there is room to debate about the relative contribution of explicit prejudice and implicit bias, but it is hard to deny that racial stereotypes can—and often do—have a serious and deleterious impact on morally salient behavior.

Philosophers have long acknowledged that we sometimes act on habits or impulses that seem misguided on further reflection, and that we sometimes make judgments that we are unwilling to reflectively endorse. But implicit biases prove fiendishly difficult to extinguish, even when we acknowledge that race should not be treated as a predictor of social status or threat (Dunham, Chen, and Banaji, in press; Gregg, Seibt, and Banaji, 2006; Huebner, 2009). This suggests a deep distinction between our reflexive and rational motivations, which most existing accounts of implicit bias see as evidence of two types of cognitive systems: a slow, controlled, inferential *system* that produces reflectively endorsed beliefs, and a heterogeneous network of systems that rapidly and reflexively generate expectations based on prior experience, yielding "attitudes and beliefs that are acquired passively without individuals' awareness and that influence subsequent judgments, decisions, and actions without intention or volition" (Dasgupta, 2013: 235). There are debates about the precise commitments of such dual-systems hypotheses, and there are many ways of spelling out the difference between these

---

[1] The numerous forms of implicit bias are likely to diverge in many ways from those I consider in this chapter. I focus primarily on the American context, and use the terms "white" and "black" as shorthand for categories to which contemporary North Americans are likely to be attuned. The mechanisms I discuss are likely to track things such as "typically African American" features, and differences in social transactions may modulate the strength and scope of these associations in ways that shape the typical characteristics of the people who are racialized as white or black.

kinds of systems (Evans and Stanovich, 2013). But for now, what matters is that some version of this hypothesis has played an integral role in structuring the investigation of implicit bias—and it is easy to see why.

The films we watch, the news we read, and the narratives that dominate the public imagination typically present racial out-groups in ways that highlight their stereotypical features. This makes an associationist hypothesis about the origin and stability of implicit bias seem plausible (Devine, 1989). If socially salient attitudes are encoded automatically and stored associatively, *exposure* to these stimuli should generate expectations about the attributes likely to be associated with particular groups. Where such associations are triggered by encounters with out-group members, this will yield biased behavior and biased judgments. Expressed schematically:

When people encounter a person, a group, or an issue they are familiar with, the attitude or belief associated with it pops into mind quickly and automatically in a split second. People may be unaware of attitude activation or only semiaware of it. But once an implicit attitude or belief is activated, it is difficult to inhibit or suppress right away and the activated attitude or belief is more likely to drive subsequent behavior, judgments, and decisions.   (Dasgupta, 2013: 236)

It has often been assumed that such attitudes are internalized gradually through repeated exposures to culturally dominant presentations of groups. And on this approach, it becomes unsurprising that such attitudes often conflict with the beliefs we later endorse consciously.

The hypothesis that associative mechanisms play an important role in the encoding and retrieval of implicit attitudes also guides a great deal of research in social psychology. Indeed, many tools for examining implicit bias are designed to track such associations. For example, participants in the *implicit association* test (IAT) are asked to rapidly categorize two groups of people (black vs. white) and two attributes ("good" vs. "bad"). Differences in response latency (and sometimes differences in error rates) are then treated as a measure of the association between the target group and the target attribute (Greenwald, McGhee, and Schwartz, 1998). Similarly, the Go/No-Go association task (GNAT) presents a target group (black people) and a target attribute (good), and uses accuracy and response latency as measures of associative strength (Nosek and Banaji, 2001). In both cases, faster responses and lower error rates are seen as evidence about the strength of non-inferential and associative computations. Such experiments reveal attitudes that are sensitive to associative considerations, and as the dual-system hypothesis predicts, these patterns persist in people who endorse egalitarian attitudes. But this is not enough to demonstrate that our biases are implemented by non-inferential and associative computations.

As Eric Mandelbaum (2015) notes, many prominent models of associative processing assume that associative representations must be encoded gradually and that they are modified only by changes in contextual or situational cues. But statistically robust effects in an IAT can be induced by asking participants to suppose that one imaginary group is bad and another is good—and this novel association can be transferred to a new group using similarly abstract suppositions (Gregg, Seibt, and Banaji, 2006). This suggests that the emergence of implicit associations does not *always* depend on the repeated pairing of group members and evaluative attributes, which would be necessary for gradual associative encoding (though these data do not rule out the possibility that *other* types of associations are formed gradually).[2] More intriguingly, abstractly induced associations cannot always be extinguished with similarly abstract suppositions. Once they are encoded, they rapidly solidify in a way that suggests one-shot learning. Furthermore, although changes in environmental contingencies *can* have a significant impact on performance in an IAT (Dasgupta, 2013; Gawronski and Bodenhausen, 2011), associative strength can also be modulated using logical and inferential strategies (Mandelbaum, in preparation). For example, reading and considering persuasive arguments about a group can significantly affect subsequent performance in an IAT (Briñol, Petty, and McCaslin, 2009); and learning that your peers have prejudiced beliefs similar to your own can enhance the accessibility of biases, modulating response times in a lexical decision task and affecting a white person's decisions about how close to sit to a black person (Sechrist and Stengor, 2001). A purely associative model would not predict either effect, though there may be ways of explaining such effects using a computational model that makes a great deal of room for associative processing. So, where does this leave us?

Unlike the beliefs we reflectively endorse, implicit attitudes arise rapidly and automatically, often outside of conscious awareness. They track some types of associative relations, and they do so in ways that are difficult to modify except by changing environmental contingencies. Such facts are commonly taken to support a dual-system hypothesis, according to which implicit attitudes are implemented by associative and affective systems, while reflectively endorsed beliefs are implemented by a controlled and inferential system. But recent data have revealed that inferential reasoning and one-shot learning can sometimes affect

---

[2] This experiment targets imaginary groups using an IAT. But as Michael Brownstein (p.c.) notes, the IAT is only one measure of implicit attitudes, and there are many ways of changing the scores on an IAT without affecting implicit bias per se. If taking an IAT is a partially controlled behavior, for example, this effect is unsurprising. I return to a similar issue in Section 3.

implicit attitudes. This would be surprising if such attitudes were implemented exclusively by associative systems. But while the existing data strongly suggest that implicit biases are not implemented *exclusively* by associative mechanisms, there is no obvious reason to suppose that only one type of mechanism is implicated in the production of implicit attitudes. Most dual-system hypotheses explicitly allow for the operation of numerous fast and automatic systems, often in parallel, but this claim is often underdeveloped. My aim in Sections 2 and 3 is to show how associative and inferential systems can *collectively* guide our behavior. To this end, I sketch a computational account of implicit biases, which is grounded in a "neurobiologically plausible and mechanistic description of how values are assigned to mental representations of actions and outcomes, and how those values are integrated to produce" morally significant decisions and morally significant behavior (cf. Crockett, 2013).

The computational theory I advance is consistent with the existing behavioral and neuroscientific data on implicit bias, and my argument is made probable by the fact that the systems I discuss play a critical role in many types of learning and decision-making. Furthermore, recent theoretical and empirical perspectives have suggested that these systems are likely to be operative in the production of reflexive and automatic moral judgments (Crockett, 2013; Cushman, 2013; Huebner, 2013; Railton, 2014). But I cannot establish *conclusively* that this is the correct story about how our implicit biases are produced and maintained. Decisive support for this computational theory therefore awaits further empirical investigation.

2 Three Kinds of System

Across the phylogenetic tree, associative learning is the primary means by which organisms represent the structure of their world, and there is reason to believe that associative learning systems play an important role in human social cognition (Crockett, 2013; Cushman, 2013; Heyes, 2012). But human decision-making is not exhausted by associative processing, and there is growing evidence that many of our decisions and actions depend on contributions from three distinct types of system, which frequently operate in parallel: associative Pavlovian systems that reflexively trigger approach and withdrawal in response to biologically salient stimuli; associative model-free systems that reflexively assign values to actions on the basis of previously experienced outcomes; and computationally expensive model-based systems that generate forward-looking decision trees to represent the contingent relationships between potential actions and outcomes and then assign values to these action-outcome pairs (Crockett, 2013). In this section I explain how each of these three systems operates in the context of human cognition more generally, and in Section 3 I return to the role that these systems are likely to play in the production and maintenance of implicit bias.

2.1 Pavlovian learning and decision-making

Pavlov famously observed that associations could be induced by ringing a bell each time he gave food to a dog; over time, the dog gradually began to salivate whenever the bell rang, even when there was no accompanying food. This widely replicated result suggests that associations linking an innate response to biologically salient rewards or punishments can be formed *passively*. Capitalizing on this fact, contemporary approaches to associative learning emphasize the role of experienced discrepancies "between the actual state of the world and the organism's representation of that state. They see learning as a process by which the two are brought into line" (Rescorla, 1988: 153). The algorithms that facilitate associative learning are error-driven: they generate predictions about the associative links between events, and update their predictions when surprising outcomes are observed; and the strength of the resulting associations is a function of updating the prior associative strength in light of the difference between a weighted average of past rewards and the most recently experienced reward (Glimcher, 2011: 15650).

Pavlovian systems can learn at different rates, depending on the kind of information they track: some systems learn gradually, and depend on repeated exposure to an associative relation; others learn rapidly, treating recent experience as authoritative. But once these systems are calibrated against a pattern of rewards and punishments, they often become inflexible (Dayan et al., 2006). To see why, it will help to consider the type of food aversion that is learned rapidly as a result of stomach discomfort (Garcia and Koelling, 1966). Such associations are difficult to extinguish, because the offending food will be avoided at almost any cost. But even if it is eaten again, the system that guides this aversion did not evolve to encode associative relations with things that do-not-make-you-sick. The unsurprising upshot is that gustatory learning evolved to rapidly encode predictions about poisonous substances, and to generate long-lasting aversions to things that are potentially poisonous.

A network of mechanisms in the ventral striatum, basolateral amygdala, and orbitofrontal cortex represent associative relations between stimuli and biologically significant events (Niv, 2009: 22), and there appear to be many different Pavlovian systems that evolved to track things as diverse as food, water, sexual reward, and social exchange. Each of these systems is narcissistic, in the sense that it only "cares" about the associative relations that are salient to its own purposes

(Akins 1996). But since biologically salient situations often involve multiple sources of reward and punishment, these systems operate in parallel, leading to competitions for the guidance of biologically and socially significant actions (Rescorla, 1988). Such competitions must be settled by systems that evaluate the extent to which some value ought to be acted on, and this is why biological cognition also requires model-free systems that can reflexively assign value to actions on the basis of previously experienced outcomes.

2.2 Model-free learning and decision-making

Not all rewards grow on trees, and even those that do must often be cultivated. Pavlovian learning on its own can attune us to the *presence* of existing rewards and punishments, but something more is necessary when we must decide which rewards to pursue. Expressed differently, Pavlovian systems encode passively associations between an innate response and a biologically salient reward, but model-free systems are necessary where we encode learned associations between actions and outcomes. Like savvy investors, we should only adopt a plan of action if doing so is likely to make us better off in the long run. This requires forming expectations about valuable outcomes, as well as estimating the likelihood of those outcomes given our chosen plan of action. Of course, it would be nice if we could carefully map out all the alternative possibilities and evaluate them before making such decisions, but the world rarely cooperates. We are often forced to make choices on the basis of our current experience, either because we lack information that would be necessary to build such a plan, or because we do not have time to construct and evaluate all the relevant models of how things *might* turn out. Nonetheless, even rapid decisions must be sensitive to the *cost of acting* and the *value of expected payoffs*. And fortunately, evolution has found a clever solution to the problem of rapid evaluative decision-making, which is commonly known as the Law of Effect: actions that tend to produce positive outcomes are repeated, while actions that tend to produce negative outcomes are avoided. In many environments, this strategy is quite successful, and it has been preserved as the core of model-free decision-making.

Beginning in the mid-1990s, research in computer science and cognitive neuroscience converged on an account of the predictive and associative algorithms that make this type of instrumental decision-making possible. Model-free algorithms were discovered, which generated predictions about future outcomes on the basis of current sensory cues. In their most general form, these algorithms were designed to compute a prediction-error signal whenever outcomes were *better* or *worse* than expected, given the current value of a reward and the expected future value of that reward—which could be computed by way of a temporal derivative (Sutton and Barto, 1998). These algorithms monitor the discrepancies between predictions and outcomes, and they adjust future predictions in light of experienced discrepancies. Over time, this yields a form of error-driven learning that allows a learner to become attuned to the stable patterns of rewards and punishments in its environment. These algorithms thus lead an entity to pursue positive outcomes while avoiding negative outcomes. Simultaneously, neuroscientists discovered phasic spiking activity of midbrain dopamine neurons that was consistent with such algorithms. This activity increased when outcomes were *better-than-expected*, decreased when outcomes were *worse-than-expected*, and was unaffected by outcomes whose time and value are accurately predicted (Montague et al., 1996; Schultz et al., 1993). Bringing these two insights together, it was suggested that these midbrain neurons function as "detectors of the 'goodness' of environmental events relative to learned predictions about those events" (Schultz, Dayan, and Montague, 1997). In the intervening years, numerous tasks, using numerous sources of reward, and species ranging from honeybees to nonhuman primates, have revealed a midbrain network that computes a multimodal and polysensory teaching signal that directs attention, learning, and action-selection in response to valuable outcomes (Schultz, 1998, 2010).

While there are still debates over the precise computational algorithms that are implemented by model-free systems, there is broad consensus that risk- and reward-based decision-making recruit a network of evolutionarily old, computationally simple systems, which allow us to produce, maintain, and revise behavioral policies by tracking patterns of reward and their predictors (Glimcher, 2011). Indeed, recent neuroscientific studies have revealed model-free systems in the midbrain and orbitofrontal cortex, which collectively implement the learning signals and motivational "umph" required to get habitual learning off the ground (Rangel et al., 2008; Liljeholm and O'Doherty, 2012). Mechanisms in the ventral striatum compute expectations when the distribution and likelihood of a reward is uncertain, while distinct circuits in the ventral striatum and anterior insula evaluate risk and compute risk-prediction-error signals (Preuschoff et al., 2006, 2008; Quartz, 2009). Another network including the orbitofrontal cortex and basal ganglia represents reward values in ways that are sensitive to both the probability of positive outcomes given recent gains and losses (Frank and Claus, 2006; Shenhav and Greene, 2010), and relative satiation (Critchley and Rolls, 1996). Finally, and most intriguingly, the failure to conform to social norms evokes activity in the ventral striatum and posterior medial prefrontal cortex (mPFC), which is consistent with a prediction-error signal whose amplitude covaries with the likelihood of adjusting behavior to restore conformity (Klucharev et al., 2009); norm conformity can even be decreased by interrupting the activity of this circuit using transcranial magnetic stimulation (Klucharev et al., 2011).

Considerations of computational economy and efficiency militate against coding for multiple sources of reward when all necessary information can be encoded more simply. As a result, model-free systems monitor for prediction errors at many points in temporally extended chains of events—which is what allows them to treat current experience as evidence for the success or failure of a long-term behavioral policy (Dayan, 2012).[3] We can ignore the mathematical and neurological complexities of these algorithms for now, as the import of this fact is fairly intuitive. Model-free systems initially respond to rewarding outcomes, but where there are clear predictors of those outcomes, they become more sensitive to the presence of those reward-predicting stimuli. For example, such a system may initially respond to the delicious taste of a fine chocolate bar. But when this taste is repeatedly preceded by seeing that chocolate bar's label, the experience of seeing that label will be treated as rewarding in itself—so long as the label remains a clear signal that delicious chocolate is on the way. Similarly, if every trip to the chocolate shop leads to the purchase of that delicious chocolate bar, entering the shop may come to predict the purchasing of the chocolate bar, with the label that indicates the presence of delicious chocolate; in which case, entering the shop will come to be treated as rewarding. And if every paycheck leads to a trip to the chocolate shop...

The upshot is that model-free systems can track predictors of rewards, predictors of predictors of rewards, and more. This allows the reward signal triggered by the predictor of a reward to *stand-in* for the value of a behavioral policy; where things go better or worse than expected, given that policy, prediction-error signals can be used to revise these behavioral policies to make valuable outcomes more likely (Balleine, Daw, and O'Doherty, 2008). But these are error-driven algorithms, and they can *only* adjust behavior where things go better or worse than expected. This type of learning is sometimes quite successful, as it is when the receipt of a reward is wholly contingent upon the actions taken in its pursuit. Indeed, as systems that treat the earliest successful predictor of rewards as *stand-ins* for the success of a long-term behavioral policy, they will be relatively

[3] Changes in the phasic spiking rates of dopamine neurons are consistent with an ability to track exponentially weighted sums of previous rewards, and computational models reveal that this activity yields a prediction-error signal that can be adjusted to fit a temporally extended policy in light of the experienced value of recent rewards (Glimcher, 2011: 15653). This is why the repeated experience of the predictor of a reward leads to a shift in the phasic activity of these neurons: rather than firing immediately after a reward is received, they fire when the earliest predictor of that reward is observed.

successful in any environment where action-outcome contingencies are relatively stable.

Where ecological and social pressures produce stable environmental contingencies, the Pavlovian systems discussed in Section 2.1 will yield motivations to approach beneficial things and to avoid harmful things. Similarly, when ecological and social pressures produce stable environments where an agent can expect the future to be relevantly like the past, model-free systems will facilitate the formation of behavioral policies that bring about good results in the long run. But like Pavlovian learning, model-free systems rely on error-driven associative processes that are difficult to modify once they are fixed, and they tend to yield suboptimal outcomes "where traditionally rewarding actions lead to undesirable outcomes, or vice versa" (Crockett, 2013: 363).

More troublingly, the mere adoption of a new behavioral policy, which is grounded on new predictions about action-outcome contingencies, can leave prior predictions in place—although these associations may fade into the background. For example, failing to find one's favorite chocolate bar may lead to the purchase of a different one, yielding a new preference and a new behavioral policy. But this shift in behavioral policies may leave the associative link between the original label and chocolate bar intact, since no errors were ever detected in *that* predicted link. Moreover, since statistical regularities do not always align with our reflectively held ideals, such systems can get us into trouble. Pavlovian and model-free systems are designed to get the patterns of environmental contingencies and the patterns of action-outcome contingencies right. So where an environment is organized in ways that leads us to pursue bad ends, we must adopt other decision-making strategies, and preferably strategies that allow us to act with forethought, choosing between different potential courses of action by anticipating future outcomes (cf. Prinz, 2002: 4).

2.3 Looking forward, and model-based decisions

One way of acting with forethought is by repurposing model-free systems to evaluate *merely possible* situations, and this strategy appears to be operative in human cognition. In a recent experiment where stock values were changed *after* decisions about whether to buy them had been made, activity in the ventral caudate was sensitive to differences between how much *could have been* won and how much actually was won (Lohrenz et al., 2007). This activity is consistent with a fictive-error signal; that is, a signal that reflexively compares actual outcomes against *things that might have been*. Such fictive-error signals provide an initial way for us to test our actions before carrying them out; and the systems that produce these signals are integrated with the Pavlovian and model-free systems discussed previously. However—and this point will be key when we return to implicit biases—these fictive-error signals are computed by model-free systems, and they compete with the signals computed by other model-free systems, contributing to the guidance of action by strengthening or weakening the force of existing associations. In a striking demonstration of this fact, it was shown that the brains of smokers produce and ignore fictive-error signals in ongoing behavioral choice (Chiu et al., 2008). The competitions between associative processes reveal important computational limitations on human decision-making, and they will be significant to my discussion of the architecture of implicit bias in Section 3. But before addressing this issue, I must address a final class of decision-making systems that are present in human cognition.

We are not simply stimulus-response machines. While it is often difficult to do so, we can sometimes construct and evaluate counterfactual models of the world that allow us to predict the consequences of our actions before we act. Indeed, there is growing evidence that systems dedicated to model-based reasoning allow us to produce decision trees that represent the value of various potential action-outcome pairs, and then search these trees to determine which actions are likely to produce the best outcomes overall (Crockett, 2013: 363).[4] This process relies on mechanisms in the prefrontal cortex that represent stored goals and values in working memory. And while model-based decisions can be more accurate and flexible than those produced by predictive learning systems, "their computation is costly in terms of neural resources and time" (Niv, 2009: 21). Furthermore, situational or endogenous variables can modulate the salience of our goals, values, and ideals, and they often do where they conflict with representations produced by simpler associative systems (Braver and Cohen, 2000). This is important, as there are many cases where the outputs of model-based systems will not converge on the same decision that would be made on the basis of Pavlovian or model-free values—and conflicts between these systems must be settled by way of comparative evaluations that determine which representation is most salient in the current situation (Dennett, 1991; Huebner, 2014; Selfridge, 1959). Increased activity in PFC and insula is often observed when a decision is made under risk or uncertainty; and increased activity of the ventromedial PFC is often observed when distinct reward and avoidance values must be converted into a "common currency" to allow for a comparative evaluation (Levy and

---

[4] I cannot defend the claim that such systems operate by constructing and evaluating decision trees in this chapter, as doing so would take us far afield from my central argument. At present, tree-based searches offer the most promising account of model-based cognition (cf. Crockett, 2013; Daw et al., 2011; Huys et al., 2012).

Glimcher, 2011; Montague and Berns, 2002; Montague, Hyman, and Cohen, 2004). By contrast, activity is increased in the dorsolateral PFC when ongoing behavior is organized in light of existing goals or values (D'ardenne et al., 2012; Miller and Cohen, 2001; Knoch et al., 2008); and there is evidence that the insula serves as the interface between model-based, model-free, and Pavlovian systems, which allows for the silencing of these systems when computational resources are abundant (Bechara, 2001; Moll et al., 2006).

There is a great deal of evidence that our decisions, as well as our behavior, are typically produced by aggregating the "votes" cast by Pavlovian, model-free, and model-based systems in support of their preferred actions (Crockett, 2013; Daw et al., 2011; Huys et al., 2012). According to this view, the attitudes we express at a particular time depend causally on the outputs of multiple systems. This yields a more dynamic account of attitudes, as their contents can shift as we triangulate stable model-based representations against the dynamic evaluative representations that are encoded by Pavlovian and model-free learning systems. In the remainder of this chapter I argue that our implicit and explicit attitudes are also likely to reflect the combined influence of these three types of computationally and psychologically distinct evaluative systems. This is often hard to see, because the "attitudes" examined by social psychologists are often stabilized as components of large-scale behavioral dispositions (cf. Machery, this volume). In part, I will argue, this is because there are robust regularities in the world to which Pavlovian and model-free systems can readily become attuned. By pulling apart the relative contributions of these systems to our biased decisions and behavior, I hope to make it clear how both inferential and environmental interventions can contribute to changes in our behavior; and I hope to provide some insight into the reasons why various short-term and long-term interventions on bias are as successful as they are. But first I must explain how implicit biases could be produced and sustained by Pavlovian, model-free, and model-based mechanisms.

3 A Plausible Architecture for Implicit Bias

We reflexively see human behavior as indicative of psychological dispositions (Gilbert and Malone, 1995), and the information we encode about group membership allows us to rapidly draw inferences about the features of group members on the basis of incredibly sparse information. This capacity is part of our evolutionary inheritance (Mahajan et al., 2011), and it emerges early in development. By the age of 4, children already make inferences about psychological properties on the basis of group membership (Diesendruck and Eldror, 2011), and they will even use linguistic labels designating group membership to guide inferences about the psychological and behavioral traits of new members (Baron et al., 2013). Our tendency to classify others is triggered by the presentation of even minimal information (e.g. "you belong to the red group"), and this feature of our psychology would be difficult, if not impossible, to eliminate. But there is a great deal we can do to moderate its impact, for this capacity is subserved by a content-poor mechanism that must be calibrated against environmental feedback to yield biases. Expressed differently, while we may have evolved to distinguish between in-groups and out-groups, it is unlikely that we evolved to treat race, gender, and ability as grouping criteria—and doing so requires setting the parameters on general-purpose mechanisms for social cognition. This is where the three systems I have discussed become critically important.

Let us start with Pavlovian systems. Intriguingly, images of group members with shared physical characteristics are insufficient to license category-based inference in 4-year-olds (Baron et al., 2013). But the fact that they do not yet show this tendency should not be too surprising if learning about groups on the basis of visual information recruits Pavlovian algorithms that can be attuned to the co-variations between observed physical features and the experience of biologically significant reactions (e.g. fear, threat, dislike, or reward). Since there is no intrinsic relationship between race and danger, learning these reactions has to occur in a rather roundabout way. But there are evolutionarily old mechanisms that allow us to track the emotional reactions of our friends and family, and we can treat these signals as indications of which things are threatening or dangerous. Of course, we also reflexively monitor the dangers and rewards presented in the media where the members of racialized out-groups are often represented as sources of danger, threat, or sexual reward. Pavlovian mechanisms could slowly attune to these racialized representations, yielding attitudes grounded on fear, disgust, and sexual lust. Were racialized out-groups *only* experienced as sources of threats and dangers, the predictive algorithms employed by Pavlovian systems would yield fully calcified associations that would always guide behavior in light of (often mistaken) predictions about the dangers, threats, and rewards that interactions with out-groups will afford. But even less totalizing representations could drive strong avoidance reactions, which could lead us to suppress behavior and avoid situations where we predict (often mistakenly) that an aversive outcome is likely.[5]

---

[5] While such associations are likely to be pervasive, they are unlikely to be totalizing. While young black men may be tracked as threats, they may also be tracked as successful athletes; and young black women are likely to be primarily treated as sexual objects. In short, even the Pavlovian associations encoded by a person are likely to be a heterogeneous lot, and this will cause all sorts of problems in attempts to intervene on these representations. I return to this point in Section 4.

The hypothesis that some implicit biases are implemented by Pavlovian algorithms gains support from the fact that faces of racialized out-group members trigger increased activity in the amygdala (see Stanley, Phelps, and Banaji, 2008 for a review). This effect is even observed when white participants are exposed subconsciously to photographs of black people (Cunningham et al., 2004). Although the amygdala has long been thought to play an important role in fear conditioning, more recent data suggest that it also evaluates the biological and social *salience* of stimuli in ways that track more abstract patterns of risk and reward (Adolphs, 2010). Amygdala lesions reduce loss aversion, increase risk-taking and social curiosity, and make people who appear unapproachable and untrustworthy *seem* more trustworthy and approachable (Adolphs, Tranel, and Damasio, 1998; Demartino, Camerer, and Adolphs, 2010). And connections to the striatum allow the amygdala to generate an avoidance signal based on the risks associated with socially and biologically significant stimuli. I contend that when the faces of racialized out-group members trigger increased activity in the amygdala, this is likely to be because participants are reflexively evaluating potential dangers, risks, and indicators of trustworthiness when they observe the face of a member of a racialized out-group.[6]

In socially relevant interactions, multiple Pavlovian associations may be relevant to rapid decision-making and the guidance of behavior. A variety of partially overlapping associations could be encoded for the members of a particular racial group, and numerous associations will often be applicable to a single person (since every person belongs to multiple groups). In this case, risk categorization would become a dynamic process in which numerous factors are monitored in parallel and evaluated for salience relative to a particular task (Quadflieg and Macrae, 2011: 221; Rescorla, 1988). Where multiple Pavlovian associations are relevant to ongoing behavior, competitive algorithms must be employed to determine which associative representations are most salient in light of current task-demands. So approach and avoidance responses depend on the value of particular associations, as well as the extent to which distinct representations converge or diverge from one another. When multiple associations converge on a single response, that response will be facilitated, but where there are conflicts between associations, responses will be slower to come on-line (Huang and

---

[6] As Brownstein (p.c.) notes, this hypothesis predicts that people who have not been exposed to racialized environments would not show this type of response. This is right, but I am not sure how it could be tested in our current world. That said, there are data suggesting that *familiar* faces of well-respected blacks do not trigger this same response in white participants; and there is reason to believe that this may reveal an effect of top-down control, such that the evaluations carried out by Pavlovian systems are inhibited as a result of familiarity (cf. Stanley, Phelps, and Banaji, 2008).

Bargh, 2014). As a result, the excitatory and inhibitory relations between multiple associations become a critical variable in explaining many kinds of human behavior. Faces that display typically African-American features will elicit stronger stereotype activations than faces with less prototypical features (Blair et al., 2002); images of people wearing clothing that are atypical for an out-group member are less likely to evoke racialized judgments (Barden et al., 2004); and seeing a person in an unexpected setting tends to evoke less biased responses (Wittenbrink, Judd, and Park, 1997). Expressed simply, whether "looking young, black and male will elicit the activation of stereotypic beliefs along any (or all) of those dimensions depends on his unique appearance and the situation in question" (Quadflieg and Macrae, 2011: 223). I maintain that this is partly because of the complex relations between the underlying Pavlovian associations.

If this is right, environments that contain multiple overlapping sources of racialized reward and punishment will allow Pavlovian systems to attune to environmental contingencies in ways that sustain robust and stable behavioral dispositions. At the same time, we should expect the operation of these systems to be sensitive to individual differences in learning history, and the strength of encoded associations will be modulated by individual differences in impulsivity as well as risk aversion. In line with the hypothesis that tasks like the IAT and the GNAT provide evidence about the strength of associations, we find general trends that are modulated by differences between populations, as well as contextual and situational cues (Greenwald et al., 2009). We also find that different populations and different tasks evoke different patterns of activity in the amygdala (Kubota, Banaji, and Phelps, 2012). These data are, however, also consistent with downstream effects on model-free and model-based evaluations. Indeed, existing models of social cognition suggest that signals from Pavlovian systems can suppress behavior that would otherwise be produced by model-free systems, and they can "prune" the decision trees produced by model-based systems by eliminating options that are "too aversive" (Crockett, 2013).[7] So before assuming

---

[7] What would it take to show that these effects were the result of integrating multiple competing representations, as opposed to revealing a simple effect of Pavlovian processing? As I argue in the remainder of this section, there are both conceptual as well as empirical arguments that speak in favor of the competitive processing hypothesis. Since model-based, model-free, and Pavlovian processes *can*, and *often do* operate in parallel, it would be surprising if they did not do so in this case. Of course, alternative computational models may some day be developed, which would speak decisively in favor of more localized Pavlovian effects. But at present, the most promising "computational approaches to decision-making account for choices by adding up model-based, model-free, and Pavlovian action values, and then converting those values into action probabilities using a softmax function, essentially treating the three systems as separate experts, each of which "votes" for its preferred action (Crockett, 2013: 364). While this fact is not decisive, I hope that the arguments

that the effects revealed by these tasks are a simple function of Pavlovian processing, we must consider the possibility that non-Pavlovian systems also play an important role in the production and stability of implicit bias.

Model-free systems are also associative, as they monitor experience for prediction errors and continually adjust their predictions in light of experienced rewards and punishments. But as I noted in Section 2.3, these systems are also sensitive to fictive-error signals, which allow for the adjustment of behavior in light of simulated outcomes, and to other abstract forms of social instruction (Crockett, 2013; Dayan, 2012). For example, when we use linguistic labels and other minimal types of information to guide *inferences* about the unobserved features of group members, this process must initially depend on the use of abstract representations, and perhaps even model-based computations. This is probably the reason why such tasks typically recruit activity in regions of the medial PFC that are commonly associated with *abstract social reasoning* (Cooper et al., 2012; Mitchell, McCrae, and Banaji, 2006). But connections between the amygdala and mPFC allow these more abstract impressions to rapidly be offloaded onto model-free systems. Expressed simply, signals from the mPFC can modulate approach and avoidance behavior to drive the rapid construction of behavioral policies (Kim et al., 2011). For example, in a novel categorization task, the solidification of biases that can be tracked using an IAT occurs quite rapidly (Dunham, Chen, and Banaji, in press). As people carry out this task, they must mentally rehearse the new action-outcome associations, and in so doing they are likely to reflexively generate course-grained mental simulations that can train model-free systems. After all, model-free systems respond to real as well as imagined feedback, and these systems do not know the difference between the two. Finally, since there are no signals that errors are being made in the novel categorization task—indeed, the participants are categorizing just as they are supposed to—this process of offloading could easily yield a self-perpetuating system, where the resonance between the initial forms of abstract reasoning and the new model-free policies become evidence that everything is going as planned.

In real-world environments, this situation is complicated by the fact that robust patterns of social feedback also line up with these simulations, causing habitual responses to solidify, and making it difficult to get rid of these associations using only model-based interventions. Model-free systems can track more abstract relations between actions and outcomes, and they can generate behavioral policies that are sensitive to social norms rather than perceived or imagined

---

I advance in the remainder of this section lend credence to this hypothesis. (Thanks to Jennifer Saul and Michael Brownstein for pushing me to clarify this issue).

threats (Klucharev et al., 2009, 2011). In typical situations, the result of this process is likely to be quite troubling. Problematic biases are often encoded through a process of verbal and behavioral instruction, which is used—carelessly—to teach children about how *we* respond to the members of racialized out-groups; warnings are made about the threats and dangers posed by an out-group, and about the situations in which these dangers are likely to arise. Model-free systems learn from this type of social instruction, and this could lead to the production of *habits* that attach negative (and more rarely, positive) values to engagements with the members of racialized out-groups. Where this type of information resonates with Pavlovian processing, or with consciously held beliefs that are also formed as a result of this instruction, this process could rapidly transform social feedback into patterns of habitual response. Where behavioral policies track social norms that systematically disadvantage racialized out-groups, the prediction errors that would be relevant to the adjustment of these policies must take the form of evidence that the norms are different than expected (i.e. they must reveal that the predicted statistically normal practices were not in fact statistically normal!); for these backward-looking mechanisms, the fact that a particular group is exploited or dehumanized will always be irrelevant—for error-driven learning is only sensitive to statistical norms. But in spite of the dangers of this process of training model-free systems by way of simulations or direct instruction, the fact that this is possible also suggests that it may be possible to *retrain* model-free systems using other types of simulations—and I return to this point in Section 4. But first, I address the potential role of model-based systems, which could be used to guide behavior in accordance with our reflectively endorsed goals and values.

As I noted in Section 3, model-based systems can produce and search through decision trees, allowing us to determine whether a particular action will align with, for example, our commitment to egalitarian values. These systems can operate consciously or subconsciously, mapping out various potential actions and evaluating the extent to which they satisfy our stored representations of goals and values; and as a result, they could generate value-driven aversions to racist behavior and exploitation, as well as preferences for the promotion of anti-kyriarchal ideals. I maintain that this is one of the primary reasons why studies of implicit bias often reveal increased activity in the dorsolateral PFC and anterior cingulate cortex (ACC) when people attempt to suppress their biases (Stanley, Phelps, and Banaji, 2008). The ACC is commonly activated in situations that trigger conflicts between multiple evaluative systems; and in this case, there is likely to be a conflict between biased Pavlovian and model-free representations, and more egalitarian ideals. The activity of the dorsolateral PFC, by contrast, indicates the deployment of working memory representations, which are employed in modeling and evaluating potential actions in light of our goals and values. There is evidence that these working memory systems in the PFC allow us to exercise control over ongoing behavior, using bias signals to modulate the activity of other evaluative systems in light of our representations of goals and values (Miller and Cohen, 2001). This provides a way for implicit associations to be regulated using model-based evaluations. But importantly, model-based systems operate in parallel to model-free and Pavlovian systems, and most biologically and socially salient choices will represent the combined influence of multiple computationally distinct systems (Crockett, 2013).

Therefore, it is significant that these systems could produce conflicting pulls toward everything from the positive value of norm conformity (understood as attunement to locally common patterns of behavior), to the aversive fear associated with an out-group, and the desire to produce and sustain egalitarian values, among many other situation relevant values. Where the outputs of these systems diverge, each will cast a vote for its preferred course of action; where some of these votes are negative, this will yield a bias toward behavioral inhibition (though the size of this effect will always depend on the strength of these votes, as well as the excitatory and inhibitory relations between multiple representational systems); where there is conflict between the outputs of multiple systems, we will see the familiar increase in response latency revealed by measures like the IAT and the GNAT. The key point is that model-based, model-free, and Pavlovian systems can exert inhibitory and excitatory effects on one another, and that this fact is likely to have a significant effect on behavior (Huebner and Rupert, 2014). In the IAT and GNAT, the task-demands may generate a working-memory signal that conflicts with the representations produced by Pavlovian and model-free systems. This would then yield a difference in latency for counterstereotypical associations, because there is a conflict between distinct decision-making systems. But the point is not merely that there is a conflict between these systems, which is where the familiar analysis stops. By approaching the data from a perspective that highlights the existence of multiple competing systems, which are carrying out different types of computations, we can begin to understand a puzzling piece of data that is rarely discussed in the literature on implicit bias.

Patients with focal lesions in vmPFC show less bias in implicit association tasks, but they make explicit judgments that are indistinguishable from controls (Milne and Grafman, 2001). The most promising computational models of mPFC suggest that these circuits play a critical role in translating the reward and avoidance values computed by model-free and Pavlovian systems into a common currency that can be triangulated against currently active goals (Levy and Glimcher, 2011; Montague and Berns, 2002). Damage to these circuits yields a pronounced tendency to make impulsive decisions on the basis of currently active task-demands. For example, people with lesions to vmPFC make high-risk decisions in the face of ongoing economic losses, and they accept risky bets even where they know that their odds of winning are vanishingly small (Clark et al., 2008; Saver and Damasio, 1991). They also tend to accept more unfair offers in ultimatum games, suggesting an inability to adjust the value of accepting such offers against the reflexively computed value of punishing someone who behaves unfairly (Koenigs and Tranel, 2007). I maintain that the data reported by Milne and Grafman (2001) are also plausibly explained by the failure to integrate multiple values. Specifically, while stereotypical values encoded by Pavlovian and model-free systems are still available to guide some behavior, damage to mPFC prevents these values from being integrated with the currently salient goal of matching faces to evaluative categories.[8] In this experiment, though perhaps not in every other case, the impact of Pavlovian and model-free values is swamped by the salience of the goal-directed representations that are operative in the task.

Building on this suggestion, we can begin to see why inferential processing sometimes has an effect on implicit bias (Mandelbaum, 2015), and why inferential processes are less useful when working memory resources are depleted as a result of increased stress or because of increases in cognitive or affective load. People who are *strongly committed* to egalitarian goals and values show an increased capacity to inhibit or suppress the influence of stereotypes on their judgments. When people with chronic egalitarian goals attempt to compensate for their previously expressed biases, those with the strongest commitments to egalitarian values are less likely to exhibit implicit biases (Moskowitz et al., 1999). A similar effect is also present in tasks measuring shooter-bias (Glaser and Knowles, 2008), which is even more striking since these goals impact incredibly rapid responses that must be made rapidly. Together, such data suggest "that a chronic motivation is capable of dominating even the strongest and fastest-acting conflicting responses" (Bargh, 2006). But even without such chronic motivations, people can use consciously held goals to temporarily modulate reflexive responses. For example, a stimulus that typically evokes negative attitudes (such as a rat) can be *treated* as having a positive value in the context of a

---

[8] Crockett (2013) notes that serotonin functioning modulates the salience of Pavlovian computations. If the model I am sketching is roughly correct, manipulations of serotonin should also modulate implicit bias, but the relevant hypotheses have yet to be tested.

currently active goal; but as soon as this goal is inactive, the valence of that stimulus will revert to its default state (Ferguson and Bargh, 2004).

There is evidence, however, that even minor stress can "flip a switch" that can lead us to abandon computationally taxing model-based processing, and to rely on computationally cheaper forms of model-free or Pavlovian processing (Crockett, 2013; Schwabe and Wolf, 2013). While it is commonly noted that associative processing dominates judgment and decision-making under stress or cognitive load, this reveals a deep fact about the architecture of human cognition, and more specifically about the importance of more chronic goals in bias-relevant decision-making. The increased load imposed by making rapid judgments can increase reliance on Pavlovian associations and model-free processing, and this is likely to be the reason why many people are slower to offer egalitarian responses when asked to rapidly classify stereotype-consistent claims as true or false (Wegner, 1994). It is also likely to be the reason why stress might affect everything from the likelihood of arresting or prosecuting someone to decisions about the severity of a sentence, as well as rapid judgments about whether a black person is carrying a gun or behaving in a threatening manner (each of which appears to be a case where implicit biases have a significant impact). While chronic goals can help to moderate these responses, it is unwise to assume that they always will.

Beyond this fact, we must remember that the computational architecture of implicit bias is likely to be incredibly complex. Most socially significant decisions require sifting through numerous sources of information to distill multiple parallel possibilities into a single value that can guide action (Bargh, 2006; Levy and Glimcher, 2011; Montague and Berns, 2002). Even in the best of cases, where we are not under stress, and where we are not facing an increase in cognitive or affective load, the extent to which we rely on a particular association, or the extent to which our decisions are guided by a particular value, will be sensitive to a wide range of situational factors that guide the online construction of action-guiding representations. As the brain attempts to find a way to sift through all of the representations that are relevant to our ongoing behavior, it must rely on a wide variety of pressures and contextual cues that arise in a particular situation. Thus, cigarette smokers who show a negative implicit attitude toward smoking are less likely to display this attitude when it has been a long time since they smoked a cigarette (Sherman et al., 2003). While the pursuit of nicotine rewards can often be inhibited by the model-based value assigned to not smoking, the value of that reward varies with changes in the neurochemical and social context in which a judgment must be made. In the same way, the negative Pavlovian values associated with walking through a particular neighborhood, or seeing someone who is wearing a particular type of clothing, may lead to decisions that privilege associative processing over consciously endorsed goals—yielding a biased aversion, or much worse. Precisely how such computations are carried out will depend on the context in which a decision must be made. If so, this would have serious implications in moral psychology, since both the strength and accessibility of implicit biases will vary across contexts.

I maintain that the strength of various associations, the impact of particular model-free policies and model-based goals, and the inhibitory and excitatory relations between multiple systems are crucial variables that ought to be taken into account in developing a mechanistic account of how implicit biases are produced (cf. Rupert, 2011). In light of this fact, we should expect low between-measure correlations for different ways of examining implicit bias. Different tasks will not always be measuring a single, unified thing, which is properly called an attitude (Machery, this volume). Instead, these tasks are likely to track the influence of multiple causal factors, all of which are sensitive to individual differences in reinforcement history, experimental context, and corresponding differences in the temporary processing goals evoked by a particular task. I contend that Machery (this volume) and Holroyd and Sweetman (this volume) are right to be skeptical of the claim that implicit bias is a unitary cognitive phenomenon. And I hold that Machery is likely to be right that what emerges in an individual are stable dispositional traits. My core claim is that these traits are likely to be produced and sustained by the complex and dynamic interaction between model-based, model-free, and Pavlovian systems, as well as the world to which the learning systems we rely on are attuned. By focusing on this fact, I suggest that we can begin to develop a more plausible account of where and when strategies for intervening on implicit biases are likely to prove successful, and my aim in Section 4 is to sketch an account of the most plausible types of intervention on implicit bias.

4 Three Types of Imagination

Suppose that our experience of the world is filtered through the lens of a massively parallel computational system that continually integrates the outputs from numerous representational mechanisms, each of which only produces representations that are salient to the tasks they have evolved and developed to tackle. Some of these mechanisms process information relevant to our current goals and values, others process information that arises through episodic memories or counterfactual reasoning, and still others generate low-level predictions about reward-based or action-outcome contingencies. On this view, it "is as if the mind constantly explodes the outside world into multiple parallel possibilities for action, but must then reduce and distill these back for use in a world in which you can only do one thing at a time" (Bargh, 2006: 158). We rely on integrative mechanisms that obscure the massively parallel processing that lies behind our decisions and motivations. As Early Modern philosophers commonly recognized, this yields many confused representations of the world in which we live and act (*confundere:* mingled together). In many cases, these representations make it easy to assume that interventions focused on our immediate experience will have a significant effect on our future behavior. So, we imagine better ways to live and act, we commit to egalitarian worldviews, and we try to be better people. But as the literature on implicit bias suggests, such strategies are often insufficient to modify our behavioral dispositions; and to the extent that we fail to moderate or suppress our implicit attitudes, we often find ourselves acting on the basis of habit, or reactive fear—and often, as a matter of our encounters with the world, we find ourselves compelled to pursue worse things though we see that better ones are available (Spinoza, 2002: 320).

In part, our failures to moderate and suppress our implicit biases derive from the fact that we are unaware of the causes of our behavior, and our attempted interventions leave many of the model-free and Pavlovian systems that guide our behavior untouched. They do little more than add another voice to the cacophony of representations that collectively guide our behavior. In some cases, this helps. An extra voice sometimes tips the balance toward more egalitarian behavior. But since model-free and Pavlovian systems are calibrated against the pervasive stereotypes and oppressive power relations that permeate our world, they continually push us back toward bad habits and problematic ideologies—an effect that is more pronounced when we are tired, stressed, annoyed, or under a high cognitive load; and we live in a world that fosters these states. When the awareness of our biases fades, we often find ourselves—as a result of our encounters with the world—compelled to act in ways that we cannot reflectively avow. So I maintain that the only way to effectively intervene on our implicit biases, and to free us from the problematic constraints imposed by Pavlovian and model-free processing, is to modify the internal and external environments to which our automatic behavior is attuned.

4.1 Just use your imagination

Many implicit attitudes are situational adaptations that are attuned to features of the racist, sexist, and heteronormative communities in which we are immersed (Dasgupta, 2013: 240). But if error-driven learning mechanisms make such attunement possible, they will also make it possible to shift these attitudes by changing the patterns of socially salient stimuli to which we are exposed. In a striking confirmation of this fact, Dasgupta and Greenwald (2001) presented people with images and short biographies of admired and respected African Americans (e.g. Martin Luther King Jr and Michael Jordan), and deeply despised white Americans (e.g. Jeffrey Dahmer and Timothy McVeigh). They then used an IAT (which participants tended to view as a hand–eye coordination task) to show that implicit racial bias was significantly decreased in people exposed to these stimuli—more strikingly, the effect persisted 24 hours later. Gawronski and Bodenhausen (2006: 698) claim that this effect is likely to have occurred because task demands led to enhanced activation of pre-existing associations related to black people; and this hypothesis gains support from the fact that evaluations of well-known people depend, at least in part, on whether they are categorized on the basis of their race or another socially salient feature: Michael Jordan elicits positive evaluations when he is categorized as an athlete, but negative evaluations when he is categorized as an African American (Mitchell, Nozek, and Banaji, 2003). There is also a great deal of evidence demonstrating that priming a person with a socially salient category facilitates associative processing in an IAT (Gawronski and Bodenhausen, 2006). And the situation in which such decisions are made does have a significant biasing effect on the integration of associative representations. But something is not quite right with this hypothesis. Why should thinking about Michael Jordan and Martin Luther King Jr affect the categorization of unfamiliar faces, and why should it have this effect 24 hours later when people are not reminded of the primes and believe that the IAT is really a hand–eye coordination task? There is every reason to believe that these participants would have had other pre-existing associations related to black people, and that many of these associations would have affected response time in the other direction. On the assumption that they did not see the racial primes as related to the initial IAT, there is little reason to suppose that the same pre-existing associations that were deployed in the first phase of the task would be triggered the next day.

The account of implicit bias I advanced earlier offers insight on this point. Gawronski and Bodenhausen (2006: 698) are right that using priming tasks can impact the competitions between multiple systems. But they do not see the possibility of using imaginative representations to co-opt associative learning mechanisms and to adjust our reactions in ways that align them with our reflectively held ideals. The model-free systems implicated in some types of associative processing are sensitive to both actual and fictive-error signals, and they are responsive to simulated experiences as well as more abstract forms of social instruction and inferential processing—though precisely how successful these types of interventions are remains an open question. Reading a brief narrative and briefly imagining the life of Martin Luther King Jr may therefore modulate existing associations by updating the stored value of race-relevant contingencies. Expressed schematically, prefrontal working memory systems operate in parallel to the midbrain systems that guide model-free learning, and can amplify or dampen reward signals by way of bidirectional circuits linking these areas; imaginative engagements with out-groups can trigger the operation of these systems in ways that have a significant impact on our biases. As Johnson et al. (2013) show, reading a brief narrative about a *strong* Muslim woman's response to being assaulted in a subway station effectively reduces implicit bias, especially in people who are not antecedently disposed to engage in perspective-taking.

In a sense, narrative engagement is a familiar strategy for intervening on implicit attitudes, and it shares much in common with the kind of cognitive and dialectical behavioral therapy that has been designed to retrain our implicit attitudes (cf. Huebner, 2009). There is even evidence that we can rely on repeated and directed exposure to the non-stereotypical properties of a stereotype-target to influence automatic judgments (cf. Kawakami et al., 2000). But this is not the only way that we can intervene on the internal environment to which our biases are attuned. Implementation intentions have also been shown to have a similar effect, using only a brief rehearsal of an *if–then* action plan that specifies a trigger-cue and an outcome (e.g. *If I see a person, then I will ignore his race!*). Mentally rehearsing an implementation intention three times yields a form of *reflexive action control*, much like the kind of control evoked by chronic egalitarian values and other shifts in value-driven processing suggested previously, and it can significantly decrease shooter bias and modulate the latency of responses in IATs and GNATs (Mendoza, Gollwitzer, and Amodio, 2010; Webb, Sheeran, and Pepper, 2012). Such results initially seem surprising, but I maintain that they are likely to be the result of encoding novel action-plans in working memory, which can be used to up-regulate or down-regulate the salience of existing associations (Miller and Cohen, 2001). The operation of mechanisms in the ventromedial PFC, which translate the reward and avoidance values computed by multiple systems into a common currency, can be strongly impacted by the presence of an action plan (Levy and Glimcher, 2011; Montague and Berns, 2002). Through bidirectional connections between the PFC and the midbrain, the outputs of model-based computations up-regulate and down-regulate the salience of existing associations in light of our goals and values.

This all seems like good news, as such interventions are simple, and they could have a strong impact on the computations that guide biased judgments and biased behavior. But these strategies are limited, and each depends on a relatively local intervention. It would take superhuman cognitive resources to moderate and suppress all our biases in this way, especially where ongoing feedback from the racist world in which we live continually pushes against this system. As long as we are able to focus on egalitarian goals, prevent them from decaying over the course of our everyday experience, and activate implementation intentions when they are called for, such strategies will operate in ways that help to reshape our habits and reflexive evaluations. But if my model is approximately right, we should also expect there to be other systems pushing back, and since the patterns of associative relations we experience in our world are often difficult to track it will be difficult to moderate and suppress the impact of all of these factors on our decisions and behavior. This, I take it, is the main insight of contemporary Spinozist theories of belief fixation (e.g. Gilbert, Tafarodi, and Malone, 1993; Huebner, 2009; Mandelbaum, submitted). The systems that guide our implicit attitudes are likely to "reflect whatever local environments they are chronically immersed in," and while brief exposures to counterstereotypical situations or local adjustments to our goals and values produce a brief reduction of bias, we will eventually revert to local norms and prior biases (Dasgupta, 2013: 271). The effectiveness of these strategies are thus likely to be compromised whenever computational resources are slim, when we are distracted, and when we are experiencing a stressful situation—and all these situational variables can cause us to backslide into a reliance on Pavlovian and model-free associations that are attuned to the biased structure of our world.

4.2 Niche construction and prefigurative imagination

My account of implicit attitudes suggests that biased stereotypes arise because there is something "right" about them; but in many cases, the only thing that is "right" about them is that they pick out statistical regularities in our experience, which are produced and sustained by patterns of systematic, deeply entrenched, institutionalized bias (e.g. there *are* fewer women in STEM fields, blacks *are* more likely to be arrested, and racialized images pervade the media images we are most likely to encounter). Unfortunately, this is all that backward-looking error-driven learning systems can see, and it is all that they can care about. So as we watch or read the news, watch films, rely on tacit assumptions about what is likely to happen in particular neighborhoods, or draw elicit inferences on the basis of the way in which a person is dressed, we cause ourselves to backslide into our implicit biases. No matter how calm, vigilant, and attentive to our biases we try to be, I maintain that we will be unable to moderate or suppress all our problematic implicit biases until we eliminate the conditions under which they arise. But with an understanding of the mechanisms that guide reinforcement learning, we can begin to see a way *forward* to developing more robust strategies for intervening on our implicit biases.

To my mind, Nilanjana Dasgupta (2013: 247) has made the most important *ethical* contribution to the rapidly growing literature on implicit bias. As she notes, "environments that facilitate positive contact with members of stereotyped groups create and reinforce positive implicit associations, thereby counteracting implicit bias." Those who live in diverse environments, where members of out-groups are encountered in a diverse range of situations, show lower rates of implicit bias and more egalitarian reflective attitudes (Dasgupta and Rivera, 2008). Such environments not only reduce implicit bias; "they also increase people's support for public policies and legislation focused on fixing structural bias and extending equal rights to all groups" (Dasgupta, 2013: 247). But the core insight is that we should not simply attempt to eliminate biases, we should attempt to develop more egalitarian attitudes. To do this we must first live in a world that institutes more egalitarian practices. Of course, we do not inhabit such a world, and many people will only experience the members of racialized out-groups through the distorting and one-dimensional lens of the mainstream media, or through encounters that are easily coded as interactions with "co-workers" or "friends-of-friends" instead of interactions with "black people." Since a person may elicit a positive evaluation when he is categorized in some ways, while still triggering a negative evaluation when he is categorized as an African American, such encounters are unlikely to impact our behavioral dispositions in their full generality (Mitchell, Nozek, and Banaji, 2003). This is why we cannot be content with a world dominated by racist associations. In such worlds, bias will often seep into our thoughts and behavior.

Fortunately, we are rapid niche constructors, and we can manipulate *our world* in ways that make it represent new things for us. We have long worked to make the world smart so that we can be dumb in peace (Clark, 1998: 80), and the strategies that we have used to do this must be deployed in the context of our morally and socially significant attitudes as well if we want to eliminate implicit and explicit bias. We can cultivate egalitarian commitments; and we can construct relationships with like-minded people who will help us to defend and promote egalitarian attitudes. On this ground we can work to build a world that is not grounded on racist (sexist, heteronormative, or ableist) attitudes or beliefs (cf. Haslanger, 2000). To build such a world, we must attempt to reject dominant social norms, challenge existing social institutions, and develop practices that are better than those we have come to expect. But we face a real difficulty in this regard. Error-driven learning helps us to calibrate our behavior against existing norms, and we find norm compliance intrinsically rewarding and norm violation intrinsically aversive. Over the course of our evolutionary history, these facts have had an undeniable benefit (Zawidzki, 2013); but our propensity toward norm conformity and overimitation have also made us conservative organisms that are willing to work to replicate the oppressive forms of social organization that dominate our world. So the type of niche construction that is required to overcome our racial biases calls for another type of imagination, which capitalizes on our ability to transform one another's attitudes, beliefs, and behavioral dispositions.

If we want to *overcome* implicit bias, and if we want to become the sorts of agents who are not dominated by reactions that we cannot reflectively avow, we must engage in collective prefigurative practices designed to create a world where our reflexive reactions are already calibrated against our reflectively held goals and values. We cannot do this on our own, as we always need others to nudge us back toward better practices when we backslide into the racist (sexist, heteronormative, and ableist) thoughts and behaviors that are *statistically normal* in the world that surrounds us. We need to build a new and better world in the shell of the old one, and we need to build relationships and forms of social engagement that embody the world we want to live in. This type of practice is forward-looking, and it requires making creative use of the model-based mechanisms that allow us to imagine alternative possibilities; but it also requires trying to live as if an egalitarian world exists before one actually does. These prefigurative practices can become a collective form of *mindshaping* (Mameli, 2001; Zawidzki, 2013): as we build the world we want to inhabit, we will thereby generate new expectations about how we should live, and these expectations will cause our reflexive learning mechanisms to attune to the work we are trying to bring about. Expressed differently, I contend that we can only develop egalitarian attitudes by living in an egalitarian world. As paradoxical as it seems, this is the most promising strategy for overcoming implicit bias.

Acknowledgments

The argument presented here has benefited greatly from a number of conversations with Cassie Herbert, Dan Kelly, Rebecca Kukla, Nabina Liebow, Eric Mandelbaum, and Susanne Sreedhar. I am also grateful for the helpful feedback, on earlier drafts of the chapter, from Michael Brownstein, Ruth Kramer, and Jennifer Saul.

References

Adolphs, R. (2010). "What does the amygdala contribute to social cognition?" *Annals of the New York Academy of Sciences* 1191(1): 42–61.

Adolphs, R., Tranel, D., and Damasio, A. (1998). "The human amygdala in social judgment." *Nature* 393(6684): 470–4.

Akins, K. (1996). "Of sensory systems and the 'aboutness' of mental states." *The Journal of Philosophy* 93: 337–72.

Balleine, B., Daw, N., O'Doherty, J. (2008). "Multiple forms of value learning and the function of dopamine." In Glimcher, P. W., Fehr, E., Camerer, C., and Poldrack, R. A. (eds.), *Neuroeconomics: Decision Making and the Brain*. London: Academic Press: 367–87.

Barden, J., Maddux, W., Petty, R., and Brewer, M. (2004). "Contextual moderation of racial bias: The impact of social roles on controlled and automatically activated attitudes." *Journal of Personality and Social Psychology* 87: 5–22.

Bargh, J. A. (2006). "What have we been priming all these years? On the development, mechanisms, and ecology of nonconscious social behavior." *European Journal of Social Psychology* 36(2): 147–68.

Baron, A., Dunham, Y., Banaji, M., and Carey, S. (2013). "Constraints on the acquisition of social category concepts." *Journal of Cognition and Development* 15(2), 238–68.

Bechara, A (2001). "Neurobiology of decision-making." *Seminar in Clinical Neuropsychiatry* 6: 205–16.

Blair, I., Judd, M., Sadler, M., and Jenkins, C. (2002). "The role of Afrocentric features in person perception: Judging by features and categories." *Journal of Personality and Social Psychology* 83: 5–25.

Braver, T. S. and Cohen, J. D. (2000). "On the control of control: The role of dopamine in regulating prefrontal function and working memory." *Control of Cognitive Processes: Attention and Performance* 18: 713–37.

Briñol, P., Petty, R. E., and McCaslin, M. J. (2009). "Changing attitudes on implicit versus explicit measures: What is the difference?" In Petty, R. E., Fazio, R. H., and Briñol, P. (eds.), *Attitudes: Insights from the New Implicit Measures*. New York, NY: Psychology Press: 285–326.

Chiu, P., Lohrenz, T., and Montague, P. (2008). "Smokers' brains compute, but ignore, a fictive error signal in a sequential investment task." *Nature Neuroscience* 11(4): 514–20.

Clark, A. (1998). *Being There: Putting Brain, Body, and World Together Again*. Cambridge, MA: MIT Press.

Clark, L., Bechara, A., Damasio, H., Aitken, M., Sahakian, B., and Robbins, T. (2008). "Differential effects of insular and ventromedial prefrontal cortex lesions on risky decision-making." *Brain* 131(5): 1311–22.

Cooper, J., Dunne, S., Furey, T., and O'Doherty, J. (2012). "Dorsomedial prefrontal cortex mediates rapid evaluations predicting the outcome of romantic interactions." *The Journal of Neuroscience* 32(45): 15647–56.

Correll, J., Urland, G., and Ito, T. (2006). "Event-related potentials and the decision to shoot: The role of threat perception and cognitive control." *Journal of Experimental Social Psychology* 42(1): 120–8.

Critchley, H. and Rolls, E. (1996). "Hunger and satiety modify the responses of olfactory and visual neurons in the primate orbitofrontal cortex." *Journal of Neurophysiology* 75: 1673–86.

Crockett, M. (2013). "Models of morality." *Trends in Cognitive Science* 17(8): 363–6.

Cunningham, W., Johnson, M., Raye, C., Gatenby, J., Gore, J., and Banaji, M. (2004). "Separable neural components in the processing of black and white faces." *Psychological Science*, 15(12): 806–13.

Cushman, F. (2013). "Action, outcome and value: A dual-system framework for morality." *Personality and Social Psychology Review* 17(3), 273–92.

D'Ardenne, K., Eshel, N., Luka, J., Lenartowicz, A., Nystrom, L., and Cohen, J. (2012). "Role of prefrontal cortex and the midbrain dopamine system in working memory updating." *PNAS* 109: 19900–9.

Dasgupta, N. (2013). "Implicit attitudes and beliefs adapt to Situations: A decade of research on the malleability of implicit prejudice, stereotypes, and the self-concept." *Advances in Experimental Social Psychology* 47: 233–79.

Dasgupta, N. and Greenwald, A. (2001). "On the malleability of automatic attitudes: combating automatic prejudice with images of admired and disliked individuals." *Journal of Personality and Social Psychology* 81(5): 800–14.

Dasgupta, N. and Rivera, L. (2008). "When social context matters: The influence of long-term contact and short-term exposure to admired outgroup members on implicit attitudes and behavioral intentions." *Social Cognition* 26(1): 112–23.

Daw, N., Gershman, S., Seymour, B., Dayan, P., and Dolan, R. (2011). "Model-based influences on humans' choices and striatal prediction errors." *Neuron* 69: 1204–15.

Dayan, P. (2012). "How to set the switches on this thing." *Current Opinion in Neurobiology* 22: 1068–74.

Dayan, P., Niv, Y., Seymour, B., Daw, N. (2006). "The misbehavior of value and the discipline of the will." *Neural Networks* 19: 1153–60.

De Martino, B., Camerer, C. F., and Adolphs, R. (2010). "Amygdala damage eliminates monetary loss aversion." *PNAS* 107(8): 3788–92.

Dennett, D. (1991). *Consciousness Explained*. Boston: Little Brown Books.

Devine, P. (1989). "Stereotypes and prejudice: their automatic and controlled components." *Journal of Personality and Social Psychology* 56(1): 5.

Diesendruck, G. and Eldror, E. (2011). "What children infer from social categories." *Cognitive Development* 26: 118–26.

Dovidio, J., Kawakami, K., Johnson, C., Johnson, B., and Howard, A. (1997). "The nature of prejudice: Automatic and controlled processes." *Journal of Experimental Social Psychology* 33: 510–40.

Dunham, Y., Chen, E., and Banaji, M. (in press). "Two signatures of implicit intergroup attitudes: Developmental invariance and early enculturation." *Psychological Science*.

Evans, J. and Stanovich, K. (2013). "Dual-process theories of higher cognition: Advancing the debate." *Perspectives on Psychological Science* 8: 263–71.

Ferguson, M. and Bargh, J. (2004). "Liking is for doing: The effects of goal pursuit on automatic evaluation." *Journal of Personality and Social Psychology* 87: 557–72.

Frank, M. and Claus, E. (2006). "Anatomy of a decision." *Psychological Review* 113: 300–26.

Garcia, J. and Koelling, R. A. (1966). "Relation of cue to consequence in avoidance learning." *Psychonomic Science* 4: 123–4.

Gawronski, B. and Bodenhausen, G. (2006). "Associative and propositional processes in evaluation: An integrative review of implicit and explicit attitude change." *Psychological Bulletin* 132(5): 692–731.

Gawronski, B. and Bodenhausen, G. (2011). "The associative-propositional evaluation model: Theory, evidence, and open questions." *Advances in Experimental Social Psychology* 44: 59–127.

Gilbert, D. and Malone, P. (1995). "The correspondence bias." *Psychological Bbulletin* 117(1): 21.

Gilbert, D., Tafarodi, R., and Malone, P. (1993). You can't not believe everything that you read. *Journal of Personality and Social Psychology* 65: 221–33.

Glaser, J. and Knowles, E. D. (2008). "Implicit motivation to control prejudice." *Journal of Experimental Social Psychology* 44(1): 164–72.

Glimcher, P. (2011). "Understanding dopamine and reinforcement learning: The dopamine reward prediction error hypothesis." *Proceedings of the National Academy of Sciences* 108 (Supplement 3): 15647–54.

Greenwald, A., McGhee, D., and Schwartz, J. (1998). "Measuring individual differences in implicit cognition: The Implicit Association Test." *Journal of Personality and Social Psychology* 74: 1464–80.

Greenwald, A., Poehlman, T., Uhlmann, E., and Banaji, M. (2009). "Understanding and using the Implicit Association Test: III. Meta-analysis of predictive validity." *Journal of Personality and Social Psychology* 97(1): 17–41.

Gregg, A., Seibt, B., and Banaji, M. (2006). "Easier done than undone: Asymmetry in the malleability of implicit preferences." *Journal of Personality and Social Psychology* 90: 1–20.

Haslanger, S. (2000). "Gender and race: (what) are they? (What) do we want them to be?" *Noûs* 34(1): 31–55.

Heyes, C. (2012). "Simple minds: A qualified defence of associative learning." *Philosophical Transactions of the Royal Society B* 367: 2695–703.

Huang, J. and Bargh, J. (2014). "The selfish goal: Self-deception occurs naturally from autonomous goal operation." *Behavioral and Brain Sciences* 34(1): 27–8.

Huebner, B. (2009). "Troubles with stereotypes for Spinozan minds." *Philosophy of the Social Sciences* 39(1): 63–92.

Huebner, B. (2013). "Do emotions play a constitutive role in moral cognition?" *Topoi* 1–14.

Huebner, B. (2014). *Macrocognition*. New York: Oxford University Press.

Huebner, B. and Rupert, R. (2014). "Massively representational minds are not always driven by goals, conscious or otherwise." *Behavioral and Brain Sciences* 37(2): 145–6.

Huys, Q., Eshel, N., O'Nions, E., Sheridan, L., Dayan, P., and Roiser, J. (2012). "Bonsai trees in your head: How the Pavlovian system sculpts goal-directed choices by pruning decision trees." *PLoS Computational Biology* 8(3): e1002410.

Johnson, D., Jasper, D. Griffin, S., and Huffman, B. (2013). "Reading narrative fiction reduces Arab–Muslim prejudice and offers a safe haven from intergroup anxiety." *Social Cognition* 31(5): 578–98.

Kawakami, K., Dovidio, J., Moll, J., Hermsen, S., and Russin, A. (2000). "Just say no (to stereotyping)." *Journal of Personality and Social Psychology* 78(5): 871–88.

Kim, M., Loucks, R., Palmer, A., Brown, A., Solomon, K., Marchante, A., and Whalen, P. (2011). "The structural and functional connectivity of the amygdala: From normal emotion to pathological anxiety." *Behavioural Brain Research* 223(2): 403–10.

Klucharev, V., Hytönen, K., Rijpkema, M., Smidts, A., and Fernández, G. (2009). "Reinforcement learning signal predicts social conformity." *Neuron* 61: 140–51.

Klucharev, V., Munneke, M., Smidts, A., and Fernández, G. (2011). "Downregulation of the posterior medial frontal cortex prevents social conformity." *Journal of Neuroscience* 31: 11934–40.

Knoch, D., Nitsche, M. A., Fischbacher, U., Eisenegger, C., Pascual-Leone, A., and Fehr, E. (2008). "Studying the neurobiology of social interaction with transcranial direct current stimulation." *Cerebral Cortex* 18(9): 1987–90.

Koenigs, M. and Tranel, D. (2007). "Irrational economic decision-making after ventromedial prefrontal damage." *Journal of Neuroscience* 27: 951–56.

Kubota, J., Banaji, M., and Phelps, E. (2012). "The neuroscience of race." *Nature Neuroscience* 15(7): 940–8.

Levy, D. and Glimcher, P. (2011). "Comparing apples and oranges." *Journal of Neuroscience* 31: 14693–707.

Liljeholm, M. and O'Doherty, J. P. (2012). "Contributions of the striatum to learning, motivation, and performance: An associative account." *Trends in Cognitive Science* 16(9): 467–75.

Lohrenz, T., McCabe, K., Camerer, C., and Montague, P. (2007). "Neural signature of fictive learning signals in a sequential investment task." *PNAS* 104: 9493–8.

Machery, E. (this volume). "De-Freuding Implicit Attitudes."

Mahajan, N., Martinez, M., Gutierrez, N., Diesendruck, G., Banaji, M., and Santos, L. (2011). "The evolution of intergroup bias: Perceptions and attitudes in rhesus macaques." *Journal of Personality and Social Psychology* 100: 387–405.

Mameli, M. (2001). "Mindreading, mindshaping, and evolution." *Biology and Philosophy* 16(5): 595–626.

Mandelbaum, E. (2015). "Attitude, inference, association: On the propositional structure of implicit bias." *Noûs.* DOI: 10.1111/nous.12089.

Mandelbaum, E. (submitted). "Thinking is believing."

Mendoza, S., Gollwitzer, P., and Amodio, D. (2010). "Reducing the expression of implicit stereotypes: Reflexive control through implementation intentions." *Personality and Social Psychology Bulletin* 36(4): 512–23.

Miller, E. and Cohen, J. (2001). "An integrative theory of prefrontal cortex function." *Annual Review of Neuroscience* 24: 167–202.

Milne, E. and Grafman, J. (2001). "Ventromedial prefrontal cortex lesions in humans eliminate implicit gender stereotyping." *Journal of Neuroscience* 21(12): 1–6.

Mitchell, J., Macrae, C., and Banaji, M. (2006). "Dissociable medial prefrontal contributions to judgments of similar and dissimilar others." *Neuron* 50(4): 655–63.

Mitchell, J., Nosek, B., and Banaji, M. (2003). "Contextual variations in implicit evaluation. *Journal of Experimental Psychology: General* 132: 455–69.

Moll, J., Krueger, J., Zahn, R., Pardini, M., Oliveira-Souza, R., de., and Grafman, J. (2006). "Human fronto-mesolimbic networks guide decisions about charitable donation." *PNAS* 103: 15623–8.

Montague, P. and Berns, G. (2002). "Neural economics and the biological substrates of valuation." *Neuron* 36: 265–84.

Montague, P., Dayan, P., and Sejnowski, T.J. (1996). "A framework for mesencephalic dopamine systems based on predictive Hebbian learning." *Journal of Neuroscience* 16: 1936–47.

Montague, P., Hyman, S., and Cohen, J. (2004). "Computational roles for dopamine in behavioural control." *Nature* 431(7010): 760–7.

Moskowitz, G., Gollwitzer, P., Wasel, W., and Schaal, B. (1999)." Preconscious control of stereotype activation through chronic egalitarian goals." *Journal of Personality and Social Psychology* 77(1): 167–84.

Niv, Y. (2009). "Reinforcement learning in the brain. *The Journal of Mathematical Psychology* 53(3): 139–54.

Nosek, B. and Banaji, M. (2001). "The go/no-go association task." *Social Cognition* 19(6): 625–64.

Preuschoff, K., Bossaerts, P., and Quartz, S. (2006). "Neural differentiation of expected reward and risk in human subcortical structures." *Neuron* 51: 381–90.

Preuschoff, K., Quartz, S., and Bossaerts, P. (2008). "Human insula reflects risk predictions errors as well as risk." *Journal of Neuroscience* 28: 2745–52.

Prinz, J. (2002). *Furnishing the Mind: Concepts and their Conceptual Basis.* Cambridge, MA: MIT Press.

Quadflieg, S. and Macrae, C. (2011). "Stereotypes and stereotyping: What's the brain got to do with it?" *European Review of Social Psychology* 22: 215–73.

Quartz, S. (2009). "Reason, emotion, and decision-making." *Trends in Cognitive Science* 13: 209–15.

Railton, P. (2014). "The affective dog and its rational tale." *Ethics* 124(4): 813–59.

Rangel, A., Camerer, C., and Montague, R. (2008). "A framework for studying the neurobiology of value-based decision-making." *Nature Reviews Neuroscience* 9: 545–56.

Rescorla, R. (1988). "Pavlovian conditioning: It's not what you think it is." *American Psychologist* 43: 151–60.

Rupert, R. (2011). "Embodiment, consciousness, and the massively representational mind." *Philosophical Topics* 39(1): 99–120.

Saver, J. and Damasio, A. (1991). "Preserved access and processing of social knowledge in a patient with acquired sociopathy due to ventromedial frontal damage." *Neuropsychologia* 29: 1241–9.

Schultz, W. (1998). "Predictive reward signal of dopamine neurons." *Journal of Neurophysiology* 80: 1–27.

Schultz, W. (2010). "Dopamine signals for reward value and risk." *Behavior and Brain Function* 6: 24.

Schultz, W., Apicella, P., and Ljungberg, T. (1993). "Responses of monkey dopamine neurons to reward and conditioned stimuli during successive steps of learning a delayed response task." *Journal of Neuroscience* 13: 900–13.

Schultz, W., Dayan, P., and Montague, P. (1997). "A neural substrate of prediction and reward." *Science* 275: 1593–9.

Schwabe, L. and Wolf, O. (2013). "Stress and multiple memory systems: From 'thinking' to 'doing'." *Trends in Cognitive Sciences* 17(2): 60–9.

Sechrist, G. and Stengor, C. (2001). "Perceived consensus influences intergroup behavior and stereotype accessibility." *Journal of Personality and Social Psychology* 80(4): 645–54.

Selfridge, O. (1959). "Pandemonium: A Paradigm for Learning." *Mechanisms of Thought Processes: Proceedings of a Symposium at the National Physical Laboratory.* London: Her Majesty's Stationary Office: 513–31.

Shenhav, A. and Greene, J. (2010). "Moral judgments recruit domain-general valuation mechanisms to integrate representations of probability and magnitude." *Neuron* 67: 667–77.

Sherman, S., Rose, J., Koch, K., Presson, C., and Chassin, L. (2003). "Implicit and explicit attitudes toward cigarette smoking: The effects of context and motivation." *Journal of Social and Clinical Psychology* 22: 13–39.

Spinoza, B. (2002). *Complete Works.* S. Shirley (trans.). London: Hackett.

Stanley, D., Phelps, E., and Banaji, M. (2008). "The neural basis of implicit attitudes." *Current Directions in Psychological Science* 17(2): 164–70.

Sutton, R. and Barto, A. (1998). *Reinforcement Learning: An Introduction.* Cambridge: MIT Press.

Webb, T., Sheeran, P., and Pepper, J. (2012). "Gaining control over responses to implicit attitude tests: Implementation intentions engender fast responses on attitude-incongruent trials." *British Journal of Social Psychology* 51: 13–32.

Wegner, D. (1994). "Ironic processes of mental control." *Psychological Review* 101: 34–52.

Wittenbrink, B., Judd, C., and Park, B. (1997). "Evidence for racial prejudice at the implicit level and its relationship with questionnaire measures". *Journal of Personality and Social Psychology* 72: 262–74.

Zawidzki, T. (2013). Mindshaping: A New Framework for Understanding Human Social Cognition. Cambridge, MA: MIT Press.

1.3

The Heterogeneity of Implicit Bias

Jules Holroyd and Joseph Sweetman

The term 'implicit bias' has very swiftly been incorporated into philosophical discourse. Our aim in this chapter is to scrutinize the phenomena that fall under the rubric of implicit bias. The term is often used in a rather broad sense to capture a range of implicit social cognitions, and this is useful for some purposes. However, here we articulate some of the important functional differences between phenomena identified as instances of implicit bias. We caution against ignoring these differences, as it is likely they have considerable significance—not least for the sorts of normative recommendations being made concerning how to mitigate the bad effects of implicit bias.

1 The Disparate Phenomena called 'Implicit Bias'

Philosophical attention has galvanized around the notion of implicit bias in recent years. Roughly, studies show that individuals harbour many implicit associations between mental constructs, such as 'salt' and 'pepper', or 'white' and 'good'. Sometimes associations concerning stigmatized social groups influence a decision or action. An implicitly biased decision or action is one that expresses or embodies implicit features of cognition, which distort or influence that behaviour. For example, the implicit association between the race category 'white' and evaluative term 'good' can influence people to judge more positively a CV with a white-sounding name on it than the same CV with a black-sounding name (Dovidio and Gaertner, 2000). Philosophers have been particularly concerned with those implicit processes that influence behaviour in undesirable and often discriminatory ways. Some of the questions that philosophers have been interested in are: what are the ethical implications of acknowledging the influence of implicit bias on decision and action? What are the consequences for our understanding of agency, responsibility, and how we ought to act? What is epistemologically problematic about the operation of implicit bias? What kinds of material changes in the world are needed to address and mitigate the likely operation of implicit bias? (See e.g. Kelly and Roedder, 2008; Machery, Faucher, and Kelly, 2010; Holroyd, 2012; Gendler, 2011; Haslanger, 2008.)

What, exactly, is implicit bias? Understanding this is an important step in sensibly addressing these other questions. Our concern is that broad character-izations of implicit bias have led to misleading generalizations, and normative recommendations that may either be counterproductive, or at least less useful than they could be—so we will argue.

Let us start by observing some of the ways in which the term has been characterized and used. In her influential paper 'Implicit bias, stereotype threat and women in philosophy', Jennifer Saul characterizes implicit bias as

unconscious biases that affect the way we perceive, evaluate, or interact with people from the groups that our biases 'target'.   (2013: 40)

This is a useful functional definition: implicit biases are whatever unconscious processes influence our perceptions, judgements and actions—in this context, in relation to social category members (women, blacks, gays, for example).[1] How-ever, there is some evidence that suggests that implicit biases are not always 'unconscious'. It is contentious that the participants are unaware of the cognition that is being implicitly measured in tasks such as the IAT (De Houwer, 2006; Monteith and Voils, 1998). Work on the correction of implicit race bias specif-ically suggests that some awareness of implicit bias is possible, if not likely (Wegener and Petty, 1995). It would not be surprising, given the argument to follow, if there were variations in awareness of different implicit associations. The debate about awareness of implicit processes is interesting, but is not our focus here. (For a discussion, see De Houwer, 2006; Fazio and Olson, 2003, Hann et al., 2013; Holroyd, 2014; see also Gawronski, Hofmann, and Wilbur, 2006).

More importantly for the focus of this chapter, the functional definition we have started with here leaves open the matter of precisely what processes constitute implicit bias, and in particular whether we are dealing with a singular entity or a range of psychological tendencies.

A further concern is that this usage seems to permit ambiguous use of the notion of implicit bias: sometimes 'implicit bias' is used to refer to an *output* such as a biased decision or judgement (for example: '[i]t seems very likely, then, that philosophers will display implicit bias against women'; Saul, 2013: 43). It is also

---

[1] Saul's focus is principally on harmful implicit biases, but she notes that there are a range of idiosyncratic and unproblematic biases.

used in a way that appears to refer to a mental state or process. This can be seen in remarks concerning people 'hav[ing] implicit biases' (Saul, 2013: 55). We think this encourages the tendency to suppose that there is a unified process or state ('implicit bias') that produces a distorting influence on judgement and action (also referred to as 'implicit bias').[2]

Elsewhere, the term 'implicit bias' has been used even more expansively. In addressing the epistemological implications of implicit bias, Tamar Gendler (2011) discusses the phenomena of racial categorization, stereotype threat, and the cognitive depletion that subjects experience after interracial interactions, all under the rubric of 'implicit bias'. In this context, then, implicit bias is being used to pick out a range of social cognitions (and affective states), including but not limited to, unconscious activation and application of stereotypes (involving conscious feelings of anxiety/threat), automatic categorization (of things or people into groups which are perceived as sharing properties), and effortful activity (such as suppression of biased responses or stereotyping).

We contend that whilst in some contexts this kind of expansive understanding of implicit bias can be useful (Section 2), it also has significant limitations and tends to obscure important differences between implicit associations (Sections 3 and 4).

2 The Usefulness of an Expansive Concept

For three reasons, this broad usage makes considerable sense. First, the processes at issue in (for example) Gendler's treatment of the issue are all automatic, difficult to discern from introspection, difficult to bring under reflective control, and as a result not governed by the same norms of reasoning as are reflective states (such as occurrent beliefs and desires). It is useful to identify a set of processes that share these features, and contrast them with the kinds of reflective processes to which philosophers have typically attended. This enables attention to be drawn to the large range of mental activity not encompassed by a focus only

---

[2] Perhaps this conflation of output and cognitive content reflects the confusion over awareness mentioned above. While there is no evidence that people lack conscious awareness of the cognitive content measured by implicit measures, there is evidence to suggest that, under certain conditions, this content may impact other processes and behaviours outside of conscious awareness (Gawronski et al., 2006; Hann et al., 2013). As such, the question of whether implicit bias is unconscious depends on whether one is referring to content or output. More precisely, the evidence seems to suggest that it is the content that may, under some circumstance, be outside of conscious awareness. One of the key points we make in this chapter is that distinguishing differing content is important in under-standing implicit processes—the way content (i.e. mental representations/associations) impacts on behaviour (output).

on reflective, deliberative cognition, and the importance of recognizing this range and its role in our mental lives.[3]

Secondly, functional definitions such as Saul's are helpful if one is concerned—as is important—with articulating the widespread *effects* of implicit biases, and the worries that arise in relation to these. For example, if we want to focus on and articulate the patterns of discrimination in which implicit biases might be implicated, then attending closely to the nature of the implicit cognitions them-selves is not the priority task. If the priority is in articulating those effects rather than looking at the processes that produce those effects and ways of combating them, then it is reasonable to talk of implicit bias as simply whatever implicit processes produced those effects. Such a priority is important in gaining recog-nition of the pervasive nature of the problem. (One cannot encourage people to adopt strategies to combat the problem if they do not agree that there is a problem.)

Another consequential reason for subsuming a number of phenomena under the notion of implicit bias is that it makes it more likely that certain important claims about implicit bias are true. For example, Saul makes the general claim that 'human beings are strongly influenced by a range of disturbing and often unconscious biases' (2013: 40). And indeed, this claim is likely to be true if the notion of implicit bias is broadly construed to include a range of implicit social cognitions. The claim that 'we are all likely to be implicitly biased' (Saul, 2013: 55) will be true if 'implicitly biased' refers to a range of phenomena extending to a number of different negative and socially consequential implicit social cognitions.[4]

We do not mean to suggest that there is any sleight of hand here: gaining traction in addressing the effects of implicit bias requires garnering agreement on the claim that almost all of us will need to reconsider the ways in which our judgements and actions may be influenced—ways we would find surprising and perhaps uncomfortable. For these purposes, a broad characterization of implicit bias is legitimate and useful.

---

[3] One might argue that existing notions already perform these useful functions, such as those of automaticity or system 1 functioning. However, the notions of implicit social cognition, automati-city, and system 1 processes are all examples of dual-process models of the mind with the distinctions between these terms simply reflecting the particular area of cognitive psychology (i.e. memory, attention, and decision making, respectively) that gave rise to them. (For an excellent account of this history, see Gawronski and Payne, 2010.)

[4] That is: for a particular bias, b, it may not be probable that an individual has that bias—but for a range of biases, b1-bn, it is probable that an individual has a bias in that range. So it remains true that all individuals are likely to have some biases.

However, we think that there are two dangers in the philosophical discourse about implicit bias (which amplify each other). Firstly, we want to suggest that there are some dangers in regarding 'implicit bias' as a catch-all for a range of implicit (and not so implicit) social cognitions; doing so permits generalizations that may not be warranted. Secondly, we want to raise concerns about the tendency to overlook the ways in which processes that fall under the rubric of implicit bias may differ, either functionally or structurally, because attending to these differences probably has important implications for the normative recommendations made about how to combat problematic implicit biases.

This tendency is reinforced by the philosophical discourse concerning implicit bias, which speaks to 'the effects of implicit bias', 'the ethical implications of implicit bias', 'the epistemological implications of implicit bias', and so on. (For examples of such usage, see Gendler, 2011; Saul, 2013; Machery et al., 2010; Holroyd, 2012). This kind of discourse implies that the concern is with a certain homogeneous phenomenon (implicit bias) and its effects, and plays down the idea that there might be differences within the phenomena falling under the rubric of implicit bias.

It is our contention that, for some purposes, these differences matter. Perhaps most importantly, the differences matter to the kinds of normative recommendations needed concerning how to mitigate or remove the influence of implicit biases.

3 Implicit Processes and Different Kinds of Implicit Association

Philosophers are not alone in making assumptions about the unified nature of the phenomena. Amodio (2008) observes that 'researchers [including empirical psychologists] have generally assumed that implicit stereotyping and evaluation arise from the same underlying mechanism' (7). In the following sections we articulate the reasons to suppose that implicit bias is functionally heterogeneous, and that this heterogeneity matters considerably. We also consider the reasons for holding that the processes underpinning implicit biases are heterogeneous, but raise concerns about one dimension along which these processes have been distinguished.

In the literature from empirical psychology, we find reference to 'implicit processes' rather than implicit biases (Amodio and Mendoza, 2010; Nosek, Hawkins, and Frazier, 2012; for a review, see Gawronski and Payne, 2010). This suggests that what is at issue is a set of processes which share the property of being 'implicit'—generally (and not uncontestedly[5]) under the radar of reflect-ive introspection, difficult to bring under reflective control, and quick and efficient.

Amodio (in accordance with most other psychologists working in this domain, e.g. Fazio, 2007; Greenwald et al., 2002) understands these implicit processes essentially to consist in the utilization of 'associations stored in memory' (2010: 364). Associations[6] are discerned by tests such as the implicit association test (IAT) and affective priming task (Fazio et al., 1995). In the IAT (the most popular implicit measure) the implicit associations present in an individual's cognitive structures are revealed in the swiftness of response in categorizing concepts into pairs. A range of experimental tests aims to reveal individuals' associations, and thereby identify factors that may play a role in perception, judgement, and action, but which go unreported in reflective (explicit) statements of what guided behaviour, either because of self-presentation worries (Fazio and Olson, 2003) or simply because such associations are not readily detectable by the agent (see Brownstein and Saul, this volume, for a description of implicit measures such as the IAT).

What kinds of associations are at issue here? A number of central cases of implicit bias have concerned philosophers (there are numerous studies, but these have received significant attention). The associations between social category and stereotypic or negative notions are cause for particular concern. Such associations have variously been found to guide the evaluation of CVs, produce shooter bias, and affect interracial interactions (see e.g. Saul, 2013; Kelly and Roedder, 2008; Machery et al., 2010). Are the same associative mechanisms, or kinds of mech-anism, involved in each of these cases? Do the associations all function in the same way, or are there important differences?

We advance two claims here: first, that evidence indicates that different associations have different characteristics. Accordingly, there is reason to doubt that all generalizations about implicit bias can be substantiated, and to be

---

[5] See e.g. Monteith, Voils, and Ashburn-Nardo (2001); De Houwer (2006); Fazio and Olson (2003); Nosek et al. (2012).

[6] The idea that memory, and the mind more broadly, is associative is a long-held view in philosophy. Subsequently, psychologists and neuroscientists concerned with learning and memory have adopted this idea. However, there is work to suggest that this associative picture of mind may be fundamentally flawed (see Gallistel, 2008; Gallistel and King, 2009; Gallistel and Matzel, 2013). While discussion of this point is outside the scope of the present chapter, we feel it important to acknowledge and to make clear that our argument is not fundamentally based on an associative picture of the mind. Regardless of the way memory is organized and instantiated in the brain, we believe that it is a mistake to suppose that the cognitive processes at work in implicit biases are all relevantly similar.

cautious about talk of 'implicit bias' simpliciter. Secondly, drawing on the work of Amodio (2008) and Amodio and Devine (2006), we consider whether it is appropriate to understand that one dimension along which implicit bias differs, both in terms of content and underpinning structure, is in terms of whether implicit associations are semantic or affective. These terms refer to ways of categorizing kinds of associative process: firstly, according to whether the content of the association concerns the meaning of the associated constructs, or the positive or negative affect accompanying a construct; and secondly, in terms of the processes underpinning these different contents. We argue that this distinction is problematically deployed in their empirical studies, and so whilst we might endorse the general claim that implicit associations differ functionally, in respect of how they seem to operate in relation to other beliefs and behaviours, we do not endorse the more specific claim that these differences are captured or predicted by either contents, or an underlying structure, that is understood in terms of the semantic/affective distinction. However, if the claim about functional difference is right, there will be important consequences for making generalizations about implicit bias. In particular, there are implications for the general recommendations made concerning how to mitigate implicit bias, which we address in the Section 4.

3.1 Biases behaving differently: two kinds of heterogeneity

At first glance, it seems clear that the studies that have been focused upon involve different associations. Some studies test for gendered associations, others test for associations with racial categories, others still for age, sexuality, and religious or ethnic groups, and respective associations.[7] Clearly, there are different associations involved in the studies reported on. The strength of implicit associations between the following categories (inter alia) have been tested:

- Gender (gendered words: she, woman/he, man) and words associated with leadership (manager, director/worker, assistant) (Webb, Sheeran, and Pepper, 2010).
- Sexuality (images of gay and heterosexual kisses) and positive and negative words (Payne, Cooley, Loersch, and Lei, ms.).

---

[7] Other implicit associations that have little directly to do with social identity have also been studied, such as associations concerned with health and other foods, with objects of fear (such as snakes), and so on. Whilst these associations have garnered less interest from philosophers, they have been important in advancing understanding of the kind of cognitive processes at work in these implicit attitudes and in developing clinical interventions for addiction and various psychopathologies.

- Race (black and white name primes) and personal preferences (like/dislike) (Olson and Fazio, 2004); black and white faces and positive and negative words (Amodio and Devine, 2006).
- Gendered pronouns (he/she) and job titles (nurse, mechanic) (Banaji and Hardin, 1996).
- Ethnic/religious group words (Muslim/Scottish) and words associated with terror, or peace (Webb, Sheeran, and Pepper, 2010).

It is obvious that there are different associations involved here; the relevant associations hold between relata with different content. But even this obvious fact is obscured by talk of 'implicit bias' simpliciter, without note of which associations are in play. Attending to this prompts us to ask what these differences in content amount to; should we expect all of these associations to behave in similar ways? We claim that there is reason to suppose not, and that this has implications for philosophical discussion about, and practical recommendations relating to, implicit biases. One explanation for the functional differences we outline in Section 3.2 appeals to the difference in contents. This means that it would be of utmost importance to attend to the content of implicit biases, rather than talk about implicit bias in generalized terms, if one is concerned to outline the effects, and ways of combating discriminatory behaviours.

A second kind of explanation might appeal to different processes involved in implicit cognition. For example, some have argued that there is reason to suppose that the various implicit measures are accessing discreet and non-unified implicit associations (such that they do not all cluster together to form an 'implicit attitude'), or perhaps different kinds of implicit processes. The IAT is one amongst a number of implicit measures; that is, tests which attempt to 'get at' individuals' implicit associations (such as their implicit race associations). A number of authors have pointed out that individuals' scores across implicit measures weakly correlate (that is, showing an implicit association on one measure does not correlate with showing an implicit association on another measure). For example, Fazio and Olson (2003) cite various studies in which they observe the 'disappointing correlations among various implicit measures', and report that 'in our own lab we have repeatedly failed to observe correlations between IAT measures and priming measures of racial attitudes' (277).

In a survey article, Nosek et al. (2007) argue that one of the best explanations for this weak correlation is simply the range of processes being tested for by the various implicit measures:

[t]he relations may also reflect heterogeneity of cognitive processes that contribute to the various measures. The term *implicit* has become widely applied to measurement methods

for which subjects may be unaware of what is being measured, unaware of how it is being measured, or unable to control their performance on the measure. Identification of the cognitive processes that contribute to different measures will promote a more nuanced description and categorization of methods based on the particular processes that they engage. (277)

The idea for our present purposes is that the lack of correlation between implicit measures, as Nosek claims, is explained by the different processes or cognitive structures that each measure is tapping into. Nosek et al. suggest:

The next generation of research in implicit cognition will likely revise the simple implicit–explicit distinction and introduce a more refined taxonomy that better reflects the heterogeneity of cognitive processes that are collectively termed *implicit*. (267)

Accordingly, there are two ways in which implicit biases might be heterogeneous. Firstly, we may observe functional heterogeneity in the way that different implicit associations operate (perhaps explainable by differences in content); and secondly, there may be heterogeneity in the processes underpinning different implicit associations. In this chapter we remain agnostic as to whether the heterogeneity manifest in implicit associations is attributable to different content or to different underlying processes. (Whilst the content explanation could do the explanatory work, it is possible that better formulated understandings of the structural differences might also have explanatory power.) Our main contention is that philosophers also need to be alert to the dimensions of heterogeneity in the ways that implicit biases operate, and possible distinctions between different kinds of implicit cognitive processes, that might explain this, for two reasons. Firstly, because evidence supporting such a taxonomy is relevant to precisely what generalizations can be made about implicit associations. Secondly, because the way that the distinctions are drawn may themselves require philosophical scrutiny. We return to this point in Section 3.2.

Regarding the first concern, about the generalizations that are warranted, one illustration of this pertains to the claims that philosophers have variously made about individuals being afflicted by implicit bias *irrespective* of their explicit beliefs. But there is reason to suppose that this generalization cannot be made. With respect to some associations, this claim seems true: in tests for implicit associations between gendered pronouns (he/she) and stereotypical roles (nurse/secretary), Banaji and Hardin (1996) found no difference in the extent of implicit biases between individuals who, on self-report measures, scored either high or low in sexist beliefs (139). In contrast, in studies reported in Devine (2002), it appears that individuals who held non-prejudiced behaviour to be important in itself display less race bias on race IATs (which require pairing black and white face or names with positive or negative words); that is, the explicit beliefs and attitudes an individual held did seem to correlate with the degree of implicit bias they manifested. (See also Nosek et al., 2007 (277–8) for discussion of the cases in which self-report measures seem to correlate with implicit attitudes.)

Crucially, the heterogeneity of implicit biases in this respect means that some generalizations about the relationship of implicit associations to explicit beliefs— such as that implicit biases are independent of explicit attitudes—cannot be substantiated.

We have in this section distinguished between two ways in which implicit biases might be heterogeneous: functionally, or in terms of the underlying processes. We provided some evidence that supports functional heterogeneity, and indicated the reasons for which some have suggested that there may be heterogeneity in terms of the underlying processes involved. Of course, one explanation for these bits of evidence could be simply that the experimental designs did not always produce or measure the effects that they should or could have (cf. Nosek et al., 2007: 276). Nonetheless, the findings should give reason to exercise caution about claims that are general in nature, and that make recommendations for the regulation of bias that suppose general applicability of such recommendations. In Sections 3.2.1–3.2.3 we provide further considerations in support of the claim that the best explanation of this heterogeneity is not experimental deficit, but rather differences between implicit associations and their operation.

3.2 Distinct associations with distinct behavioural influence

We have identified associations that are obviously, on the face of it, different. We have noted that some of these biases appear to stand in different relationships to explicit beliefs. This suffices for our central message of caution regarding the generalizations that can be made about implicit biases (a message we shall elaborate in Section 4). At least in this respect, then, generalizations about implicit biases are mistaken. This is significant, as there is a tendency to suppose that implicit biases are unrelated to explicit beliefs, and this may have further implications for how questions such as control, responsibility, and accountability are considered.

In this section we consider a further way in which implicit associations may differ; namely, with respect to the influence they exert on different kinds of behaviour. This dimension of functional heterogeneity has been articulated in the context of empirical studies that aim to differentiate between different underlying processes: 'semantic' and 'affective' associations. If we take these experimental results at face value, then there would be reason to suppose that it identifies some underlying structure to the heterogeneous implicit processes. However, we argue that there are reasons to worry about this distinction, and that it should not, as presently articulated, be endorsed. This does not, however, undermine our central claim that implicit biases differ in important ways; there seems to be some important functional heterogeneity, though it is not best captured in terms of semantic and affective associations. Moreover, our discussion reinforces the claim that philosophers should attend to the ways in which psychologists are distinguishing different implicit biases. We explore the implications of this claim in the final section.

We start by presenting the further dimension of functional heterogeneity, then explain—and critique—the conceptual framework used to articulate this in terms of the heterogeneous underlying structures, by empirical psychologists.

3.2.1 DISTINCT ASSOCIATIONS

Amodio and Devine (2006) attempted to isolate the operation of different associations, and test for the presence of each. In order to do this, they constructed two race IATs. One was designed to test for associations between race and certain stereotypic traits: white/black, and mental (e.g. brainy, smart, educated) or physical (athletic, agile, rhythmic) constructs. They supposed that individuals might hold these implicit associations (such as a stronger association between *black* and physical constructs and between *white* and mental constructs) without also having negative attitudes or affect associated with that racial category (in common and imprecise parlance, an individual might hold a stereotype without having negative attitudes or disliking the stereotyped individuals). The second IAT was designed to test for these latter, negative affect-laden associations by asking participants to pair black or white faces with pleasant or unpleasant constructs (respectively: *love, loyal, freedom; abuse, bomb, sickness*).[8]

The striking—and crucial for our purposes—finding was this: 'the participants' scores on the two IAT's were uncorrelated' (Amodio and Devine, 2006: 14). That is to say, the extent to which individuals expressed the mental/physical associations *was not correlated* with scores on the second IAT for negative implicit attitudes.

Why is this significant? Firstly, it suggests that the two associations were in some subjects operating independently (Amodio and Devine, 2006: 655). Whilst we might expect many implicit associations to go in step (for example, we might expect an individual who implicitly associates black men with danger to also have

---

[8] This kind of attitude (stereotyping without negative affect) is termed 'benign racism' in analyses of racism. See e.g. Garcia (1996).

implicit negative affect—fear—towards them), this study indicates that at least some implicit associations about the same group are held independently. (Note that this observation is more readily made once we attend carefully to the different contents of implicit associations, obscured by generalized speak of 'implicit bias'.)

Secondly, these findings indicate that there may be variation across individuals with respect to which associations are operative in producing implicitly biased perceptions, judgements of, or actions towards a particular group. For any implicit association, some individuals may have it and others may not (which is consistent with the variation in affective association found in studies by Devine et al., 2002). But the presence of (e.g.) one kind of implicit race association does not entail the presence of other forms of implicit race associations[9]—and conversely, the absence of one implicit association does not entail that one is free from other problematic implicit race biases.

Even if much of the time, or in many subjects, implicit associations work in concert, if there are distinct associations then it will be important to understand further the ways in which they may differ. This is of crucial import, given the differential behavioural outputs that these two implicit associations correlated with, which we now describe.

3.2.2 DISTINCT INFLUENCES ON BEHAVIOUR

Not only did the studies indicate that different implicit associations were not correlated; they also indicated that the different associations uniquely predict different behavioural outcomes. In the study by Amodio and Devine (2006), participants were asked to make judgements about the competences of a potential test partner, and then asked to sit and wait for their test partner to enter the room. The—in fact, fictive—test partner was indicated to be African American. Seating distance was measured as a behavioural indicator of positive or negative affect. Experimental participants who displayed strong associations on the race IAT for the mental/physical constructs, described in Section 3.2.1, made judgements about the competence of their test partner consistent with stereotypes (such as competence on questions about sports and popular culture, rather than mathematics). But these kinds of association did not predict greater seating distance from the test partner. On the other hand, manifestation of strong negative evaluative associations on the affect-based IAT uniquely predicted

---

[9] As Alex Madva has pointed out (correspondence), it might permit us to infer the increased probability of other sorts of implicit race association, even if the correlation is low.

seating distance (greater negative associations correlated with greater seating distance), but not judgements of competence.[10]

So, one association seems to be implicated in the judgements and evaluations individuals made, the other in approach or avoidance behaviours. This provides further support for the worry we raise: that certain generalizations about predicted behaviours cannot be made across various implicit associations. Note that this is not at all surprising when we consider associations that differ in their target: we would not expect gender associations to predict behavioural outcomes regarding racial interactions. What is noteworthy here is that different race associations (that is, associations that concern the same target social identity) are operating independently and with different behavioural predictions.[11]

If different implicit associations seem to exert influence on different kinds of behaviour, then understanding this will be important in formulating strategies that aim to combat implicit bias. In relation to the particular associations at issue here, for example, if one is involved in a task such as evaluation of an individual's competence or intelligence, then mitigating the associations between race and mental or physical constructs that may influence that judgement will be of particular importance. On the other hand, if one is concerned with increasing the amount and quality of intergroup contact, one might focus on limiting or changing negative affective associations. We return to this point in Section 4.1.

3.2.3 A DIMENSION OF HETEROGENEITY: SEMANTIC AND AFFECTIVE ASSOCIATIONS?

The experimental results we have just presented support our thesis that implicit associations are functionally heterogeneous and may not readily admit of the sorts of generalization that have been made (concerning behavioural predictions and their relation to explicit beliefs, for example). However, these results are framed in empirical psychology in terms of two different kinds of association: semantic and affective. The idea is that this identifies a systematic difference in content, which is underpinned by a structural heterogeneity (along which the

---

[10] It is worth noting the study by Macrae et al. (1994), which seems to indicate that stereotypes can affect seating distance. Participants in whom stereotypes were activated sat further from the stigmatized individual. Is this finding in tension with that by Amodio and Devine (2006)? We think not. It is important to observe that the stereotype at work in the study by Macrae et al. was that of 'skinhead', which is likely to involve various associations (fear, hostility, aggression) that are more similar to the negative evaluative associations found to predict greater seating distance in the study by Amodio and Devine. Moreover, this finding drives home our overall point that it is difficult to make generalizations across different kinds of association. Attention must be paid to how different contents may produce different behavioural predictions and outcomes.

[11] Thanks to Alex Madva for emphasizing the importance of this point.

functional heterogeneity may be explained). The mental/physical constructs are identified as 'semantic' associations. Other examples of this kind of association are salt/pepper and woman/she. The unpleasant/pleasant constructs (used on the second IAT described in Section 3.2.1) are identified as 'affective' associations—those that have an affective valence. Other associations put into this category include those for which one relata is evaluative, either generally ('good/bad') or in more specific ways ('attractive/disgusting'). Generalizations about these two kinds of association, concerning their influence on behaviour, how they might be learned or unlearned, are then made. Here we have not adopted this way of conceptualizing the distinction, nor supposed that the differences described in the previous sections are underpinned by such a distinction—either in content, or in underpinning processing—and are reluctant to do so for the following reasons.

Firstly, even if we endorse heterogeneity in content, considerations of parsimony counsel against explaining these differences in terms of different underlying associative processes. That implicit associations dissociate, and generate different behavioural predictions, could be explained in terms of the content of the associations, without recourse to distinct underlying mechanisms.

Secondly, however, even at the level of contents, the distinction posited is itself problematic. Whilst it is coherent to draw such a distinction (between those associations which have affective content and those which do not), the way this distinction is deployed is problematic. For one thing, it seems inappropriate to characterize one side of the distinction as 'semantic'. How should we best make sense of the idea of a 'semantic' association? This category has been used to identify associations that hold between 'semantically related concepts' (Amodio, 2008: 8). But that idea seems deployed problematically in the study described in Sections 3.2.1 and 3.2.2: the stereotypic association is not adequately characterized as a matter of the semantic meaning of *black* or white; nothing in the *meaning* of these terms is associated with mental or physical constructs (in contrast, the meaning of *woman/she* clearly is semantically related; a paradigm case of semantic relationship is between 'bachelor' and 'unmarried man'). The characterization might aim to pick out the fact that certain semantic content has become associated with the racial category, such that the two are associated in mind. But this does not help us to pick out one side of the distinction, as paradigm relata of affective associations (*good*, *attractive*, and so on) have semantic content which comes to be associated with one social group.

Perhaps what is at issue is the contents of a *schema* (or stereotype) for different racial categories (and other aspects of social identity) (Haslanger, 2008). Schemas are characterized by Haslanger as 'a patterned set of dispositions in response to one's circumstances' (212). Might we understand semantic associations in terms of the contents of a schema, saying that if included in a schema, an association (a kind of pattern of thought) is semantically associated? The problem is that it is not at all clear that schemas do not include the sorts of association that have been classified as 'affective', as dispositions to respond could just as well be under-pinned by affect as by cognitive understandings. Haslanger is here drawing on Valian (2005), who denies that schemas have affective content. Valian writes that on her account, schemas are 'cold'. Her account 'is purely cognitive rather than emotional or motivational' (198). We believe our point to show that Valian's understanding of schemas, which is narrower than Haslanger's, to be mistaken in excluding affective content, if that is to include the negative affect that attaches to evaluative terms such as 'good', 'bad', 'loyal', 'evil', and so on.

All this raises worries for characterizing one side of the distinction as 'seman-tic'. But the difficulty is not simply that this way of describing the distinction seems inapt; rather, the distinction does not seem to cut where it needs to in order for Amodio and Devine to draw their conclusions about the heterogeneity of content, or underlying processes (as affective or semantic). If the distinction is supposed to be between associations with semantic content and those without, then this distinction was not adequately captured by their experimental design, because some associations that are supposed to be on the affective side have semantic content (good, disgusting, and so on).

Perhaps the distinction captured by their experimental design is supposed to be between associations that are affectively valenced (with positive or negative affective 'pull') and those that are not. Some who endorse the primacy-of-affect thesis, according to which all concepts held have *some* valence, might worry about this characterization: everything, it seems, would fall into the 'affective' category. One might reject that worry: perhaps the 'affective' associations can be identified as those that produce affect above a certain threshold. Even still, whilst this may present us with a conceptually coherent way of drawing the distinction that the categories do not seem to be exclusive seems to pose difficulties for the thesis that there are two distinct kinds of content, which operate on two different underlying structures, about which generalizations and predictions can be made. This is especially so because the experimental studies utilize notions which incorporate both semantic content and affect (good/bad, attractive/disgusting, and so on).

Even those terms that are supposed to indicate semantic associations in Amodio and Devine's studies (intelligence, athleticism, smart) have both evalu-ative and semantic content (the characteristics are positive, good, features). So, we might at this stage claim that such a distinction is coherent (if not best described as 'semantic' and 'affective'), but that the studies by Amodio and

Devine do not exclusively track this distinction, insofar as the supposedly seman-tic associations had affective content, and the supposedly affective associations had semantic content. Given this, their deployment of the distinction cannot be used to support the claim that there are two kinds of association that generate distinct behavioural predictions.

An analogy can help us to make this point. Suppose one wanted to evaluate children's well-being, and one supposed that a dimension that might explain different levels of well-being is whether a child has an active father in their life, or is raised by a single parent. One might construct a study to evaluate this hypothesis. But that distinction on which the hypothesis rests is deployed problematically, and cannot be explanatorily useful in predicting different out-comes, because (obviously) some single parents are fathers. In order to test the hypothesis, the study would have to compare the outcomes of those children who did not have an active father, and those who did. If there are different outcomes in children's well-being, some other way of understanding and describing the circumstances that might make that difference must be sought. By the same token, the distinction between semantic and affective distinctions cannot be posited as explanatorily useful in explaining different outcomes (e.g. different behavioural influences) if some so-called semantic associations investigated are also strongly affect-laden. In order to test the hypothesis, the study would have to compare associations which are not affect-laden with those which are. Until the distinction is deployed in a way that really does investigate distinct instances of each sort of implicit association, the findings cannot support the claim that the heterogeneity consists in two independent and distinct processes: affective and semantic.

Given these concerns, we do not here endorse the idea that what distinguishes different implicit associations (and any different underlying mechanisms) is that some are semantic and others affective. We should not endorse this as accurately capturing heterogeneous underlying processes involved in implicit biases. This is consequential for the notions that are at work in empirical psychology: we suggest that this distinction has been unsatisfactorily deployed. If Nosek is right that more fine-grained understandings of the cognitive processes involved in implicit cognition are needed, then so is more attention to the way that these processes are conceptualized and deployed in empirical studies.

Is it worth attempting to construct further studies which investigate this distinction? We have indications that different implicit associations generate different behavioural predictions. Whether this is a function of the affective content of the association, or indeed a distinct process particular to affective-laden associations, remains an open question—one worth pursuing insofar as it is worth finding out what sorts of generalization can be made, and on what basis (the content of associations, or processes underlying them). It is not impossible to imagine how that distinction could be adequately operationalized. For instance, one might imagine an experimental paradigm in which the positive and negative words are replaced with (neuro)physiologically induced feelings of pleasure vs. displeasure on which to make more 'purely' affective categorizations. These could be contrasted with associations without affect (or with only a very low affective content). Such an undertaking is fraught with practical difficulties, but is not, in principle, impossible to implement. It is beyond the scope of this chapter to develop any full proposals for such efforts, but we would encourage psychologists and others to consider the possible ways of proceeding. Perhaps only if systematic content differences were then discerned might it be appropriate to consider claims about the underlying processes for the distinct content differences.

For present purposes, we need not establish that there are differences in terms of distinct and heterogeneous implicit processes. Rather, our aim is to draw attention to the fact that there are important functional differences with respect to some implicit associations—some of which are in terms of the degree of affect, which seems to make a difference (perhaps it is not the only thing that makes a difference) to the behavioural predictions generated. At present, experimental evidence supports the claim that implicit associations differ in some respects, such that some generalizations about implicit bias are unsupported. But, we have argued, it is not warranted to identify the respects in which they differ to be with regard to the associations being carved into two kinds: semantic or affective.

There remain two possibilities. One is to hold that implicit biases operate on fundamentally the same sort of process, but that they are dissociable and can functionally differ significantly in various dimensions (with respect to degree of awareness, relationship to explicit belief, behavioural predictions). Another is to hold that there are multiple processes involved in the category of implicit biases, and that these different processes correspond to the different features we have highlighted. At this stage, we do not believe that the considerations we have marshalled speak in favour of one or other of these theses—but there is much further work to be done on this topic.

3.3 Summary

We began by showing that experimental results illustrate functional differences which mean that it will be difficult to make certain generalizations about the phenomena that fall under the rubric of 'implicit bias'. These functional differences may be explicable in terms of content, or in terms of heterogeneity of underlying structure, such as whether the associations are affect-laden or not.

However, the way experimental studies have deployed the distinction between different kinds of association mean that those conclusions cannot provide support for there being two distinct kinds of process. It remains an open question what best explains the functional differences observed. That there are functional differences, however, is not in doubt. This claim is supported by the following considerations: the differences in content and the failure of correlation across implicit measures; the different relationship of implicit associations to explicit beliefs; and the different behavioural predictions generated by different implicit associations. To the extent that there is reason to believe that these functional differences are explained by heterogeneous cognitive processes, however, we suggest that further work is to be done in making precise the nature of this heterogeneity and deploying it in experimental design.

We have already alluded to the fact that these findings will have implications for philosophical discourse about implicit bias. In Section 4 we explain in more detail what we take these implications to be, and make specific recommendations about how philosophical discussions about implicit bias can accommodate these concerns.

4 Implications of the Heterogeneity of Implicit Bias

In this section we draw out the key implications of recognizing the functional heterogeneity of implicit bias.

4.1 Avoiding misleading generalizations, specific normative recommendations

The first implication of the aforementioned discussion pertains to the kinds of theoretical claims that have been made about implicit bias. Philosophers have reported on implicit bias in rather general terms, frequently talking of 'implicit bias' simpliciter or 'implicit race bias', rather than noting the particular kinds of association at issue. For clarity's sake, it would be useful to articulate the specific associations at issue. What particular stereotypical constructs are they associated with? Are evaluative associations at issue? What degree of negative affect is involved? One reason for which it is important to do so is that there are implications for the kinds of normative recommendations philosophers make about strategies for combating implicit bias.

Such strategies generally fall into two categories (see Jolls and Sunstein, 2006). Insulating strategies aim to put in place mechanisms that prevent bias from being activated by insulating individuals from the information that might activate them. For example, anonymizing CVs or essays means that evaluators do not have the information (about the gender, age, or race, and so on, of the evaluated individual) that might trigger implicit associations that distort judgement or influence behaviour. This sort of strategy, therefore, need not be sensitive to the functional heterogeneity of implicit bias, insofar as it simply prevents bias triggering information from reaching the individual.

Mitigating strategies are those that attempt to limit any effects of implicit bias where activation and influence remains a possibility (because insulation from bias relevant information is not feasible). Mitigation might occur either by hindering the activation of the bias, or if it is activated, by blocking its influence upon judgement or action. For example, in interview contexts, where at least some salient social identities of an individual are not possible to 'cover up' or 'anonymize', steps need to be taken to reduce the likelihood of any implicit associations being activated, or if activated, from having an effect on judgement or action. Such steps might involve the deliberate exposure to counterstereotypical exemplars (so as to inhibit the activation of stereotypical associations) (Joy-Gaba and Nosek, 2010), or having agreed upon the weightings of criteria for evaluation (so that the influence of bias—which can lead merit to be redefined to accommodate bias—might be corrected) (Uhlmann and Cohen, 2005), or even pre-interview 'retraining' of behavioural disposition, so that avoidance dispositions are replaced with approach responses (Kawakami et al., 2007).

We argue that recommendations about the kind of mitigating strategies that should be undertaken need to be sensitive to the content of implicit associations likely to be at work, and the kind of behavioural outcome at issue. For example, the limited experimental findings outlined in Section 3.2 suggest that some implicit associations will influence judgement rather than approach/avoidance behaviours, and others will have greater influence on such behaviours (but less so on evaluative judgements). If this is right, then it is possible that a mitigating strategy might misfire by targeting an implicit association that is less likely to be influential in that particular context. For example, in light of the findings described in Section 3.2, we might say that if one is aiming to mitigate the influence of implicit associations on interracial interactions (which may involve approach/avoidance behaviours, such as seating distance) it would be a mistake to focus mitigating strategies on the implicit associations between mental/physical constructs and race (for example, by utilizing counterstereotypical exemplars to that stereotype). The strength of those associations did not correlate with greater seating distance (avoidance behaviour). Conversely, strategies which require individuals to reprogramme certain approach or avoidance responses to overcome implicit race biases might target negative affect (as has been shown in Kawakami et al., 2007) and make for smoother interracial interactions, but it is not clear that they will be effective in mitigating the influence of implicit associations that feed into evaluations of competence or academic aptitude. For example, the IATs that measured the effects of approach/avoidance response reprogramming, in Kawakami et al. (2007), tested for impact on associations with generally positive (love, cheer, happy) and negative (pain, hate, evil) constructs, rather than for specific stereotypical associations such as those in Amodio and Devine (2006). Indeed, there is reason to suppose that certain strategies that may challenge negative affect would not be at all effective in mitigating stereotypical associations: the use of positive exemplars to challenge negative affect might nonetheless encode associations that affirm some other stereotypes. (For example, using Wilt Chamberlain or Michael Jordan as a positive exemplar might entrench the stereotypical associations concerning between black and physical, rather than mental, constructs.)

Given the need for more information about the ways in which different implicit associations might operate differently, we are hesitant to make concrete proposals about how best to mitigate biases. Indeed, as more research reveals the different cognitive processes that may explain such functional differences, more research will be needed on what strategies are relevant to different implicit associations. However, our key claim is that it is important to be alert to the possibility that different associations are in play, and that adopting one strategy for mitigating implicit bias (e.g. exposure to counterstereotypical exemplars) is likely to be at best partial, and may address only some of the possible associations that could lead to implicitly biased outcomes. An awareness of how different strategies are effective in combating different implicit associations should counsel in favour of more comprehensive strategies for mitigating implicit biases.

Moreover, there are implications for individuals reflecting on whether they need to undertake such strategies. Precisely because implicit associations have been found to operate independently of each other, simply because an individual has been found not to have one implicit association (e.g. one IAT result that does not show an implicit race bias) does not mean that they do not have another quite similar one. As Alex Madva aptly expresses it (in correspondence): 'Maybe a given doctor has good interpersonal interactions with black people but still doesn't give them appropriate drug prescriptions. Just because you lack one racial bias doesn't mean you're off the hook.' Likewise, undertaking one bias-mitigating strategy does not mean that others will not remain operative. Recognizing the complexity of implicit associations, how they are related, and their functional heterogeneity, has important implications for evaluating one's own susceptibility to, and strategies for mitigating, the influence of bias.

4.2 Four recommendations

Research programmes into the way in which the different kinds of association differ and interact are ongoing. On the basis of the argumentation in this chapter, we first make the recommendation to empirical psychologists that the distinction between affective and semantic associations be revisited, and how it is experimentally deployed reconsidered. Moreover, because of the functional heterogeneity of implicit biases, and because of the difficulty of understanding how they might work together when multiple biases are all in play, it is important that the effects of implicit bias and interventions to tackle it be based on evidence beyond that garnered from psychology laboratories. We need to base recommendations for real-world interventions on rigorous field-experimental work.

We have three more recommendations for philosophers continuing to work on the range of important issues raised by the empirical findings about implicit bias. First, we recommend caution with respect to generalizations that are made about implicit bias. Whilst some generalizations are true and useful, we have drawn on evidence that indicates that other such generalizations are at best misleading.

Second, with respect to the formulation and implementation of normative claims concerning how to mitigate the effects of implicit biases, we recommend approaches that acknowledge the functional differences between implicit biases, and different strategies that might be needed to combat each of them. Attention to the different associations that might be involved in a given context, and the specific strategies that might be needed to combat the different kinds of implicit association, is needed. (We might aver that employing as many strategies as possible is the best plan, but, whilst a reasonable inference, this is as yet empirically unsupported.)

Finally, when writing about implicit bias, whilst the shorthand and general term 'implicit bias' can be useful, it would often be of helpful (both for assessing the truth of the claims made, and the likely efficacy of normative recommendations drawn from the claims) if the particular kinds of association at issue are articulated. This will assist in the identification of the association at issue, the contexts in which that particular association is likely to be particularly problematic, and the kinds of mitigating strategy that are likely to be efficacious. Recognizing and accommodating the heterogeneity of implicit bias may be an important step in effectively combating its effects.

References

Amodio, D. M. (2008). "The social neuroscience of intergroup relations." *European Review of Social Psychology* 19: 1–54.

Amodio, D. M. and Devine, P. G. (2006). "Stereotyping and evaluation in implicit race bias: Evidence for independent constructs and unique effects on behavior." *Journal of Personality and Social Psychology* 91: 652–61.

Amodio, D. M. and Mendoza, S. A. (2010). "Implicit intergroup bias: Cognitive, affective, and motivational underpinnings." In Gawronski B. and Payne, B. K. (eds.), *Handbook of Implicit Social Cognition*. New York, NY: Guilford Press: 353–74.

Banaji, M. and Hardin, C. (1996). "Automatic stereotyping." *Psychological Science* 7: 136–41.

De Houwer, J. (2006). "What are implicit measures and why are we using them." In Wiers, R. W. and Stacy, A. W. (eds.), *The Handbook of Implicit Cognition and Addiction*. Thousand Oaks, CA: Sage: 1–28.

Dovidio, J. F. and Gaertner, S. L. (2000). "Aversive racism and selection decisions: 1989 and 1999." *Psychological Science* 11: 319–23.

Devine, P. G. et al. (2002). "The regulation of explicit and implicit race bias: The role of motivations to respond without prejudice." *Journal of Personality and Social Psychology* 82(5): 835–48.

Fazio, R. H. (2007). "Attitudes as object-evaluation associations of varying strength." *Social Cognition* 25: 603–37.

Fazio, R. H., Jackson, J., Dunton, B., and Williams, C. (1995). "Variability in automatic activation as an unobtrusive measure of racial attitudes: A bona fide pipeline?" *Journal of Personality and Social Psychology* 69: 1013–27.

Fazio, R. H. and Olson, M. A. (2003). "Implicit measures in social cognition research: Their meaning and use." *Annual Review of Psychology* 54: 297–327.

Gallistel, C. R. (2008). "Learning and representation." In Menzel R. (ed.), *Learning Theory and Behavior*; vol. 1 of *Learning and Memory: A Comprehensive Reference*. Oxford: Elsevier: 227–42.

Gallistel, C. R. and King, A. (2009). *Memory and the Computational Brain: Why Cognitive Science will Transform Neuroscience*. New York: Blackwell/Wiley.

Gallistel, C. R. and Matzel, L. D. (2013). "The neuroscience of learning: Beyond the Hebbian synapse." *Annual Review of Psychology* 64: 169–200.

Garcia, J. L. A (1996). "The heart of racism." *Journal of Social Philosophy* 27(1): 5–46.

Gawronski, B., Hofmann, W., and Wilbur, C. J. (2006). "Are 'implicit' attitudes unconscious?" *Consciousness and Cognition* 15: 485–99.

Gawronski, B. and Payne, B. K. (eds.) (2010). *Handbook of Implicit Social Cognition: Measurement, Theory, and Applications*. New York: Guilford Press.

Gendler, T. S. (2011). "On the epistemic costs of implicit bias." *Philosophical Studies* 156(1): 33–63.

Greenwald, A. G., Banaji, M. R., Rudman, L. A., Farnham, S. D., Nosek, B. A., and Mellott, D. S. (2002). "A unified theory of implicit attitudes, stereotypes, self-esteem, and self-concept." *Psychological Review* 109: 3–25.

Hahn, A., Judd, C. M., Hirsh, H. K., and Blair, I. V. (2013). "Awareness of implicit attitudes." *Journal of Experimental Psychology: General* 143: 1369–92.

Haslanger, S. (2008). "Changing the ideology and culture of philosophy: Not by reason (alone)." *Hypatia* 23(2): 210–22.

Holroyd, J. (2012). "Responsibility for Bias." *Journal of Social Philosophy* Special issue, ed. Crouch, M. and Schwartzman, L.

Holroyd, J. (2014). "Implicit bias, awareness and epistemic innocence." *Consciousness and Cognition* Special Issue on Imperfect Cognitions, ed. Bortolotti, L. and Sullivan-Bisset, E.

Jolls, C. and Sunstein, C. (2006). "The law of implicit bias." *California Law Review* 94: 969–96.

Joy-Gaba, J. A. and Nosek, B. A. (2010). "The surprisingly limited malleability of implicit racial evaluations." *Social Psychology* 41: 137–46.

Kawakami, K., Phills, C. E., Steele, J. R., and Dovidio, J. F. (2007). "(Close) distance makes the heart grow fonder: Improving implicit racial attitudes and interracial interactions through approach behaviors." *Journal of Personality and Social Psychology* 92(6): 957–71.

Kelly, D. and Roedder, E. (2008). "Racial cognition and the ethics of implicit bias." *Philosophy Compass* 3(3): 522–40.

Machery, E., Faucher, L., and Kelly, D. (2010). "On the alleged inadequacies of psychological explanations of racism." *The Monist* 93: 228–54.

Macrae, C. N., Bodenhausen, G. V., Milne, A. B., and Jetten, J. (1994). "Out of mind but back in sight: Stereotypes on the rebound." *Journal of Personality and Social Psychology* 67(5): 808–17.

Monteith, M. and Voils, C. (1998). "Proneness to prejudiced responses: Toward understanding the authenticity of self-reported discrepancies." *Journal of Personality and Social Psychology* 75(4): 901–16.

Monteith, M. J., Voils, C. I., and Ashburn-Nardo, L. (2001). "Taking a look underground: Detecting, interpreting and reacting to implicit racial biases." *Social Cognition* 19(4): 395–417.

Nosek, B. A., Hawkins, C. B., and Frazier, R. S. (2012). "Implicit social cognition." In Fiske, S. and Macrae, C. N. (eds.), *Handbook of Social Cognition*. New York, NY: Sage: 31–53.

Nosek, B., Greenwald, A., and Banaji, M. (2007). "The Implicit Association Test at age 7: A methodological and conceptual review." In Bargh, J. (ed.), *Automatic Processes in Social Thinking and Behaviour*. New York, NY: Psychology Press: 265–92.

Olson, M. A. and Fazio, R. H. (2004). "Reducing the influence of extrapersonal associations on the implicit association test: Personalizing the IAT." *Journal of Personality and Social Psychology* 86: 653–67.

Payne, B. K., Cooley, E., Loersch, C., and Lei, R. (ms.). "Who owns implicit attitudes? Testing a meta-cognitive perspective."

Saul, J. (2013). "Implicit bias, stereotype threat and women in philosophy." In Jenkins F. and Hutchison, K. (eds.). *Women in Philosophy: What Needs to Change?* Oxford: Oxford University Press: 39–60.

Uhlmann, E. L. and Cohen, G. L. (2005). "Constructed criteria redefining merit to justify discrimination." *Psychological Science* 16(6): 474–80.

Valian, V. (2005). Beyond Gender Schemas: Improving the Advancement of Women in Academia, *Hypatia* 20(3): 198–213.

Webb, T. L., Sheeran, P., and Pepper, J. (2010). "Gaining control over responses to implicit attitude tests: Implementation intentions engender fast responses on attitude-incongruent trials." *British Journal of Social Psychology* 51(1): 13–32.

Wegener, D. T. and Petty, R. E. (1995). "Flexible correction processes in social judgment: The role of naive theories in corrections for perceived bias." *Journal of Personality and Social Psychology* 68: 36–51.

1.4

De-Freuding Implicit Attitudes

Edouard Machery

Ask any social psychologist about the important discoveries made in her field over the last twenty years, and the odds are that she will mention the discovery of implicit attitudes: the alleged finding that, in addition to the attitudes people are aware of having and are able to verbalize (called "explicit attitudes"), people also have unconscious attitudes toward the same objects (called "implicit attitudes"), which may be in tension with their explicit attitudes.[1] Attitudes toward races have been of interest in this research tradition, and social psychologists claim to have found that, in addition to the attitudes toward blacks, Asians, and so on that people are able to report, they also have unconscious racial attitudes that may be discordant with their explicit attitudes. In particular, people who sincerely claim to be unbiased toward blacks happen to be often implicitly biased against them. When someone sincerely asserts that she does not prefer whites to blacks, she expresses her egalitarian attitude toward blacks, but this explicit attitude does not exhaust her racial attitudes: she is also likely to have an unconscious negative attitude toward them. (For philosophical discussion, see e.g. Kelly and Roedder, 2008; Kelly, Machery, and Mallon, 2010; Machery, Faucher, and Kelly, 2010; Brownstein and Madva, 2012; Saul, 2013.)

What kind of things are attitudes? According to the dominant picture in social psychology and in philosophy, attitudes are mental states. Explicit attitudes are mental states that people can be conscious of, while implicit attitudes are mental states that people are typically unaware of having. Because this picture is somewhat reminiscent of Freud's conception of human mental life—an arena where conscious and unconscious desires fight to control behavior—I will call this

---

[1] For reviews, see Fazio and Olson (2003); Nosek et al. (2007a); Crano and Prislin (2008); Rudman, Phelan, and Heppen (2007); Stanley, Phelps, and Banaji (2008); Gawronski and Payne (2010); Nosek, Hawkins, and Frazier (2011).

picture "the Freudian picture of attitudes." The goal of this chapter is to show that this Freudian picture is deeply misguided. I will argue that attitudes are not mental states at all; rather, they are traits. Furthermore, because the distinction between what is explicit and what is implicit is meaningful only when applied to mental states, it makes no sense to speak of implicit and explicit attitudes.[2] Thus, there are no implicit attitudes, social psychologists' consensus notwithstanding. Finally, when people make assertions such as "I do not prefer whites to blacks," they are genuinely expressing a mental state, but this mental state is not an attitude. I call this new picture of attitudes "the trait picture." In the remainder of this chapter I will clarify this new picture, and will show its superiority over the Freudian picture of attitudes.

Here is how I will proceed. In Section 1 I will flesh out the Freudian picture of attitudes; in Section 2 I will explain the trait picture of attitudes in detail; in Section 3 I will provide an argument for the latter and against the former; and in Section 4 I will briefly respond to six objections.

1 The Freudian Picture of Attitudes

1.1 What is an attitude?

The first thing to do is to disambiguate the term "attitude," since it is used differently in social psychology and in the philosophy of mind. In the philosophy of mind, attitudes, or propositional attitudes, are relations to propositions that are typically thought to differ functionally. Beliefs, desires, wishes, and hopes are the typical examples of propositional attitudes. In social psychology and in the areas of philosophy interested in implicit attitudes or biases, "attitude" does not refer to propositional attitudes. Rather, attitudes are simply likings or dislikings of things. In what follows, I will use "attitude" in this latter sense.

Attitudes are individuated by two properties: their valence (whether the attitude is positive and negative and how strong it is), and their formal object, i.e. what they are about. They are distinguished from other two-place psychological relations (e.g. attention) by the nature of their formal objects, by their valence, and by their functional properties—what brings them about and what they bring about.

Likings and dislikings need not be propositional: their formal objects can be individuals and classes, though one can also have attitudes for or against

---

[2] The view defended here differs from the view of those, like Fazio and de Houwer, who hold, first, that in contrast to the hypothesis that there are two constructs—implicit and explicit attitudes—there is only one construct (i.e. people's attitudes), second, that these attitudes are measured directly and indirectly, and third, that these attitudes are mental states.

propositions (e.g. that Obama is president or that the Yankees win the World Series). The formal objects of these likings and dislikings need not exist actually; one can have attitudes toward non-existents. For instance, many people have pro-attitudes toward god. These formal objects are also very diverse: they range from individuals, such as persons (e.g. Barack Obama), to kinds, such as age groups (e.g. elderly), races and ethnicities (e.g. African Americans), gays, people with disabilities, and obese individuals, to behaviors such as smoking, to abstractions, such as female authority, political orientation (e.g. liberals vs. conservatives), and brands (e.g. Coke vs. Pepsi).

Social psychologists have examined attitudes about many different kinds of formal object; indeed, social psychology emerged as a subdiscipline in the 1920s to measure attitudes of various kinds, with particular interest in those attitudes that have economic or political significance (Thurstone, 1928; Danziger, 1994: ch. 8). Recent work on so-called explicit and implicit attitudes has followed this trend, with research on the hypothesized implicit attitudes toward, e.g., political ideas (e.g. Arcuri et al., 2008), obese individuals (e.g. Teachman et al., 2003), smoking (e.g. Sherman et al., 2003), and brands such as Coca-Cola and Pepsi (e.g. Maison, Greenwald, and Bruin, 2004).

1.2 Implicit and explicit attitudes

As noted in the introduction to this chapter, contemporary psychologists routinely distinguish two types of attitude: explicit and implicit. Two dimensions distinguish them: automaticity and introspectability. An attitude is more automatic to the extent that its influence on behavior and on other mental states is not under intentional control, and an attitude is more introspectable to the extent that people can become aware of its nature by introspection. Explicit attitudes are taken to be those attitudes that are introspectable and whose influence on behavior and mental states can be under intentional control, while implicit attitudes are taken to be those attitudes that are not introspectable and that influence behavior and mental states automatically.

For the sake of simplicity, I will assume that automaticity is a single dimension, but the notion of automaticity may in fact correspond to distinct phenomena, as argued by Bargh (1994). I will also take for granted the claim that implicit attitudes are correctly described as being opaque to introspection, although this is not entirely uncontroversial (Gawronski, Hofmann, and Wilbur, 2006). Automaticity and introspectability are also conceptually and, perhaps, empirically orthogonal dimensions. In particular, people could be aware of some attitudes without being able to control their influence. Finally, these two dimensions have been the focus of different research traditions in psychology. To caricature a bit, cognitive psychologists have been more interested in automaticity and control (e.g. Shiffrin and Schneider, 1977), while social psychologists have usually focused on introspectability.

Despite their differences, explicit and implicit attitudes have in common that they are both supposed to be mental states. Implicit attitudes are mental states that people cannot control and do not have introspective access to; explicit attitudes are mental states that people can control and introspect.[3] What does it mean to say that explicit and implicit attitudes are mental states? There are various mutually compatible ways to address this question. First, to say that attitudes are mental states is to say that they have the same ontological status as emotions (e.g. anger), beliefs, judgments, desires, intentions, and wishes. Second, mental states can be occurrent.[4] Fear, anger, an occurrent belief, an occurrent desire, and so on, are psychological events that cause further psychological events (other occurrent beliefs, some intentions, and so on). Third, because I endorse non-reductive materialism and because I take brain states to be the ontological basis of most, if not all, human mental states, to say that implicit and explicit attitudes are mental states is to say that each occurrent attitude is a (possibly extremely complex and distributed) brain state. So, in principle, one could open your head and point toward your occurrent implicit and explicit attitudes, exactly as one could point toward your occurrent fear when you shrink away from a dangerous-looking snake.

We thus obtain the following picture of the mind from social psychology and philosophy: attitudes—likings and dislikings—are mental states, and thus brain states, that are either introspectable and controllable or beyond introspection and control; both kinds of attitude vie for the control of human behavior and psyche. Although they are rarely fully explicit about their ontological commitments, psychologists embrace this picture when they speak of "retrieving attitudes" from memory, "accessing attitudes," or "activating" them.[5] Mental states are the kind of things that get retrieved from memory, accessed, or activated. Thus,

---

[3] One might doubt that explicit attitudes are always under intentional control. However, while explicit attitudes are not always *actually* controlled (e.g. influenced by one's motives, reasoning, and so on), in contrast to implicit attitudes, they are supposed to be *potentially* controlled.

[4] Beliefs, desires, and so on, need not be occurrent. Even when one does not entertain the belief that Paris is in France, one has this belief in a dispositional sense.

[5] Some social psychologists deny that there is a single mental state that is people's implicit attitude. Rather, on their view, behavior is caused by many different kinds of mental state, some of which are conscious while others are not, some of which are associative while others are propositional, some of which are controllable while others are not, and so on. This view is not the target of the present chapter. In many respects, it is similar to the trait view of attitudes developed in Section 2. For the target of this chapter, each (either implicit or explicit) attitude is a unitary mental state.

in an influential article on the dual model of attitudes, according to which people can have two distinct and possibly competing attitudes, Wilson, Lindsey, and Schooler (2000: 102) write (italics mine):

People can have dual attitudes, which are different evaluations of the same attitude object, one of which is an automatic, implicit attitude and the other of which is an explicit attitude. The attitude that people endorse at any point in time depends on whether they have the cognitive capacity to *retrieve* the explicit attitude and whether the explicit attitude *overrides* the implicit one.

Many philosophers have also embraced this picture of attitudes. For instance, Gendler (2008a: 642) writes (italics mine):

A paradigmatic alief [Gendler's term for implicit attitudes] is *a mental state* with associatively linked content that is representational, affective and behavioral, and that is activated—consciously or nonconsciously—by features of the subject's internal or ambient environment. *Aliefs may be either occurrent or dispositional.*

Kriegel (2012: 475) concurs with Gendler (italics mine):

[A]n alief is *a mental state* whose *occurrence causally explains* our behaviour in cases where our behaviour does not match our beliefs, but may be operative as well when our behaviour does match our beliefs.

Because so-called implicit attitudes are not introspectable, psychologists have developed various tasks to measure their strength: the implicit association test, the affective priming task, the semantic priming task, the Go/no Go task, the affect misattribution procedure, the extrinsic affective Simon task, to name only the most well-known measures (for review, see De Houwer et al., 2009; De Houwer and Moors, 2010). These tasks are called "indirect" measures because they quantify attitudes indirectly by examining various states (e.g. hormone level) and behaviors assumed to be automatically influenced by them.

It will be useful to describe two of these measures. The implicit association task (IAT), which was first developed by Greenwald (Greenwald, McGhee, and Schwartz, 1998), is the most well known measure of the hypothesized implicit biases.[6] The implicit association task is a sorting task, which typically involves four distinct categories, divided into two pairs. For instance, an implicit association task may involve the category pair black and white (called "target concepts") on the one hand, and good and bad (called "attribute dimensions") on the other. The exemplars of the categories black and white can be pictures of black and white faces, while exemplars of the other two categories are individual words,

---

[6] For discussion, see de Houwer (2001); Nosek, Greenwald, and Banaji (2005, 2007); Lane et al. (2007); Greenwald et al. (2009).

such as "wonderful," "glorious," and "joy" for good, and "terrible," "horrible," and "nasty" for bad. Subjects must sort the exemplars as fast as they can. Importantly, subjects are required to sort them into the four categories using only two response options. For instance, they could be told to press "*e*" when presented with any exemplar of good or any exemplar of black, and press "*i*" when presented with any exemplar of bad or any exemplar of white. Furthermore, the task is multi-stage (often comprised of five stages), and the response options ("*e*" and "*i*") are assigned to different categories in different stages. One stage may require a response to exemplars of good or black with "*e*" and exemplars of bad or white with "*i*," while the next stage assigns bad or black to "*e*" and good or white to "*i*." If a subject sorts exemplars faster and more accurately when good and white share a response option than when good and black share a response option, this fact is interpreted as an indirect measure of a stronger association between the two categories good and white, and hence a relative, implicit preference for whites over blacks. Implicit association task scores are of course a relative, rather than absolute, measure of attitude.

Fazio's evaluative priming task, also called "the bona fide pipeline" (Fazio et al., 1995), works differently. Participants are presented with primes that belong to two (or more) categories of interest—for instance, pictures of white or black faces—before being asked to categorize evaluative adjectives ("wonderful," "disgusting") as being good or bad. Subjects' latencies in response to negative adjectives after having seen the primes belonging to category 1 and to category 2 are compared. People are thought to have a negative attitude toward category 1 if they are faster at categorizing negative adjectives after having seen a prime of category 1 than a prime of category 2, and the difference between these two conditions measures people's implicit attitude. The basic insight behind the procedure is that, when a prime automatically elicits a valenced reaction, subjects are ready to classify words that elicit a congruent reaction.

1.3 A familiar picture

The picture of the mind endorsed by the likes of Wilson, Gendler, and Kriegel should be familiar enough, since it has a very long pedigree. First and foremost, it is somewhat reminiscent of Freud's psychodynamic views.[7] For Freud, desires are either conscious (people are aware of having them and can verbalize them) or unconscious (people are unaware of having then). The latter desires are

---

[7] This is not to deny that there are many differences between Freud's psychoanalytic views and the dominant picture of attitudes in social psychology. In particular, Freud had a tripartite picture involving the id, the ego, and the super-ego, and was concerned with desires.

unconscious because people repress them. Conscious and unconscious desires vie for the control of human behavior, and the influence of unconscious desires can be noticed in many aspects of people's lives. To identify unconscious desires, psychoanalysts have developed several indirect measures, including the interpretation of dreams, the interpretation of verbal slips, and the Rorschach test.

In philosophy, the Freudian picture of attitudes has an even longer history, since it is reminiscent of Plato's psychology in *Phaedrus* and in Book 4 of *The Republic* (1956), as noted by Gendler (2008b). In the latter work, Socrates and Glaucon focus on a puzzling psychological phenomenon: the occurrence of a desire for something and of an aversion toward it in a single mind. To explain this phenomenon, Socrates is led to conclude that the mind has different parts, which can lead to competing desires and aversions on the grounds that "the same thing will never do or undergo opposite things in the same part of it and towards the same thing at the same time; so if we find this happening, we shall know it was not one thing but more than one" (436, b6-c1). Despite obvious differences, the different parts of the mind hypothesized by Socrates are somewhat reminiscent of Freud's unconscious and conscious desires and of social psychologists' implicit and explicit attitudes.

2 The Trait Picture of Attitudes

According to the Freudian picture, attitudes are mental states that vary in terms of their automaticity and introspectability. By contrast, according to the trait picture, attitudes are not mental states, but rather traits—things like courage, prudence, or evenhandedness. Because they are traits, they are neither explicit nor implicit. The goal of this section is to clarify these claims.

2.1 What is a trait?

There are at least two ways of clarifying the notion of a trait.[8] First, examples help identify what kind of things traits are. Starting with folk psychology, honesty is a trait. A person's honesty (somewhat) predicts her behavior in a large range of situations. Honesty is not a mental state. It does not occur; it is not realized in the brain, though it obviously depends on brain states.[9] Traits are also posits of scientific psychology. Personality dimensions, such as the five dimensions of the

---

[8]   To my knowledge, Allport (1937) introduced the notion of "trait."

[9]   It is important not to confuse realization with any dependence relation. A property occurrence (an event) realizes another property occurrence only if they are identical, and a property type is realized by another property type only if every occurrence of the former is identical to the occurrence of the latter. It makes little sense to view courage as something that can occur. When people act

OCEAN model—openness to experience, conscientiousness, extraversion, agree-ableness, and neuroticism—are traits. They (imperfectly) predict behavior in a range of situations. None of these dimensions is "in the head." There are numerous other traits in psychology, such as the need for cognition—people's tendency to engage in effortful cognitive activities (e.g. Cacioppo and Petty, 1982). Some traits (e.g. courage and modesty)—particularly those posited by folk psychology—have a moral dimension, but not all.

In addition to providing examples, one can characterize traits more abstractly. I propose the following characterization:

A trait is a disposition to perceive, attend, cognize, and behave in a particular way in a range of social and non-social situations. Within a species, there are individual differences with respect to a particular trait; some organisms have more of it, others less. This variation can be measured, and it is predictive of their behavior and cognition.[10]

On this characterization, traits are dispositions. Dispositions can be broad- or narrow-track. Solubility is a narrow-track disposition, since it is manifested in a single way. Broad-track dispositions manifest themselves differently in many different situations—perhaps in an indefinite number of situations. Traits are broad-track dispositions. These dispositions are not simply behavioral. A trait is not merely a disposition to behave in a particular manner in a range of situations. Traits are also psychological dispositions, which manifest themselves in the emotions, attention patterns, beliefs, desires, and so on, that people have in a range of situations.

This characterization of traits applies to the examples just provided. Courage is a disposition to behave and cognize. Courageous people face danger in the right way, and they also do not succumb to fear. They are motivated to face dangerous situations. Courage manifests itself in a myriad of ways in many different kinds of situation. People are more or less courageous, and a person's courage (imper-fectly) predicts her behavior. The same is true of the personality dimensions such as openness to experience.

Importantly, traits are not mental states. As noted earlier, mental states can be occurrent; the occurrent/dispositional distinction applies to them. Because they can occur, they can be the relata of (token) causal relations. In contrast to mental states, traits do not occur, and thus do not enter in token causal relations, though they can occur in type causal relations. Because traits cannot be occurrent events,

---

courageously in a given occasion, it is not because courage has occurred in their mind, but rather because some emotions, values, or beliefs are influencing their behavior.

[10] This characterization is not a definition.

they are not identical to occurrent brain states. Thus, a person's courage is not something that occurs and has specific effects when it occurs; someone's extraversion is not realized by a particular (even very complex) brain state; and you would not find a person's need for cognition if you opened her brain. However, traits depend on mental states and mental processes. A person's degree of courage depends on her moral beliefs (e.g. whether fear is shameful), on the nature of her fear reactions, on the strength of her pride, on her capacity for self-control, and so on. I call the set of mental states and processes that determine the strength of a trait "the psychological basis" of this trait. More formally, the psychological basis of a trait is the set of mental states and processes that is sufficient for the possession of a trait to a particular degree. Typically, it includes very different kinds of mental states and processes. Thus, the psychological basis of courage includes moral beliefs, emotions, and self-control processes. Several distinct sets of mental states may be sufficient for the possession of a trait to a particular degree. Obviously, the psychological basis varies from trait to trait, and one is typically ignorant of most components of the psychological basis of a trait.

2.2 Attitudes are traits

According to the trait picture of attitudes, and in contrast to the Freudian picture, attitudes are traits. They are broad-track dispositions to behave and cognize (have thoughts, attend, emote, and so on) toward an object (its formal object) in a way that reflects some preference. To have a positive attitude toward liberals is to be disposed to interact with liberals in a way that reflects a positive evaluation and to have positive thoughts and emotions about them.

Just like any other trait, attitudes have a psychological basis. They depend on a motley assortment of mental states and processes. A negative racial attitude toward blacks may depend on moral beliefs (e.g. for most of us the belief that racism is wrong or, for some racists, the belief that racism is right), on non-propositional associations between concepts (e.g. an association between the concept of a black man and the concept of danger), on emotions (e.g. fear when confronted with black men), and on weak self-control. This psychological basis is as heterogeneous as the psychological basis of courage. Some of the components may be conscious (perhaps some moral beliefs), while others (including associations between concepts) are likely to be inaccessible to introspection.

If attitudes are traits, one may wonder what is measured by the indirect measures of attitudes that have been developed by social psychologists over the years. According to the trait picture of attitudes, indirect measures quantify components of the psychological bases of attitudes—particularly components that are not accessible to introspection. For instance, a negative attitude toward black people plausibly depends on non-propositional associations between concepts (perhaps in addition to propositional beliefs). The implicit association test may be measuring the strength of such associations, for instance, the association between the concept of danger and the concept of a black man. The affect misattribution procedure may be measuring one's automatic emotional responses to the formal objects of one's attitudes such as one's automatic fear reaction to black men.[11] On this view, different indirect measures of a trait typically measure different components of its psychological basis. For instance, the affect misattribution procedure and the implicit association test may respectively measure automatic emotional reactions and concept associations. Furthermore, because attitudes depend on these measured components, indirect measures approximately measure the strength of the resulting attitude. The more influential a measured component is in determining the strength of a trait, the better this approximation. If the automatic fear reaction to black men is an influential determinant of one's negative attitude toward black people, then the affect misattribution procedure would provide a reasonably accurate estimate of one's attitude toward black people.

2.3 Quid of explicit and implicit attitudes?

What remains in this framework of the distinction between implicit and explicit attitudes? First, the distinction between what is explicit and what is implicit does not apply to traits, but only to mental states. Some mental states are introspectable, others are not, and the distinction between what is introspectable and what is not can thus be meaningfully applied to mental states (e.g. one's belief about the shameful nature of fear). Dispositions to behave and cognize (e.g. courage) are not like that. Just like other dispositions (e.g. flammability or solubility), they are not themselves observable—only their manifestations are—and they cannot be the targets of introspection.[12] One can come to know the strength of a disposition to behave and cognize by inferring it from its manifestations or from the mental states on which it depends, but not by introspection. As a result, according to the trait picture of attitudes, attitudes are neither explicit nor implicit. While the attitudes themselves are neither implicit nor explicit, some components of their psychological bases may well be implicit—automatic and not open to introspection—and others explicit—under intentional control and

---

[11] This is probably an oversimplification. An indirect measure may be influenced by several components of the psychological basis of an attitude.
[12] This point assumes that introspection has an observational character.

open to introspection. Beliefs about black people may be explicit, while associations between the concept of a black man and the concept of danger may be implicit.

If there are no explicit attitudes, then what are speech acts like "I like black people" expressing? According to the Freudian picture of attitudes, they express an explicit attitude. The trait picture of attitudes denies this. Such speech acts can have various functions. They can be expressive, expressing a conscious emotional reaction. They are then similar to expressive speech acts such as "Yummy!" and "LOL!" They can also be directive, expressing commands directed to oneself. On that view, when one says "I like black people," one is ordering oneself to like black people. They are then similar to "Focus!" They can also be expressions of a commitment to a moral norm. If that is the case, when one says "I like black people," one is really expressing a commitment to the norm of racial egalitarianism. Finally, they can express conscious assessments of the strength of one's attitudes. When one says "I like black people," one can express a judgment, namely, an assessment of the valence and strength of one's attitude toward black people. When one says "I like Pepsi," one can express an assessment of the valence and strength of one's attitude toward Pepsi. This judgment is not an attitude; it is about an attitude.[13] It can be more or less accurate; it can be wildly inaccurate. When the topic is not morally or socially charged (e.g. brands), people are likely to assess their attitudes accurately, but they are less likely to assess them accurately when it is morally or socially charged (e.g. races in the USA).

People plausibly rely on different strategies to assess the nature and strength of their attitudes. They may often consider the introspectable elements of the psychological basis of the relevant attitude. For instance, the assessment of one's racial attitudes may be based on the moral belief that all races are equal. People plausibly introspect different components of the psychological basis of an attitude in different contexts. In some contexts, they may pay attention to their fear reaction toward black men rather than to their moral beliefs. Because different components are introspected in different contexts, attitude self-assessment may vary across contexts. Bem's (1972) self-perception theory is also useful to explain how one assesses the valence and strength of one's attitudes. According to Bem, people form beliefs about their traits by observing their past and present overt behaviors in the relevant situations. For instance, if someone

---

[13] Perhaps one could object to the idea that such speech acts report an assessment of one's attitudes on the grounds that if they were, then people would simply adjust their assessments, after taking an IAT. This objection underestimates how much people can be in denial or how easy it is to dismiss unpleasant evidence. Take courage, for instance: cowards can still maintain that they are courageous even after multiple instances of cowardice.

remembers that an evening, in a dark alley, she crossed the street to avoid walking past five young black men, she will be less likely to ascribe to herself a positive attitude toward black people.

To make this characterization of speech acts such as "I like black people" more intuitive, it is useful to consider assertions such as "I am very courageous." It would make no sense to distinguish implicit courage from explicit courage, and to propose that "I am very courageous" expresses people's explicit courage. Rather, when I make this speech act, I am sometimes committing myself to the norm of courage; sometimes, I am merely assessing the strength of my courage; I am making a judgment about my courage. This judgment may be based on the introspection of my moral beliefs about fear (e.g. the belief that fear is shameful) or on past memories of craven behaviors in the face of danger. It is more or less accurate.

Let us now turn briefly to implicit attitudes. According to the trait picture, there are no implicit attitudes, though again, some components of the psychological bases of attitudes may be implicit. So, there is no such thing as implicit racism or implicit sexism. Again, considering traits like courage makes this point very intuitive. Let us suppose I am a complete coward, and that I often run away in fear in the face of imagined dangers. Nonetheless, I have a high opinion of my courage, and I often sincerely assert "I am very courageous." Would we make sense of this situation by stipulating the existence of two forms of courage— explicit courage and implicit courage? I think not. Instead, we would say that I am not courageous, and that the assessment of my courage is very misguided. According to the trait picture, the same is true of racism, sexism, and other attitudes.

3 An Argument for the Trait Picture of Attitudes

Sections 1 and 2 merely clarified the Freudian and trait pictures of attitudes, and I have so far given no argument for the superiority of the latter over the former. At best, I have highlighted the intuitive nature of the trait picture by drawing an analogy with traits such as courage. The goal of Section 3 is to remedy this situation by proposing an argument to the best explanation for the trait picture of attitudes.

Arguments to the best explanation begin with describing some empirical phenomena. They then hold that a particular hypothesis among a set of hypotheses provides the best explanation of these phenomena. They then (inductively) conclude that this hypothesis is true. Arguments to the best explanation are not uncontroversial (for discussion, see Harman, 1965; Van Fraassen, 1989; Lipton,

1991; Schupbach and Sprenger, 2011), but I will take their inductive validity for granted in this chapter.

In the present context, the argument is that the trait picture of attitudes provides a compelling, unifying account of a disparate array of otherwise puzzling findings in the literature on implicit attitudes. In what follows, I describe four findings, some of which are not sufficiently acknowledged by philosophers, and I argue that the trait picture best explains each of them.

3.1 Low correlations between indirect measures

As noted in Section 1, contemporary psychologists have developed many indirect measures of people's alleged implicit attitudes. An important finding is that the correlations between these measures are extremely low. Nosek et al. (2007, 274) write:

> Bosson, Swann, and Pennebaker (2000) observed weak relations among seven implicit measures of self-esteem, including the IAT (r values ranged from -0.14 to 0.23). Also, a number of studies have compared the IAT with variations of evaluative priming and found weak relations.

For instance, Sherman et al. (2003) report that correlations between various forms of implicit association test and of evaluative priming vary from -0.11 to 0.11. None of these correlations is significant, and their sizes are very small.

This result is puzzling if the Freudian picture of attitudes is correct. According to this picture, implicit attitudes are a distinct kind of mental states that are quantified by indirect measures. Because any measure is noisy, there is naturally an upper bound to the correlation between any two measures (which is equal to the product of their reliability). But if different indirect measures really tapped into the same implicit attitude, we would expect much larger correlations than those found. By contrast, the trait picture of attitudes predicts this result. According to this picture, indirect measures typically tap into different components of the psychological bases of attitudes. There is no reason to expect these components to correlate with one another. For instance, the association between the concepts of a black man and of danger may be strong, even if someone has only a weak automatic fear reaction to black men (or vice versa). As a result, indirect measures should often correlate poorly with one another.

A proponent of the Freudian picture of attitudes may respond in one of three ways. First, she could insist that the low correlations between indirect measures are due to their low reliability. In Cunningham, Preacher, and Banaji (2003), people's true implicit association test scores and their true evaluative priming scores are modeled as latent variables that are measured by repeated applications of the implicit association test and of the evaluative priming test. When these scores are modeled this way, their correlation increases to about 0.5. In addition, Cunningham et al. (2003) developed a model where the latent variables standing for implicit association test scores and evaluative priming scores were themselves measuring a single latent variable, which stood for people's implicit attitude. This model fitted the data well. Cunningham et al. (2003) concluded that the low correlations between the indirect measures do not show that these measures tap into different things. However, there are at least two reasons to resist this conclusion. Their modeling is not comparative: they do not compare the fits of a model in which indirect measures are indicators of a single attitude and a model in which they are indicators of two distinct attitudes. In addition, various manipulations can influence the size of these correlations (see Olson and Fazio, 2003, discussed in Section 3.2), suggesting that the low correlation between indirect measures is not primarily due to noisy measures, but to the fact that they are measuring different things.

Second, a proponent of the Freudian picture of attitudes may reply that there are in fact several distinct implicit attitudes, corresponding to the different indirect measures. This response would be a stark departure from the usual description of implicit attitudes. It is also bad scientific practice to postulate a theoretical entity for every measure.

Third, she may respond that only one of the indirect measures (e.g. the implicit association test) really measures implicit biases. That other measures fail to correlate with it only shows that they are inaccurate measures (for relevant discussion, see Bar-Anan and Nosek, 2012). However, it is unclear which of the indirect measures should be judged to measure implicit attitudes accurately. Surely, social psychologists do not seem to agree that one of the measures is the correct measure.

3.2 Variation in the correlations between indirect measures

Research suggests that the size of the correlation between two indirect measures can be manipulated. As seen in Section 1, in Fazio's evaluative priming task, participants are primed with instances of categories of interest, for instance, with pictures of black faces and white faces. An important feature of this task is that subjects' attention is not drawn to the categories to which the faces used as primes belong. Rather, subjects are invited to focus on the distinctive features of each face, since they are told that they will be tested for their capacity to recognize each face. By contrast, in the category-based version of evaluative priming (Olson and Fazio, 2003), subjects are told to pay attention to the race of the faces they are primed with. In Olson and Fazio (2003), scores obtained with the usual evaluative priming task did not correlate with participants' implicit association test scores, while the scores obtained with the category-based evaluative priming task did.

The variation in the correlation between indirect measures is not predicted by the Freudian picture of attitudes, but it is simply explained by the trait picture of attitudes if the usual and category-based versions of evaluative priming tap into different components of the psychological bases of attitudes. If the category-based version of evaluative priming happens to tap into the same component as the implicit association test, then a large correlation would be expected.

3.3 Variation in the indirect measures of attitudes

While Sections 3.1 and 3.2 focused on the correlation between different indirect measures, this section focuses on the contextual variation in the measurement of a hypothesized implicit attitude by means of a particular indirect measure. A robust finding is that indirect measures are extremely labile, and that measurement varies from context to context, depending on subtle features of subjects' environment. Rydell and Gawronski (2009: 1118) write that "previous research has shown that automatic evaluations can be highly context-dependent" (see also Gawronski and Sritharan, 2010). Here are some examples of this context-dependence. Dasgupta and Greenwald (2001) have shown that exposing American subjects to admired African Americans (e.g. Denzel Washington) and to despised white Americans (e.g. Jeffrey Dahmer) make their implicit association test scores less pro-white. Blair, Ma, and Lenton (2001) report that asking subjects to generate mental images of stereotypical and counterstereotypical women influences their implicit association test scores. Rudman and Lee (2002) report that listening to violent and misogynistic rap music increases the pro-white bias of American subjects' implicit association test scores toward African Americans. Similarly, associating African Americans with valued activities (e.g. barbecuing) and with disvalued activities (e.g. gang activities) influences implicit association test scores (Wittenbrick, Judd, and Park, 2001). Schaller, Park, and Mueller (2003) provide evidence that implicit association test scores of people who believe in a dangerous world are higher with respect to the danger posed by black people when the test is taken in a dark room. Lowery, Hardin, and Sinclair (2001) have shown that interacting with a black experimenter reduces pro-white implicit association test scores, and Richeson and Ambady (2001) have shown that expecting to interact with a socially superior woman makes men's implicit association test scores negatively biased against women, while expecting to interact with a socially equal or inferior woman makes them positively biased toward women. Peck et al. (2013) have provided evidence that IAT scores about races decrease when white subjects are put in a virtual reality environment where their own skin appears dark.

The Freudian picture is consistent with the context-dependence of the measurement of the hypothesized implicit attitudes since mental states can be more or less strongly activated as a function of different contextual factors. So, the advantage of the trait picture over the Freudian picture is not that the former, but not the latter, predicts contextual variation. Rather, its advantage is that it is better equipped to predict the nature of this context-dependence, that is, to predict which contextual factors are likely to influence the measurement of attitudes. The Freudian picture postulates a new kind of mental state—implicit biases—and as a result it is unclear why some contextual factors rather than others (why darkness?) would influence their activation. By contrast, the trait picture hypothesizes that attitudes depend on psychological bases that encompass good old-fashioned mental states and processes, such as emotions, self-control, and so on, and that indirect measures tap into some of these components.[14] Because we know a lot about these mental states—there is after all a lot of research on emotions and on what influences them—the trait picture leads us to predict which factors should modulate the measurement of attitudes by means of indirect measures. For instance, because darkness heightens stress in humans and other diurnal species, it should modulate implicit association test scores if this test measures, or is somehow influenced by, stress.

3.4 The low predictive validity of indirect measures

When one hears philosophers, psychologists, and science popularizers talk about implicit attitudes—particularly implicit racism and implicit sexism—one may get the erroneous impression that indirect measures of attitudes are excellent predictors of biased behavior, since implicit attitudes are called upon to explain many social ills. The truth is, however, quite different. Two recent meta-analyses (Greenwald et al., 2009; Oswald et al., 2013) suggest that the predictive validity of the implicit association test is extremely low. The predictive validity of other indirect measures is unclear, since there is to my knowledge no relevant meta-analysis. Some studies suggest that Fazio's evaluative priming task has some predictive validity, but the extent of this predictive validity remains unclear (e.g. Ferguson, 2008; Spruyt et al., 2007). Supposing that the findings about the IAT generalize to other indirect measures, it would seem that, while indirect measures do predict behavior, they are poor predictors. According to Greenwald

---

[14] Relatedly, it is worth noting that the trait picture involves fewer ontological commitments than the Freudian picture because it does not require the introduction of a new kind of mental state.

et al. (2009), the partial correlations between implicit association test scores and behaviors range from 0.1 to 0.2, depending on the formal object of the attitudes (e.g. about 0.2 for intergroup relations and 0.15 for gender/sexual orientation). Improving on Greenwald et al.'s methodology, Oswald et al. (2013) report even weaker partial correlations.

The Freudian picture of attitudes would lead us to expect indirect measures to be imperfectly related to behavior, since any measure is noisy and since the hypothesized implicit biases are only one of the causal determinants of behavior (in addition to the hypothesized explicit attitudes, people's intentions, and so on). However, the very low predictive power of indirect measures fits better with the trait picture of attitudes than with the Freudian picture, since the correlations between indirect measures and behavior should be larger on the latter than on the former. On the Freudian picture of attitudes, indirect measures of, for example, the attitude toward black people tap a single mental state, namely, the implicit attitude toward black people. By contrast, on the trait picture, a particular indirect measure taps into one of the many components that determine behavior, such as emotions, associations between concepts, and so on. So, where the Freudian picture posits a single determinant of behavior (i.e. the implicit attitude), the trait picture posits many (i.e. the components of the psychological basis of an attitude). An indirect measure should be worse at predicting behavior on the trait picture than on the Freudian picture (in fact it should be a poor predictor) because it only measures one of the many components of the psychological basis of an attitude—e.g. automatic emotional reactions.

3.5 Upshot

There is no doubt that each of the four phenomena described in this section could be explained by a proponent of the Freudian picture of attitudes if she resorted to various ad hoc assumptions, but the proponent of the trait picture does not need to hypothesize this array of assumptions; instead, these phenomena naturally follow from the trait picture. Thus, the trait picture provides the best explanation of an important set of phenomena about attitudes.

4 Objections and Responses

4.1 Traits are not useful posits in psychology

One could first express doubts about the trait picture on the grounds that traits are not useful posits in psychology and that they have been extensively criticized in social and personality psychology. In particular, the correlation between, on the one hand, the traits postulated over the years by psychologists and, on the other, behavior, seems to be rarely larger than 0.3 (for discussion, see e.g. Mischel, 1968; Ajzen and Fishbein, 1977), and behavior is influenced by mundane features of the environment (for discussion of the situationist literature in a philosophical context, see Doris, 2002).

However, first, it would be very curious for contemporary psychologists embracing the Freudian picture of attitudes to appeal to the situationist critique of the notion of trait, since this critique cuts equally against the notion of attitude. Attitudes suffer from exactly the same problems as traits; in particular, they predict behavior poorly. Calling some attitudes "implicit" and others "explicit" changes nothing about this problem.

But perhaps some critics would reject both the Freudian picture *and* the trait picture of attitudes. Their criticism of the appeal to the notion of trait would not be part of a defense of the idea that attitudes are mental states, and their concerns with the notion of trait should be addressed head on. This can be done quickly. To conclude from the situation–person debate in social and personality psychology that the notion of trait should be rejected is to misinterpret the outcome of twenty years of controversy (Ross and Nisbett, 1991). Properties of the person and situational features both influence behavior. In particular, Epstein (1979, 1980) has shown that when one aggregates over behaviors and individuals, measures of traits are actually predictive of behavior. On average, people who score differently on valid measures of genuine traits behave differently.

4.2 Is a science of attitudes possible?

One may think that the very phenomena I used to undermine the Freudian picture also speak against the trait picture, and in fact cast doubt on the very possibility of a science of attitude, be they conceived as mental states or as traits. In particular, if indirect and direct measures do not agree with one another and if measurement varies across contexts, then it would seem that attitudes cannot be measured—which raises questions about whether they are real at all.

This is naturally not the place for a detailed defense of the psychology of attitudes, and I am happy to merely endorse the conditional claim that if there is to be a scientific psychology of attitudes, they are better conceived as traits than as mental states. On the other hand, for at least some objects, measured attitudes are predictive of aggregate behavior. Furthermore, it may be that attitudes are only to be found for some objects. For instance, it may be that in some domains (e.g. races) people do not harbor any broad-track psychological and behavioral dispositions, and thus, that they have no attitudes to be measured. Finally, the issue may be less with the notion of attitudes than with the current measures of attitudes, or at least with some of them. Because of the low predictive validity of the IAT, it just seems to be a poor method for measuring people's attitudes. The same conclusion would apply to the indirect measures that have been developed over the last twenty years if their predictive validity is not substantially larger than the IAT's.

4.3 Traits and mental states

The contrast I have drawn between traits and mental states assumes that mental states are the kind of things that can occur. However, some philosophers, such as Schwitzgebel (2002), hold that beliefs are dispositions, while philosophers such as Ryle (1949) have characterized all mental states, including emotions, as dispositions. For them, then, it is not necessary for something to be a mental state that it be able to occur. If this view is correct, I may have been too quick to conclude that attitudes are not mental states from the fact that they are traits.

There are several lines of response to this objection. I could insist that mental states are the kind of things that can occur and argue that Schwitzgebel, Ryle, and others have mischaracterized beliefs, emotions, and so on. I could instead insist that mental states are the kind of things that can occur and argue that Schwitzgebel's, Ryle's, and others' arguments show that beliefs, emotions, and maybe some other putative mental states are not genuine mental states after all. Finally, I could argue that even if Schwitzgebel's, Ryle's, and others' arguments show that some mental states do not occur, the contrast between the Freudian and the trait pictures is still significant, since, while attitudes may then be mental states in some sense (where being a mental state does not require being able to occur), they are not mental states in another sense (where being a mental state requires being able to occur). I develop this third line briefly in what follows.

For the philosophers and psychologists whose views are discussed in this chapter, attitudes are not dispositions. For them, attitudes are states of individuals that can be occurrent and that have causes and effects when they occur.[15] They are the kind of things that can be retrieved from memory, accessed, or activated. So, whether or not some mental states such as beliefs are dispositions, the trait picture differs from the Freudian picture in asserting that attitudes are not the kind of mental states that can occur.

In addition, contemporary philosophers who view beliefs as dispositions typically do not deny that there are mental states that are properly characterized as non-dispositional. For instance, Schwitzgebel does not view beliefs as simply

---

[15] Dispositional propositional attitudes are of course dispositions, but they are dispositions to be occurrent beliefs, desires, and so on.

behavioral dispositions, but as behavioral and psychological dispositions (see, particularly, 2002: 252). On this view, then, not all mental states are to be identified with dispositions. Hence, there is still a genuine contrast to be drawn between viewing attitudes as traits and viewing them as those mental states that can occur.

So, only radical views, such as Ryle's, raise an issue for the contrast drawn between the Freudian and the trait picture of attitudes, but these radical views are extremely implausible, though this is not the place to discuss them at any length. They are also in tension with much of contemporary psychology, which does not identify mental states such as emotions or motives with dispositions.

4.4 Implicit and explicit traits?

One could perhaps challenge the idea that the distinction between what is explicit and what is implicit cannot be applied to attitudes as traits. First, could it not be the case that an individual has two distinct attitudes toward the same object (conceived as traits)? Consider Jekyll and Hyde: the same individual has different behavioral and psychological dispositions, hence different traits, when he is Jekyll and when he is Hyde. While this case is fictional and would be pathological if it were real, perhaps people can have distinct traits in different contexts or situations. Couldn't one be very open to experience in some contexts, but not in other contexts? Couldn't one be disposed to act and cognize in relation to, say, sweets in a way that expresses a positive evaluation when blood glucose levels drop too low, and in a way that expresses a negative evaluation otherwise? If this is the case, it seems possible to apply a distinction related to (though perhaps not identical with) the contrast between what is implicit and what is explicit to traits in general, and attitudes in particular. Perhaps the nature of one of the distinct attitudes, but not the other, can be easily known. That is, perhaps the valence and strength of the former attitudes, but not of the latter, can be reliably inferred. If so, the former attitude could be said to be explicit and the latter implicit.

First, even if this proposal were correct, the Freudian picture, which treats attitudes as mental states instead of traits that depend on a heterogeneous psychological basis, would still be mistaken, and the distinction between what is explicit and what is implicit would have to be seriously redefined. Second, while this proposal is certainly coherent and may be correct in psychiatric cases (e.g. in the case of multiple personality disorder), it is not needed to explain the phenomena that the original distinction between implicit and explicit attitudes (in particular, people sincerely reporting being unbiased, while showing biases on indirect measures) was meant to explain.

4.5 Ambivalent attitudes?

One may wonder what the trait picture has to say about ambivalent attitudes—
that is, about situations where people have both a positive and a negative liking of
some object. The trait picture does not deny that people sometimes have positively and negatively valenced mental states about the same object (e.g. two
distinct, differently valenced emotions). On the other hand, the trait picture
denies (except perhaps in pathological cases) that people have ambivalent attitudes. If the hypothesized coreferential, differently valenced mental states do not
lead to a broad-track disposition to behave and cognize in a way that expresses
either a positive or a negative preference, then people simply do not have an
attitude toward the relevant object. They will act and cognize in a way that
expresses a positive preference in some contexts and a negative preference in
other contexts, and their aggregate behavior cannot be predicted (even imper-
fectly) by postulating a trait.

4.6 Impact on the psychology of attitudes?

One may wonder what impact the proposed replacement of the Freudian picture
with the trait picture of attitudes has on the psychology of attitudes in general and
on the research on the hypothesized implicit attitudes in particular. Does this
proposal mean that twenty years of research on implicit attitudes should be
rejected? Or rather, does it leave much of this research intact? And if the
proposed replacement has little impact on psychologists' empirical research, is
it really substantial?

Much of the empirical research on implicit attitudes can be reframed within
the trait picture. For instance, the claim that people's implicit attitudes can
diverge from their explicit attitudes amounts to the finding that, for at least
some formal objects, people are poor at assessing their attitudes. Furthermore,
this proposal is not trivialized by the fact that current research can be translated,
so to speak, into the framework of the trait picture. How empirical research is
conceptualized matters, since erroneous conceptualizations lead to false debates.
For instance, if attitudes are mental states, the question arises of their causal
relations with other antecedents of human behaviors, such as motives and
intentions. Are occurrent attitudes causes of motives and intentions, and,
through them, of behaviors? Rather, are they directly causing behavior in addition to motives? Such questions are misguided if attitudes are traits.

However, embracing the trait picture of attitudes should lead us to reassess the
recent empirical research on implicit attitudes in one important respect. If
attitudes are these broad-track dispositions that are expressed in many different

domains, a good measure of attitudes should have predictive validity. It should predict how people behave and think or feel in a range of circumstances. For instance, a good measure of racial attitudes should predict how people behave and think or feel in racially charged circumstances. Those indirect measures that have very low predictive validity (e.g. the IAT) should be viewed with circumspection. They may simply be bad measures of people's attitudes. The field of attitude research in psychology may be too quick to embrace the IAT and possibly other indirect measures too.

Conclusion

In this chapter I have compared two different ways of thinking about the nature of attitudes: as mental states and as traits. The trait picture of attitudes provides the best explanation of an array of otherwise puzzling findings. Finally, if attitudes are truly traits, then the distinction between implicit and explicit attitudes is meaningless.

Acknowledgments

I am grateful for comments by Michael Brownstein, Luc Faucher, Bryce Huebner, Dan Kelly, Carole Lee, Neil Levy, Alex Madva, and Jennifer Saul.

References

Ajzen, I. and Fishbein, M. (1977). "Attitude-behavior relations: A theoretical analysis and review of empirical research." *Psychological Bulletin* 84: 888–918.

Allport, G. W. (1937). *Personality: A Psychological Interpretation*. Oxford: Holt.

Arcuri, L., Castelli, L., Galdi, S., Zogmaister, C., and Amadori, A. (2008). "Predicting the vote: Implicit attitudes as predictors of the future behavior of decided and undecided voters." *Political Psychology*, 29: 369–87.

Bar-Anan, Y. and Nosek, B. A. (2012). "A comparative investigation of seven implicit measures of social cognition." <http://papers.ssrn.com/sol3/papers.cfm?abstract_id=2074556>.

Bargh, J. A. (1994). "The four horsemen of automaticity: Awareness, efficiency, intention, and control in social cognition." In Wyer, R. S. and Srull, T. K. (eds.), *Handbook of Social Cognition*. Hillsdale, NJ: Erlbaum: 1–40.

Bem, D. J. (1972). "Self-perception theory." In Berkowitz, L. (ed.), *Advances in Eperimental Social Psychology*. New York: Academic Press: 1–62.

Blair, I. V., Ma, J. E., and Lenton, A. P. (2001). "Imagining stereotypes away: The moderation of implicit stereotypes through mental imagery." *Journal of Personality and Social Psychology* 81: 828–41.

Bosson, J. K., Swann Jr, W. B., and Pennebaker, J. W. (2000). "Stalking the perfect measure of implicit self-esteem: The blind men and the elephant revisited?" *Journal of Personality and Social Psychology* 79: 631–43.

Brownstein, M. and Madva, A. (2012). "The normativity of automaticity." *Mind and Language* 27: 410–34.

Cacioppo, J. T. and Petty, R. E. (1982). "The need for cognition." *Journal of Personality and Social Psychology* 42: 116–31.

Crano, W. D. and Prislin, R. (eds.) (2008). *Attitudes and Attitude Change.* New York, NY: Psychology Press.

Cunningham, W. A., Preacher, K. J., and Banaji, M. R. (2003). "Implicit attitude measures: Consistency, stability, and convergent validity." *Psychological Science* 12: 163–70.

Danziger, K. (1994). *Constructing the Subject: Historical Origins of Psychological Research.* Cambridge: Cambridge University Press.

Dasgupta, N. and Greenwald, A. G. (2001). "On the malleability of automatic attitudes: Combating automatic prejudice with images of admired and disliked individuals." *Journal of Personality and Social Psychology* 81: 800–14.

De Houwer, J. (2001). "A structural and process analysis of the Implicit Association Test." *Journal of Experimental Social Psychology* 37: 443–51.

De Houwer, J. and Moors, A. (2010). "Implicit measures: Similarities and differences." In Gawronski, B. and Payne, B. K. (eds.), *Handbook of Implicit Social Cognition.* New York: The Guilford Press: 176–96.

De Houwer, J., Teige-Mocigemba, S., Spruyt, A., and Moors, A. (2009). "Implicit measures: A normative analysis and review." *Psychological Bulletin* 135: 347–68.

Doris, J. (2002). *Lack of Character.* Oxford: Oxford University Press.

Epstein, S. (1979). "The stability of behavior: I. On predicting most of the people much of the time." *Journal of Personality and Social Psychology* 37: 1097–126.

Epstein, S. (1980). "The stability of behavior: II. Implications for psychological research." *American Psychologist* 35: 790–806.

Fazio, R. H., Jackson, J. R., Dunton, B. C., and Williams, C. J. (1995). "Variability in automatic activation as an unobtrusive measure of racial attitudes: A bona fide pipeline?" *Journal of Personality and Social Psychology* 69: 1013–27.

Fazio, R. H. and Olson, M. A. (2003). "Implicit measures in social cognition research: Their meaning and use." *Annual Review of Psychology* 54: 297–327.

Ferguson, M. J. (2008). "On becoming ready to pursue a goal you don't know you have: Effects of nonconscious goals on evaluative readiness." *Journal of Personality and Social Psychology* 95: 1268.

Gawronski, B., Hofmann, W., and Wilbur, C. J. (2006). "Are 'implicit' attitudes unconscious?" *Consciousness and Cognition* 15: 485–99.

Gawronski, B. and Payne, B. K. (2010). *Handbook of Implicit Social Cognition.* New York, NY: Guilford Press.

Gawronski, B. and Sritharan R. (2010). "Formatin, change, and contextualization of mental associations: Determinants and principles of variation in implicit measures." In Gawronski, B. and Payne, B. K. (eds.), *Handbook of Implicit Social Cognition.* New York, NY: The Guilford Press: 216–40.

Gendler, T. S. (2008a). "Alief and belief." *Journal of Philosophy* 105: 634–63.

Gendler, T. S. (2008b). "Alief in action (and reaction)." *Mind and Language* 23: 552–85.

Greenwald, A. G., McGhee, D. E., and Schwartz, J. L. (1998). "Measuring individual differences in implicit cognition: The implicit association test." *Journal of Personality and Social Psychology* 74: 1464–80.

Greenwald, A. G., Poehlman, T. A., Uhlmann, E. L., and Banaji, M. R. (2009). "Understanding and using the Implicit Association Test: III. Meta-analysis of predictive validity." *Journal of Personality and Social Psychology* 97(1): 17–41.

Harman, G. H. (1965). "The inference to the best explanation." *The Philosophical Review* 74: 88–95.

Kelly, D., Machery, E., and Mallon, R. (2010). "Race and racial cognition." In Doris, J. M. and the Moral Psychology Research Group (eds.), *The Moral Psychology Handbook*. Oxford: Oxford University Press: 463–72.

Kelly, D. and Roedder, E. (2008). "Racial cognition and the ethics of implicit bias." *Philosophy Compass* 3: 522–40.

Kriegel, U. (2012). "Moral motivation, moral phenomenology, and the alief/belief distinction." *Australasian Journal of Philosophy* 90: 469–86.

Lane, K. A., Banaji, M. R., Nosek, B. A., and Greenwald, A. G. (2007). "Understanding and using the implicit association test: IV. Procedures and validity." In Wittenbrink, B. and Schwarz, N. (eds.), *Implicit Measures of Attitudes*. New York, NY: The Guilford Press: 59–102.

Lipton, P. (1991). *Inference to the Best Explanation*. London: Routledge.

Lowery, B. S., Hardin, C. D., and Sinclair, S. (2001). "Social influence effects on automatic racial prejudice." *Journal of Personality and Social Psychology* 81: 842–55.

Machery, E., Faucher, L., and Kelly, D. (2010). "On the alleged inadequacies of psychological explanations of racism." *The Monist* 93: 228–54.

Maison, D., Greenwald, A. G., and Bruin, R. H. (2004). "Predictive validity of the Implicit Association Test in studies of brands, consumer attitudes, and behavior." *Journal of Consumer Psychology* 14: 405–15.

Mischel, W. (1968). *Personality and Assessment*. New York, NY: Wiley.

Nosek, B. A., Greenwald, A. G., and Banaji, M. R. (2005). "Understanding and using the Implicit Association Test: II. Method variables and construct validity." *Personality and Social Psychology Bulletin* 31: 166–80.

Nosek, B. A., Greenwald, A. G., and Banaji, M. R. (2007). "The Implicit Association Test at age 7: A methodological and conceptual review." In Bargh, J. A. (ed.), *Social Psychology and the Unconscious: The Automaticity of Higher Mental Processes*. New York: Psychology Press: 265–92.

Nosek, B. A., Hawkins, C. B., and Frazier, R. S. (2011). "Implicit social cognition: from measures to mechanisms." *Trends in Cognitive Sciences* 15: 152–9.

Nosek, B. A. et al. (2007a). "Pervasiveness and correlates of implicit attitudes and stereotypes." *European Review of Social Psychology* 18: 36–88.

Olson, M. A. and Fazio, R. H. (2003). "Relations between implicit measures of prejudice: What are we measuring?" *Psychological Science* 14: 636–9.

Oswald, F. L., Mitchell, G., Blanton, H., Jaccard, J., and Tetlock, P. E. (2013). "Predicting ethnic and racial discrimination: A meta-analysis of IAT criterion studies." *Journal of Personality and Social Psychology* 105: 171–92.

Peck, T. C., Seinfeld, S., Aglioti, S. M., and Slater, M. (2013). "Putting yourself in the skin of a black avatar reduces implicit racial bias." *Consciousness and Cognition* 22: 779–87.

Plato (1956). "The Republic." In Rouse, W. H. D. (trans.), *Great Dialogues of Plato*. London: Penguin Books.

Richeson, J. A. and Ambady, N. (2001). "Who's in charge? Effects of situational roles on automatic gender bias." *Sex Roles* 44: 493–512.

Ross, L. and Nisbett, R. E. (1991). *The Person and the Situation: Perspectives of Social Psychology*. New York, NY: Mcgraw-Hill.

Rudman, L. A. and Lee, M. R. (2002). "Implicit and explicit consequences of exposure to violent and misogynous rap music." *Group Processes and Intergroup Relations* 5: 133–50.

Rudman, L. A., Phelan, J. E., and Heppen, J. B. (2007). "Developmental sources of implicit attitudes." *Personality and Social Psychology Bulletin* 33: 1700–13.

Rydell, R. J. and Gawronski, B. (2009). "I like you, I like you not: Understanding the formation of context-dependent automatic attitudes." *Cognition and Emotion* 23: 1118–52.

Ryle, G. (1949). *The Concept of Mind*. Chicago, IL: University of Chicago Press.

Saul, J. (2013). "Scepticism and implicit bias." *Disputatio* 5(37): 243–63. <http://www.disputatio.com/wp-content/uploads/2013/11/Saul_Jennifer-Scepticism-and-Implicit-Bias.pdf>.

Schaller, M., Park, J. H., and Mueller, A. (2003). "Fear of the dark: Interactive effects of beliefs about danger and ambient darkness on ethnic stereotypes." *Personality and Social Psychology Bulletin* 29: 637–49.

Schupbach, J. N. and Sprenger, J. (2011). "The logic of explanatory power." *Philosophy of Science* 78: 105–27.

Schwitzgebel, E. (2002). "A phenomenal, dispositional account of belief." *Noûs* 36: 249–75.

Sherman, S. J., Rose, J. S., Koch, K., Presson, C. C., and Chassin, L. (2003). "Implicit and explicit attitudes toward cigarette smoking: The effects of context and motivation." *Journal of Social and Clinical Psychology* 22: 13–39.

Shiffrin, R. M., and Schneider, W. (1977). "Controlled and automatic human information processing: II. Perceptual learning, automatic attending and a general theory." *Psychological Review* 84: 127–90.

Spruyt, A., Hermans, D., De Houwer, J., Vandekerckhove, J., and Eelen, P. (2007). "On the predictive validity of indirect attitude measures: Prediction of consumer choice behavior on the basis of affective priming in the picture–picture naming task." *Journal of Experimental Social Psychology* 43: 599–610.

Stanley, D., Phelps, E., and Banaji, M. (2008). "The neural basis of implicit attitudes." *Current Directions in Psychological Science* 17: 164–70.

Teachman, B. A., Gapinski, K. D., Brownell, K. D., Rawlins, M., and Jeyaram, S. (2003). "Demonstrations of implicit anti-fat bias: The impact of providing causal information and evoking empathy." *Health Psychology* 22: 68–78.

Thurstone, L. L. (1928). "Attitudes can be measured." *American Journal of Sociology* 33: 529–54.

Van Fraassen, B. C. (1989). *Laws and Symmetry*. Oxford: Oxford University Press.

Wilson, T. D., Lindsey, S., and Schooler, T. Y. (2000). "A model of dual attitudes." *Psychological Review* 107: 101–26.

Wittenbrink, B., Judd, C. M., and Park, B. (2001). "Spontaneous prejudice in context: Variability in automatically activated attitudes." *Journal of Personality and Social Psychology* 81: 815–27.

1.5

Stereotype Threat and Persons

Ron Mallon

Stereotype threat is the threat each of us faces in a situation in which our behavior or performance might be interpreted as confirming a stereotype about a group to which we belong. Stereotype threat is typically studied in the lab by priming a subject's group affiliation in advance of the subject's performance of a task at which a group stereotype represents the group as comparatively worse. Surprisingly, even subtle primes can produce significant degradations of performance on a range of tasks including, notably, standardized tests. And work on stereotype threat suggests that such threat occurs for a variety of sorts of group identity, including race and ethnicity (e.g. Steele and Aronson, 1995; Gonzales, Blanton, and Williams, 2002), gender (Shih et al., 1999), and socioeconomic status (Croizet and Claire, 1998). These and similar findings are exciting, as they promise to provide a partial explanation for persistent inequalities in educational performance, and a burgeoning body of evidence is now exploring interventions to minimize or eliminate it (Yeager, Walton, and Cohen, 2013; Yeager and Walton, 2011).

As with many other-directed implicit biases, stereotype threat is often explained by social psychologists as the result of automatic and sometimes unconscious mental states and processes. For instance, one sort of explanation has it that stereotype threat occurs when a situation primes or "activates" a stereotypical representation that, in turn, triggers an automatic process that *interferes* with successful performance; for example, by increasing cognitive load for subjects (e.g. Croizet et al., 2004). The stereotype, here, is simply some representation of the putatively typical features of a category, but the associations it represents need not be believed.

These explanations are of a piece with a much broader "dual-process" movement in psychology, and in philosophy as well, that emphasizes explanations of mental and behavioral phenomena by appeal to *System 1* mental states and processes that operate automatically or reflexively, without consuming "central" or "executive" resources such as intention or willpower. In contrast to the explanations emphasizing System 1 mental states and processes are those that feature *System 2* mental states and processes: representational states that involve slow, reflective, calculative reasoning.[1]

A growing body of work in empirically informed moral psychology has suggested that, for better or worse, recognition of the importance of System 1 processes poses a challenge to more traditional, reason-based explanations of thought and behavior that are common elsewhere in the social sciences, in social philosophy, and throughout much of the humanities (e.g. Doris, 2009, forthcoming; Greene, 2007; Haidt, 2001). System 1 explanations may not appeal to propositional attitudes such as beliefs and desires at all, nor need they characterize processes governed by rational transitions; indeed, many theorists emphasize that System 1 processes can give rise to behavior in response to stereotypes that are not themselves believed or endorsed, via processes that are merely associations or activations. The result is thought and behavior that we do not and cannot rationally endorse (Doris, 2009). Because, in some sense yet to be explained, they characterize mental life below "the level of the person," I shall call such explanations *subpersonalist*, and I will contrast them with reason-based *personalist* explanations. Because explanation in terms of System 1 processes is often a species of subpersonal explanation, it seems that personalist explanations appeal to System 2. And, indeed, the sorts of intentional states and rational processes to which personalist explanations advert look to be just the sorts of mental states hypothesized to constitute System 2. Indeed, these representational states and rational transitions look to be substantially continuous with those hypothesized by the personalist explanations of "commonsense" or "folk" psychology— the belief-desire psychology that ordinary people ordinarily use to explain and predict and intervene on the ordinary thoughts and behaviors of persons.

While it is tempting to stop there, equating the subpersonal with System 1 and the personal with System 2, doing so carries some unwanted theoretical baggage. For instance, System 1 processes are often conceived to operate automatically and unconsciously, while System 2 processes are willful and conscious. In contrast, the "subpersonal" vs. "personal" distinction concerns the extent to which our ordinary "personal"-level idioms of explanation, prediction, and intervention can be appropriately applied to the mental states and processes in question. Insofar as these idioms can be applied to automatic and unconscious mental states or

---

[1] For various dual-process accounts, see e.g. Chaiken and Trope (1999); Bargh and Chartrand (1999); Gendler (2008); Stanovich (2004); Kahneman (2011).

processes, there will be no neat mapping of subpersonal/personal onto System 1 and System 2, but equally—and this is a point we return to at the end—there will be no neat inference from System 1 mental states or processes to the failure of personal explanation. For now, it is enough to note that the correspondence between these two distinctions can be more or less rough, depending upon how, exactly, their details are spelled out.

Why care about the distinction between personal and subpersonal explanations? One general worry is simply that subpersonalism threatens to undermine all personalist explanations either by falsifying them or by excluding them (cf. Churchland, 1981; Stich, 1983; Kim, 1998). In this vein, many philosophers will remember Jerry Fodor's declaration:

If commonsense intentional psychology really were to collapse, that would be, beyond comparison, the greatest intellectual catastrophe in the history of our species...
(Fodor, 1987: xii)

Of course, even if one agrees with Fodor about the centrality of commonsense intentional explanation to our folk and scientific projects, one might allow that commonsense intentional states play little role in the explanation of stereotype threat.

Nonetheless, evidence for sweeping conclusions accumulates piecemeal, and defenders of folk psychology would do well to attend to subpersonalist claims from the dual-process literature.

My project here is motivated by a concern related to, but more specific than, Fodor's. Explanations adverting to persons and their reasons are intimately bound up with our treating persons *as persons*, for example, in holding them to be reason-governed and responsible (Strawson, 1962). Approaching stereotype threat as something that bypasses our capacities as believing, desiring, and intending agents, results in explanations that alienate us, leaving us unable to recognize ourselves in the explanations that result, and ultimately, this distorts our understanding of prospects for intervention as well, making successful interventions seem like "magic" (Yeager and Walton, 2011). The result is a gap between many explanations of stereotype threat in the literature and the interventions that are proposed to alleviate it.

In this chapter I explore and articulate both personal and subpersonal interpretations of stereotype threat, and I suggest that subpersonal accounts of stereotype threat are incomplete because they fail to account for phenomena better explained by a personalist interpretation. My aim is not to completely displace subpersonal explanations, for I expect accounting for all the phenomena connected with stereotype threat will require a range of mechanisms, both personalist and subpersonalist. Rather, in arguing for a central role for personalist explanations, I hope to highlight the explicability of stereotype threat and many successful interventions on it in light of our intuitive grasp of rational actors in socially threatening situations.

Here is how I proceed. In Section 1 I review several seminal studies documenting the existence of stereotype threat. Then, in Section 2, I distinguish personalist and subpersonalist accounts of stereotype threat in more detail, and review some subpersonalist social psychological explanations. In Section 3 I draw attention to some personalist explanations in the social sciences and humanities, and briefly sketch a personalist account of stereotype threat. In Section 4 I draw on a range of evidence to argue for a personalist account of the mental states that trigger stereotype threat. Then, in Section 5, I argue for a personalist construal of the processes underlying stereotype threat. Finally, in Section 6, I offer some concluding thoughts.

1 What Is Stereotype Threat?

Not all stereotype threat is concerned with objective performance on set tasks. Pioneering stereotype threat researcher Claude Steele (2010) named his book on stereotype threat *Whistling Vivaldi*, after the practice of Brent Staples, an African American editorialist for *The New York Times*. While in graduate school at the University of Chicago, Staples realized that strangers he passed in the park were intimidated by his approach—that of an African American male. He moved to defuse the threat he posed by whistling a tune by Vivaldi. This disrupted others' stereotypical interpretation of him, putting them (and in turn, him) at ease. This is stereotype threat since Staples was under threat of confirming the stereotype of a frightening African American male and changed his behavior to defuse it. Here, however, I am concerned with the narrower phenomenon of stereotype threat effects upon performance. Consider a few examples.

The term "stereotype threat" was introduced by Steele and Aronson in their influential paper "Stereotype threat and the intellectual test performance of African Americans" (1995). In one illustrative study they give a test comprised of items from the verbal section of the Graduate Record Examination (GRE) to black and white college students. In one "diagnostic" condition the test was described as "diagnostic of intellectual ability," while in a second "nondiagnostic" condition it was described as "a laboratory problem-solving task that was nondiagnostic of ability" (799). Steele and Aronson found that blacks in the diagnostic condition performed significantly worse than whites in the diagnostic condition, and also worse than blacks or whites in the nondiagnostic condition

(Study 2). Black participants in the diagnostic condition completed fewer items with less accuracy.

A few years later, Shih, Pitinsky, and Ambady (1999) followed up on this research, but with a twist: they manipulated more than one dimension of identity. In one study they offered a quantitative test to a group of undergraduate Asian American women with very high average quantitative SAT scores. In one condition, subjects were given a questionnaire that primed their gender identity, and in a second they were given a questionnaire that primed their ethnic identity. In a third, no identity was primed by the questionnaire. Shih and colleagues predicted that gender-priming would put subjects under stereotype threat and, as in Steele and Aronson's study, test performance would be impaired. But while women are stereotyped as less quantitatively skilled, Asians are stereotyped as more so. In fact, they found that for both accuracy and number of correctly completed items, the gender-primed subjects were outperformed by the controls, who were outperformed by the ethnicity-primed subjects.[2]

In another fascinating study, Stone, Lynch, Sjomerling, and Darley (1999) extended findings of stereotype threat to athletic performances and to white subjects. In a pair of experiments, they showed that black Princeton undergraduates' performance on a golf test suffered relative to controls if the task was presented as "diagnostic of sports intelligence," but white Princeton undergraduates suffered relative to controls if the task was presented as a measure of "natural athletic ability." The idea is that the black subjects performed worse under threat of confirming a deleterious stereotype about black intelligence, while white subjects performed worse under threat of confirming a deleterious stereotype about white athletic ability.

Does any of this matter in the real world? Stricker and Ward (2004) manipulated the elicitation of demographic information either before or after a real standardized Advanced Placement Calculus examination offered by the Educational Testing Service. While they cautiously suggested no effect, according to Danaher and Crandall's (2008) reanalysis of the data, moving the information section to the end of the examination lowered the scores of men and raised those of women (decreasing the overall gender gap by 33%)![3]

---

[2] A number of social psychology results have come under scrutiny in recent years as the result of systematic attempts to replicate results in social psychology. Moon and Roeder (2014) attempted to replicate Shih, Pittinsky, and Ambady's (1999) study and failed, but Gibson et al. (2014) have succeeded in replicating the effect. It seems likely that debate about the replicability of the effect will continue for some time. While the controversy is obviously relevant for the issues I discuss, I do not explore it in detail here.

[3] Similar results were obtained on a Computerized Placement Test (CPT).

Taken together, these studies, along with numerous others, have documented effects of stereotypes on performance that are of interest to a broad range of practical and social concerns. But what explains these phenomena?

2 Subpersonalism about Stereotype Threat

There is no consensus among social scientists on the exact explanation of stereotype threat, and some suggest or defend complex, multi-mechanism accounts (e.g. Steele and Aronson, 1995: 799; Schmader et al., 2008). Nonetheless, it seems that there is some agreement about the *shape* of the explanation; namely, that the explanation will be substantially subpersonalist.

In Section 1 I suggested that personalists explain behaviors (and their consequence) by appeal to mental states that rationally produce other mental states and behaviors. Subpersonalists, in contrast, appeal to states and processes that I have suggested are "below the level of the person." But we need to precisify these rather vague ideas further for our discussion of stereotype threat. We have suggested that the distinction between personalists and subpersonalists about stereotype threat depends both upon the nature of the mental states that trigger the threat, and of the processes that those mental states initiate.

Specifically, personalists suggest that the *mental states* are (implicit or explicit) *propositional attitudes* like beliefs and desires—states that can act as, and interact with, *reasons* for thinking and doing certain things—and the *processes* are rational mental transitions and rational practical reasoning. And we can characterize a subpersonalist thesis for each of these—one that treats the mental states as *mere* representations (toward which no believing attitude need be taken) and the processes that connect mental states with one another and behavior as automatic and *merely* causal.[4] That gives us four theses. Two are about mental states:

Mental-State Personalism (MSP):   Stereotype threat occurs when a situation activates *propositional attitudes* (e.g. *beliefs*) about one's category and situation.

Mental-State Subpersonalism (MSS):   Stereotype threat occurs when a situation activates mere *representations* about one's category and situation.

And two are about processes:

Process Personalism (PP):   Stereotype threat occurs when triggers initiate rational processes of thought and action that interfere with normal or optimal performance.

---

[4] Indeed, some characterizations of automatic processes characterize them as associative processes which are understood as experientially produced networks of mutual activation among representations. See Dacey (2015).

Process Subpersonalism (PS):   Stereotype threat occurs when triggers initiate an automatic, causal process that interferes with normal or optimal performance.

Attention to these distinctions is certainly reflected in the psychological literature (e.g. Gawronski and Bodenhausen, 2006), in part because the distinction corresponds to some articulations of "dual-process theory," but it is sometimes unclear exactly how to interpret social psychological work in terms of it, and often individual theorists and particular papers can suggest multiple interpretations. Still, my aim here is not to critique any particular theorist, but to understand and raise questions for what I take to be the pervasive subpersonalism in the social psychological literature, including the literature on stereotype threat. Interpretatively, I suggest that the social psychological literature is subpersonalist *sometimes* in the first, mental-state sense, and *typically* in the second, process sense.

2.1 Mental-state subpersonalism

Stereotype threat effects are triggered by a representation (e.g. a stereotype or belief) activated by a situation. Discussions of stereotype threat in social psychology suggest three possible sorts of triggers: the first subpersonalist, and the second two personalist.

On the subpersonalist, *stereotype activation* interpretation, mere activation of (and not having a belief attitude toward the proposition expressed by) a representation that represents category members as not good in the performance domain is sufficient to degrade performance.

On the personalist, *strategic belief* interpretation, stereotype threat is triggered by a belief about how others will interpret or react to one's performance. There are many varieties of such strategic belief. For example, one may experience fear or anger in response to the belief that *one's performance will be taken as evidence for the confirmation of a negative stereotype by others*. Or one might experience lowered motivation because of a belief that *one will be held to a lower standard because of one's category membership*.

And on the personalist, *stereotype belief* interpretation: stereotype threat is triggered by the stereotype itself being *believed* by the experiencer of threat.

Most work on stereotype threat psychology suggests that the first or second is the case, and suggests, sometimes explicitly, that the third is not the case. In this section I will consider the first, returning to the other two personalist possibilities in Section 4.

We can see an example of the stereotype activation interpretation in Shih et al. (1999), who view their work as an attempt to expand the work on the powerful effects of automatic and unconscious activation ... and self-application of stereotypes by examining whether the implicit activation of particular identities can facilitate as well as debilitate academic performance.   (80)

Here they advert to a range of influential work on stereotypes that suggests a subpersonal route to behavioral changes, including one famous study from Bargh, Chen, and Burrows (1996), who primed their subjects with words that were associated with being old. Bargh and colleagues subsequently documented a subsequent reduction in walking speed (as compared to subjects not so primed) by subjects departing the experiment.

This extraordinarily influential study by Bargh and others has recently come under fire because of failures to replicate the phenomenon by Doyen et al. (2012) and Pashler et al. (2011). Doyen et al. have argued that the original effect stemmed from experimenter expectations. While the status of the experiment by Bargh et al. remains a continued subject of debate, there is nonetheless a range of stereotype threat data in which it seems that mere priming of a representation produces effects on performance that seem to result simply from unconscious enactment of stereotype content. As Shih et al. (2002) write: "... across a variety of domains, nonconscious priming of stereotypes has been found to cause individuals to think and act in stereotype-consistent ways" (638).

Notice that, like Bargh et al. (1996), none of the experimental probes in the stereotype work reviewed above explicitly mention the content of the stereotypes presumed to subsequently play a role in modifying performance. For example, Shih et al. (1999) ask subjects to indicate their ethnicity or gender, but they do not explicitly evoke the negative or positive connotations of these stereotypes. And work by, say, Steele and Aronson (1995) or Stone et al. (1999) does not even go that far. These probes merely suggest that the tasks at hand are diagnostic in a domain.[5]

In each of these cases, stereotype threat seems to begin with mere activation of a stereotypical representation, and does not clearly implicate the representation being believed.[6]

---

[5] Nearly a decade later, Schmader et al. (2008) similarly wrote that stereotype threat begins with merely "activating negative stereotypes about a social identity one possesses" (337). Later (and following Gawronski and Bodenhausen, 2006), they suggest the importance of *beliefs* about one's situation, including evaluations of the importance of the target domain and beliefs about one's group and oneself, but they seem to understand these beliefs as simply activated representations (e.g. 339ff).

[6] Gendler (2008) makes this explicit by coining the term *alief* for these states that are not beliefs, but are still representational and influence behavior in virtue of their content.

2.2 Process subpersonalism

Work on stereotype threat suggests considerable agreement among social psychologists surrounding a subpersonal interpretation of the process that degrades performance. Such process subpersonalists typically hold that the threatening situation initiates some process that automatically (and nonrationally) interferes with normal performance. Consider two sorts.

2.2.1 BEHAVIORAL INTERFERENCE: STEREOTYPE IMITATION

As we have just noted, Shih and colleagues (1999, 2002), following work by Bargh and others (e.g. Bargh, Chen, and Burrows, 1996; Bargh and Chartrand, 1999), interpret stereotype threat as the product of a process in which subtle priming of stereotypical representations automatically gives rise to imitative processes in which the representational content of the stereotype is expressed in behavior, and even if doing so is against the intentions of the subject.

The picture here is that there are two processes that determine behavior, and that in cases of stereotype threat, the two are in competition. The detrimental stereotype degrades performance in a domain even while other mechanisms (including those involving executive control) may operate to promote them.

2.2.2 COGNITIVE INTERFERENCE: FINITE RESOURCES

Steele and Aronson's (1995) paper offers a range of possible explanations for stereotype threat, many of which have been explored in further research. They write:

The stereotype loads the testing situation with an extra degree of self- threat, a degree not borne by people not stereotyped in this way. This additional threat, in turn, may interfere with their performance in a variety of ways: by causing an arousal that reduces the range of cues participants are able to use...by diverting attention onto task-irrelevant worries...by causing an interfering self-consciousness...or overcautiousness...   (799)[7]

These explanatory hypotheses amount to endorsements of a sort of process subpersonalism on which the situation activates mental states that interfere with optimal or normal processing of the task. While this article dates from the early days in the exploration of stereotype threat, Steele and Aronson's own best guess was that

---

[7] This passage continues to consider a personalist hypothesis: "Or, through the ability-indicting interpretation it poses for test frustration, it could foster low performance expectations that would cause participants to withdraw effort" (799). This last hypothesis, which is not Steele and Aronson's considered view, is an example of personalist theorizing.

stereotype threat caused an inefficiency of processing much like that caused by other evaluative pressures. Stereotype-threatened participants spent more time doing fewer items more inaccurately—probably as a result of alternating their attention between trying to answer the items and trying to assess the self-significance of their frustration.

(809)

Stereotype threat effects on performance have been conceived, from the outset, primarily as an effect of an automatic process or processes interfering with performance.

Some more recent work has continued very much in the vein of Steele and Aronson's (1995) proposals, but with an increasing body of evidence and theoretical sophistication in its support. Schmader, Johns, and Forbes (2008) model stereotype threat's effects on cognitive and social performance as involving three distinct though causally intertwined pathways:

1. A physiological stress response that impairs prefrontal cognition.
2. Added cognitive load produced by actively monitoring one's own performance.
3. Added cognitive load produced by efforts to suppress other responses to threat (e.g. stereotype threat, self monitoring).

Crucially, all three of these pathways disrupt performance on cognitive and social tasks by taxing or disrupting a finite common resource—working memory—that is required by the controlled reasoning processes that subserve performance of complex cognitive and motor tasks.

Steele and Aronson (1995) and Schmader et al. (2008) suggest that a threating situation activates some automatic process that, in turn, competes for or depletes some cognitive resource, degrading performance on tasks that also draw on that resource.

Taken together, these two sorts of model—behavioral interference or cognitive interference—register ways in which activation of automatic processes by representations may give rise to disruptions of performance on a range of tasks. I now turn to sketching an alternative, personalist explanation of stereotype threat.

3 Personalist Explanations of Stereotype Threat

As I suggested at the outset, personalist explanations explain behavioral phenomena by appeal to reasons that persons have, where this involves appeal to agents' "propositional attitudes"—their beliefs, desires, and other intentional mental states. They assume that such mental states produce other mental states and behaviors via rational transitions including simple logical entailments. They are, thus, explanations that appeal to agents, beliefs, desires, and choices.

3.1 Personalist explanations in social science and social theory

While there is little work interpreting stereotype threat in personalist terms, personalist explanations that advert to intentional mental states, behaviors, and rational transitions among them are at the heart of a huge proportion of explanations in the humanities and the social sciences, ranging from the history of ideas, to cognitive behavioral theory, to rational choice theory (Rosenberg, 1995).

Consider a prominent example from within social psychology itself: Carol Dweck's influential work on "fixed" vs. "growth" mindsets. Over the past several decades, Dweck has amassed a host of evidence that how individuals think about their capacities as either already fixed, or as capable of further growth, influences their subsequent performance on a range of tasks (Dweck 1999). Individuals with a "fixed" mindset respond to adversity with lost interest and motivation, while a "growth" mindset leads to a more active and engaged working through of difficulties.

On Dweck's own account of her findings, subjects' withdrawal of effort, attention, and identification from a task amounts to a rational response to subjects' beliefs about who and what they are and the nature of the situation in which they find themselves. If one expects to gain nothing from a task but negative feedback about one's already fixed properties, withdrawing from the task seems perfectly rational. And Dweck's work fits easily as an example of rational, personalist explanation.[8]

While much of Dweck's research program does not explicitly concern categories of persons such as race, ethnicity, or sex, the connection is not hard to draw. To the extent that membership in these categories carries assumptions that category members share one or more distinctive properties that explain category-typical differences and that are fixed by nature, we can conjecture that self-directed categorization would rationally lead one to withdraw effort, attention, and identification from the task in just the way Dweck's subjects do.

Consider a different personalist example from a different social science: the controversial theory of "acting white." Introduced by Fordham and Ogbu (1986), the theory of "acting white" attempts to explain the differential scholastic

---

[8] Because personalist explanations can be neutral with respect to whether the mental states or processes occur consciously, Dweck's personalism is consistent with conscious or unconscious (but rational) influence of standing "mindset" attitudes.

performance of African Americans by appeal to the idea that they stigmatize academic performance as "acting white." The theory has been influential, though a study in North Carolina (Tyson, Darity, and Castellino, 2005) found little evidence that the theory can serve as a general explanation of differential academic performance. A more recent study by Fryer and Torelli (2010), however, found evidence consistent with the theory in U.S. high schools. Fryer and Torelli constructed a metric of individual popularity, and charted that against their grade point average.

The effects were striking. Black students in public high schools whose GPA rises towards a 4.0 suffer a decline in popularity that has no parallel among white students (but is less pronounced than the fall-off faced by Hispanic students). Crucially, according to the theory, these students are simply reacting to the shared social meanings of the identities that are available—meanings that suggest to them that academic success is characteristic of whiteness and in some way inappropriate for black or Hispanic students. Exactly how the belief that academic achievement is "acting white" leads to lower popularity is unclear from these data, but the theory of "acting white" suggests that it is a product of interpersonal strategizing, making choices about one's aims in part by calculating the probable reactions of others. For present purposes, we note that it is rational to downplay school performance if higher performance comes at social costs or if it is seen as intrinsically more costly or difficult. Thus, the theory of "acting white" interprets African American students as making reasonable choices given their situations and beliefs.

One puzzling aspect of stereotype threat is the seemingly self-confirming nature of the representations involved: in stereotype threat, a community's stereotypical representation of categories of person as good or bad at an activity can actually produce the comparative differences represented. Work by Hacking (1995a, 1995b, 1998) on the "looping effect of human kinds" has explored phenomena that have this puzzling aspect—phenomena in which a community's representation of a category as being a certain way causes category members to instantiate the representation.[9] He suggests a wide range of categories of person or action that members of the category come to have the properties that they do in part because they are represented as so having them. For instance, Hacking (1995a) suggests that patients diagnosed with "multiple personality disorder" or "dissociative identity disorder" in fact intentionally (though perhaps sincerely) enact a culturally promulgated "script" of symptoms in order to acquire certain social benefits or recognition that they find reinforcing. As this script changed, as

---

[9] Saul (2011) suggests stereotype threat as an instance of looping effects.

when theorists began to believe that more and more personalities or "alters" could be found within each patient, the behavior of those categorized changed as well, confirming this new belief (77).

Drawing upon these general ideas, Appiah (2005) offers a similar account of racial identity:

Once labels are applied to people, ideas about people who fit the label come to have social and psychological effects. In particular, these ideas shape the ways people conceive of themselves and their projects ... the label plays a role in shaping the way the agent makes decisions about how to conduct a life.   (66)

Both Hacking's and Appiah's analyses explain differential features of category members by appeal to intentional agents making choices within the situations in which they find themselves.

These examples from social science and social philosophy are personalist in that they emphasize belief (in contrast to the activation interpretation) and rational calculation resulting in action. These personalist explanations are thus apparently very different from the subpersonalist explanations at work in social psychology. But could we offer a personalist explanation of stereotype threat?

3.2 Personalism about stereotype threat

Personalist explanations, as I use the term here, endorse both mental-state personalism and process personalism. What would such an explanation look like?

We have already seen one personalist example: Staples' recognition that he was under stereotype threat and his strategic choice to "whistle Vivaldi." Here, his behavior is captured straightforwardly in personalist terms.

Limiting ourselves to the case of performance contexts, here is one possibility. If a threatening situation leads one's situation-relevant beliefs and desires to become occurrent, prompting one to withdraw attention or effort from the task at hand, then a personalist explanation would seem appropriate. For instance, one might withdraw because one expects to be unsuccessful (because of *stereotype belief*), or because one expects that others have low expectations or will even hold one's performance against one (varieties of *strategic belief*). Each of these offers a personal explanation of stereotype threat involving appeal to propositional attitudes and rational processes. But is there any evidence to support personalism about stereotype threat?

There is some evidence that stereotype threat produces withdrawal from activities. Stone (2002), for instance, showed that subjects that were identified with a domain under stereotype threat withdrew from practice sessions that would have improved overall performance. And there is some evidence that expectations of success or failure can have immediate consequences on perform- ance as well. Cadinu et al. (2003) carried out an experiment that directly manipu- lated subjects' expectations of performance in tests under stereotype threat by telling women subjects directly that women perform worse, or better, or no differently than men on a logical–mathematical examination. Women who received negative information about their capacities both expected to do worse, and did do worse, than women in the other conditions (Experiment 1).

But these studies face many others apparently supporting a subpersonalist approach. I now turn to offer considerations for mental-state personalism and process personalism separately, and in more detail.

4 Could Personalism about Mental States in Stereotype Threat be True?

Begin with personalism about the mental states that trigger stereotype threat. We have mentioned two personalist interpretations of triggering beliefs present in the literature: strategic belief and stereotype belief.

4.1 Personalist interpretations

Steele himself emphasizes the interpretation of a situation as involving threat (e.g. Steele, 1997). On this view, it seems that stereotype threat begins with a strategic belief about one's situation—a belief not in the content of the stereotype itself, but rather, in the fact that the situation itself is stereotype-relevant, and that one's performance runs the risk of confirming a deleterious stereotype. This threat produces fear, anxiety, anger, or attentional monitoring—states that exert add- itional cognitive load on subjects under stereotype threat. This is a personalist construal of the relevant mental state (for Steele, belief that the situation is threatening), but it carries no commitment to belief in the stereotype itself.

While Steele emphasizes the role of negative emotions such as fear and anxiety—emotions that are plausibly triggered by beliefs about dangerous or out-of-control features of a situation—other sorts of belief about one's interper- sonal situation could also conceivably play a role. For example, beliefs about what is expected of one and what one can be blamed for intersect with category beliefs in complex ways. To the extent that stereotype threat is triggered by beliefs about how others will react to various possible actions one can undertake (and their probable outcomes), stereotype threat will be belief-driven rather than merely representation-driven.

An alternative, personalist instigating mental state is belief in the stereotype itself; viz. the belief that, for example, one's race or sex or class is a reliable indicator of one's ability to perform a task successfully. If one believes that one is not likely to be good at a task, that by itself could create a range of reasons to withdraw from the task. It can lead to the belief that one will not do well, as well as the belief that others do not expect one to do well.

While there is some ambiguity about whether beliefs or mere representations trigger stereotype threat, many social psychologists seem to assume that the stereotype itself plays its role in stereotype threat in virtue of its status as a *representation* instead of in virtue of its status as a belief. That is, they assume that subjects need not believe a stereotype in order for activation of it (along with other representations or beliefs) to trigger stereotype threat effects on performance.[10] Sometimes, the possibility of a dissociation between explicit belief and the stereotypical representation itself is explicitly asserted, as when Steele and Aronson (1995) insist of stereotype threat that "for the person to be threatened in this way, he need not even believe the stereotype" (798; cf. Steele, 2010). This anecdotal suggestion seems borne out by the fact that, in a range of key stereotype threat studies (e.g. Steele and Aronson, 1995; Shih et al., 1999), subjects are themselves talented in the performance domain. These subjects seem subject to stereotype threat despite having good evidence of their own ability to succeed in the domain.

4.2 Empirical evidence against mental-state subpersonalism

Perhaps the best evidence against mental-state subpersonalism is that stereotype threat seems to be under the control of subjects' beliefs about the situation and themselves. Consider first that subjects' susceptibility to stereotype threat depends upon their standing beliefs about themselves and their situation. For example, subjects who endorse the content of the stereotype are more susceptible to stereotype threat (Schmader, Johns, and Barquissau, 2004). In addition, many interventions suggest that changing subjects' beliefs alleviates stereotype threat.

For example, employing Dweckian interventions, Aronson changed students' beliefs about the malleability of their capacities for success in tested domains, leading to increased engagement and improved grade point averages (Aronson, Fried, and Good, 2002). This is consistent with the idea that stereotype threat itself is produced, in part, by the interpretation of feelings of frustration or difficulty as evidence of one's inadequacy to the task.

---

[10] An exception may be Schmader et al. (2008), who note that belief in a deleterious stereotype is correlated with susceptibility to stereotype threat. However, they explain this connection on the grounds that where there is such a belief, the associative connection between a group and a stereotype domain is strong (338).

Similarly, Cohen, Steele, and Ross (1999) reduce student's perceptions of bias by leading them to interpret negative feedback as evidence of their teacher's high standards instead of as evidence that casts doubt on the fairness of the situation (as in interpersonal threat) or on the student herself (as in stereotype belief). Yeager et al. (2014) designed an intervention around this idea, and report substantial boosts of black seventh-graders' GPAs. By changing the beliefs that guide the interpretation of negative feedback, these interventions improved performance.

Johns et al. (2005) boosted women's scores on a statistics examination simply by informing them about stereotype threat as the examination was offered, changing their interpretation of any difficulties experienced.

We have seen that Cadinu et al. (2003) manipulated expectations about test success and changed subjects' performance. Similarly, Good, Aronson, and Harder (2008) manipulated women mathematics students' expectations under stereotype threat by assuring them that:

This mathematics test has not shown any gender differences in performance or mathematics ability. The test has been piloted in many mathematics courses across the nation to determine how reliable and valid the test is for measuring mathematics ability. Analysis of thousands of students' test results has shown that males and females perform equally well on this test. In other words, this mathematics test shows no gender differences.   (22)

Those students subsequently performed better on a practice examination than control students who had not read the paragraph.

In each of these cases, performance is boosted, apparently by altering subjects' beliefs about their situation. The best (though hardly the only) explanation of this, I suggest, is that stereotype threat is triggered by subjects' beliefs rather than by stereotypical representations that are merely activated, and that altering those beliefs alters the outcomes to which they contribute.[11] What kinds of beliefs are they?

4.3 *What beliefs?*

We have distinguished strategic beliefs about what others will think or do from stereotype beliefs—beliefs in the stereotype itself. This is a distinction based on the content of the beliefs. Are they about what others will think or do? Or are they about features of the category itself?

---

[11] It remains possible that the interventions interrupt stereotype threat effects not by surgically intervening on the same mental states that produce it, but rather by disrupting it in some other way—for example, by swamping it with unrelated, but positive, boosts to performance.

The range of different interventions on beliefs that modify effects of stereotype threat on performance suggests that some combination of beliefs about the situation and beliefs about the category to which one belongs are relevant. Crucially, however, the empirical evidence just considered also suggests that one important aspect of what is believed is the deleterious content of the stereotype itself. This is suggested first by the correlation between susceptibility to stereotype threat and belief in the stereotype itself (Schmader, Johns, and Barquissau, 2004). But it is also suggested by the success of Dweckian interventions that seem to alter subjects' understandings of themselves (Aronson et al., 2002) rather than interpersonal features of the situation they are in.

These interventions change subjects' interpretations of what academic domains mean, and how encountered difficulty is to be interpreted; but they do not obviously change subjects' beliefs about how others in the situation might or might not view their performance as confirming or disconfirming a stereotype. In fact, the intervention in Johns et al. (2005) actually increases subjects' belief that the experimenter expects women to do worse than men on the examination. This makes sense because in teaching subjects about stereotype threat, the experimenter explicitly raises the issue. Despite this increase, subjects' test performance also improves (suggesting that a belief in interpersonal threat was not crucial in that case).

That belief in the stereotype plays an important role is, in fact, quite plausible even in situations in which fear of interpersonal judgment is in play, for in these situations the threat seems logically, and plausibly psychologically, connected to belief in the stereotype itself. Emotions such as fear and anxiety, and other automatic, emotional reactions to threat, are plausibly reactions to beliefs that a situation is threatening. However, without doubt about one's capacity to succeed in a specific performance, these situations need not be threatening. They might be, for example, opportunities to shatter negative misconceptions. Academic performance situations, where objective measures of success and failure are in play, look to be threatening to the extent that one has doubts about one's ability to perform successfully. Such doubts plausibly increase with one's belief that the stereotypical content might be true.

5 Could Process Personalism be True?

While some psychologists interpret the mental states that give rise to stereotype threat in personalist terms, many agree that stereotype threat occurs when a representation triggers a subpersonal automatic process that interferes with successful performance. However, there are difficult questions for an exclusively subpersonalist interpretation of these processes.

One question for the process subpersonalist regards the efficacy of interventions in producing stereotype "lift" that boosts performance, like that in Shih et al. (1999). Recall there that subjects used stereotype threat to lower the scores of Asian women reminded that they are women, and raise the scores of those reminded that they are Asian. But how is this boosting possible?

Notice that the personalist has an apparently straightforward answer: activating category-negative beliefs leads to some sort of disengagement or discounting of the task, while activating category-positive beliefs leads to greater engagement or motivation on the task. Crucially, for the personalist, the explanation of degradation of performance and enhancement of the performance are symmetrical: they involve the same mechanism operating on different beliefs.

How can the process subpersonalist account for results like this? The stereotype imitation theorist has a ready answer. Shih et al. (1999) hold that mere activation of a representation can lead to facilitation of imitatative behaviors—behaviors that lead to negative performance in one case, and positive in another. Thus, when the representation is negative, it degrades performance. And when it is positive, it enhances it. Again, a symmetrical explanation.

However, there are reasons to be skeptical of this explanation. First, we have already noted that this explanation appeals to a process that crucially involves a subpersonal interpretation of the mental states that give rise to stereotype threat, and we have already seen reason to doubt that this is correct. So, to choose just one example, the intervention by Johns et al. (2005) does not seem to alter subjects' underlying stereotype representation at all, but it does reduce stereotype threat effects on mathematics performance.

In addition, the claim that priming a representation facilitates imitation is itself questionable. We noted above the debate over Bargh et al.'s (1996), and these have resulted in more general ongoing controversy about priming data. However, even if we allow that such priming data are replicable, it is not clear that the imitative model is the correct interpretation of them. For instance, one apparently successful replication of priming for *being old*, by Cesario et al. (2006), suggests a different, nonimitative interpretation of the mechanism involved. Cesario et al. reproduce the effect from Bargh et al. (1996), but show that slower walking directly correlates with positive attitudes toward the aged. Subjects with negative attitudes did not exhibit it (Experiment 2). This evidence suggests that the primed content prepares subjects for actions, not simply by imitating a representation, but in combination with their background beliefs and evaluations. If so, then the "stereotype imitation" mechanism is too simple a story of the process underlying these results, and it seems implausible as a model for stereotype threat as well.

In the absence of the stereotype imitation account, though, it is hard to see how the process subpersonalist can offer a symmetrical explanation of degradation and boosting of performance. Consider again, for instance, Steele and Aronson's suggestion that stereotype threat emerges from anxiety taxing cognitive resources. While that explains decreased performance, it seems that there needs to be a different mechanism involved in boosting performance. But that is just to say that process subpersonalists have a less elegant account than personalists.

It might be thought that this is too quick. Interference accounts of the sort suggested by Steele and Aronson (1995) or Schmader et al. (2008) could also offer a symmetrical explanation. One possibility is that in cases manipulating inter-sectional identities like that in Shih et al. (1999), all the subjects, including the unprimed control subjects, experience baseline stereotype threat that leads to an interfering state like fear or anxiety. Boosted subjects lower their levels of interfering anxiety while threatened subjects raise it, and the corresponding improvement or degrading of performance results.

However, this seems ad hoc. After all, these subjects always have two identities: one that boosts mathematics performance and the other that disrupts mathematics performance. Given that, why should anxiety rather than no anxiety be the default state? Consider also that boosting seems possible among subjects that are not under stereotype threat. For example, Danaher and Crandall (2008)—analyzing Stricker and Ward's (2004) data—note a decrease in male scores on AP Calculus examinations when they are asked about their gender after an examination rather than before it.[12] Ultimately, however, more study is needed to understand these issues definitively.

Finally, automatic states may have a role to play which is not captured by subpersonalist accounts of the process degrading performance: they may simply realize or instantiate intentional evaluations. Consider again, for example, Steele's suggestion that stereotype threat effects are products of anxiety or fear. (There is some evidence that some stereotype threat is mediated by anxiety: Osborne, 2001; Delgado and Prieto, 2008.) The existence of such emotional mediators does not

---

[12] Subjects may have baseline anxiety caused not by stereotype threat, but by the testing situation itself. In this case, "boost" would lower the anxiety, and threat would raise it. But the mechanisms would be different. Boost would lower anxiety because the anticipation of success negates the belief that produces the anxiety. But threat would raise anxiety because of the perception of the additional risk of interpersonal judgment. So, while both would be mediated by anxiety, the way they interact with anxiety is quite different.

show that cognitive load theorists are correct, for it does not show that the states produce degraded performance via exhausting cognitive resources (even if they do). They might, for instance, produce degraded performance by reducing the subjects' subjective evaluation of the activity—by making the activity itself aversive, for instance. Personalists can allow that a task that produces anxiety or fear (or other aversive automatic reactions) may lead subjects to discount, disengage with, or otherwise downregulate from performance domains. This would provide an explanation of degraded performance that was accompanied by automatic activation but capturable within an intentional idiom: the subject did not want to do the activity.[13]

But this possibility seems to violate the dual-process supposition that frames much of the theorizing about stereotype threat and other implicit biases, for it suggests that automatic processes may subserve personalist as well as subpersonalist responses. How is this possible?

Although much social psychological work is framed in dual-process terms, there is a different, canonical way of conceiving of the place of rational thought in the architecture of the mind that has played a crucial role in shaping cognitive science—as one of several different "stances" or "levels of explanation" (Marr, 1982; Pylyshyn, 1984; Newell, 1982; Dennett, 1987). Within this schema, personal explanations may pick out events and mechanisms that are describable by multiple theories or at multiple other levels of explanation. So one event could be both, say, a *deciding not to pursue this task further* or a *computation of expected utility* and also an *experiencing of anxiety* or a *shift in dynamic patterns in one's neuronal network*.

This "levels of explanation" architectural conception is very different from a dual-process account, for while dual-process frameworks conceive of System 1 and System 2 as competitive, a levels-of-explanation framework suggests that events are subject to an asymmetric cascade of distinct explanations in which higher levels of explanation have explanations at lower levels, but not necessarily the reverse. So higher-level, intentional explanations may well be realized in part by lower-level processes, though processes will not always be realized by higher-level states.

Returning to our suggestion, it is simply that some automatic processes—for example, emotional activations—might realize personalist explanations at a

---

[13] There are empirical questions about this interpretation. Some stereotype threat researchers have suggested that being under stereotype threat increases subjects' motivation in the task domain (e.g. Jamieson and Harkin, 2007, 2009). I set this aside here, noting only that this explanation competes not only with a certain variety of personalist, but also with the other impersonalist accounts I discuss here.

lower level of explanation. They might not be instances of interference with performance. A proper appreciation of the architectural options should allow this as a possibility.

6 Explaining Stereotype Threat

There is a vast and burgeoning body of data in support of various, often competing explanations of stereotype threat, and a complete explanation of the various phenomena described in the empirical literature will surely involve reference to multiple different explanatory mechanisms. My aim here has been to explore how these data inform, and can be informed by, our folk conception of ourselves as rational agents, and I have pursued this exploration by distinguishing various explanatory options along personalist and subpersonalist dimensions.

Like the literature on other-directed implicit bias, work on stereotype threat suggests limits to our rational governance—limits that may grow out of dual-process conceptions of mental architecture endemic in social psychology. In contrast to this trend, I have argued that there are key phenomena that suggest an important role for personalist mechanisms—including both mental states and processes—in the explanation of stereotype threat.[14] In the case of mental states, I have argued that stereotype threat is plausibly triggered by beliefs and that one of the triggering beliefs in stereotype threat is belief (or partial belief) in the truth of the stereotype itself. This implies that intervening to alter these beliefs ought to change stereotype threat effects on performance as well—something I think the experimental literature bears out. And in the case of processes, I have reviewed some experimental evidence that directly favors a personalist explanation of stereotype threat, though I have also suggested that subpersonalist explanations have trouble with the parsimonious explanation of stereotype "lift."

I have gone through this trouble not because I think stereotype threat is to be explained exclusively in personalist terms. Rather, as I noted at the outset, I expect that a complete explanation of stereotype threat will invoke a range of causes, both personalist and subpersonalist. But exclusively subpersonal understandings of stereotype threat can make it seem a mystery why addressing the fairness of a situation or the capacity of the experimental subject to succeed could be successful in alleviating stereotype threat or lifting performance. In essence, there is a gap between many explanations of stereotype threat in the literature and the interventions that are proposed to alleviate it. And I have argued that

---

[14] For other work in this vein, see Mandelbaum (2015).

some of these interventions are precisely those that are already widely available to us, in virtue of our intuitive grasp of rational actors in threatening situations.

Acknowledgments

I am grateful to audiences at Sheffield University, Boston University, and Sienna College, and for helpful comments and discussion from Alisa Bokulich, Michael Brownstein, Mike Dacey, Tamar Gendler, Stacey Goguen, Sally Haslanger, Chris Jenson, Eric Mandelbaum, Jenny Saul, Brian Scholl, and Gregory Walton.

References

Appiah, K. A. (2005). *The Ethics of Identity*. Princeton, NJ: Princeton University Press.

Aronson, J., Fried, C. B., et al. (2002). "Reducing the effects of stereotype threat on African American college students by shaping theories of intelligence." *Journal of Experimental Social Psychology* 38: 113–25.

Bargh, J. and Chartrand, T. L. (1999). "The unbearable automaticity of being." *American Psychologist* 54(7): 462–79.

Bargh, J., Chen, M., et al. (1996). "Automaticity of social behavior: Direct effects of trait construct and stereotype activation on action." *Journal of Personality and Social Psychology* 71(2): 230–44.

Cadinu, M., Maass, A., Frigerio, S., Impagliazzo, L., and Latinotti, S. (2003). "Stereotype threat: The effect of expectancy on performance." *European Journal of Social Psychology* 33: 267–85.

Cesario, J., Plaks, J. E., et al. (2006). "Automatic social behavior as motivated preparation to interact." *Journal of Personality and Social Psychology* 90(6): 893–910.

Chaiken, S. and Trope, Y. (1999). *Dual-Process Theories in Social Psychology*. New York, NY: Guilford Press.

Churchland, P. (1981). "Eliminative materialism and the propositional attitudes." *Journal of Philosophy* 77(2): 67–90.

Cohen, G. L., Steele, C. M., et al. (1999). "The mentor's dilemma: Providing critical feedback across the racial divide." *Personality and Social Psychology Bulletin* 25: 1302–18.

Croizet, J. and Claire, T. (1998). "Extending the concept of stereotype threat to social class: The intellectual underperformance of students from low socioeconomic backgrounds." *Personality and Social Psychology Bulletin* 24: 588–94.

Croizet, J., Després, G., et al. (2004). "Stereotype threat undermines intellectual performance by triggering a disruptive mental load." *Personality and Social Psychology Bulletin* 30: 721–31.

Dacey, M. (2015). *Simple Minded: Rethinking Associations in Psychology*. Ph.D. Thesis. Washington University in St. Louis.

Danaher, K. and Crandall, C. S. (2008). "Stereotype threat in applied settings re-examined." *Journal of Applied Social Psychology* 38: 1639–55.

Delgado, A. R. and Prieto, G. (2008). "Stereotype threat as validity threat: The anxiety-sex-threat interaction." *Intelligence* 36: 635–40.

Dennett, D. C. (1987). *The Intentional Stance*. Cambridge, MA: MIT Press.

Doris, J. (2009). "Skepticism about persons." *Philosophical Issues* 19(1): 57–91.

Doyen, S., Klein, O., et al. (2012). "Behavioral priming: It's all in the mind, but whose mind?" *PLOS One* 7(1): e29081.

Dweck, C. S. (1999). *Self-Theories: Their Role in Motivation, Personality, and Development*. Philadelphia, PA: Psychology Press.

Fodor, J. (1987). *Psychosemantics: the Problem of Meaning in the Philosophy of Mind*. Cambridge, MA: MIT Press: Bradford Books.

Fordham, S. and Ogbu, J. U. (1986). "Black students school success: Coping with the burden of acting white." *Urban Review* 18(3): 176–206.

Fryer, R. and Torelli, P. (2010). "An empirical analysis of acting white." *Journal of Public Economics* 94(5–6): 380–96.

Gawronski, B. and Bodenhausen, G. V. (2006). "Associative and propositional processes in evaluation: An integrative review of implicit and explicit attitude change." *Psychological Bulletin* 132: 692–731.

Gendler, T. (2008). "Alief and belief." *Journal of Philosophy* 105(10): 634–63.

Gibson, C. E., Losee, J., and Vitiello, C. (2014). "A replication attempt of stereotype susceptibility (Shih, Pittinsky, and Ambady, 1999): Identity salience and shifts in quantitative performance." *Social Psychology* 45: 194–8.

Gonzales, P. M., Blanton, H., et al. (2002). "The effects of stereotype threat and double-minority status on the test performance of Latino women." *Personality and Social Psychology Bulletin* 28: 659–70.

Good, C., Aronson, J., et al. (2008). "Problems in the pipeline: Stereotype threat and women's achievement in high-level math courses." *Journal of Applied Developmental Psychology* 29: 17–28.

Greene, J. D. (2007). "The secret joke of Kant's soul." In Sinnott-Armstrong, W. (ed.), *Moral Psychology*. Cambridge, MA: MIT Press. 3: 35–117.

Hacking, I. (1995a). "The looping effects of human kinds." In Sperber, D., Premack, D., and Premack, A. J., *Causal Cognition: A Multidisciplinary Debate*. New York, NY: Clarendon Press: 351–94.

Hacking, I. (1995b). *Rewriting the Soul: Multiple Personality and the Sciences of Memory*. Princeton, NJ: Princeton University Press.

Hacking, I. (1998). *Mad Travelers: Reflections on the Reality of Transient Mental Illnesses*. Charlottesville, VA: University Press of Virginia.

Haidt, J. (2001). "The emotional dog and its rational tail: A social intuitionist approach to moral judgment " *Psychological Review* 108: 814–34.

Jamieson, J. P. and Harkins, S. G. (2007). "Mere effort and stereotype threat performance effects." *Journal of Personality and Social Psychology* 93(4): 544–64.

Jamieson, J. P. and Harkins, S. G. (2009). "The effect of stereotype threat on the solving of quantitative GRE problems: A mere effort interpretation." *Personality and Social Psychology Bulletin* 35(10): 1301–14.

Johns, M., Schmader, T., et al. (2005). "Knowing is half the battle: Teaching stereotype threat as a means of improving women's math performance." *Psychological Science* 16: 175–9.

Kahneman, D. (2011). *Thinking, Fast and Slow*. New York, NY: Farrar, Straus and Giroux.

Kim, J. (1998). *Mind in a Physical World: An Essay on the Mind–Body Problem and Mental Causation.* Cambridge, MA: MIT Press.

Mandelbaum, E. (2015). "Attitude, inference, association: On the propositional structure of implicit bias." *Noûs* 49(3).

Marr, D. (1982). *Vision: A Computational Investigation into the Human Representation and Processing of Visual Information.* San Francisco, CA: W. H. Freeman.

Moon, A. and Roeder, S. (2014). "A secondary replication attempt of stereotype susceptibility (Shih, Pittinsky, and Ambady, 1999)." *Social Psychology* 45(3): 199–201.

Newell, A. (1982). "The knowledge level." *Artificial Intelligence* 18(1): 87–127.

Osborne, J. W. (2001). "Testing stereotype threat: Does anxiety explain race and sex differences in achievement?" *Contemporary Educational Psychology* 26: 291–310.

Pashler, H., Harris, C., and Coburn, N. (2011). "Elderly-related words prime slow walking." <http://www.PsychFileDrawer.org/replication.php?attempt=MTU%3D> Retrieved August 8, 2013.

Pylyshyn, Z. (1984). *Computation and Cognition: Toward a Foundation for Cognitive Science.* Cambridge, MA: MIT Press.

Rosenberg, A. (1995). *Philosophy of Social Science.* Boulder, CO: Westview Press.

Saul, J. (2011). "Maker's knowledge or perpetuator's ignorance." *Jurisprudence* 2(2): 403–8.

Schmader, T., Johns, M., et al. (2004). "The costs of accepting gender differences: The role of stereotype endorsement in women's experience in the math domain." *Sex Roles* 50: 835–50.

Schmader, T., Johns, M., et al. (2008). "An integrated process model of stereotype threat effects on performance." *Psychological Review* 115: 336–56.

Shih, M., Ambady, N., et al. (2002). "Stereotype performance boosts: The impact of self-relevance and the manner of stereotype activation." *Journal of Personality and Social Psychology* 83: 638–64.

Shih, M., Pittinsky, T. L., et al. (1999). "Stereotype susceptibility: Identity salience and shifts in quantitative performance." *Psychological Science* 10: 80–3.

Stanovich, K. E. (2004). *The Robot's Rebellion: Finding Meaning in the Age of Darwin.* Chicago, IL; London: University of Chicago Press.

Steele, C. (1997). "A threat in the air: How stereotypes shape intellectual identity and performance." *American Psychologist* 52: 613–29.

Steele, C. (2010). *Whistling Vivaldi: And Other Clues to how Stereotypes Affect Us.* New York, NY: W. W. Norton and Company.

Steele, C. and Aronson, J. (1995). "Stereotype threat and the intellectual test performance of African Americans." *Journal of Personality and Social Psychology* 69: 797–811.

Stich, S. P. (1983). *From Folk Psychology to Cognitive Science: The Case Against Belief.* Cambridge, MA: MIT Press.

Stone, J. (2002). " Battling doubt by avoiding practice: The effect of stereotype threat on self-handicapping in white athletes." *Personality and Social Psychology Bulletin* 28: 1667–78.

Stone, J., Lynch, C. I., Sjomerling, M., and Darley, J. (1999). "Stereotype threat effects on black and white athletic performance." *Journal of Personality and Social Psychology* 77: 1213–27.

Strawson, P. (1962). "Freedom and resentment." *Proceedings of the British Academy* 48: 1–25.

Stricker, L. J. and Ward, W. C. (2004). "Stereotype threat, inquiring about test takers' ethnicity and gender, and standardized test performance." *Journal of Applied Social Psychology* 34: 665–93.

Tyson, K., Darity Jr., W., and Castellino, D. R. (2005). "It's not 'a black thing': Understanding the burden of acting white and other dilemmas of high achievement." *American Sociological Review* 70(4): 582–605.

Yeager, D. S. and Walton, G. M. (2011). "Social-psychological interventions in education: They're not magic." *Review of Educational Research* 81: 267–301.

Yeager, D., Walton, G., and Cohen, G. L. (2013). "Addressing achievement gaps with psychological interventions." *Phi Delta Kappan* 94: 62–5.

Yeager, D. S. et al. (2014). "Breaking the cycle of mistrust: Wise interventions to provide critical feedback across the racial divide." *Journal of Experimental Psychology: General* 143(2): 804–24.

PART 2

Skepticism, Social Knowledge, and Rationality

2.1

Bias: Friend or Foe?
Reflections on Saulish Skepticism

Louise M. Antony

In her paper "Scepticism and implicit bias" (2013), Jennifer Saul identifies a form of skepticism—a challenge to our claims to know—that she argues is, or ought to be, "peculiarly disturbing" (2013: 2). The challenge comes from what we have learned about the operation of *implicit bias* in evaluative contexts. Studies show that as we make various evaluative decisions we are very likely being influenced by the social identity of the evaluee. Such influence has been discovered in the grading of student work (Bradley, 1993), in the review of job candidate (Steinpreis, Anders, and Ritzke, 1999; Moss-Racusin et al., 2012), in the evaluation of submissions to journals (Peters and Ceci, 1982), and even in such day-to-day decisions as whether a conversation is worth continuing (Valian, 1998). As Saul points out, the ethical implications of these findings are disturbing, especially for those of us who sincerely disavow the very prejudices that appear to be affecting our judgments.

Saul's focus, however, is the epistemological significance of these data: if we are influenced, even unconsciously, by factors that we recognize to be irrelevant to the matter under consideration, then it is likely that we are often making substantive mistakes, that we are failing to encourage some excellent students, failing to hire some excellent philosophers, and admitting or hiring philosophers who are not as good as we thought. If so, then the field of philosophy is not as good as it could be. The existence and operation of implicit bias, in other words, is detrimental to our collective philosophical goals. Because of implicit bias, we know less than we would otherwise.[1]

---

[1] Helen Longino and Elizabeth Anderson have defended a related but slightly different thesis: viz. that social *inequality* has negative epistemic effects, independently of the human attitudes and biases

This is why Saul claims that the findings about implicit bias generate a *new form* of skepticism. Traditional skepticism, Saul points out, generates doubt (or tries to) by pointing to certain *possibilities*: it says that we *might* not know because we *might* not be warranted in believing. The challenge of this new skepticism, Saul explains, is more pointed. Although not global in scope like traditional skepticism, this "Saulish skepticism" (as I shall call it) is more destructive. Saulish skepticism *actually* diminishes our warrant for many everyday judgments, and *actually* impugns the reliability of the epistemic practices on which they are based. The data about implicit bias tell us that, at least in certain domains, it is *likely* that we *are not* warranted in believing what we believe, and—worse still—it is *likely* that some of our beliefs in this domain *are false*.

One reason, then, why Saulish skepticism is "peculiarly disturbing" is that it makes real demands on us. We cannot leave the problems of implicit bias behind in the seminar room, as we can worries about brains in vats and barn façades. But just how disturbed should we be? How deep does the challenge of Saulish skepticism go?

It is tempting to construe the findings about implicit bias as pertinent only to *casual* or *incautious* reasoning—reasoning done on the fly, or in time- or resource-pressured circumstances, where practical demands require us to take lots of cognitive shortcuts. It is easy to admit that such shortcuts may involve sloppy thinking, questionable data, or both. "Sure," one might say, "in ordinary life, I tend to rely on stereotypes, to overgeneralize, and to jump to conclusions— I'm only human after all." (If one is attracted to dual systems theory,[2] one might ascribe the problem of implicit bias to the operation of System 1 cognition, which is said to run on unconsciously acquired associations, as opposed to the more careful and judicious System 2.)

Still, even if one has come to terms with our *de facto* reliance, now and then, on questionable generalizations and fallible heuristics, it is hard not to believe that there are not *some* kinds of intellectual activity immune from the effects of bias. We would like to believe that, at least during periods of calm and sober reflection, we reason cogently and on the basis of considered beliefs. If so, the thought would go, then care and attention might provide a bulwark against, or perhaps even a

---

that might be involved in creating or sustaining them. They would no doubt agree with Saul about the negative impact of bias as well. I shall be discussing Longino's arguments in some detail.

[2] See Kahneman (2011). I am not, in fact, a fan. The syndrome that characterizes System 1 thinking is displayed by at least three importantly different kinds of cognitive structures: encapsulated input systems, automatized expert judgment, and brutely associative memory.

corrective for, the implicit biases that might otherwise intrude. (System 2 can wrest control away from System 1 when it needs to!)

But alas, the problem of implicit bias cannot really be circumscribed. As its name implies, implicit bias operates beneath our introspective radar; we cannot know by reflection when or how it might be affecting our judgment. There is no reason to think that the intrusion of implicit bias is limited to quick or casual inference. Although some measures of implicit bias, like the Implicit Association Test, require subjects to make very rapid judgments, many studies (e.g. Moss-Racusin et al., 2012) involve subjects' making decisions in naturalistic settings, where we may assume they are putting forth their best efforts. The fact is, we cannot know through introspection when or how knowledge of someone's social identity is affecting our judgments. *Even we philosophers*, Saul cautions, must realize that "we may be accepting arguments we should not accept and rejecting arguments we should not reject."[3]

This stings. And it points to the second reason why Saulish skepticism is disturbing: it threatens our epistemic self-esteem. The fact that our reasoning may be influenced by factors we do not recognize and attitudes we do not endorse means that we must reckon ourselves less rational and less epistemically autonomous than we would like to be.[4] It is an interesting question in its own right how exactly implicit bias intrudes in cases where we think we are reasoning carefully and rationally. But whatever the explanation, the upshot is clear: we do not always know why we think what we think.

Exacerbating this challenge to our preferred conceptions of epistemic agency is the fact, emphasized by Saul, that even if we accept the likelihood that we are subject to implicit bias, we cannot know *a priori* what to do about it. Those who study implicit bias and its effects have come up with a variety of strategies for overcoming it, or at least for mitigating its impact on important decisions. Strikingly, though, these strategies are *not* the ones that we might have thought, *a priori*, to be the effective ones.[5] It turns out, for example, that simply *trying* to be more objective—for example, by resolving not to "pay attention" to someone's race or gender—does nothing to remove implicit bias. Efforts of this sort may actually make things worse. A person who makes a conscious attempt to set aside

---

[3] Saul (2013): 247.

[4] Some philosophers would say that we did not need the specific evidence about implicit bias to discover this—that decades of psychological research on decision-making points in the same direction. See, for example, Kornblith (2012).

[5] Miranda Fricker, in her excellent book *Epistemic Justice: Power and the Ethics of Knowing* (2007), seems at times to presume that such biases as "testimonial injustice"—the tendency to accord to members of marginalized groups less credibility than they deserve—can be corrected by careful self-observation and resolution. Perhaps, but this is not something we can know *a priori*.

certain factors may fail in doing so, but meanwhile acquire false confidence that she has succeeded in making her judgments more objective, with the unhappy result that her (still-)biased judgments have become even less corrigible than they were before.[6]

In short, it is a kind of fantasy to think that biases intrude only when our guard is down—a fantasy that permits us to think that if we were only more *careful* in our thinking, more *responsible* or more *virtuous* in our epistemic practice, things would be all right. That leaves intact the conviction that there is within each one of us some epistemic still place from which we can see clearly and judge soundly. I contend, however, that facing the deep challenge of Saulish skepticism will require us to accept that there is no such place.

As Saul explains, responsible inquiry requires us to see our own epistemic activity from an external, and somewhat mechanistic point of view. She says that we must

recognize that our epistemic capacities are prone to errors that we cannot learn about through first-person reflection; and that we must correct them using counter-intuitive mechanical techniques that draw not upon our rational agency but upon automatic and unconscious responses. (2013: 260)

I think of the point in Dennettian terms (Dennett, 1987): if we really want to prevent or to interrupt biased thinking, we must occasionally abandon the "intentional stance" toward ourselves, and take up the "design stance" instead.

In a way, this shift in approach is simply what Quine had in mind when he recommended that we take a naturalistic approach to the study of knowledge. Quine argued that we should stop trying to prescribe, *a priori*, the proper relation between data and theory, and instead make an empirical study of human knowing. This would be a matter of investigating the actual circumstances in which we learn things, and the actual processes and practices through which we learn them. "Why," he asked of Carnap,

all this creative reconstruction, all this make-believe? The stimulation of his sensory receptors is all the evidence anybody has to go on, ultimately, in arriving at his picture of the world. Why not settle for psychology? (Quine, 1969)

The sort of investigation Quine is arguing for here must necessarily put at risk assumptions about ideal epistemic strategies for creatures constituted and situated as we human beings are. Whether naturalization represents a wholesale abandonment of the normative goals of traditional epistemology is a matter of debate. What is clear, however, is that Quine's approach to the study of knowledge

---

[6] See Apfelbaum, Sommers, and Norton (2008) for a study on stereotype suppression. (Thanks to Michael Brownstein for calling this work to my attention.)

requires us to write a kind of blank check for warrant. It requires us to accord some degree of positive value to any and all features of human inquiry that conduce to epistemic success, whether or not those features conform to our *a priori* expectations of ourselves as rational agents.

This is the first point I want to make: that an adequate response to the problem of Saulish skepticism requires our taking an empirical, naturalistic approach to the study of human knowledge, and that this approach requires us to treat the matter of epistemic norms as an empirical question. We must allow for the possibility that some traditionally accepted epistemic norms will turn out to be inappropriate for creatures constituted and situated as we are. We must also allow that certain habits of thought deemed vicious will turn out to be absolutely central to human epistemic success.

My second point—and the *main* point of this chapter—is that the above-mentioned possibilities are *realities*. The main casualty of the naturalistic approach is going to be a certain conception of *objectivity*. A naturalistic approach to the study of human knowledge reveals that we should not strive to put aside all bias. Objectivity, conceived as the absence of *bias*, is an inappropriate epistemic norm for us, because bias is an essential element in human epistemic success. And when I say that bias is essential, I do not mean merely that bias is ineliminable (although it is that). I mean that bias plays a *constructive* role in the development of human knowledge; it is an enabling condition of human cognitive achievement. Without it, we would know less, not more. This fact must complicate our response to the problem of implicit bias.

Lest I be misunderstood, let me explain what I mean by bias. The term "bias," as it is commonly used, implies something morally or rationally negative.[7] I mean to use the term in its more general, normatively neutral sense, as meaning "a tendency; an inclination of temperament or outlook."[8] As I shall explain, the largest epistemic challenge facing any finite knower is the problem of *underdetermination*: there are always many, many distinct empirical hypotheses consistent with our sensory data. Accordingly, I am counting as a "bias" any structure, database, or inferential disposition that serves in a non-evidential way to reduce hypothesis space to a tractable size. Biases, in this sense, may be propositions explicitly represented in the mind, or they may be propositional content realized only implicitly, in the structure of a cognitive mechanism. They

---

[7] This definition from the Oxford English Dictionary (U.S.) is typical: <http://www.oxforddictionaries.com/us/definition/american_english/bias> (Accessed October 1, 2014).

[8] Merriam-Webster online dictionary, def. 3: <http://www.merriam-webster.com/dictionary/bias> (Accessed October 1, 2014).

may reside in subpersonal computational structures, or they may be elements of person-level beliefs or associations, fully accessible to consciousness. They may work at the level of individual cognition, or at the level of socially structured inquiry.

I realize that biases, in my sense, form a motley assortment.[9] But that is part of my point. Human perception and human cognition confront the problem of underdetermination at every stage of empirical learning, and at every stage, the solution depends on bias. If we are to confront those instances of bias that rightly concern us, we must understand the role bias plays in the proper functioning of human epistemic capacities, and the factors that enable it to play a positive role, in those cases where it does.

I have already claimed (with Saul) that the facts about implicit bias should make us give up the idea that we can determine *a priori* what norms and strategies will best improve our epistemic practice. What I am claiming now is that a broader empirical understanding of the workings of human cognition should make us give up the idea that bias is *inherently* bad. That is not at all to say that *no* biases are bad. The forms of implicit bias with which this discussion began are morally pernicious, and destructive of knowledge to boot. So if bias can be a good thing, what makes the bad biases bad? I contend that it is not the fact that they are biases—that is, it is not the mere fact that they incline us toward one judgment rather than another. Rather, it is the fact that they incline us in the wrong direction: away from the truth, rather than toward it. In terms of etiology and psychological structure, there may be no difference between a bad bias and a good one—the difference might lie only in the content of the biases and the consequences for action and judgment that come from our possessing them.[10]

We need not be discouraged by all this. It does not mean that we cannot meet the challenge of Saulish skepticism, only that we cannot meet it by attacking bias, *tout court.* We need a more selective, more nuanced approach.

---

[9] I said earlier that it was a problem for the System 1/System 2 model that the cognitive processes that meet the criteria for System 1 were importantly different from each other. Why is that not a problem with my category "biases"? Because—I am not claiming that biases constitute a natural cognitive kind—I am classifying them together *only* because they all, in one way or another, *incline* us, and I claim that this is an epistemologically important characteristic.

[10] In saying that etiology may not distinguish bad biases from good ones, I am thinking of etiology "narrowly," in terms of the sensory and cognitive processes that generate the bias. If, instead, we consider the etiology "widely," so as to include the environments in which those processes operate, then we might well be able to find an etiological criterion that distinguishes good biases from bad. If we consider normal processes of generalization, for example, it may well be that those processes, when applied in an environment shaped by sexism or racism, yield biases that are bad either epistemically or morally, or both. (Thanks to Michael Brownstein for making this suggestion.)

In what follows, I shall fill in the details of the picture I have just outlined. In Section 1, I begin by telling you why I think bias has gotten such a bad rap. The idea that bias is inherently malign is tied, I argue, to a particular type of *empiricist* conception of mind and knowledge, a legacy of logical positivism. Although this version of empiricism has few official defenders today, it still animates popular views about how knowledge works. In particular, it supports a conception of *objectivity*—objectivity as absence of bias—the assumption of which is counterproductive in our efforts to deal with Saulish skepticism and the larger issues of justice that make implicit bias a problem. In Section 2 I explain some of the findings in cognitive science that challenge this empiricist conception of the mind, and that confirm the positive role bias plays in human epistemic life. I shall conclude by highlighting some of the practical payoffs of this work: novel strategies for combating Saulish skepticism, and a new, more politically potent view of objectivity.

1 Bias, Empiricism, and Dragnet Objectivity

Why think that bias is a bad thing?

Some of my readers will remember the old American television show, *Dragnet*. This program followed the adventures of two Los Angeles police detectives: Sergeant Joe Friday and Officer Bill Gannon. The detectives were presented to us viewers as paragons of epistemic responsibility. Friday, especially, was scrupulous in his approach to every new crime. While collecting evidence, he would militate against the intrusion of speculation, sympathy, or surmise. His epistemic integrity was signified by a telling catch-phrase, uttered whenever a too-voluble witness seemed on the verge of offering a personal opinion: "Just the facts, ma'am."

Dragnet itself is now widely regarded as ridiculous—so corny it is camp—yet the epistemic values it so risibly extolled are still widely accepted, if only implicitly. Although no one would say that any real human being *could* meet the standard set by the robotic Sergeant Friday, too many of us still think we ought to *try*.

The idea that beliefs should be based exclusively on "the facts" derives from an *empiricist* conception of mind and knowledge. (There may be other rationales too, but I cannot think of any.) The term "empiricist" is used in many ways, so let me explain how I intend the term to be understood. When I speak of "empiricism," I do *not* mean just the general view that knowledge depends on experience. I mean, rather, a quite specific view about *how* knowledge is based on experience. This is a view about the structure of the mind—one that was defended by Locke,

Berkeley, Hume, and Mill in the modern period, and by logical positivists and behaviorists in the early twentieth century.[11] The main tenet of empiricism (in this strict sense) is the claim that the mind contributes nothing *substantive* to the development of knowledge. The mind, on this conception, is a neutral machine that manipulates sensory data in accordance with domain-general principles of operation.

To say that the mind's principles are "domain-general" is to say that the mental operations that take us from sensory experience to knowledge are always the same no matter what we are learning about. Empiricist theories have varied with respect to the number and types of learning mechanisms they allow. A very austere empiricism, like Skinner's behaviorism, allows only one mechanism of learning: association. A more liberal empiricism might also allow formal operations, like inference.[12] Either way, "domain-generality" is a way of spelling out the idea that knowledge comes *strictly* from experience: whatever contribution the mind makes to the development of knowledge, it is the same contribution in every case, and can thus be factored out in the etiology of empirical belief.

The mind according to the empiricist, then, is a *neutral* machine for transforming experience into belief. This is a pretty blunt view of psychology, as we shall soon see. But it is worth noting that, for the picture to work, the empiricist needs an equally blunt view of *experience*. If sense experience is to constitute "the facts," then sense experience must carry direct testimony from the external world, unadulterated by beliefs, desires, or values that the subject brings to the experiential setting. Observations must be *received*, not constructed.[13] Any substantive addition by the subject to the data of the senses would render those data equivocal; it would lessen the degree to which subsequent belief reflects the character of the world, thus corrupting the objectivity of our experience. Here, then, is a conception of *bias*: bias is anything that interferes with the neutrality of the mental machine, either by adulterating its sensory inputs, or by selectively controlling the inputs it receives.

---

[11] Though not Quine, as we shall see shortly.

[12] Skinner was not only an empiricist; he was also a reductionist about the mind. Earlier empiricists had no problem with the mind; they spoke unabashedly of "impressions" and "ideas." But Skinner wanted an account of animal behavior that abjured reference to private mental states, and so he restricted his theoretical resources to observable stimulations and observable behavioral responses. This, at any rate, was his official position; he was not able to obey his own strictures when it came to characterizing the acquisition of human language. See Chomsky (1959).

[13] In my own work on perception I defend the view that perception *begins* with informational states that have exactly these characteristics. But the *percept*—the output of perceptual processing—is a construction embodying endogenously supplied information. See my (2011).

I earlier identified, as the central challenge for any epistemology, the problem of *underdetermination*: for any finite chunk of sensory experience, there will be an infinite number of hypotheses consistent with that experience. For the empiricist, this means the problem that there can be indefinitely many distinct patterns present and extractable from any finite set of sensory inputs. But supposing the problem of underdetermination was solved, there is a second problem looming. On an empiricist view, empirical learning is essentially a matter of pattern extraction from sensory inputs. But what if an epistemic subject is not propitiously located? If a subject's surroundings are atypical, then the sensory data to which she is exposed will be unrepresentative, and the regularities she extracts will hold only in her locality, and not be true generally. I shall call this the problem of *idiosyncrasy*.

Rationalist thinkers of the early modern period dealt with the problems of idiosyncrasy and underdetermination in one fell swoop by positing innate mental structure—structure that, by some sort of prearrangement, mirrored the structure of the empirical world. (As we shall see, this turns out to be pretty much the correct story.) But since empiricists are committed to the view that the mind makes no substantive contribution to empirical knowledge, this expedient is not open to them.[14] Empiricists must solve the problem of underdetermination and dampen the threat of idiosyncrasy in some other way, and they really have only one variable to work with: *epistemic location*.

Let me explain. If knowledge is essentially a matter of sampling, then the epistemic challenge is to ensure the representativeness of the sample from which the regularities are extracted, and the only way to do that is to sample as may different epistemic locations as possible. The *more* locations one takes up, the more sensory data one accrues; the more *various* these locations, the more likely that idiosyncratic elements of any one location will be filtered out. *Literal* travel is not necessarily required—epistemic travel might equally well be a matter of taking up new perspectives on familiar things—looking through microscopes, manipulating nature in unusual ways to see what happens. Epistemic travel, in reducing idiosyncracy, might then help with the problem of underdetermination: as accidents of epistemic location are filtered out, so too, one hopes, are spurious patterns eliminated—indeed, to the extent that *perspective* is eliminated. (It is a telling irony that the same "ideal" epistemic position has been dubbed by one critic—Susan Bordo (2013)—as "the view from everywhere," and by

---

[14] Although, as we shall also see, Quine brought a bit of this idea into his empiricism—which was, for just that reason, revisionary.

another—Thomas Nagel (1986)—as "the view from nowhere.") Bias is subjective, and the subjective is bad.

I do not deny that this conception of bias—as an interfering factor in the proper operation of our epistemic faculties—has a lot of intuitive appeal. It fits many of the paradigm cases: the sexist who clings to his belief that women are bad at mathematics even in the face of clear evidence to the contrary; the venal researcher who selectively reports only the data that support her hypothesis. The problem, though, is that in utilizing this notion of bias, we tacitly endorse the conception of mind and knowledge that lies behind it, and that conception is, as I will argue, empirically bankrupt. That is bad enough. But in fact, things are worse. The empiricist view delivers not only a particular conception of bias, but also a particular norm for inquiry: Dragnet objectivity. And this is not an epistemic norm that any progressive should *want* to endorse.[15]

One way to appreciate the problems with this conception of bias, and the correlative value of Dragnet objectivity, is to examine the areas most amenable to analysis in these terms. Consider, for example, the practice of *anonymizing*. This is one of the practices shown to be dramatically effective in reducing the effects of implicit bias. One demonstration of its power comes from the world of music: the percentage of women in major symphony orchestras shot up from less than 5% in 1970 to 25% today, once it became standard practice for musicians to perform their auditions from behind an opaque screen (Goldin and Rouse, 1997). Dragnet objectivity appears to provide the practice with an epistemically sound rationale: if one is not burdened with potentially biasing information about the social identity of an evaluee, then one's judgment cannot, *ipso facto*, be improperly skewed by that information.

I concede immediately that anonymizing *does* work to eliminate implicit bias in some cases, and thus to mitigate some of the concerns that drive Saulish skepticism. Any adequate account of bias must recognize this. The problem with the empiricist notion of bias is that anonymizing is about the *only* practice that it does rationalize. The empiricist notion of bias provides no epistemic guidance— or worse, *bad* epistemic guidance—in cases where anonymizing cannot be utilized. For example: in everyday, face-to-face encounters, we are often confronted with overt markings of our interlocuter's social identity—markers that convey information that we cannot "un-know." In cases like this, what are we to do?

---

[15] To be clear: I am not saying that one's commitment to epistemic norms ought to depend on what values one holds. I am a veritist, and so think that the epistemic norms we commit to can only be warranted by reference to the goals of acquiring truth and avoiding falsehood. What I *am* saying is that it would be bad news for various progressive projects if it turned out that Dragnet objectivity actually was a good epistemic norm, by veritistic standards.

Then there are the situations in which anonymizing has drawbacks; situations in which the practice can deprive us of epistemically *pertinent* information. Consider the fact that social subordination can have effects that skew the evidential value of customary markers of achievement. Gregory Walton, Stephen Spencer, and Sam Erman (in press) have documented and actually quantified the degree to which "stereotype threat" degrades students' performance on standardized tests. If we want to take this sort of handicap into account when we evaluate college applications (for example), we must *attend* to the social identity of applicants.

Now, a defender of the ideal of Dragnet objectivity might argue that empiricism does have the resources for dealing with this sort of situation. She might say that the information Walton et al. have brought to light simply shows—empirically, as a matter of observation—that a certain measuring device (the standardized test) is inaccurate in certain situations. This is no different from obtaining evidence that a certain thermometer is inaccurate at temperatures above or below a certain degree, and it is certainly permissible, even by strict empiricist standards, to discard biased instruments in favor of more reliable epistemic tools.

Perhaps so. But there are other cases where we must abjure anonymizing practices and where things cannot be reconciled so easily with the Dragnet ideal. Consider situations in which we want to take account of the ways in which social subordination has probably handicapped members of some particular group, as when we decide to discount certain academic indicators as predictive of eventual academic success. What is different about these cases from the cases in which anonymizing is a good strategy is that in these cases, there need be no epistemically *distorting* biases in play. Part of the injury suffered by individuals in conditions of oppression is the loss of opportunity to develop and display their talents. In such cases, it is a background understanding of the pernicious effects of subordination that warrants differential treatment, not direct positive evidence of bias in one's evaluations of the proffered credentials.

Speaking more generally (and again, leaving aside the significant consideration that the empiricist view of mind is very likely false), there are serious problems with the empiricist view of bias and its correlative ideal of objectivity, from the point of view of progressive, engaged epistemology. To accede to a standard of inquiry that condemns *any* inclination toward one hypothesis or one set of interests over another, no matter the context, no matter the reason, is to impede our own efforts to repair the social damage that injustice has wrought. I have two problems in mind. The first concerns the alleged epistemic value of demographic diversity; the second concerns a dangerous belief about the actual organization of science that is encouraged by faith in the norm of Dragnet objectivity.

A view that has become increasingly popular among progressive epistemologists and philosophers of science is the view that diversity should be recognized to be an *epistemic* value. The idea is that an increase in the demographic diversity of our academies and our laboratories will lead to an increase in the quality of our scholarship and our science. If so, say proponents of the claim, then we have epistemic, as well as moral and political, grounds for supporting programs like affirmative action. But why think that demographic diversity will pay epistemic dividends?

The idea originates in feminist critiques of the *individualism* of empiricism in mainstream epistemology. The complaint is that the predominant conception of the epistemic agent is too abstract and featureless to capture important features of the human epistemic condition.[16] Helen Longino (2002), for example, has pointed out that the recommendation to take up a wide variety of epistemic positions can hardly help the individual knower. No human being can acquire enough sensory data in a single lifetime to make even a dent in the problem of underdetermination. And no matter how various any individual's epistemic locations, the sum total of her experience is still essentially a view from that one perspective.

According to Longino, then, the only way to mitigate the epistemic threats of underdetermination and idiosyncrasy is to switch our focus from individual epistemic agents to whole *communities* of knowers. Considered collectively, a community of knowers possesses a great deal more evidence than does any individual knower. If the community is sufficiently diverse, and if members of the community engage each other in the right ways, idiosyncrasies of viewpoint can be effectively filtered out. Objectivity, on this approach, becomes a *social* epistemic virtue, in the sense that it is (at least partly) determined by the composition and internal dynamics of an epistemic community, rather than a matter of individual epistemic practice.[17]

This is how Longino comes to the conclusion that we have a strong epistemic reason for seeking greater demographic diversity within our society, particularly within academic and research communities. Greater demographic variety, she argues, will produce a greater diversity of ideas, and will also increase the rigor of scientific review. Longino believes, in effect, that the *social* dynamics of epistemic

---

[16] See, for example, Alcoff and Potter (1982). Although I agree with their claim that, at that time, mainstream epistemology neglected the social dimensions of knowledge, I disagree that individualistic epistemology is necessarily problematic. See my (1995).

[17] Longino (2001: 103) goes so far as to say that an experimental result does not constitute an *observation* unless and until the result is socially vetted through replication.

practice can make up for the epistemic limitations suffered by individual human beings.[18]

I agree with much that Longino has to say about objectivity; for example, I am very sympathetic to the idea that objectivity is most properly viewed as a social epistemic virtue.[19] But Longino's epistemic argument for demographic diversity requires more than that. It depends on the assumption that variation in epistemic position is *ipso facto* salutary (2001: ch. 6). Longino accepts the key empiricist assumption that the aim of objectivity is the filtering out of subjective elements in our theorizing. She recognizes that we cannot really increase the number of perspectives available to individual agents—it is always just one per agent, however various that agent's experience—but she thinks we can get the effect of doing so by increasing the number of agents whose perspectives are in play. Enlarging and diversifying the community of knowers is her proof against idiosyncrasies in the epistemic positions of individual agents, so as to bring scientific theory into ever greater and ever purer dependence on "just the facts."

From a political perspective, this argument for the value of diversity is highly problematic. If diversity *per se* is a good thing, then it looks like we ought to support *any* diversification of the knowledge community. It seems to rationalize, for example, the demands of creationists who claim that the scientific consensus in favor of evolution is merely an artifact of the biases of the current scientific establishment. Of course, they say, you will not find many advocates of intelligent design in research universities—the evolutionists are biased against them! Similarly, it appears that we must take seriously complaints about Women's Studies and Gender Studies departments that they are packed with feminists, so that "politically incorrect" views (such as the view that women actually control men by manipulating men's sexual desire) can get no fair hearing.

I do not think that the complaints of creationists and gender essentialists have merit. My point is that backers of the view that diversity is an epistemic virtue have no tools for rebutting them.[20] If homogeneity of opinion is the problem with our currently demographically homogeneous academy, then homogeneity of opinion is a problem anywhere it develops. In fact, as many of us know, defenders

---

[18] Elizabeth Anderson (1995) is another philosopher who argues for the epistemic value of diversity. Her argument is somewhat different from Longino's: Anderson places the emphasis on the increased creativity that she believes comes from a diverse intellectual community, and cites empirical evidence that appears to support this claim. I cannot here consider Anderson's argument in detail, but I will say something about this central claim later, when I discuss criticisms of the strict empiricist view of science.

[19] But see my (1995) for qualifications.

[20] Daniel Hicks (2011) considers, but ultimately rejects, a possible reply Longino might make to this criticism. Thanks to Jennifer Saul for bringing this paper to my attention.

of progressive programs of study, like Gender Studies and Race Studies, are often attacked in just these terms. Scholars in these areas are said to be trying to "brainwash" students by "indoctrinating" them with leftist "propaganda."[21] I am not so naive as to think that attacks like these are *often* motivated by a sincere concern for objectivity in the academy, but some occasionally are, and we ought to have a responsible answer. Dragnet objectivity will not provide one.

Longino would likely object here that she is *not* presuming Dragnet objectivity—that she is not assuming that *just any* type of diversity makes for an epistemically stronger community.[22] She makes a much more specific assumption: viz. that variation in *social position* is what is epistemically salutary. So specified, her valorization of diversity does not commit her even to empiricism, and certainly not to Dragnet objectivity.

I accept that this more specific assumption of Longino's is not backed by, and thus does not require commitment to, empiricism *per se*. The problem is that it is not backed by *anything*. The assumption needs justification—it certainly does not follow from the *social importance* of race, gender, and so forth that such properties are more *epistemically* important than any other parameters of variation. One possible justification would be a kind of epistemic essentialism that Longino would never endorse—the view that women think differently from men, for example. But without such an assumption, it is hard to see why adding *demographic* diversity, in particular, would improve our ability to gain knowledge, and why adding that sort of diversity would be more salutary than adding *doctrinal* diversity of the sort demanded by creationists and opponents of critical studies.[23]

---

[21] See, for example, Patai and Koertge (2003).

[22] Longino would also say that she defends diversity as a *contextual* virtue. That is, she would say that whether diversification of the academy is a good thing or not depends on the character of the larger social context. I have a hard time understanding this notion. If there is no social stratification by gender or race, would it no longer matter if most professors and researchers were white and male? (I am not presuming that it would; I am only trying to become clear on the conditions.) Or is it that, if the academy *were* racially and sexually diverse, then it would not be necessary to diversify? That goes without saying—but it does not explain why diversification was *epistemically* necessary in the context of a racist or sexist society.

[23] One (anonymous) reader has made the suggestion that feminist standpoint epistemology might offer a non-essentialist justification for privileging gender diversity over other forms of diversity. Feminist standpoint theory holds that women who develop feminist consciousness can attain a privileged epistemic perspective, in virtue of their social positioning as central to biological reproduction but marginal with respect to their control over the social context in which reproduction occurs. (See Hartsock, 1983.) Feminist standpoint theory, if true, would certainly provide some warrant for seeking greater inclusion of appropriately situated women in certain areas of inquiry, and it would do so without appealing to any "essentially" feminine modes of thought or perception.

I have no objections to the general idea that features of one's social position can be epistemically pertinent. But there are two serious problems with feminist standpoint theory that should give pause to anyone who wants to mount an epistemic case for demographic diversity on such a basis. The first

To put the matter bluntly: the empiricist conception of bias, and the correlative notion of Dragnet objectivity, invites in the bogey of "reverse discrimination." From the empiricist point of view, bias is bias—it is never justified, not anywhere, not for any reason. It is this idea to which Chief Justice John Roberts was appealing when he struck down the racial integration plan proposed by the Jefferson County Board of Education. Writing for the plurality[24] in Meredith v. Jefferson, Roberts wrote: "The way to stop discrimination on the basis of race is to stop discriminating on the basis of race." He continued: "Racial balancing is not transformed from 'patently unconstitutional' to a compelling state interest simply by relabeling it 'racial diversity.'"[25]

I want to note—emphatically—that the failure of this epistemic argument for diversity does nothing *whatsoever* to diminish the strength of the moral and political arguments for democratizing science and the academy, nor for using race-, gender-, or class-based criteria as a means to that end. Our knowledge institutions, as they are currently constituted, neglect to a criminal degree the needs and interests of socially subordinated people. Indeed, these institutions are increasingly oriented toward the interests of the wealthiest and most powerful people in our society—a trend that is vastly accelerated by the erosion of public funding for education and research. The demographic homogeneity of the academy and the laboratory certainly reflects the racism, sexism, and economic subordination that silences voices and limits opportunities. Science surely would look different if research were driven by a recognition of human need, rather than by the love of profit.

All that said, there is another kind of epistemic argument for pursuing diversity that does work, and that is the argument from Saulish skepticism. The research on implicit bias tells us that factors of race and sex are influencing our evaluations in situations where we *antecedently* believed they were not, and in

problem is that there is strong reason to doubt that there are enough substantive commonalities among the experiences of all women to constitute a single "standpoint." This is a point that has been urged by many feminists: see, for example, Bat-Ami Bar On (1993), Susan Bordo (2013), and Elizabeth Spelman (1990). The second problem is that, even if some epistemic advantages can be garnered from occupying a given social position, that does not mean that one is epistemically advantaged *overall*. Social subordination, whether or not it confers epistemic benefits, carries epistemic costs too—illiteracy, innumeracy, and epistemic diffidence, to name but a few.

In any case, standpoint theory does not represent an endorsement of the epistemic value of *bias*. On the contrary, standpoint theory asserts that women with feminist consciousness are better positioned epistemically because they *lack* a bias—self-interested wishful thinking—that contaminates the perspective of individuals in a gender-dominant position.

[24] Justice Anthony Kennedy wrote a separate concurrent opinion. He held that, while the JCPS's plan used race in an unconstitutional way, there *were* constitutional ways of using race.

[25] <http://supreme.findlaw.com/supreme_court/docket/2006/december/05-915-meredith-v-jefferson-county-school-board.html>.

ways that flout our avowed critieria. We thus learn empirically that our current gatekeeping policies for entrance into our knowledge institutions are, very likely, advancing the interests of members of socially dominant groups at the expense of more able members of socially subordinate groups. Work like that of Walton et al. provides highly *specific* reasons for attending to particular aspects of social position.

It must be remembered, however, that once the existence of bias is discovered, it becomes an *empirical* matter how to identify and neutralize the pernicious biases that are at work. As Saul has emphasized, we cannot assume that we can figure out, *a priori*, what measures will be effective in counteracting these biases. In particular, we cannot know *a priori* that diversifying the pool of evaluators will do any good. It may *seem* obvious, for example, that increasing the percentage of women in a field will combat the kind of bias documented in the Moss-Racusin study of resume evaluation (2012). But a look at the facts shows that this is not necessarily so—Moss-Racusin found that women were just as likely to display gender bias as men.

Let me turn to the second political problem with the ideal of Dragnet objectivity; this has to do with its relation to popular conceptions of science. I have said that Dragnet objectivity is a *normative* notion, and that no one would claim that anyone does actually realize it (except, perhaps, the robotic Sergeant Friday). Nonetheless, the ideal is connected with a certain view about how structured rational inquiry, especially science, *actually* proceeds. This is a view that was taught to many of us—and still is taught today—as "the scientific method." Here is one exposition from the online pedagogical materials of a physics professor at a U.S. research university, chosen more or less at random from a Google search on the phrase "scientific method:"

I. The scientific method has four steps:
- Observation and description of a phenomenon or group of phenomena.
- Formulation of an hypothesis to explain the phenomena.
- Use of the hypothesis to predict the existence of other phenomena, or to predict quantitatively the results of new observations.
- Performance of experimental tests...

If the experiments bear out the hypothesis it may come to be regarded as a theory or law of nature...If the experiments do not bear out the hypothesis it must be rejected or modified...There is always the possibility that a new observation or a new experiment will conflict with a long-standing theory.[26]

---

[26] <http://www.teacher.nsrl.rochester.edu/phy_labs/appendixe/appendixe.html>.

This picture of the process of scientific enquiry clearly endorses Dragnet objectivity as an epistemic ideal. Dragnet objectivity simply *is* the limit notion of "scientific method," as described. In Section 2 I argue that this is no better an ideal for *social* knowledge-seeking than it is for individuals. But what concerns me here are the consequences of this ideal of science. Does it actually work?

Science, as a collective epistemic endeavor, has been wildly successful. That is, the collective human enterprise of scientific research has yielded an enormous amount of knowledge about the natural world, as well as an astonishing degree of control over it. (That is *not* to deny that there is still even more that we do not know, and it is not to deny that that the control we have gained has been very much a mixed blessing.) But it is not the case that science and scientists are successful because and to the extent that they conform to the prescriptions of Dragnet objectivity.

In fact, however, scientists do not follow the scientific method—and it is a good thing they do not. Just as is true in the case of individual human minds, collective inquiry would be less successful, rather than more, if scientists really followed such rules as "If the experiments do not bear out the hypothesis, reject it." For one thing, scientists are properly biased strongly in favor of the most fundamental principles of theories that have won consensus, and will be much more likely to attribute a recalcitrant empirical finding to experimental error or false intermediate assumptions than to consider the possibility that one of these principles are wrong. (Advocates of intelligent design are correct when they say that biologists are not willing to consider the possibility that the theory of evolution is false.)

However, as in the case of individual psychologies, there are in science bad biases as well as good ones. The history of science in the last couple of centuries is replete with cases in which the social, political, or religious beliefs of researchers led to the formulation and acceptance of theories that in fact had no empirical support whatsoever.[27] In the present day, the institutional realities of scientific research involve economic and personal incentive structures that, at the very least, bias scientists' choices of research projects,[28] and at the very worst, induce them to produce "findings" that serve the economic interests of their sponsors.[29]

---

[27] The history of research on group differences in intelligence supplies many examples. See Kamin (1974); Lewontin, Rose, and Kamin (1985); and Gould (1996).

[28] See Johnston (2008).

[29] Consider the case of Wei-Hock Soon, a scientist at the Smithsonian Center for Astrophysics. Soon has been a prominent spokesperson for climate-change denial. It was recently revealed that he has accepted more than $1.2 million from the oil industry and from the rightwing Charles G. Koch Charitable Foundation—funding that he failed to disclose in at least eleven scholarly papers. See Gillis and Schwartz (2015).

All of this should be common knowledge; but the belief that science succeeds because science and scientists *are* "objective" (in the Dragnet sense) makes critique of the human institutions of science very difficult. It is very common for progressive critics of particular programs or theories in science to be *themselves* accused of bias in bringing the biases of scientists to light. Carefully constructed critiques of the methodology or factual assumptions behind particular lines of research are dismissed as ideologically motivated slander. Feminist critics of research on gender are quite familiar with this sort of attack: the line is that feminists do not like the truth, and so "blame the messengers."[30]

I would go so far as to say that there is an *ideology* of objectivity that prevails in contemporary first-world thinking about science and scientists, and that, like all ideologies, it serves to obscure the real workings of the institutions it purports to describe, by means of a false, apparently rationalizing alternative narrative. I think an excellent first step, and possibly a necessary one, toward exploding the myth of value-free, neutral science, is to acknowledge the actual structure of human science, which does not, could not, and should not, limit itself to "just the facts."[31]

2 Why is Bias Good? Naturalism and Nativism

The twentieth-century descendent of classical empiricism was logical positivism. The signature project of the movement was Rudolf Carnap's *Der Logische Aufbau der Welt*. In that work, Carnap attempted to show how, at least in principle, a complex and rich theory of the natural world such as was emerging in physics and other natural sciences could be built up and justified on the basis of simple sensory experiences. The project foundered; it turned out be impossible to complete the construction without certain non-sensory primitive relations.

W. V. Quine, though a student and ardent admirer of Carnap, saw in the failure of the program of rational reconstruction, not just a problem for the strict empiricist theory of knowledge, but a fundamental lesson about epistemology itself. The aim of the project of rational reconstruction had always been normative, not descriptive; positivists did not claim that the actual construction of scientific theories mirrored the formal structures they described. The idea was that, however scientists actually went about their business, their results would be vindicated if it could be shown that their theories were *in principle* rationally derivable from sensory experience. But Quine raised the following question:

---

[30] John Stossel, "Boys and Girls are Different," ABC News Special, January 17, 1998.
[31] I develop this argument in more detail in my (2006).

regardless of whether a rational reconstruction succeeded in displaying *ideal* relations between sensory evidence and theoretical principles, how could a merely *hypothetical* model explain how *actual* scientific theories were justified? If scientists did not act the way the normative model said they should, what explains *their* success? And if they *can* succeed without conforming to the model, why *should* they aim to do so?

Quine's conclusion, as I mentioned earlier, was that epistemology needed to turn away from a prioristic prescription about how theory ought to be related to evidence, and set itself, instead, the explanatory project of figuring out how human beings come to construct successful theories on the basis of the evidence they have available to them. We should, Quine argued, treat knowledge as a naturally occurring phenomenon, and investigate it the same way we investigate other goings-on in the natural world.

Approaching epistemology in this naturalistic way, Quine realized that the program of rational reconstruction simply could not address what he identified as the central problem for a human epistemology: underdetermination. A rational reconstruction can appeal to as much sensory evidence as necessary; it can idealize away from temporal and spatial constraint. (And remember that the project failed, even so.) Real human scientists, however, are stuck in their immediate spatiotemporal neighborhoods. The evidence they can gather—individually, or collectively, across all of human history—will not be remotely enough to choose among all the distinct hypotheses compatible with that experience.

This is not only true in science, Quine pointed out, but also in mundane cognition. Given the substance and strength of the conclusions we actually do draw on the basis of our experience—conclusions as simple as our beliefs about the behavior of ordinary material objects—the sensory data on which these conclusions rely are paltry and equivocal. Yet despite all of this, we do seem to build reasonably adequate models of the external world, and science does progress. How?

Quine's answer: we depend on *bias*. (Admittedly, he did not quite put it this way.) At the most fundamental level, Quine pointed out, empirical learning could not proceed without our having an innate "similarity space"—a set of biases that make salient to us some rather than other properties of experienced objects. This much cognitive structure must be in place prior to experience, because it is necessary in order for us to *use* past experience as a guide to the future. Every token experience is, in its total quality, unique from every other, and so is it also, in some respect, similar to every other. If we had no native inclination to attend to some parameters of similarity to the exclusion of others, we would have to guess randomly about which similarities are important and which are not. That would mean that not only our projected generalizations, but the concepts in terms of which those generalizations are framed, would be always simultaneously open to empirical test. And in that case, inductive generalization as we think of it—learning the predictive value of observed similarities—would never get off the ground. Another thing: our inductive biases must be universal to our species. Otherwise, we would be unable to share experience in any epistemically useful way, since there would be no guarantee that my parameters of generalization would line up with yours.

This is not to say, by the way, that human similarity space is the only *possible* way that induction could ever possibly work. It may be that a supercomputer with no preset probabilities or parameters, but with vast memory stores and an enormous dataset, could extract many useful patterns in a reasonable amount of time. The point is that *we* cannot do that. We do not have the computational speed, nor the storage capacity, nor the experiential data to do what we do the way such a computer might do it. The fact that we are merrily generalizing and projecting as early as 3 months of age shows that the parameters of similarity we use are not *extracted from* patterns in our experience, but rather that we have *brought* them *to* experience.[32,33]

An innate similarity space does give us a basis for extracting patterns from experience, but what enables us to choose among the myriad different hypotheses that might explain those patterns? Here again, Quine appeals to bias. Human theorists, he argued, choose hypotheses on the basis of a smallish set of "virtues;" we prefer simpler hypotheses to more complicated ones, economical hypotheses to profligate ones, and conservative hypotheses to ones that entail radical revision of our previous beliefs. Other things equal, we also prefer hypotheses that are empirically adequate and self-consistent, although these virtues, like the others, can be traded off for sufficiently greater virtue elsewhere.[34] In itemizing these virtues, Quine meant to be speaking descriptively about the way human beings actually think. With respect to warrant, Quine was straightforward: he called these virtues "extra-empirical," to indicate that they were not in any way inferred from experience, but were rather part of the machinery necessary for making such inferences. With respect to warrant, Quine could do no better than Hume

---

[32] For a description of one of these new experimental paradigms, see Bloom (2014).

[33] Neither do these considerations show that we do not employ statistical learning algorithms. The point here is about the parameters we choose to attend to in experience, not what we do with the data once we get it. More on this later. Thanks to Edouard Machery for questions that prompted this clarification.

[34] Quine and Ullian (1978).

did in explaining how induction was "justified": viz. that we lie under a "practical necessity" of making epistemic choices in one way or another, and to the extent that the practice we adopt leads to empirical success, the practice is vindicated. "Vindication" such as this is all *ex post facto*, and not the kind of bottom-up, constructive justification that the positivists had sought.

At around the same time that Quine was writing, C. G. Hempel and Thomas Kuhn were developing similar criticisms of the conceptions of science spawned by positivism. Hempel described a view of science he called "naïve inductivism"—it was, more or less, the picture of science still promoted under the label "scientific method." Hempel criticized naïve inductivism on the grounds that it failed to capture the actual logic of confirmation. In fact, he argued, scientific hypotheses are never put to experimental test in isolation. They are always tested in conjunction with background theory and with tacit assumptions about the normalcy of experimental conditions (a point also emphasized by Quine.) A failed prediction, then, does not logically necessitate the rejection of a hypothesis—it demands only reconsideration of the whole conjunction: hypothesis, theory, and background conditions. Observations thus do not provide the sort of neutral authority that (what I call) Dragnet objectivity assigns to it.[35] Hempel, like Quine, emphasized the role of non- or extra-empirical assumptions in determining where to apportion blame when scientific predictions failed.

Thomas Kuhn (1962) focused on misconceptions about the history of science—misconceptions that were encouraged, again, by the strict empiricist idea that our science is a matter of the gradual and continuous shaping and reshaping of theory by an ever-expanding body of observational evidence—a view he called the "accretion" model of scientific change. His alternative picture assigned an even more robust role to bias in explaining both the emergence of modern science and its continued progress: a construct he called a *paradigm*. A paradigm, in Kuhn's technical sense, is a set of fundamental theoretical and methodological commitments that acquire the status of consensus within a scientific community. A paradigm, he argued, makes scientific cooperation possible by establishing a common vocabulary and a common understanding of the problematic.

Kuhn noted, however, that paradigms come at a cost: scientists cannot afford to be *open-minded*. A paradigm effectively restricts the hypothesis space within which scientists work, hiving off as either settled or as unimportant a whole raft

---

[35] This is so, even assuming that the notion of "observation" was unproblematic—an assumption that also came under (withering) attack during the same period by Quine, Putnam, and others. See, for example, Quine (1948) and Putnam (1962).

of conjectures that might have seemed, pre-paradigm, equally worthy of attention. And the restriction must be sturdy—scientists must hold on to the paradigm
with a certain amount of—and this is Kuhn's own word—*dogmatism* (1963).
They must resist revision to the central commitments of the paradigm, even in
the face of failed predictions and anomalous experiences. (In terms of Quine's
virtues: scientists working within a paradigm privilege the extra-empirical virtue
of *conservativism*—either by discounting the virtue of empirical adequacy, or by
discounting simplicity, by countenancing increasingly *ad hoc* alterations in their
theories.) Science, in other words, depends on its practitioners' displaying a fairly
high degree of bias—on their maintaining a robust disposition to regard certain
matters as not open to debate.

According to Kuhn's reading of scientific history, once a paradigm has
emerged, it is not given up until an alternative paradigm has become
available—a revolutionary rather than a reformist change. (Hence the name of
his landmark book, *The Structure of Scientific Revolutions*.) Experimental failures
and observed anomalies do not usually dislodge fundamental principles all by
themselves. For example, the Michelson–Morley experiment, which textbooks
often present as decisive disconfirmation of the idea that light moved through a
substantial medium, was performed in 1887; but Newtonian mechanics did not
begin to be seriously questioned until Einstein published his theory of special
relativity in 1905.[36]

Kuhn also argues that the existence of a paradigm makes for efficiency in
scientific education. Young scientists need not learn the history of their subjects,
nor must they prove for themselves the truth of the fundamental theoretical
principles of their fields. Kuhn went so far as to liken the modern scientific
education to the training received by a novice in a religious order—and he did not
mean the comparison to be unflattering. Indeed, his point was that the oft-cited
contrast between religious "faith" and scientific "rationality" is a bit chimerical.
Scientists are not Sergeant Fridays in lab coats; they rely everyday on assumptions
that are *for them* untested. Their commitment to the fundamental principles of
their theories is far more durable than they themselves recognize.

Kuhn's discussion of scientific education has bearing on Longino's epistemic
argument for demographic diversity in science. If Kuhn is right about scientific
education, then there is little reason to think (again, leaving aside essentialist
theories) that a student's race or gender or class identity will make much of a
difference to the set of hypotheses in play within a particular scientific field, or to
the interpretation of experimental results. The process of becoming a scientist has

---

[36] Kuhn (1962: 72–3).

a homogenizing effect, epistemically speaking. This is absolutely *not* to say that democratizing science would not have enormous effects on research agendas and on the ethics of research—I doubt that any black scientist would have allowed the Tuskegee experiment to go forward. But there is (a) no reason to think that a person of color, or a white woman, would emerge from scientific education with significantly different *doctrinal* commitments than the white men in their cohorts, and (b) no reason to think that science would be better if they did.

The relevance of all this to the issue of implicit bias is this: naturalistic studies of knowledge and of science make it clear that bias plays a constructive role in human cognition. Hempel's and Kuhn's naturalistic studies of science and scientific change make quite clear that adherence to a norm of Dragnet objectivity—if it were even possible—would be fatal to scientific progress.

As an advocate of naturalism in the study of knowledge, Quine never quite took his own counsel; he ignored the cognitivist revolution of the 1960s and 1970s, the agents of which, ironically, followed Quine's methodological playbook to the letter. Chomsky, for example, showed that behaviorist learning theory (the version of strict empiricism that dominated psychology in the early and middle parts of the twentieth century) could not explain the basic facts about human language acquisition. Behaviorism (which Quine explicitly avowed, for entirely philosophical reasons) held that all learning (by all species, across all domains) was a matter of behavioral shaping through patterns of reinforcement. Chomsky pointed out, however, that a serious look at the conditions under which human children acquired their native languages revealed that they did not receive either the types or the amounts of reinforcement they would need in order for learning theory to account for their linguistic achievements.[37] Parents typically do not give children any feedback about grammaticality; when they do, it is generally ignored by the children. Indeed, Chomsky argued, it was highly unlikely that any *general* theory of learning could account for the richness of the acquired linguistic competence on the basis of evidence actually available to children—evidence that was, relative to the cognitive structure ultimately attained, fragmentary and often misleading. What was needed to deal with this "poverty of the stimulus," Chomsky argued, was a domain-specific learning mechanism.

Accordingly, Chomsky hypothesized a specialized, native mental structure—"universal grammar" or "UG"—that served to sharply constrain the kind of grammatical rules a child could infer on the basis of her limited linguistic experience during her first three years of life. For example, UG specifies (linguists believe) that all grammatical rules must be *structure-sensitive*—they are defined

---

[37] Chomsky (1959). See also Chomsky (1975).

over functional grammatical categories rather than merely over words. This is why English-speaking children know right away, without having to make the mistake and be corrected, that questions invert predicates and subjects—"Is the toy you brought me in your suitcase?"—rather than just the first verb and the first noun—"Brought the toy you me is in your suitcase?"[38]

The idea that human minds worked by exploiting rich native learning structures, specific to specific domains, revolutionized psychology and linguistics. The study of the mind became very much the study of specialized cognitive modules, which theorists characterized in terms of native or "folk" theories of important domains. Developmental psychologists posited native mechanisms embodying knowledge of the behavior of medium-sized physical objects (Elizabeth Spelke), knowledge of the behavior of animals (Susan Carey), and knowledge of human psychology (Alan Leslie).[39]

Adopting the computationalist paradigm, vision scientists (e.g. Gregory, Rock) dealt with the "inverse problem"—the problem of how we infer a representation of three-dimensional reality from the two-dimensional retinal display—by positing "hidden assumptions" about the relation between features of the retinal image and facts about physical layout that played a role in normal visual processing.[40] In circumstances where these hidden assumptions are false, we fall prey to illusion. Consider the rotating face mask illusion.[41] A hollow mask is rotating; as it moves away from us, the side that appeared to be the front, and convex, suddenly switches, and appears to be the concave back (with corresponding changes to what initially appeared to be the back). This can be explained by reference to the "hidden assumption" that illumination is always from above.[42]

Now one consequence of our perceptual systems' heavy reliance on biases is that we human knowers must come to terms with the fact that our ability to know a great many things depends upon our being *situated* in the right sort of environment. This is the downside of dependence on bias. We must give up

---

[38] Chomsky (1975: 30–3).

[39] This research is surveyed in Spelke and Kinzler (2007).

[40] See Palmer (1999), esp. section 1.1.3. It is an open question how "hidden assumptions" are realized—it is unlikely that they are explicitly represented. The main point here is that there is a strong bias in the processing of visual information that, at the *very* least, gives the effect of an inference involving premises with these contents. For discussion of the "psychosemantics" involved, see my (2011).

[41] This illusion—and many others—can be viewed at Michael Bach's website: <http://www.michaelbach. de/ot/fcs_hollow-face/>.

[42] In the case of this particular "hidden assumption," some scientists think that what is innate is not the particular assumption that illumination comes from above, but rather the disposition to fix on some direction as the default source of illumination. See Marcus (2005).

hope of ever doing what Terry Horgan and David Henderson (2001) call "practicing safe epistemology"—we cannot expect to find epistemic strategies that would be effective in any possible world. Should we ever encounter extra-terrestrial beings with language, we should not expect that our children could acquire those languages as effortlessly as they acquire ours. We might not even be able to interpret such beings by means of explicit study—our grammatical categories and representational strategies might turn out to be parochial. Here there is a trade-off—as there so often is—between the efficiency and utility of special-purpose tools and the flexibility of general ones.

In sum: our ability to garner information from the environment by means of our senses depends upon stable but contingent features of our situation. *Biases* are the aspects of our mental machinery that track those features reliably. Biases make possible perception, language, and science. They make us less self-reliant epistemically, but in the main they play a constructive role in human cognition.

So far, I have focused on the role of native biases in the development of human knowledge. But there are acquired biases that serve us in similar ways. Many of the lessons of work on mental shortcuts can be understood in this way. Although some psychologists, such as Daniel Kahneman, have emphasized the ways in which fast, reflexive judgments can lead us astray, others, such as Gerd Giger-enzer, have argued that reflexive judgments serve us well, as long as they are issued in the right environment. Consider, for example, the "recognition heuris-tic." If you ask a classroom of German middle-schoolers to tell you which American city is bigger, San Diego or San Jose, a majority will give the right answer: San Diego. Why? Because they have *heard of* San Diego, but have not heard of San Jose. Since a city's size correlates fairly well with its fame, German students who just pick the city they recognize over the one they do not, do pretty well on this task. Ask American students the same question, though, and they will likely be at chance. These students know *too much* to be able to rely on the recognition heuristic. They recognize both cities, and so they need specific information about each one—information most people do not have at their fingertips—to be able to give the correct answer. So the recognition heuristic works well only in circumstances where (a) the individual using it knows a little, but not much, about the domain in question, and (b) there is a correlation, within that same domain, between notoriety and the property of interest. Gigerenzer calls this contingency "ecological validity"—reliability, within the proper place.

The reliability of many of our native biases depends simply upon our being situated in a certain way in our physical environment. Other biases, however, depend for their utility and reliability on our *social* environment. For human beings, epistemic codependence is ubiquitous. For one thing, an enormous amount of what we know (or think we know) comes from the testimony of others. For another, we use agreement with others as one of the chief means of assessing our beliefs. Since reliance on others is essential to our epistemic efficiency, an adequate account of knowledge must explain how this epistemic codependence contributes to our success. A large part of the story, we know, is going to be a matter of biases with *social* ecological validity.

Consider testimony. Our ability to learn through testimony does not depend much on the quality of our own skill in picking informants—we do not, despite the desperate conjectures of some internalists, condition our degree of credulity to an assessment of our witness's track record. It appears, rather, that we are simply biased toward believing what we hear, unless (though sometimes even in spite of) having positive reason to doubt.[43] A strategy like that—"if someone says it, believe it"—will lead to grief unless it is practiced in a social environment in which either people by and large tell the truth, or, when they do not, it does not matter.

It is tempting to think that reliance on cognitive biases is just a kind of crutch, and that bias-free reasoning is still a more perfect strategy, if we could only manage it. But this is not so. Giving up biases—even when we can—may simply lead to different kinds of epistemic failure, given the facts about our epistemic limitations. This is evident from work done by Gigerenzer and others on extrapolation problems. Such problems, like medical diagnoses, require us to predict future conditions on the basis of observations about the past. But which aspects of the past should we attend to, and which should we ignore?

Traditional statistical models can be built that assign significance to every factor previously shown in the past to correlate with the condition of interest. But there are two drawbacks for human beings who want to use such models. The first is *computational intractability*. Without access to a computer, deriving conclusions from a complicated statistical model can be impossible. But secondly, even in cases where a computer can obviate the tractability problem, another problem looms: the problem of *overfit*. A model that retrodicts past conditions perfectly is apt to be poor at predicting future conditions; this is because the model is *too* influenced by factors that occurred fortuitously in the past and that are unlikely to crop up regularly in the future. Such models are not *robust*.[44]

In an essay provocatively entitled "In praise of epistemic irresponsibility: How lazy and ignorant can you be?," Michael Bishop (2000) surveys a wide range of

---

[43] Michealian (2009).

[44] Gerd Gigerenzer, "Why heuristics work," *Perspectives on Psychological Science*, web edition: <http://www.slideshare.net/andreshluna/gigerenzer-why-heuristics-work>.

work comparing the performance of what he calls "irresponsible but very reliable strategies" (IRS) with the performance of both "proper strategies"—strategies built on laws of probability and logic—and human experts. The overall conclusions supported by this work are, first, that IRSs typically outperform human experts—even when the IRS in question is designed to mimic the predictive strategy of the *specific* human expert it subsequently outperforms—and second, that IRSs come extremely close to the performance of the proper models. Proper models are, for unaided human beings, intractable in application to cases of any complexity. What the relatively poor performance of the human experts shows is that our best efforts to reason according to the standard rules—our best efforts to reason in an epistemically responsible way—are less fruitful than would be the adoption of ecologically valid shortcut strategies. In short, Bishop (2000: 179) concludes: "...for a wide range of real-world problems, the most reliable, tractable reasoning strategies audaciously flout the internalist's epistemic virtues."

3 Bias: Friend or Foe, and How Can We Tell the Difference?

But if all this is so, how are we supposed to understand implicit bias? How exactly can we criticize its role in our evaluative practices? How can we integrate a normative conception of *epistemic agency* (according to which our evaluative judgments should be tuned to—and only to—the relevant facts) with a *naturalized* conception of ourselves (according to which we need shortcuts and tricks)?

I contend that understanding the etiology and operation of these constructive biases can help us, finally, in understanding and reducing biases that are pernicious.

To begin with, once we identify particular biases influencing our judgment, we can investigate their ecological validity. Here are the factors we need to consider with respect to a given epistemic practice. a) *Markers* and *targets*: what properties are we aiming to track (targets), and what properties are we using as markers of the target properties? b) *Indication relations*: do the markers in fact correlate with the target properties? Then, if a practice passes muster with respect to (a) and (b): c) what *mechanism* sustains the correlation?

The simplest case of pernicious bias is the one in which the practice fails condition (b). This is the test we would expect racial bias, gender bias, and class bias to fail, and in fact, we know that they do. In the cases that give rise to Saulish skepticism, cases of bad implicit bias, we discover that we are relying on markers that do not provide information about the pertinent target properties. Since we do not *consciously* believe that racial or gender markers do track the properties in which we are interested, we are not usually surprised to learn that, in fact, they do not. We can have direct evidence that the habit of indulging such biases, in the environments we currently inhabit, will lead to error *by our own lights*. These biases are not ecologically valid.

If our biases are leading us astray in this way, we may need to retune the perceptual *markers* of qualities in which we have a legitimate interest. Consider epistemic authority: if there has been a long period of time in which intellectual experts were almost all men, then a deep voice might have become a marker of expertise. If it is no longer the case that intellectual experts are almost always men—if there have come to be a significant number of women who are entitled to be treated as authorities, then the "deep voice" marker has gotten out of tune with the trait it once marked. We will, in this sort of case, need to contrive ways of deactivating that marker and, eventually, replacing it with one that is more reliable.

This recommendation, I realize, suggests a certain circularity: "retuning" the system of markers in the social environment will require our first making judgments about the target property, when we know that it is precisely such judgments that embody implicit bias. How do we bootstrap our way out of this problem? Ironically, it might be that we can make progress by imposing, *in these cases,* a heuristic, strategic, Dragnet standard of objectivity: mechanically noting all the "facts," and making all inference principles as explicit as possible. Thus, for example, if we realize that we are likely to underestimate the productivity of women job applicants, we can force ourselves to explicitly count the number of publications by each applicant, and to relate them to precalibrated grades.

However, the investigation of the ecological validity of biases may also turn up problems that will not fit this pattern. There are certain features of social identity that, with respect to certain target properties, *will* pass the test of condition (b). That is, there are cases where features like race, gender, or economic class *do* correlate with properties of legitimate interest, whether we like it or not. This can easily happen because of the malign effects of social subordination. For example, with respect to many skills, like musical or athletic skills, level of preparation is a good marker of the target property. But race and economic class will be strongly predictive of level of preparation in some of these areas. Very few poor children grow up to win auditions for symphony orchestra positions, because they generally have not had access to excellent instruction and fine instruments all their lives as have their more affluent peers. Tennis, which is rarely offered as an extracurricular activity at public schools, and even more rarely taught as part of physical education curricula, is one of the few sports in the U.S. that does not have a high percentage of black players. (Golf, of course, is another.)

This is where condition (c) becomes important. In an environment like the one that currently exists in the U.S., we have a situation where a marker that is, intuitively, epistemically valid is also one that correlates positively with intuitively *impertinent* aspects of social identity. The existence of this second correlation will make reliance on these impertinent factors—class or race—an ecologically valid strategy. There is no threat here from Saulish skepticism; in these cases we will not be making mistakes about *actual* qualifications if we simply relax and trust our biases. From the perspective of justice, however, we want to say that we most certainly should not relax and trust our biases. I would like to state that again: *from the perspective of justice*, we should not relax and trust our biases.

Condition (c) requires us to investigate the explanations for the tracking relations identified in connection with conditions (a) and (b). Once we have identified the *mechanisms* that keep markers and targets in phase, we can often see that the marker-target correlations are shallow and fortuitous; that is to say, they do not depend upon deep or rationally principled connections between target and marker; rather, they depend upon a pattern of social inequities that we can and ought to change. *Epistemic* reform in such cases is not the issue: the justificatory connection between level of preparation (marker) and skill (target) is completely proper.

Presumably, many, if not most, pernicious biases are adventitious in this way: they record contingent correlations that can be changed through social will, rather than deep regularities in nature. This is almost certainly the case with race, since there is every reason to doubt that the racial categories operative in contemporary society track real biological kinds. But what about gender? Gender does track (to a large extent) biologically natural kinds.[45] Does that mean that we are doomed to see the world in pink and blue? No. Gender, even if it (to some extent) tracks a biological kind, is itself a social kind. As a social kind, its function is to keep a set of socially important traits in phase with certain biological facts, and to keep those socially important traits in concordance with each other. But that function is unnecessary. We do not need social proxy categories for sex; whenever actual biological sex becomes important—when we want to reproduce, for example—we do not need gender to help us figure out who is who. Thus, one way to eliminate gender bias would be to eliminate *gender* itself.[46]

---

[45] This is not to deny the existence nor the importance of intersexuality and transidentities. It is simply to say that there is, statistically speaking, a very robust correlation between gender and biological sex, however these are understood.

[46] I develop this conception of gender, as a force that creates and maintains artificial concordances, in Antony (1998).

From a moral standpoint, then, our aim should be the creation and maintenance of equal opportunity. From an epistemic standpoint, our goal should not be to eliminate bias, but rather to manipulate the regularities in our environment so as to create a social world in which we *can* indulge our biases, without injustice.

Let me conclude this section with an example of a novel approach to dealing with at least one aspect of the problem of implicit bias—one that probably would not have emerged without solid empirical work on the nature of human generalizations.

Many philosophers and linguists are interested in the behavior of *generic* expressions. Generics often occur as "bare plurals," as in the sentence, "birds lay eggs." One interesting feature of generic claims is that they are highly counterexample-resistant. Most people judge the above sentence to be true, for example, even though they are aware, if they think about it for a second, that male birds do not lay eggs, and neither do female juveniles. That means that at any given time, it is likely that a *majority* of birds are not egg-layers. Recognizing that fact rarely makes people change their opinion: they will still agree that "birds lay eggs" is true. If our biases—whether explicit or implicit—are stored as generics, we should be doubtful that they will be weakened by mere exposure to counterexamples. For someone who accepts generics like "girls suck at math" and "blacks are good at sports," it is unlikely that encounters with female mathematics professors or athletically challenged blacks will, on their own, make much difference.

This resistance to counterexamples is especially strong in the case of what Sarah-Jane Leslie (2008) calls "striking-property generics"—generics that attribute dangerous or highly noteworthy properties to things of a certain kind. Examples include "ticks carry Lyme disease" and "sharks attack bathers." People who assert such claims are not bothered by the fact that only a tiny fraction of ticks actually carry the bacterium that causes Lyme, nor that the vast majority of sharks have never threatened a single human being.

Leslie's hypothesis is that generic claims reflect a primitive, foundational form of generalization—one that does not involve quantifiers like "all," "some," and "most." This hypothesis is supported by research into the etiology of generic beliefs. It is known that generic beliefs are formed quickly, and on the basis of relatively small samples. Also, generics tend to involve categories that are highly "essentialized." This term in psychology refers to a kind of folk metaphysics that governs a lot of our conceptualization of the natural world. To essentialize a kind is to view its members as sharing some deeply hidden property—an essence— that unifies and explains the individuals' surface properties. (This is an inchoate version of the Putnam/Boyd theory of natural kinds.) A shared essence warrants projection of properties from one observed instance of the kind to others.

Striking-property generics form especially quickly, often on the basis of one instance. Leslie explains that if a property is very dangerous, then it is important to the organism to avoid anything that might have, or that has a disposition to acquire, that property. Thus, if even one tick actually carries Lyme disease, its essence-sharing cousin ticks will all be presumed to have the capacity, or the propensity, to carry the disease as well. A hasty generalization in such cases, though it generates false positives, keeps the organism safe by preventing false negatives. A more nuanced generalization might both take too much time to acquire, and too much time to apply.

Leslie cites work by developmental psychologists Susan Gelman, Elizabeth Ware, and Felicia Kleinberg that indicates that human beings can and do use linguistic cues, as well as other forms of experience, to learn which categories support generic claims: for example, children who are told stories involving made-up categories like "zarpie" will generalize more readily if the term is introduced in a linguistic context like this:

Zarpies like ice cream

than one like this:

This zarpie likes ice cream.[47]

Putting these findings all together, Leslie (forthcoming) offers an account of the genesis of (at least one mode of) social prejudice. Many social-group attributions are made using the linguistic construction "X is a Φ:" "Joe is a Jew," "Ahmed is a Muslim," "Sally is a woman." The use of this characteristically generic construction sets up the kinds Jew, Muslim, and woman as candidates for essentialized kinds. Then, if one member of one of these kinds displays a striking property, a striking-property generic can result: "Muslims are terrorists." Since striking-property generics are especially resistant to counterexample, they will not be dislodged simply by the thinker's encountering people who do not fit the emerging stereotype. This calls into question whether the empiricist suggestion of deliberately confronting oneself (or a bigoted other) with counterexamples will, even over time, be effective in eliminating prejudice.

There are strategies for counteracting or dismantling biases that have the sort of etiology Leslie describes. The most effective regimen, according to Leslie, is extensive, cooperative, and equitable engagement with persons of the stereotyped

---

[47] Gelman, S. A., Ware, E. A., and Kleinberg F. "Effects of generic language on category content and structure" (under review at the time of Leslie's writing). Leslie also cites work by Susan Gelman and Gail Heyman (1999) that supports the view that linguistic cues have a role in explaining children's tendencies to essentialize *social* categories.

group in some kind of joint project. But the etiological specifics suggest that even a shallow linguistic reform might, to some extent, disrupt or prevent the formation of pernicious, striking-property generics: avoiding the use of generic noun phrases when making attributions of features of social identity. Thus, instead of ascribing social identity properties by means of labeling nouns or generic constructions, we can use adjectives or descriptive phrases:

Instead of *labeling* a person as *a Muslim*, we might instead *describe* the person—if needed—as, say, *a person who follows Islam*, thus emphasizing that *person* is the relevant kind sortal, and that *following Islam* is a particular property that the individual happens to possess.   (ms.: 37–8)

In sum: Saulish skepticism is a phenomenon that shows us the need to take a naturalized approach to the study of human inquiry, and a naturalized approach reveals that bias is an essential and constructive factor in our ability to know our world. That fact does not doom our efforts to eliminate pernicious forms of bias. On the contrary, gaining an understanding of how and when bias is our friend will enable us to act more effectively when it becomes our foe.

References

Alcoff, L. and Potter, E. (1982). "Introduction: When feminisms intersect epistemology." In *Feminist Epistemologies*. London: Routledge: 1–14.

Anderson, E. (1995). "The democratic university: the role of justice in the production of knowledge." *Social Philosophy and Policy* (Cambridge Journals) 12(2): 186–219.

Antony, L. M. (1995). "Sisters, please, I'd rather do it myself: A defense of individualism in feminist epistemology." *Philosophical Topics* 23(2): 59–94.

Antony, L. M. (2006). "The socialization of epistemology." In Goodin, R. and Tilley, C. (eds.), *The Oxford Handbook of Contextual Political Studies*. Oxford: Oxford University Press: 58–77.

Antony, L. M. (2011). "The openness of illusions." *Philosophical Issues, Special Issue on Direct Realism* 21(1): 25–44.

Apfelbaum, E. P., Sommers, S. R., and Norton, M. I. (2008). "Seeing race and seeming racist? Evaluating strategic colorblindness in social interaction." *Journal of Personality and Social Psychology* 95: 918–32.

Bar On, B.-A. (1993). "Marginality and epistemic privilege." In Alcott, L. and Potter, E. (eds.), *Feminist Epistemologies*. New York, NY: Routledge: 83–100.

Bishop, M. (2000). "In praise of epistemic irresponsibility: How lazy and ignorant can you be?" *Synthese* 122(1/2): 179–208.

Bloom, P. (2014). *Just Babies*. London: Broadway Books.

Bordo, S. (2013). "Feminism, modernism, and gender skepticism." In *Feminism/Postmodernism*, ed. Nicholson, L. London: Routledge: 133–56.

Bradley, C. (1993). "Sex bias in student assessment overlooked?" *Assessment and Evaluation in Higher Education* 18(1): 3–8.

Chomsky, N. (1959). "A review of B. F. Skinner's *Verbal Behavior.*" *Language* 35(1): 26–58.

Chomsky, N. (1975). *Reflections on Language.* New York, NY: Pantheon.

Dennett, D. (1987). "Three kinds of intentional psychology." In *The Intentional Stance.* Cambridge, MA: MIT Press: 43–68.

Fricker, M. (2007). *Epistemic Justice: Power and the Ethics of Knowing.* Oxford: Oxford University Press.

Gelman, S. A. and Heyman, G. D. (1999). "Carrot-eaters and creature-believers: The effects of lexicalization on children's inferences about social categories." *Psychological Science* 10: 489–93.

Gigerenzer, G. "Why heuristics work." *Perspectives on Psychological Science,* web edition: <http://www.slideshare.net/andreshluna/gigerenzer-why-heuristics-work>.

Gillis, J. and Schwartz, J. (2015). "Deeper ties to corporate cash for doubtful climate researcher," *The International New York Times,* February 21. <http://www.nytimes.com/2015/02/22/us/ties-to-corporate-cash-for-climate-change-researcher-Wei-Hock-Soon.html>.

Goldin, C. and Rouse, C. (1997). "Orchestrating impartiality: The impact of 'blind' auditions on female musicians." *NBER Working Paper No. 5903.* <http://www.nber.org/papers/w5903>.

Gould, S. J. (1996). *The Mismeasure of Man.* New York, NY: W. W. Norton.

Hartsock, N. (1983). "The feminist standpoint: Developing the ground for a specifically feminist historical materialism." In Harding, S. and Hintikka, S. B. (eds.), *Discovering Reality.* Dordecht: Reidel: 283–310.

Hicks, D. (2011). "Is Longino's conception of objectivity feminist?" *Hypatia* 26(2): 333–51.

Horgan, T. and Henderson, D. (2001). "Practicing safe epistemology." *Philosophical Studies* 102: 227–58.

Johnston, J. (2008). "Conflict of interest in biomedical research." In Crowley, M. (ed.), *From Birth to Death and Bench to Clinic: The Hastings Center Bioethics Briefing Book for Journalists, Policymakers, and Campaigns.* Garrison, NY: The Hastings Center: 31–4. <http://www.thehastingscenter.org/Publications/BriefingBook/Detail.aspx?id=2156>.

Kahneman, D. (2011). *Thinking Fast and Slow.* New York, NY: Farrar, Straus, and Giroux.

Kamin, L. (1974). *The Science and Politics of IQ.* London: Routledge.

Kornblith, H. (2012). *On Reflection,* Oxford: Oxford University Press.

Kuhn, T. (1962). *The Structure of Scientific Revolutions.* Chicago, IL: University of Chicago Press.

Kuhn, T. (1963). "The function of dogma in scientific research." In Crombie, A. C. (ed.), *Scientific Change: Historical Studies in the Intellectual, Social and Technical Conditions for Scientific Discovery and Technical Invention, from Antiquity to the Present.* London: Heinemann: 347–69.

Leslie, S.-J. (2008). "Generics: cognition and acquisition." *Philosophical Review* 117(1): 1–49.

Leslie, S.-J. (Forthcoming). "The original sin of cognition: Fear, prejudice, and generalization," *Journal of Philosophy.*

Lewontin, R., Rose, S., and Kamin, L. (1985). *Not in Our Genes.* New York, NY: Pantheon Books.

Longino, H. (2001). *The Fate of Knowledge in Social Theories of Science.* Princeton: NJ: Princeton University Press.

Longino, H. (2002). *Science as Social Knowledge: Values and Objectivity in Scientific Inquiry.* Princeton: Princeton University Press.

Marcus, G. F. (2005). "What developmental biology can tell us about innateness." In Carruthers, P., Laurence, S., and Stich, S. (eds.), *The Innate Mind: Structure and Content.* Oxford University Press: 23–35.

Michealian, K. (2009). "On memory and testimony." Doctoral dissertation, University of Massachusetts at Amherst.

Moss-Racusin, C. A., Dovidio, J. F., Brescoli, V. L., Graham, M. J., and Handelsman, J. (2012). "Science faculty's subtle gender biases favor male students." *Proceedings of the National Academy of Sciences* 109(41): 16474–9.

Nagel, T. (1986). *The View from Nowhere.* Oxford: Oxford University Press.

Palmer, S. E. (1999). *Vision Science: From Photons to Phenomenology.* Cambridge, MA: MIT Press.

Patai, D. and Koertge, N. (2003). *Professing Feminism: Education and Indoctrination in Women's Studies.* Lanham, MD: Lexington Books of Rowman & Littlefield.

Peters, D. P. and Ceci, S. I. (1982). "Peer-review practices of psychological journals: The fate of published articles submitted again," *Behavioral and Brain Sciences* 5: 187–95.

Putnam, H. (1962). "What theories are not." In Nagel, R., Suppes, P., and Tarski, A. (ed.) *Logic, Methodology and Philosophy of Science: Proceedings of the 1960 International Congress.* Stanford, CA: Stanford University Press: 215–27.

Quine, W. V. (1948). "On what there is." *Review of Metaphysics* 2(5): 21–36.

Quine, W. V. (1969). "Epistemology naturalized." In *Ontological Relativity and Other Essays.* New York, NY: Columbia University Press: 69–90.

Quine, W. V. and Ullian, J. S. (1978). *The Web of Belief.* New York, NY: McGraw-Hill.

Saul, J. (2013). "Scepticism and implicit bias." *Disputatio* 5: 37.

Spelke, E. and Kinzler, K. D. (2007). "Core knowledge." *Developmental Science* 10(1): 89–96.

Spelman, E. (1990). *Inessential Women.* Boston, MA: Beacon Press.

Steinpreis, R., Anders, K. A., and Ritzke, D. (1999). "The impact of gender on the review of the curricula vitae of job applicants and tenure candidates: A national empirical study." *Sex Roles* 41(7/8): 509–28.

Valian, V. (1998). *Why So Slow? The Advancement of Women.* Cambridge, MA: MIT Press.

Walton, G., Spencer, S. J., and Erman, S. (2013). "Affirmative meritocracy." *Social Issues and Policy Review* 7(1): 1–35.

2.2

Virtue, Social Knowledge, and Implicit Bias

Alex Madva

1 Introduction

Research suggests that most citizens of liberal democracies embrace egalitarian goals but nevertheless exhibit predictable patterns of implicit social bias in, for example, hiring and legal decisions. Recently, Gendler (2008; 2011) and Egan (2011) have argued that implicit biases put us in a kind of tragic normative dilemma, in which we cannot jointly satisfy all of our moral and epistemic requirements. Their arguments are, in part, responses to alarming evidence that the strength of implicit biases correlates with the knowledge individuals have of prevalent stereotypes, regardless whether they reflectively reject or endorse the content of those stereotypes.[1] Simply knowing what the stereotypes are seems to make individuals more likely to act in biased ways.

These findings suggest an opposition between social knowledge and virtue. If mere knowledge of stereotypes hinders the possibility of acting ethically, should an individual with egalitarian goals aim to forget all she knows about discrimination and stereotypes? Returning to such a state of ignorance would incur serious costs. In such a state, she would not, for example, be in a position to recognize the injustices individuals suffer in virtue of being perceived in a stereotypical light.

---

[1] The term "stereotype" can be problematic and misleading, because some of the cognitive processes underlying objectionable stereotypes also underlie unobjectionable and even rational forms of social cognition. Valian (1998) adopts the less charged term "schema," while Beeghly (2013) argues that we should broaden our understanding of "stereotypes" to include both rational and problematic forms of social cognition. For my purposes, the negative connotation of stereotypes is useful for keeping in view that I am talking about a class of somehow *bad* or *undesirable* states. I agree with Antony (2002) that distinguishing the "good" stereotypes from the "bad" is fundamentally an empirical question. See also Brownstein and Madva (2012a,b).

If, then, she ought not surrender her social knowledge, must she simply learn to live with the unfortunate effects that knowledge has?

I argue that this apparent opposition is misguided. Social knowledge as such poses no obstacle to virtue, but rather the relative *accessibility* of such knowledge does. In psychology, accessibility refers to "the ease with which a particular unit of information is activated or can be retrieved from memory" (Morewedge and Kahneman, 2010: 435). In some sense, certain bits of knowledge "come to mind" more readily than others. I intend to argue that the seeming tension between virtue and knowledge of stereotypes arises primarily insofar as that knowledge becomes too readily accessible. It is possible for social agents to acquire knowledge about the existence and effects of stereotypes, while working effectively toward being more virtuous, so long as that knowledge remains relatively *in*accessible.

This paper focuses on the problematic effects of social knowledge on the mental life and behavior of *individuals*, and, in turn, on what individuals can do about it. To consider what individuals can do is not to assume that the wrongs associated with implicit bias are primarily "individual" rather than "social." The harms and inequities suffered by individuals on the basis of race and gender depend to a great extent on social-institutional forces, and institutional change is necessary for redressing those harms. But institutions are composed both of a set of rules and laws as well as a set of individuals, and, if we want to bring about lasting change, we have to understand the roles that each plays in contributing to these large-scale harms. I focus on the role of individuals here. I intend to address what sorts of institutional policies might be warranted in light of these phenomena in future work.[2]

In what follows I recount the moral-epistemic dilemma posed by Gendler and Egan (Section 2). They argue that working toward the *ethical* ideal of being unprejudiced will inevitably incur certain "*epistemic* costs." I then critically examine the notion of an epistemic cost (Section 3), and describe how an agent could, in principle, pursue her ethical aims without incurring any (Section 4). Working toward this ideal ethical and epistemic state is no mere pipe dream, but depends on an agent's ability to regulate the accessibility of her social knowledge. I explain how the regulation of accessibility is key for resolving the dilemma (Section 5). I then describe a range of concrete strategies that individuals can implement to better approximate the moral-epistemic ideal (Section 6). Finally,

---

[2] See e.g. Valian (1998, 2010) for many of the best institutional interventions for addressing gender bias in professional contexts; Kalev et al. (2006) for an informative meta-analysis of existing strategies to promote diversity; Levinson and Smith (2012) for a collection of essays on implicit racial bias and legal theory; and Anderson (2010, 2012a) for pioneering work on prejudice and political philosophy.

I consider in greater detail one of the contexts in which our ethical and epistemic aims are alleged to come into conflict (specifically, deciding whether to consider the racial composition of neighborhoods in setting home insurance premiums; Section 7). This is very much the beginning of a larger treatment of these issues. A satisfactory account of how social knowledge is accessed, and how to thwart the pernicious influence that such knowledge can have on judgment and action, requires answering a series of interrelated questions in epistemology, ethics, and psychology. My hope is to shed some light on which questions we should be asking and make tentative proposals about how to answer them.

2 A Moral-Epistemic Dilemma?

The point of departure for Gendler and Egan (the "dilemmists," as I will call them) is empirical research on the undesirable effects that social knowledge can have on behavior. For example, Correll et al. (2002) found that the magnitude of individuals' implicit racial bias did not correlate with their self-reported racial beliefs but did correlate with their reports of what most white Americans believe.[3] In other words, it seems that merely knowing what *many others believe* about a group leads individuals to act in some respects as if they themselves believed it too.

Another problematic type of social knowledge might be knowledge of statistical regularities of demographic variation, such as average differences between social groups in crime rates and mathematics SAT scores (Gendler, 2011: 56). Take, for example, evidence suggesting that a woman sitting at the head of a table is often less likely to be identified as the group leader than a man in the same position (Porter and Geis, 1981). As Valian (1998: 127) explains:

failing to perceive a woman at the head of the table as the leader may have no discriminatory impetus behind it. On average, a woman is less likely to be a leader of a group than a man is . . . Observers may be responding to the situation only on the basis of what is most likely, and men are more often leaders, wherever they sit. It is also important to notice, though, that regardless of the reason, a female leader sitting at the head of a table loses out compared to a male leader . . . She is less likely to obtain the automatic deference that marks of leadership confer upon men. Her position will be weakened—even if observers do not intend to undermine her authority.

It seems that the knowledge that women are less likely to occupy leadership positions makes people (men and women alike) less likely to *treat* women as

---

[3] See Arkes and Tetlock (2004) for a review. See Nosek and Hansen (2008), Jost et al. (2009), and Uhlmann et al. (2012) for responses to Arkes and Tetlock's interpretation of implicit measures as reflecting *nothing but* innocuous cultural knowledge.

leaders. In other words, merely knowing *what is statistically likely* about a group leads individuals to act in some respects as if those statistical generalizations were *normative*, as if members of that group *ought* to be treated in a certain way (e.g. as if marks of leadership confer authority to men but not women). The general upshot seems to be that merely knowing certain social facts makes individuals more likely to act in biased ways. In what follows, I will, for ease of presentation, use the phrase "knowledge of stereotypes" as an umbrella term to refer jointly to all of these potentially problematic forms of social knowledge.[4]

The dilemmists claim that findings like these put us in an inescapable moral-epistemic bind, suggesting that cases will inevitably arise in which social categories are *epistemically* relevant but *ethically* objectionable. On one side of the dilemma, we have a range of epistemic goods, e.g. knowing about prevalent stereotypes, others' beliefs, demographic facts, and so on. On the other side, we have a range of ethical goods, e.g. treating people fairly, with respect, as individuals, and so on. Pursuing the former seems to compromise the latter. As Gendler (2011: 57) writes: "Living in a society structured by race appears to make it impossible to be both rational and equitable."

Roughly, the dilemmists offer three ways in which we might respond to these findings, all of which come at a price:

We can use the categories unreflectively, and wind up with a bunch of bad stereotype-concordant inferences, judgments, attitudes, etc. Alternatively, we can use the categories, but spend a bunch of cognitive resources suppressing or immediately excising the bad stereotype-concordant inferences, judgments, attitudes, etc. Finally, we can avoid using the categories, and fail to code up the base rate information.   (Egan, 2011: 72)

In other words, the possible responses seem to be:

(STATUS QUO)   To continue unreflectively using stereotypes, or perhaps even come to reflectively endorse their content;
(SUPPRESSION)   To try to actively suppress the expression of our stereotypical thoughts and impulses;
(IGNORANCE)   To aim to ignore or forget the stereotypes altogether.[5]

I assume that STATUS QUO does not strike my readers as an attractive option. It amounts to waving the white flag in the fight against prejudice. The drawbacks of

---

[4] I speak of "knowledge," rather than mere "awareness," of stereotypes, because epistemic justification is at issue. There is no moral-epistemic dilemma if the beliefs in question are false or unjustified. I ignore complications regarding whether true justified belief counts as knowledge.

[5] They describe the dilemma and the three possible responses in slightly different ways at different times (Gendler, 2008: 578; 2011: 37–8, 57; Egan, 2011: 72–3). Egan notes that these responses need not be mutually exclusive.

SUPPRESSION, according to the dilemmists, are that continually monitoring and suppressing our stereotypical thoughts threatens to make us so cognitively exhausted that we become less effective in reaching our other epistemic aims. It might even be self-defeating.[6] By trying to become ethically better we might become epistemically worse. But what about IGNORANCE? Suppose that we could erase knowledge of stereotypes from our minds, and by doing so, eliminate all the implicitly biased behaviors that harm ourselves and others. Our automatic, intuitive responses would be perfectly aligned with our reflective commitments. Egalitarian sunshine of the spotless mind. What would be the downside?

The dilemmists suggest that this option would also be epistemically suboptimal. We would lose out on information; namely, knowledge of what others believe, of demographic regularities, and so on (Gendler, 2011: 56). By losing this information we suffer an epistemic cost. Ultimately, the dilemmists seem to think that this cost is worth bearing, and that we should embrace some combination of SUPPRESSION and IGNORANCE.[7] But in what sense is IGNORANCE an epistemic cost? For that matter, what is it to *be* an epistemic cost? Answering this requires taking a stand on some broader issues in epistemology, which I do in Section 3. I then propose, in Section 4, that the dilemmists have either misdescribed IGNORANCE, insofar as we need not forget about stereotypes altogether in order to prevent their pernicious influence on behavior, or that they have failed to countenance a fourth option; namely, of *regulating* the cognitive accessibility of stereotypes, such that we can recall them when they are relevant and ignore them when not.

3 The Aims of Knowledge

Our epistemic aim is not to know *everything*.[8] Perhaps this is contentious, but it does not seem true that we have an omnipresent epistemic goal to achieve

---

[6] As when trying not to think about a white bear makes you think about a white bear. See Follenfant and Ric (2010), Huebner (2009), and Madva (2012: 103–4, 158–65) for discussion of several ways that efforts to resist stereotype-consistent thoughts and behaviors can backfire.

[7] Egan (2011: 78). Much of my concern here has to do with the claim that these responses are inherently epistemically costly. I doubt the dilemmists and I would disagree much over which practical strategies to pursue in order to make our behavior more aligned with our ethical aims, but rather over whether pursuing these strategies would force us to compromise our epistemic aims. I have benefited greatly from reading a longer, unpublished manuscript of Gendler (2011), in which she considers some of these ethically valuable but (putatively) epistemically costly strategies in greater depth.

[8] Many of my epistemological claims in what follows are indebted to Kim's (2012, 2014) account of goal-dependent, "all-else-neglected" rationality. Kim argues that the ideal of "all-things-considered"

universal knowledge of all the facts there are. This is true neither of our everyday epistemic practices nor of our scientific inquiries (nor of our theories of the theory of knowledge).

Given that we are not out to know it all, the sheer loss of information is not, just as such, an epistemically bad turn of events. There are lots of facts we simply do not care about, such as whether the number of oxygen atoms in the room is even or odd. Doubtless there are many facts out there that we do not care about but *should*.[9] I should invest more effort than I do in determining how big my carbon footprint is and what I can do to reduce it. At the same time, however, there are lots of facts we *do* care about but should not. I know plenty of facts that I could do just as well without. Once upon a time it seemed important to memorize all the lyrics to the opening theme song of *The Fresh Prince of Bel-Air*, but I would gladly trade in that knowledge now to free up mental space for something else. How many hours did I spend learning to write in cursive as a child, only for it to become an almost perfectly useless skill as an adult? Whether bits of knowledge like these are worth seeking or keeping is not a matter of their intrinsic value, but of their value relative to some further aim. I think that memorizing that theme song seemed important to me because I hoped it would impress my friends, but knowing the lyrics is of little use to me now (except at retro or campy dance parties).

To consider examples nearer to the topic at hand, take our basic cognitive dispositions to sort people into categories. From the beginnings of infancy, we start making distinctions between in-groups and out-groups, and forming specific expectations about how respective members of these groups will behave (Valian, 1998; Leslie, forthcoming). These cognitive dispositions are surely indispensable, enabling us to deal with the overwhelming complexity of information in the world as well as the underwhelming poverty of information that confronts us at any given moment. We could not accomplish much of anything without them; they serve some pretty fundamental aims. Nevertheless, to grant that these cognitive dispositions are indispensable *on the whole* is not to say that their exercise on any particular occasion is useful or accurate. While there are plenty of

rationality (of taking *everything* into account) is ultimately incoherent. In some respects, I am trying to apply his general theory of rationality to the particular case of knowledge of stereotypes.

[9] Sometimes our ignorance reflects a motivated and systematic avoidance of information. See Mills' (1997: 18) discussion of the "epistemology of ignorance, a particular pattern of localized and global cognitive dysfunctions (which are psychologically and socially functional), producing the ironic outcome that whites will in general be unable to understand the world they themselves have made." I consider the moral culpability that individuals might bear for subtle acts of selective attention and ignorance elsewhere (Madva, 2012: ch. 3).

useful categories and regularities that we pick up on, there are plenty of useless ones to which we devote undue attention and plenty of useful ones that we miss altogether.

Consider the relative difficulty people have in recognizing the faces of out-group members, which Gendler (2011) discusses at length. One component of this out-group recognition deficit seems to be that participants fail to notice individuating facial features and devote undue attention to others' out-group status. This recognition deficit occurs for faces from different races as well as from different *classes*: middle-class white participants have a harder time recognizing faces seen in "impoverished contexts" than in "wealthy contexts" (Shriver et al., 2008). They hone in on the poverty of the social context (which is, given the task at hand, irrelevant) at the expense of noticing the idiosyncratic facial features that would enable recognition later.

Recent evidence suggests that as soon as children begin to appreciate these group differences, they also begin to invest them with spurious significance, e.g. by implicitly *preferring* in-groups over out-groups, and high-status social groups over low (Dunham et al., 2013). Anti-out-group biases begin to form during the first months of infancy (Ziv and Banaji, 2012) and remain surprisingly stable through adulthood. Yet while it is relatively easy to imagine how a default disposition to, say, prefer the company of the rich and powerful might be adaptive from an evolutionary perspective (e.g. because hangers-on could share in their abundant resources), such a disposition is pretty clearly bogus from a normative perspective (be it epistemic or ethical). Many in-group preferences form during childhood, but decades of research also suggest that assigning adults into patently arbitrary groups can rapidly generate in-group preferences as well (Ashburn-Nardo et al., 2001).

Perhaps the most notorious and egregious examples of investing social categories with undue epistemic significance are the so-called "fundamental" and "ultimate" attribution errors, both of which involve systematic asymmetries in the beliefs we tend to form about causes of behavior. We are more likely to seek out personality-based explanations—and ignore situational factors—when we try to understand the bad behavior and mistakes made by others (the fundamental error; Jones and Nisbett, 1971), especially when they are out-group members (the ultimate error! Pettigrew, 1979), but exhibit the reverse tendency when it comes to explaining the mistakes made by us and our affiliates. For example, a white manager might assume that a black employee's lateness is due to laziness, while his white comanager's lateness is due to unforeseeable traffic delays caused by a car accident.

Such cases of excessive attention to certain categories, and inattention to others (which are perhaps more predictive and relevant), comprise but a few examples of a more general feature of our epistemic state: that we know and attend to lots of things we should not, and do not know and ignore lots of things we should. There are lots of facts that we would do just as well to forget or ignore because our preoccupation with them prevents us from seeking out and remembering information more relevant to our ends. This is not to assume that it is always straightforward to determine which information is relevant for which aims, but the difficulty of figuring out what is relevant cuts both ways. It is not as if we should just think about as much as we can, as the phrase "all things considered" suggests. Considering as much as we can because anything could be relevant is obviously going to be self-defeating. Considering patently irrelevant information, e.g. considering whether Pluto should be counted as a planet while deciding whether to turn left or right at a busy intersection, is, on its face, a bad epistemic practice, not just a gratuitous one. Sometimes it is worthwhile to err on the side of considering too much rather than too little, but doing so is nevertheless *to err*, to make (or increase the risk of making) a certain sort of mistake. It is to consider something that is "beside the point" or "neither here nor there," i.e. irrelevant to the truth of the proposition in question.

I grant that, at the level of scientific and communal pursuits, it might very often be preferable to err on the side of taking in too much information rather than too little. (Bring on Big Data!) Something that we take to be irrelevant now might turn out to be important down the line. Perhaps, then, we should make an extra effort to be inclusive in how many hypotheses we entertain, how much data we gather, and so on, but it obviously does not follow that we ought to take "every" hypothesis seriously, gather "all" possible data on a hypothesis, or treat everything that seems irrelevant as if it were relevant (if such norms even make sense). The history of science is replete with examples of our propensity to fixate on less predictive categories and overlook more relevant ones. We can safely say that the extensive efforts once devoted to finding a Philosopher's Stone that would turn lead into gold were wrongheaded. Such efforts were less guided by any sort of rational, inductive considerations than by fantasies of wealth and power.[10] More recently, it is absurd how much empirical attention is devoted to uncovering potential evolutionary, biological, or neuroscientific explanations for the under-representation of women in certain fields, e.g. the current hypothesis that pre-natal hormone exposure predisposes girls to be innately less *interested* in quantitative subjects than boys (Jordan-Young, 2010). Scientists are earnestly

---

[10] This is, of course, not to indict alchemy *in general*, the history of which is intricately tied to chemistry and medicine (Principe, 2012), but only to find fault with one of its notoriously misguided pursuits.

investigating the possibility that prenatal testosterone makes boys *like mathematics more* than girls (a possibility that is ostensibly more "PC" than the hotly debated proposal that testosterone makes boys *better* at mathematics). While the effects of prenatal hormone exposure on interest in mathematics is an empirical question like any other, the extensive efforts devoted to uncovering such gender differences seem misplaced, especially given the overwhelmingly credible, empirically well-supported alternative explanations in terms of social and institutional factors. It is epistemically unwarranted to devote *so much* attention to these hypotheses. Indeed, this is plausibly a case of attribution errors writ large, in that researchers are searching for explanations in terms of enduring features of our gendered brains instead of our situations.[11]

The upshot is that the loss (and the acquisition) of information is not epistemically good or bad in itself, but only so relative to some more particular aims or values. Is it an epistemic deficiency not to know the names of foreign countries and their leaders? If you want to be a public official, definitely yes. If you just want to run a chain of pizza restaurants, perhaps no. Maybe there are *some* things worth knowing for their own sake, without qualification, such as the Form of the Good envisioned by Plato. But stereotypes do not fall into that category.

4 The Right Thought at the Wrong Time?

Stereotypes might seem to be just the sorts of items we would be eager to forget. Insofar as they are often false or misleading, who needs them? Unfortunately, matters are not so simple. For one thing, it is not obvious that stereotypes are generally false (although they may still often be misleading), as in Valian's discussion of how individuals tend not to assume that a woman at the head of the table is a leader.[12] We can, however, bracket questions regarding their

---

[11] Note also that Gendler and Egan frame the moral-epistemic dilemma in terms of a single individual's cognitive limitations, not in terms of the communal advancement of scientific knowledge. The dilemma arises on the assumption that an individual can notice and track only a sharply circumscribed number and range of properties, and must therefore glom onto those properties that give her the most inductive bang for her cognitive buck. By contrast, communal pursuits of knowledge are not so sharply constrained in this way. This asymmetry between individual and communal epistemic constraints explains why scientific endeavors can afford, and even benefit from, taking in ostensibly irrelevant information, while it is typically epistemically perilous for individuals to do the same.

[12] See Beeghly (2013) for further discussion. Another common error is to radically over- or underestimate the relevant probabilities (e.g. sharks are more likely to attack people than are other creatures of the sea, but radically less likely to do so than most people believe). I believe the sort of hyperaccessibility I discuss here plays a major role in distorting estimations of probability, but I will not take up that issue here.

accuracy, because it is clearly important for individuals with egalitarian aims to know about stereotypes *at least insofar* as such knowledge enables them to recognize cases when someone suffers by virtue of being perceived in a stereotypical light.[13] For example, suppose a job candidate is not hired because the employer judged, on the basis of an objectionable stereotype, that people from the job candidate's race or gender are ill-qualified for the job. We lose the ability to identify the wrong that was done if we cannot make reference to the stereotype.

Stereotypes are worth knowing, then, not for their own sake but for specific purposes. Does the importance of retaining our knowledge of stereotypes rule out an option like IGNORANCE? It does insofar as we ought not forget about stereotypes *altogether*, but maybe we do not really need to. We simply need to be able to think about the stereotypes for certain purposes and in certain contexts, and not in others. We go epistemically astray insofar as our knowledge of stereotypes is *accessed* or *activated* in the wrong contexts and for the wrong ends.

The dilemma with which we began, however, was ethical as well as epistemic. Knowledge of stereotypes seems to make us act out of step with our considered ethical commitments. However, a second look at the data suggests that *mere possession* of knowledge of stereotypes does not just as such tend to lead to implicitly biased behavior—any more than mere possession of knowledge of the *falsity* of stereotypes tends to lead to implicitly *unbiased* behavior. Typically, studies that find relationships between implicit bias and social knowledge are about *highly accessible* knowledge of *culturally prevalent* stereotypes (Arkes and Tetlock, 2004). The problem is not mere social knowledge, but rather *hyperactive* social knowledge, agitating our minds in moments when it ought to keep silent. The normative costs of social knowledge arise primarily insofar as that knowledge becomes too accessible. We ought to access the stereotypes when they are relevant, and ignore them when not. I take the operative "ought" here to be both epistemic and ethical. We should, if possible, embrace the response of giving up some measure of cognitive access to our social knowledge. Clearly, this does not actually amount to returning to a state of total ignorance about social stereotypes. The aim is not to unlearn what we know, and thereby surrender (potentially valuable) knowledge. We want to reduce the accessibility of knowledge of stereotypes, such that it is not the first thing that comes to mind, but not lose access to it altogether. It seems, then, that the dilemmists have mischaracterized IGNORANCE (and perhaps SUPPRESSION as well, as some of the evidence I introduce in Section 6 suggests). Alternatively, it might be more accurate to conclude that

---

[13] There will be many cases when it is important to know about stereotypes. This case is among the least objectionable.

the list of three possible responses offered by the dilemmists is incomplete, and I am recommending a fourth option.[14] While the dilemmists refer to accessibility at several points (Gendler, 2011: 37; Egan, 2011: 74), they seem not to appreciate the possibility of *regulating* the accessibility of our social knowledge in order to have that information available when and only when we need it.

So how might this be possible? By way of suggesting how it is, I say something, first, about how this sort of cognitive access is understood in psychology (Section 5), and second, about what we as individuals can do to *change* the accessibility of our knowledge—in particular, our knowledge of stereotypes and other problematic social information (Section 6).

5 Primer on Accessibility

A substantial body of research shows that our decisions and actions are often swayed by the bits of knowledge that are most "accessible." In some sense, some ideas come to mind more "readily" or "easily" than others. For example, I know that in the United States, individuals of Asian descent are stereotyped to excel in mathematics. I also know that this stereotype is less prevalent in Canada.[15] Although I have not taken a test measuring my implicit associations between Asians and mathematical ability, I should assume that I am like most Americans (including Asian Americans) and that the American stereotypes of Asians are more accessible to me than the Canadian ones; I have been repeatedly exposed to the former and not the latter. (Nor do I predict that my biases would shift were I to cross the border from Vermont to Quebec.) Knowledge of Asian–mathematics stereotypes has been so pounded into our heads as to become *chronically accessible*. It comes too often and too easily to mind; the mere perception of a cue related to Asians or mathematics might activate it (although we might not be fully aware that such a stereotype has been activated, or of how it influences our thoughts and behaviors).

---

[14] Thanks to Erin Beeghly and Alice Crary, who separately urged this reformulation.

[15] I learned this from a study on the accessibility of mathematics-aptitude stereotypes for women of Asian descent. Shih et al. (1999) found that Asian American female undergraduates whose "Asian identity" had surreptitiously been made salient performed better on a mathematics test than those whose "Female identity" had been made salient and those who received no priming. Researchers ran the same study with high school students in Vancouver, Canada, and found that in this case activating an Asian identity *degraded* mathematical performance. The mathematics-aptitude stereotype may be less prevalent in Vancouver because "the Asian community is largely recently immigrated" (82). Another possible explanation, mentioned by an anonymous referee, is the high proportion of individuals of Asian heritage in Vancouver. A recent estimate suggested that 43% of people living in Vancouver's metropolitan area are of Asian descent (Todd 2014).

Over the years we learn many stereotypes that do not stick in the same way. I was once told that black people think that "white people smell like wet dogs when they come out of the rain." Hearing this certainly made an impression, but I can safely say that I have never tested it or modified my automatic dispositions (such as they are) to sniff or avert my nose around members of different races who have just come out of the rain, nor to act insecurely around non-white people after I myself have just come out of the rain. Aside from being the first example that comes to mind when I try to think of a silly stereotype, this item of knowledge is *not* chronically accessible.

Knowledge can also be *temporarily* or *transiently accessible*. Suppose that upon arrival in Montreal, a number of locals, including a guide at the tourism information desk, offer me this inside tip: "You know, in Montreal, the elderly are exceptionally good drivers. You should always try to hail taxis driven by very old people while you're here." I might briefly, for the next fifteen minutes or so, show some increased disposition to look favorably upon cab drivers of advanced years, but it is unlikely that my newfound knowledge (of what the Montréalais believe of the elderly) would have any enduring effect on my behavior. I might recall the information from time to time, but it would not remain close to the mental surface. Given my extensive socialization into a world where the elderly are routinely depicted as bad drivers, this newfound knowledge would exert little influence on my day-to-day dealings. Similarly, if you imagine yourself in a post-apocalyptic world in which all the flowers are poisoned with radiation and the insects are the only healthy things to eat, your typical preference for roses over roaches will briefly be reversed.[16] You will, on some measures, temporarily show an implicit preference for insects over flowers. But this sort of imaginative exercise will not transform you into a bug lover if you were not one already; the thoughts and feelings that come most readily to mind when you think of insects will, in a few days at the most, be much as they were before. In cases like these, a bit of knowledge is just transiently accessible, briefly rendered salient by virtue of some anecdote or exemplar.

It is fair to wonder, however, what this talk of accessibility really *means*. The natural ways of explaining it are metaphorical. Something is accessible, e.g. if it is hovering "in the back of your mind." Psychological definitions of accessibility are

---

[16] See Foroni and Mayr (2005), although Han et al. (2010) found that, while these transient effects occur for the standard IAT that uses words such as "pleasant/unpleasant," they do not occur for the "personalized" IAT that uses the words "I like/I don't like." Han et al. argue that the standard IAT often measures mere "extrapersonal associations" (roughly akin to mere knowledge of prevalent stereotypes believed by others), whereas others (Nosek and Hansen, 2008) take the grammatical sentences of the personalized IAT to induce greater self-regulation.

not entirely perspicuous either. Morewedge and Kahneman (2010: 435) define accessibility as "the ease with which a particular unit of information is activated or can be retrieved from memory." I have some intuitive sense of what they are talking about, but the notion of "ease of access" is rather obscure. One thing this definition brings out is that accessibility is intimately tied to the notion of *knowledge activation*. Eitam and Higgins (2010: 951) define accessibility and activation reciprocally:

When initially conceived, accessibility referred to the ease with which a mental representation *could* be activated by external stimulation, and activation meant that a representation *has* been accessed for use...In other words, a mental representation's accessibility referred to the amount of external stimulation needed for it to shift from a latent state (available in the mind but currently inactive) to an active one (involved in current thought and action).

Again, I more or less know what they mean, but these definitions are just cycling through synonyms: it is accessible in the sense that it is available; available in the sense that it is easily retrieved; easily retrieved in the sense that it is easily activated.

Reflecting on how accessibility is measured goes some way toward illuminating what it is. In effect, a bit of knowledge is said to be more accessible to the extent that an individual is more likely to recall it upon request, or to recall it faster. (Thus, the moral-epistemic dilemma arises in part because stereotypes are too likely and too quick to reach the mental surface.) Accessibility is then often defined computationally as "the probability of retrieval."[17] "Ease" of retrieval is thereby replaced with "probability." This definition, however, still invokes "retrieval," which is effectively synonymous with "access" (as if to say, "retrieve-ability refers to the probability of retrieval"). Terms like "retrieval" do little more than relabel commonsense notions of *remembering* in terms of a storage-space metaphor.[18] The underlying psychological constructs and

---

[17] See Bahrick (1971). Thanks to Edouard Machery for emphasizing this.
[18] Fine-grained distinctions between these terms (accessibility, availability, activation, retrieval, recall) are sometimes made, but I ignore them here. Another concern is that it is completely non-obvious why *probability* and *speed* of recall should be lumped together as two measures of a single construct, accessibility. An anonymous referee suggested that this problem could be addressed by defining accessibility in terms of the *cues* that bring a piece of information to mind. The referee rightly emphasizes the importance of cues, e.g. one person might only (be likely to) remember *p* given a specific prompt, whereas another might (be likely to) remember *p* across a broad range of cues. Perhaps, then, we should understand accessibility as a triadic relation between a person, a proposition, and a cue (or set of cues). However, this point does not help to solve the problems noted here, e.g. why to lump together probability and speed of recall. For each triad, we can ask how likely a subject *S* is to encounter cue *c*, how likely *S* is to remember *p* given *c*, how quickly *S* will remember *p* given *c*, and so on. All of these come apart. *S* might be extremely reliable at remembering *p* across a

operations remain murky. For now, perhaps the best way to understand accessibility is to understand how to *change* it.

6 The Malleability of Accessibility: Concrete Strategies

Reducing the accessibility of our knowledge only constitutes a normative cost, whether epistemic or ethical, if we cannot access that knowledge when we need it. If we can intervene to influence the accessibility of our knowledge in the right way, we can mutually satisfy (or at least come significantly closer to mutually satisfying) our epistemic as well as ethical aims. Can we do this?

It is not just wishful thinking to envision lining up the relative accessibility of our knowledge with our ethical aims. There is a significant tradition of research suggesting that accessibility is often highly goal-dependent.[19] What most readily comes to mind is often a function of what is most relevant to our aims. Some of the most important aims in this regard are those of being fair and egalitarian, as I explain later in this section. But there are surprising ways in which other aims can help us reduce the accessibility of stereotypes as well.

For example, one way to block the activation of stereotypical thoughts seems to be to adopt the aim of being *creative*. Stereotypical thinking is *typical* thinking; it is unoriginal. Agents who are motivated to think creatively will automatically ignore stereotypical associations. In Sassenberg and Moskowitz (2005), some participants were put in a "creative mindset" by being asked to recall a few occasions in which they had been creative. Participants next performed a lexical decision task, which required them to identify as fast as possible whether letters on a computer screen made up a real word or not. They saw either a black or

broad range of cues, but comparatively slow to do so, e.g. *S* is a champion at leisurely solving crossword puzzles but a miserable failure at time-sensitive memory tasks, such as the quiz show *Jeopardy!*. There are many facts which I have no chance of recalling except when given a highly specific cue, but which, given that cue, I may recall extremely quickly, e.g. I may (instantly) remember the thirtieth word of a song lyric only when I hear the recording of the song leading up to it. For many songs, the probability that I will remember the next line may be extremely low, but if I do remember it at all, I will remember it quickly. And so on.

[19] See Kunda and Spencer's (2003) goal-dependent theory of stereotype activation, which they define as "the extent to which a stereotype is accessible in one's mind" (522). For reviews, see Moskowitz (2010) and Uhlmann et al. (2010). Eitam and Higgins (2010) seek to explain accessibility *entirely* in terms of the "motivational relevance" of a bit of knowledge to an agent, and even recommend replacing the term "accessibility" with "relevance" (e.g. distinguishing "chronic" from "transient" relevance: 960). Given its obscurity, abandoning the term "accessibility" might be wise, but is "relevance" an obvious improvement? That equally fraught term/concept threatens to muddle description with prescription, i.e. the distinction between what agents happen to take to be relevant and what actually (as a normative matter) *is* relevant. I use the term "relevance" here exclusively in the normative sense.

white male face immediately followed by a nonsense word, a stereotype-consistent word, or a stereotype-irrelevant word. For example, an image of a black face followed by the word "rhythmic" would be a stereotype-consistent pairing. Those who had been primed to be creative were significantly slower to identify stereotype-consistent words than stereotype-irrelevant words, whereas participants in other conditions exhibited the reverse tendency. The stereotypical associations were irrelevant to the task of distinguishing words from non-words, and the goal of being creative enabled participants to ignore that irrelevant but otherwise chronically accessible knowledge. Being in a creative mindset prevented the stereotypes from being the first thoughts to come to mind.[20] Research on inducing a creative mindset is especially striking because there is no evidence that the manipulation saps cognitive resources or leads to the problematic "rebound" effects associated with the conscious or unconscious monitoring of unwanted thoughts (Sassenberg et al., 2004). As Sassenberg and Moskowitz (2005: 507) explain, "being primed with creativity allows for generating original ideas because one is able to think differently without the unwanted side effects of suppressing thoughts triggered by the intention to suppress them." The evidence suggests that a creative mindset really does reduce the accessibility of stereotypes, rather than simply motivating participants to refrain from applying stereotypes after they come to mind.

In that case, the goal to be creative was more or less unwittingly activated. Are there conscious, intentional strategies for influencing accessibility? This may be exactly the effect of implementation intentions, which are if–then plans that link a specific cue to a specific response, such as: "If I feel a craving for cigarettes, then I will chew gum!" Concrete plans specifying when, where, and how an action will be performed are far more effective than unspecific plans, such as: "I should cut down on smoking!" Webb and Sheeran (2008) argue that these if–then plans work in part by making the specified cue more accessible. Participants who formed an if–then plan to retrieve a coupon after the experiment exhibited heightened access to the "if" components of the plan on a lexical decision task like the one just described. They were also almost twice as likely to follow through

---

[20] This study may point to certain *aesthetic* implications of research on implicit cognition. Recommending that we should resist relying on stereotypes in art might ring in some ears as advocating the oppression of artistic creativity. But studies like this suggest that stereotypes are precisely *not* creative. Of course, creativity is a complex phenomenon. For example, an artist—or a comedian (Anderson, 2012b)—can appeal to a stereotype in order to subvert it. My point is simply that research on social cognition does not bespeak any fundamental opposition between our aesthetic and ethical aims (any more than it does between our epistemic and ethical aims). Reducing the accessibility of stereotypes might even *improve* creativity by preventing us from falling back on hackneyed depictions of members of social groups.

on retrieving the coupon than were participants who did not form an if–then plan. In contexts where we know we are wont to attend to the wrong categories, we can form if–then plans to guide our attention to the right ones.

The influence of implementation intentions on "shooter bias" is a case in point. Participants must press a button labeled "shoot" when they see an image of a person holding a gun, and "don't shoot" when they see a person holding a cell phone. Many participants, including African Americans, are faster and more likely to "shoot" unarmed blacks than unarmed whites. Mendoza et al. (2010) found that participants' shooter bias was significantly reduced after they formed intentions, such as: "If I see a gun, then I will shoot!" This intention plausibly makes the relevant cue (the gun) more accessible, and makes the irrelevant cues (such as the race of the person holding it) less accessible. In fact, there is no *more* relevant cue than the gun in this context. Participants are directing their attention to the precise property required by the task, so, given the dilemmists' assumption that our cognitive finitude requires us to focus on just a few features, this strategy incurs pure epistemic benefit with no cost. Stewart and Payne (2008) found that participants who formed the intention to think the word "safe" when they saw a black face also showed significantly less implicit racial bias. Thinking counter-stereotypical thoughts seems to reduce the accessibility of stereotypical ones.

Insofar as we already know the content of many stereotypes, and we are learning more and more about the contexts in which stereotypes do harm, then we can formulate if–then plans that pick out those contexts and specify responses. In the case of shooter bias, researchers identified a context in which racial stereotypes are highly accessible, and specified responses that counteract the stereotype. Generally speaking, in cases where stereotypes are apt to do harm, the right if–then plans might have a structure roughly along the lines of: "If I perceive a member of group G in context C (acting in way W, or being treated in way Y), then I will perform action A!" During Q&A after a lecture in December 2011, Louise Antony proposed that a person concerned to avoid overinterrupting women could form the plan: "If she's talking, then I won't!"

Many of these plans will be *other-directed*, in that they regard how we treat others, but we can also form *self-directed* plans to arm ourselves against potentially harmful environmental cues and stereotype threat. For example, a person stereotyped to underperform in mathematics can block the negative effects of stereotype threat by forming the plan: "And if I start a new problem, then I will tell myself: I can solve it!" Bayer and Gollwitzer (2007) found that participants who rehearsed this plan solved significantly more problems on a test of logical reasoning than those who rehearsed other plans, such as: "And I will tell myself: I can solve these problems!"

I mentioned that the accessibility of knowledge is highly goal-dependent, but I have not discussed the goals most relevant to reducing the accessibility of stereotypes: namely, the aims to be fair and unbiased. There is substantial evidence that these aims are effective as well, whether they are held chronically or transiently (Moskowitz, 2010). The goal to be unprejudiced can be induced, for example, by having participants contemplate a time when they *failed* to live up to this ideal. Some agents seem to have chronic egalitarian goals that are automatically activated when they find themselves in a situation in which they or others might be inclined to act in a biased way. Perhaps they have internalized the plan, "If I see injustice, then I will fight it!"

Figuring out precisely which if–then plans to adopt is a substantive project, but I see no reason to be pessimistic about taking that project pretty far. For example, perhaps one appropriate plan might be: "If I see a woman at the head of the table, then I will treat her like a leader!" Then again, perhaps the plan ought to refer generically to a *person* at the head of the table, which could help reduce the influence of other sorts of biases, e.g. regarding race, class, and disability.[21] However, if men are generally more likely to be seated at the heads of tables, then referring generically to a person might simply reinforce our initial disposition to assume men are leaders. I am skeptical that the "person" formulation would incur such unforeseen, undesirable consequences, but it is an open empirical matter. My broader point is that, like all heuristics and rules of thumb, no simple if–then plan (or collection of such plans) will provide a universally accurate guide to true belief or right action. Implementation intentions are not a magical cure-all for discrimination. Nor will they empower us to transcend human finitude and fallibility. Whichever plans we identify as most effective for advancing our aims, there will always be tradeoffs, with certain plans working better in certain contexts and for certain purposes but not others.

As far as I can tell, however, these tradeoffs need not be between our ethical and epistemic aims. The initial dilemma was that knowledge of stereotypes led to unethical behavior, and that ethical improvement would incur epistemic costs. Supposing that implementation intentions lead to ethical improvement, do they bring the costs of SUPPRESSION and IGNORANCE in tow?

Employing these if–then plans constitutes a *kind* of self-control, but they do not sap our limited cognitive resources. Implementing them is not a matter of engaging in SUPPRESSION—or, to the extent that they do involve SUPPRESSION, then that option need not be as epistemically costly as the dilemmists suggest. Rehearsing them is easy and, once formed, putting them into action often

---

[21] Thanks to Jenny Saul for helping me think through this example.

requires little or no additional effort. Gollwitzer and Sheeran (2006) go so far as to call them "instant habits." Of course, there will be limitations to how radically an if–then plan can reconfigure our ingrained dispositions, but there is no question that these plans provide a powerful way to influence the accessibility of our knowledge. Another way to reduce the accessibility of stereotypes is to *practice*, e.g. repeatedly affirming counterstereotypes. For example, repeatedly pressing a button labeled "YES" in response to counterstereotypical stimuli, such as a black face paired with the word "friendly," significantly reduces stereotype accessibility (Kawakami et al., 2000).

Moreover, these interventions do not cause participants to completely forget about stereotypes. It is implausible that a person with the right retraining, mindset, or if–then plan would somehow cease to know the contents of prevalent stereotypes. She would not suddenly profess ignorance about stereotypes regarding, say, Asians and mathematical aptitude. She might, however, have a harder time coming up with a list of such stereotypes out of the blue.[22] This is, I suggest, essentially what we are pursuing in trying to line up the accessibility of our knowledge with our ethical aim of treating others fairly.

I by no means intend to suggest that implementing these and other strategies will swiftly transport us to an ideal state of moral-epistemic virtue where we can access our knowledge at all and only the right times and where all our impulses and habits will be effortlessly unprejudiced. Rehearsing these if–then plans and training procedures are, I submit, the anti-prejudicial equivalent of using flash-cards to memorize a new vocabulary. The expectation is not that adopting these cue-behavior rules of thumb will transform us into ethically and epistemically ideal agents, any more than memorizing a set of rules and words will transform an individual into a fluent speaker of a second language.[23] Nevertheless, these if–then plans enable us to make meaningful progress in that direction, towards lining up our accessible social knowledge with our considered aim of being egalitarian—without incurring epistemic costs. We can significantly close the distance between our current sorry state and our normative ideals, and, in closing this distance, we need not make a forced choice between pursuing ethical and epistemic aims.

---

[22] I doubt this has been tested, but I predict that such debiased participants would be able to check off a list of stereotypes put in front of them, but be less able to generate an extensive list of such stereotypes without prompting. Some evidence suggests, however, that open-ended list-generating is an unreliable indicator of stereotype knowledge and accessibility (Nosek and Hansen, 2008).

[23] For more on the analogy between egalitarian agency and linguistic fluency, see my (2012: ch. 4).

7 Tragic Cases?

In Section 6 I emphasized cases, such as the influence of a creativity mindset, where stereotypes are irrelevant. What happens when stereotypes *are* relevant to the task at hand? Not to trivialize the issue, but that is when we should access them. The dilemmists, however, seem to have cases in mind where stereotypes are, specifically, epistemically relevant but ethically objectionable.

A prominent case that Gendler and Egan discuss is Tetlock et al.'s (2000) study on "forbidden base rates." Participants were asked to imagine an executive setting the premiums on home insurance in various neighborhoods. All participants were told that some of the neighborhoods were higher risk than the others. Some participants were also told that the high-risk neighborhoods were predominantly black, while others received no information about race. Here is the entire scenario participants read in the race-relevant condition:

Dave Johnson is an insurance executive who must make a decision about whether his company will start writing home insurance policies in six different towns in his state. He classifies three of the towns as high risk: 10% of the houses suffer damage from fire or break-ins each year. It turns out that 85% of the population of these towns is Black. He classifies the other three towns as relatively low risk: less than 1% of the houses suffer fire or break-in damage each year. It turns out that 85% of the population of these towns is White.   (Tetlock et al., 2000: 860–1)

Participants who were not given any race-related information tended to say that the executive should charge a higher insurance premium for the houses in the high-risk neighborhoods, but those given the information about race insisted that he should charge the same premium for all (this was especially true for politically liberal participants). Gendler (2011: 55) refers to this as "a kind of epistemic self-censorship on non-epistemic grounds." Tetlock et al. (2000: 853) suggest that these "people are striving to achieve neither epistemic nor utilitarian goals," and specifically compare this case to the classic base-rate neglect literature (854).

However, it is not clear why we should think of this as a dilemma between epistemic and non-epistemic (moral) requirements. In fact, we do not know which requirements are at issue, because we do not know which problem the participants took themselves to be solving. We do not know what their *aims* were. The participants were not, for example, told in advance that they should make the decision in the best economic interests of the insurance executive. All they were told was that "the research goal was to explore how people make judgments" (860). Plausibly, the participants who just read about high-risk neighborhoods and insurance premiums, without any reference to race, thought the task *was* just how to maximize profits, or something similar. But once race was introduced, they may very well have thought the task was how best to avoid being prejudiced, or even how to compensate for systemic racial injustice! This is quite plausible in light of how *overt* the reference to race was. Even Tetlock et al. explain that

liberals did not indiscriminately embrace any justification for not using the base rates. Liberals viewed the pragmatic or empirical grounds offered for dismissing the base rates as implausible. They were not more inclined to challenge the statistics or to argue that the best long-term profit-maximizing strategy is to charge the same price. Instead, liberals invoked a straightforward moral defense against policies that harmed the already disadvantaged.   (863–4)

Relative to the aim of preventing racial injustice, there is nothing epistemically deficient about discounting the background information about high-risk neighborhoods. Participants may have been explicitly *counting* that information as part of the justification for charging the same premiums, because this policy would prevent the exacerbation of injustice. To be clear, I am not proposing that some participants adopted the "epistemic" aim of maximizing profits while others adopted the "ethical" aim of redressing injustice. Both groups had "epistemic" aims in the sense that they were trying to form true justified beliefs (about, respectively, how to make money and how to avoid placing additional burdens on those already disadvantaged). The real test would be if participants who had categorically adopted the goal of maximizing profits still overlooked this information when race was introduced.

If I am right about the Tetlock study, then its failure to constitute a genuine moral-epistemic dilemma is telling. Such cases might be harder to find than one might think. What seemed like a moral-epistemic dilemma might be no dilemma at all, because a *morally tinged aim sets the epistemic agenda*. There is nothing inherently wrong with the epistemic agenda being set by a moral aim; there has got to be some aim or other, and it might as well be a moral one. Consider, for example, the long tradition of research seeking to identify factors that predict death-sentencing. Recently, Eberhardt and colleagues (2006) found that death-sentencing "is influenced by the degree to which a Black defendant is perceived to have a stereotypically Black appearance" (383), and Williams and Holcomb (2004) found that a death sentence is significantly more likely in cases when the victim is white and female. Of course, knowledge of these predictive factors is not being pursued "for its own sake," but because we want to know whether the practice of capital punishment is *fair*. If the race and gender of defendants and victims are strong predictive factors, that gives us reason to believe that the practice is not fair. The purely epistemic project of acquiring true beliefs about the factors that predict death sentences is, in other words, set in motion by ethical aims.[24]

I believe that there can be tragic normative conflicts with no ideal solution, such as Sartre's classic example of the individual torn between fighting in the revolution and staying home to take care of his ailing mother, and I will not offer a principled argument against the possibility of similar unresolvable conflicts arising between ethics and epistemology. I submit, however, that we have not been given definitive examples of these which pit the ethical fight against prejudice against the epistemic project of identifying the properties that give us the most inductive bang for our buck. Insofar as genuine conflicts between epistemic and ethical aims do arise in lived experience, solving them may often not be a matter of choosing which to pursue and which to sacrifice, but reconsidering the merits of the aims themselves. I have assumed that we are holding our aims fixed, but they themselves can be called into question. If our ethical and epistemic aims conflict, that may signal that we are operating with the *wrong* aims. Participants who ignored the information about high-risk neighborhoods may not have been compromising their epistemic aims; they may have been (rationally) revising them.

I hope these considerations suggest that the dilemma is less of a theoretical nature, about the principled impossibility of jointly satisfying competing normative requirements, and more of a practical nature, about what we can do concretely to thwart the pernicious influence that knowledge of stereotypes has on our judgment and behavior. There is reason to be optimistic that we can improve along this ethical front, and that we can do so without compromising our epistemic aims, if only we try.

Acknowledgements

Thanks to Erin Beeghly, Michael Brownstein, Katie Gasdaglis, and Christia Mercer for extensive feedback on drafts, and to Jenny Saul both for insightful and encouraging comments on various drafts and for organizing the wonderful Implicit Bias and Philosophy Workshops at the University of Sheffield, where I first presented many of these ideas in April 2012. I benefited greatly from the questions at my talk, especially from Miranda Fricker, Edouard Machery, and Ron Mallon, and learned much from the other brilliant psychologists and philosophers I met. I am also grateful for feedback at the Wittgenstein Workshop at the New School for Social Research in September 2012, especially from Alice Crary and Janna Van Grunsven; at the Townsend Fellows seminar at UC-Berkeley, where I learned much from Michael Nylan's comments; and during my Spring 2013 seminar at Berkeley, especially from Shannon Doberneck, Jeremy Pober, and Jen White.

---

[24] See Anderson (2004) for more on the role of "value judgments" in science.

References

Anderson, E. (2004). "Uses of value judgments in science: A general argument, with lessons from a case study of feminist research on divorce." *Hypatia* 19(1): 1–24.

Anderson, E. (2010). *The Imperative of Integration*. Princeton, NJ: Princeton University Press.

Anderson, E. (2012a). "Epistemic justice as a virtue of social institutions." *Social Epistemology* 26(2): 163–73.

Anderson, L. (2012b). "Why so serious? An inquiry into racist jokes." Presentation for the Implicit Bias and Philosophy Workshop, University of Sheffield, April 2012.

Antony, L. (2002). "Quine as feminist: The radical import of naturalized epistemology." In Antony, L. M., Witt, C., and Atherton, M. (eds.)., *A Mind of One's Own, Feminist Essays on Reason and Objectivity*, 2nd edn. Boulder, CO: Westview Press: 110–53.

Arkes, H. R. and Tetlock, P. E. (2004). "Attributions of implicit prejudice, or 'would Jesse Jackson 'fail' the Implicit Association Test?'" *Psychological Inquiry* 15: 257–78.

Ashburn-Nardo, L., Voils, C.I., and Monteith, M. J. (2001). "Implicit associations as seeds of intergroup bias: How easily do they take root?" *Journal of Personality and Social Psychology* 81: 789–99.

Bahrick, H. P. (1971). "Accessibility and availability of retrieval cues in the retention of a categorized list." *Journal of Experimental Psychology* 89(1): 117–25.

Bayer, C. and Gollwitzer, P. M. (2007). "Boosting scholastic test scores by willpower: The role of implementation intentions." *Self and Identity* 6: 1–19.

Beeghly, E. (2013). *Seeing Difference: The Epistemology and Ethics of Stereotyping*. PhD dissertation, University of California, Berkeley.

Brownstein, M. S. and Madva, A. M. (2012a). "Ethical automaticity." *Philosophy of the Social Sciences* 42(1): 68–98.

Brownstein, M. S. and Madva, A. M. (2012b). "The normativity of automaticity." *Mind and Language* 27(4): 410–34.

Correll, J., Park, B., Judd, C. M., and Wittenbrink, B. (2002). "The police officer's dilemma: Using ethnicity to disambiguate potentially threatening individuals." *Journal of Personality and Social Psychology* 83(6): 1314–29.

Dunham, Y., Chen, E., and Banaji, M. R. (2013). "Two signatures of implicit intergroup attitudes: Developmental invariance and early enculturation." *Psychological Science* 24: 860–8.

Eberhardt, J. L., Davies, P. G., Purdie-Vaughns, V. J., and Johnson, S. L. (2006). "Looking deathworthy: Perceived stereotypicality of black defendants predicts capital-sentencing outcomes." *Psychological Science* 17(5): 383–6.

Egan, A. (2011). "Comments on Gendler's 'The epistemic costs of implicit bias.' *Philosophical Studies* 156: 65–79.

Eitam, B. and Higgins, E. T. (2010). "Motivation in mental accessibility: Relevance of a representation (ROAR) as a new framework." *Social and Personality Psychology Compass* 4(10): 951–67.

Follenfant, A. and Ric, F. (2010). "Behavioral rebound following stereotype suppression." *European Journal of Social Psychology* 40(5): 774–82.

Foroni, F. and Mayr, U. (2005). "The power of a story: New, automatic associations from a single reading of a short scenario." *Psychonomic Bulletin and Review* 12(1): 139–44.

Gendler, T. S. (2008). "Alief in action (and reaction)." *Mind and Language* 23(5): 552–85.

Gendler, T. S. (2011). "On the epistemic costs of implicit bias." *Philosophical Studies* 156: 33–63.

Gollwitzer, P. M. and Sheeran, P. (2006). "Implementation intentions and goal achievement: A meta-analysis of effects and processes." In Zanna, M. P. (ed.), *Advances in Experimental Social Psychology*. New York, NY: Academic Press: 69–119.

Huebner, B. (2009). "Trouble with stereotypes for Spinozan minds." *Philosophy of the Social Sciences* 39: 63–92.

Jones, E. E. and Nisbett, R. E. (1971). "The actor and the observer: Divergent perceptions of the causes of behavior." In Jones, E. E., Kanouse, D. E., Kelley, H. H., Nisbett, R. E., Valins, S., and Weiner, B. (eds.), *Attribution: Perceiving the Causes of Behavior*. Morristown, NJ: General Learning Press: 79–94.

Jordan-Young, R. (2010). *Brain Storm: The Flaws in the Science of Sex Differences*. Cambridge, MA: Harvard University Press.

Jost, J. T., Rudman, L. A., Blair, I. V., Carney, D. R., Dasgupta, N., Glaser, J., and Hardin, C. D. (2009). "The existence of implicit bias is beyond reasonable doubt: A refutation of ideological and methodological objections and executive summary of ten studies that no manager should ignore." *Research in Organizational Behavior* 29: 39–69.

Han, H. A., Czellar, S., Olson, M. A., and Fazio, R. H. (2010). Malleability of attitudes or malleability of the IAT? *Journal of Experimental Social Psychology* 46: 286–98.

Kalev, A., Dobbin, F., and Kelly, E. (2006). "Best practices or best guesses? Assessing the efficacy of corporate affirmative action and diversity policies." *American Sociological Review* 71(4): 589–617.

Kawakami, K., Dovidio, J. F., Moll, J., Hermsen, S., and Russin, A. (2000). "Just say no (to stereotyping): Effects of training in the negation of stereotypic associations on stereotype activation." *Journal of Personality and Social Psychology* 78: 871–88.

Kim, B. (2012). *The Context-Sensitivity of Rationality and Knowledge*. PhD dissertation, Columbia University, New York.

Kim, B. (2014). "The locality and globality of instrumental rationality: The normative significance of preference reversals." *Synthese*. Advance online publication, doi 10.1007/s11229-014-0529-8.

Kunda, Z. and Spencer, S. J. (2003). "When do stereotypes come to mind and when do they color judgment? A goal-based theoretical framework for stereotype activation and application." *Psychological Bulletin* 129(4): 522–44.

Leslie, S. J. (forthcoming). "The original sin of cognition: Fear, prejudice, and generalization." *The Journal of Philosophy*.

Levinson, J. D. and Smith, R. J. (eds.) (2012). *Implicit Racial Bias Across the Law*. Cambridge: Cambridge University Press.

Madva, A. M. (2012). *The Hidden Mechanisms of Prejudice: Implicit Bias and Interpersonal Fluency*. PhD dissertation, Columbia University, NY.

Mendoza, S. A., Gollwitzer, P. M., and Amodio, D. M. (2010). "Reducing the expression of implicit stereotypes: Reflexive control through implementation intentions." *Personality and Social Psychology Bulletin* 36(4): 512–23.

Mills, C. W. (1997). *The Racial Contract*. Ithaca, NY: Cornell University Press.

Morewedge, C. K. and Kahneman, D. (2010). "Associative processes in intuitive judgment." *Trends in Cognitive Sciences* 14(10): 435–40.

Moskowitz, G. B. (2010). "On the control over stereotype activation and stereotype inhibition." *Social and Personality Psychology Compass* 4(2): 140–58.

Nosek, B. A. and Hansen, J. J. (2008). "The associations in our heads belong to us: Searching for attitudes and knowledge in implicit evaluation." *Cognition and Emotion* 22(4): 553–94.

Pettigrew, T. F. (1979). "The ultimate attribution error: Extending Allport's cognitive analysis of prejudice." *Personality and Social Psychology Bulletin* 5(4): 461–76.

Porter, N. and Geis, F. L. (1981). "Women and nonverbal leadership cues: When seeing is not believing." In Mayo C. and Henley, N. (eds.) *Gender, Androgyny, and Nonverbal Behavior*. New York: Springer: 39–61.

Principe, L. M. (2012). *The Secrets of Alchemy*. Chicago, IL: University of Chicago Press.

Sassenberg, K., Kessler, T., and Mummendey, A. (2004). "When creative means different: Activating creativity as a strategy to initiate the generation of original ideas." Unpublished manuscript, Friedrich-Schiller University, Jena, Germany.

Sassenberg, K. and Moskowitz, G. B. (2005). "Don't stereotype, think different! Overcoming automatic stereotype activation by mindset priming." *Journal of Experimental Social Psychology* 41: 506–14.

Shih, M., Pittinsky, T. L., and Ambady, N. (1999). "Stereotype susceptibility: Identity salience and shifts in quantitative performance." *Psychological Science* 10: 80–3.

Shriver, E. R., Young, S. G., Hugenberg, K., Bernstein, M. J., and Lanter, J. R. (2008). "Class, race, and the face: Social context modulates the cross-race effect in face recognition." *Personality and Social Psychology Bulletin* 34(2): 260–74.

Stewart, B. D. and Payne, B. K. (2008). "Bringing automatic stereotyping under control: Implementation intentions as efficient means of thought control." *Personality and Social Psychology Bulletin* 34: 1332–45.

Tetlock, P. F., Kristel, O., Elson, B., Green, M., and Lerner, J. (2000). "The psychology of the unthinkable: Taboo trade-offs, forbidden base rates, and heretical counterfactuals." *Journal of Personality and Social Psychology* 78(5): 853–70.

Todd, D. (2014). "Vancouver is the most 'Asian' city outside Asia. What are the ramifications?" Staff Blog, *The Vancouver Sun*, March 28.

Uhlmann, E. L., Brescoll, V. L., and Machery, E. (2010). "The motives underlying stereotype-based discrimination against members of stigmatized groups." *Social Justice Research* 23(1): 1–16.

Uhlmann, E. L., Poehlman, T. A., and Nosek, B. A. (2012). "Automatic associations: Personal attitudes or cultural knowledge?" In Hanson, J. D. (ed.), *Ideology, Psychology, and Law*. New York, NY: Oxford University Press: 228–60.

Valian, V. (1998). *Why so Slow? The Advancement of Women*. Cambridge, MA: MIT Press.

Valian, V. (2010). "What works and what doesn't: How to increase the representation of women in academia and business." In *Gender Change in Academia*. Wiesbaden: VS Verlag für Sozialwissenschaften: 317–28.

Webb, T. L. and Sheeran, P. (2008). "Mechanisms of implementation intention effects: The role of goal intentions, self-efficacy, and accessibility of plan components." *British Journal of Social Psychology* 47: 373–95.

Williams, M. R. and Holcomb, J. E. (2004). "The interactive effects of victim race and gender on death sentence disparity findings." *Homicide Studies* 8(4): 350–76.

Ziv, T. and Banaji, M. R. (2012). "Representations of social groups in the early years of life." In Fiske, S. T. and Macrae, C. N., *The SAGE Handbook of Social Cognition*, London: Sage: 372.

2.3

Stereotype Threat, Epistemic Injustice, and Rationality

Stacey Goguen

Like anyone, blacks risk devaluation for a particular incompetence, such as a failed test or a flubbed pronunciation. But they further risk that such performances will confirm the broader, racial inferiority they are suspected of. Thus, from the first grade through graduate school, blacks have the extra fear that in the eyes of those around them their full humanity could fall with a poor answer or a mistaken stroke of the pen.

(Steele, 1992)

Stereotype threat is most well known for its ability to hinder performance. However, it can result in a wide range of harmful effects, such as stress, anxiety, and self-doubt. These additional effects are as important and central to the phenomenon as its effects on performance. As a result, stereotype threat has more far-reaching implications than philosophers have discussed previously. In particular, the phenomenon has a number of unexplored "epistemic effects." These are effects on our epistemic lives—i.e. the ways we engage with the world as actual and potential knowers. In this chapter I argue that we need to employ a broader account of stereotype threat and show how such an account helps us better understand the implications of a specific epistemic effect: self-doubt. Certain kinds of self-doubt can constitute an epistemic injustice, and this sort of self-doubt can be exacerbated by stereotypes of irrationality. As a result, self-doubt from stereotype threat can erode our faith in ourselves as full human persons and as rational, reliable knowers. Thus, stererotype threat can affect more than just our ability to perform to our potential. It can also affect our very sense of self. Furthermore, using a broader account will allow us to better investigate the epistemological implications of stereotype threat, as well as the full extent of its reach into our lives.

1 The Full Effects of Stereotype Threat

Stereotype threat is, as its name implies, a psychological threat that is triggered by a negative stereotype. It is "the resulting sense that one can [...] be judged or treated in terms of the stereotype" (Steele, Spencer, and Aronson, 2002: 389). Specifically, it occurs when an individual becomes aware, consciously or unconsciously, that their behavior in a specific social arena, or "domain," could render salient a negative stereotype about them or their social group. At worst, their behavior could be interpreted as confirming the stereotype.[1] The most well known effect of stereotype threat is an unintentional decrease in performance—usually on evaluative tasks, such as difficult tests. This is "the underperformance effect." As an example, the first set of studies on stereotype threat found that Black[2] students performed worse on a GRE-like test when they were told that the test could measure their intelligence. For those students, this framing brought to mind and made salient the cultural stereotype that Black individuals are possibly not as intelligent as members of other racial groups, especially White individuals (Steele and Aronson, 1995). This underperformance effect was absent when Black students were told that the test did not measure anything, but merely showed the researchers different problem-solving strategies that people use. The stereotype about intelligence did not come to mind in the latter case, or if it did, it was unthreatening, because it was said to not apply to the testing situation.

This underperformance effect is significant, but it is, to borrow a metaphor from Rachel McKinnon (in a draft of 2014), the mere tip of the stereotype threat iceberg. The phenomenon has a whole host of effects besides underperformance. Psychologists have recently summarized them as such:

Stereotype threat also yields reduced self-efficacy (Aronson and Inzlicht, 2004), lowered confidence that one will do well in the stereotyped domain (Stangor et al., 1998); lowered aspirations to pursue stereotype-relevant careers (Davies et al., 2002; Davies et al., 2005); and negative physical and psychological health consequences, including increased general anxiety (Ben-Zeev et al., 2005; Bosson et al. 2004), blood pressure (Blascovich et al., 2001), and feelings of dejection (Keller and Dauenheimer, 2003). (Shapiro and Aronson in Stangor and Crandall, 2013, 97)

---

[1] This is a broader formulation of stereotype threat than is usually given. Often, psychologists characterize stereotype as the specific worry that one might confirm a stereotype through one's performance. This narrower definition describes what happens during underperformance, but as I will argue, that is not the only important effect of stereotype threat. Therefore, I use a broader definition that more precisely encompasses all of stereotype threat's effects.

[2] I capitalize the initial letters of "Black" and "White" when using those words as racial categories to denote that they are complex group identifiers, and not mere descriptions of skin color.

Besides this laundry list of additional effects, stereotype threat is also purported to cause "psychological disengagement" and "domain avoidance." Disengagement is, roughly, a reduction in motivation to participate or succeed in a domain, such as a general sphere of life (intellectual pursuits), an academic subject (mathematics), a hobby (video games), or even a particular social scene (nerd culture). Disengagement is a psychological withdrawal, which lessens the degree to which an individual cares how well they do in the given domain.[3] Domain avoidance, on the other hand, is roughly when individuals physically avoid or socially distance themselves from a domain.[4]

Psychologists have not paid nearly as much attention to these effects as they have to underperformance, though most seem to be aware of at least some of them, as evinced by review articles such as the one quoted above. Moreover, stereotype threat's effects on stress, motivation, and aspiration are not new information. Claude Steele, one of the first major researchers of stereotype threat, has argued since the first studies on the phenomenon that there is a "two-pronged consequence of stereotype threat—undermining both performance and aspirations" (Davies, Spencer, and Steele, 2005, 278).[5] For as long as researchers have known about the underperformance effect, they have also known that there are effects that go beyond performance. These other effects have received less attention than underperformance has, but psychologists have voiced no major misgivings over whether they exist. Therefore, it is a well-established fact that stereotype threat has many different effects besides just lowering performance. But if that is the case, then why have these other effects been largely deemphasized?

2 A Fuller Account of Stereotype Threat

Although psychologists have known that these other effects exist, it is not evident whether all psychologists take them to be central effects of the phenomenon, in the same way that the underperformance effect is taken to be a primary or central part of stereotype threat. For instance, Steele, Spencer, and Aronson (2002) frame domain avoidance and disengagement as a "response" or "acute reaction" to

---

[3] For research on disengagement, see Major et al. (1998); Crocker, Major, and Steele (1998); Steele, Spencer, and Aronson (2002); von Hippel et al. (2005); Smith, Sansone, and White (2007); Nussbaum and Steele (2007); and Forbes, Schmader, and Allen (2008).

[4] For research on domain avoidance, see Davies et al. (2002); Steele, Spencer, and Aronson (2002); Davies, Spencer, and Steele (2005); Oswald and Harvey(2000/2001); Osborne and Walker (2006); Steele, James, and Barnett (2002); Murphy et al. (2007); Gupta and Bhawe (2007).

[5] For Steele's comments on motivational effects, see Steele (1992, 1997); Steele and Aronson (1995); Steele, Spencer, and Aronson (2002).

stereotype threat (407–8). This framing might suggest that disengagement and domain avoidance are not direct effects of the phenomenon, but rather are indirect effects. They are perhaps, more precisely, descriptions of how people psychologically respond to stereotype threat or try to cope with it. By contrast, the underperformance effect would not be such a coping strategy, but rather a direct effect of the cognitive mechanisms that stereotype threat initiates.[6]

The problem with the sort of account just mentioned, which posits underperformance as the lone, central, or direct effect of the phenomenon, is that it ends up being too arbitrarily narrow. Singling out and emphasizing underperformance may be a useful operationalization for certain experimental studies, and it may be a useful narrative for securing funding for research. However, treating underperformance as the primary effect of stereotype threat is not a good theoretical basis for a comprehensive account of the phenomenon. An expanded framework that equally encompasses the effects beyond performance provides better conceptual connections to related psychological phenomena. Furthermore, an expanded account opens up avenues of both psychological and philosophical research that a focus on underperformance would likely obscure.

First, stereotype threat is not synonymous with the underperformance effect, even though the consistent focus on underperformance can make it seem so. That is, not everyone who experiences stereotype threat experiences the underperformance effect. As Steele, Spencer, and Aronson (2002) note, "Does this mean that stereotype threat always undermines the performance of stereotype-threatened test-takers? No" (388). For instance, individuals are more likely to experience underperformance when they are engaging in difficult evaluative tasks.[7] When subjects perform tasks that are on the easier side, they sometimes outperform students who are not primed for a negative stereotype.[8] Researchers posit that similar cognitive mechanisms are responsible for these different effects of under- and overperformance. Roughly, the mind goes into overdrive when it experiences stereotype threat—which is a boon when one is trying to crank out answers to easy questions, but a hindrance when one is engaging in more difficult

---

[6] There are still some open questions concerning which exact cognitive mechanisms cause this decrease in performance, but research has been leaning towards an integrated account of several different processes. For instance, some argue that, "situations of stereotype threat set in motion both automatic processes that activate a sense of uncertainty and cue increased vigilance toward the situation, one's performance, and oneself; as well as controlled processes aimed at interpreting and regulating the resulting negative thoughts and feelings that the negative stereotype can induce" (Inzlicht and Schmader, 2011: 35).

[7] For research on motivation mediating underperformance, see Steele and Aronson (1995); Aronson et al. (1999: 31); Jamieson and Harkins (2007); Fogliati and Bussey (2013: 312–13).

[8] See Oswald and Harvey (2000/2001).

tasks that require intense focus and careful attention. Insofar as we take stereo-type threat to be the set of social-psychological conditions that cause the mind to go into overdrive, then stereotype threat is affecting both the students who underperform on hard tasks, and the students who overperform on easy tasks. Therefore, the set of all people who experience stereotype threat is larger than the set of people who experience the underperformance effect. So stereotype threat is not reducible to underperformance.

Furthermore, effects such as disengagement and domain avoidance deserve to be considered direct effects of stereotype threat as much as underperformance does. Though one can frame disengagement and domain avoidance as, instead, individuals' coping strategies in response to a psychological threat, we can actually do the same for underperformance. In fact, work on the concept of psychological threat more generally suggests that all of stereotype threat's effects can be tied to various strategies individuals use to cope with such threats. Specifically, Steele, Spencer, and Aronson (2002) propose a broader framework for thinking about psychological threats to our self-worth that revolve around our social identities, of which stereotype threat is an example. They call this broader classification of threat "social identity threat," which is defined as, "the psychological state that occurs when people are aware that they have the potential to be viewed negatively or devalued because of their membership in a particular social group" (Townsend et al., 2011: 151).[9] Under the social identity threat framework, stereotype threat is just all instances of social identity threat that are triggered by a stereotype. It is, as I defined it at the beginning of this chapter, any instance where an individual responds to the fact that a certain stereotype has the potential to devalue them in their current setting.

People who experience disengagement and domain avoidance are just as aware of this potential for devaluation as are the people who experience underperform-ance. Thus, we can view these three effects (disengagement, avoidance, and underperformance) as manifestations of different coping strategies that people undertake in response to potentially being devalued. The person who disengages is the person who responds by lowering their esteem of the stereotyped domain, which allows them to protect their self-worth from devaluation. The person who avoids the domain all together prevents the threat from becoming an actualized devaluation. And the person who underperforms is the person who tries to avoid devaluation by proving the stereotype wrong, at least in this instance.

To illustrate these three reactions, imagine a domain that is rife for creating stereotype threat. For instance, imagine a large undergraduate mathematics class,

---

[9] See also Steele, James, and Barnett (2002).

with three women who have signed up to take the class. Imagine that when these three women become primed for stereotype threat—that is, when they become aware that people could compare their performance to the stereotype that women are bad at mathematics—they all react in different ways. One woman drops the class, preferring to major in English than deal with the stress and pressure that the mathematics stereotype creates. She engages in domain avoidance. The second woman stays in the class, but sits in the back most days with her arms crossed; she only half-heartedly participates in the class, because doing so allows her to deflect any implication that her performance in this class says something important about her intellectual capabilities qua woman. She engages in disengagement. The third woman, however, tries to ensure that the negative stereotype cannot be applied to her. She shows up and buckles down for each test—for if she does well enough, she will escape the reach of this particular stereotype. However, if this is a hard class, then her efforts will likely backfire due to the set of cognitive processes that have been set into motion. She is the student who experiences underperformance.

Interestingly, in this picture of stereotype threat, underperformance is even less of a direct effect than disengagement or domain avoidance. Disengagement and domain avoidance are direct responses to the threat of devaluation. Underperformance, however, is not such a direct response. Instead, it is an unintentional side-effect of a response, which is trying to disconfirm the negative stereotype through increased motivation to perform well. Therefore, if we want to extend our conceptual umbrella far enough out to include underperformance as a central effect of stereotype threat, then disengagement and domain avoidance should certainly be under that umbrella too. All three of them are part of individuals' reactions to threats of devaluation that are triggered by the presence and possible salience of a negative stereotype.[10] Therefore, they are equally all effects of stereotype threat. Again, it is too arbitrary to claim that the motivation to disconfirm a stereotype (which is what puts people at risk for underperformance) is the only reaction that truly counts as stereotype threat, whereas the other reactions are something else. If stereotype threat is, at heart, a certain kind of threat that is triggered by a stereotype, then all reactions to that threat should equally count as effects of this phenomenon.

Expanding our picture of stereotype threat to encompass these effects beyond performance opens up multiple projects for philosophical scholarship on stereotype threat. One such opportunity is, as McKinnon (2014) and others have

---

[10] See Thoman et al. (2013) for a model of stereotype threat that explicitly emphasizes these motivational effects as being central to the phenomenon.

mentioned, to consider how effects such as disengagement and domain avoidance may play a role in the underrepresentation of certain groups in certain domains. For instance, they may play a role in the underrepresentation of women and other marginalized groups in philosophy. Thus far, work on the underrepresentation of women in philosophy that discusses stereotype threat (e.g. Antony, 2012; Saul, 2013) only considers how the underperformance effect may influence the number of women in the field. It is just as likely, however, that disengagement and domain avoidance are also playing a key role in whether women successfully pursue a major or career in the profession.

To grasp how these other effects might be affecting issues of underrepresentation, I think it is helpful to lay the groundwork for another project: fleshing out stereotype threat's epistemological implications. Stereotype threat has many more "epistemic costs" than scholars have realized. By epistemic cost I mean any negative effect on a facet of our lives that deals with how we gain, retain, and disseminate knowledge. When Gendler (2011) first explored the possible epistemic costs of stereotype threat, she only considered the costs that stem from the underperformance effect. But effects such as disengagement and domain avoidance carry their own costs—ones that are heavier than those attributed to underperformance.[11]

Philosophers have taken a few steps towards exploring some of these costs. For instance, McKinnon (2014) discusses the epistemic ramifications for people who experience domain avoidance and attributional ambiguity. Ron Mallon (this volume) touches on the implications of decisions individuals make in response to stereotype threat. And though Haslanger (2014) does not explicitly address stereotype threat, she discusses the costs to epistemic agency from chronic degradation that stems from social stigma—which is something to which stereotype threat could plausibly contribute. These investigations are beginning to map out the full scope of stereotype threat, but we still have a ways to go. Over and above the epistemic costs just mentioned, stereotype threat can also have subtle but powerful consequences for the very foundations of our epistemic lives: our sense of ourselves as rational and reliable human knowers, and as full persons.

---

[11]   Again, underperformance itself is an important and damaging effect. Subtle differences in test scores can reverberate through our lives, affecting our levels of education, our employment, the social circles we run, who we meet and marry, and so on. I do not want to downplay that part of the story. What I want to do is argue that there are equally important and worrisome stories besides that one. Particularly, when it comes to the epistemological story of stereotype threat, underperformance simply does not seem to play that central a role. Other effects, however, such as disengagement, domain avoidance, stress, and self-doubt, have very critical roles to play.

In the following sections I give a preliminary account of how stereotype threat can undermine the very foundations of our epistemic life by diminishing our sense of our humanity or rational personhood. I do this by looking at the ramifications of a specific effect of stereotype threat: self-doubt. Though self-doubt is not necessarily the most damaging or destructive effect of the phenomenon, it gives us a window into just how deeply stereotype threat can affect our epistemic lives and our very sense of ourselves. Having a sense of this depth is important for pursuing other philosophical projects that stem from an expanded and fuller account of stereotype threat. I will discuss some of those projects at the end of this chapter.

3 The Epistemic Costs of Self-Doubt

Not all doubts are created equal. Some may be a frustrating or unsettling experience, but are of little long-term consequence. For instance, we may doubt whether we locked the front door before leaving our home. We may be frustrated by this doubt and what it implies for our memory, but often we are not overly concerned in any significant way. We can easily write it off as an isolated error, or as a common flaw in human memory.

Gendler (2011) discusses such minor doubts in her preliminary exploration of stereotype threat's epistemic costs. She observes that the cognitive mechanisms that lead to underperformance could do so in part by temporarily causing people to lose confidence in their knowledge—knowledge such as whether 11 x 11 is 121, or whether *sunt* is the third person plural of *esse* (50). She holds out hope that these sorts of doubts, as epistemic costs, can be "deeply interesting" to epistemologists. She fleshes out one way that these doubts might be interesting, which is in their hybrid nature of being caused by a process that has physiological and reason-based components. However, if one is not particularly interested in the difference between physical "bumps and bounces" versus mental "beliefs and arguments" leading to self-doubt, then stereotype threat may not look deeply interesting at all. Fortunately, what Gendler describes is not the only sort of doubt that stereotype threats cause. It can cause other sorts of self-doubt, which I think is of immense interest to many epistemologists—particularly those interested in social epistemology, which focuses on the influence of social identity and the epistemic interactions between people.

Some doubts are interesting, not because of what causes them, but because of what they themselves set into motion. For instance, to use a classic philosophical example, if we could sincerely doubt something such as whether we have two hands, that doubt would have serious ramifications for our epistemic life. If we are in sincere doubt of a fact like that, we probably will (and probably should) also start doubting other, more fundamental propositions about ourselves, such as whether we are capable of reliable perception. Wittgenstein (1951) makes this very observation in *On Certainty*: "If a blind man were to ask me 'Have you got two hands?' I should not make sure by looking. If I were to have any doubt of it, then I don't know why I should trust my eyes" (125). A doubt about our hands implies a doubt about our eyes, and really our brain too. That is, some doubts are interesting because they can create a cascade of further, more serious doubts. They can spillover into deeper, more important aspects of ourselves.

"Spillover" is a concept used by psychologists to refer to stereotype threat's ability to affect additional domains other than the one specifically targeted by a stereotype.[12] For instance, a negative stereotype about a group's ability in mathematics can affect that group's behavior in not just mathematics (via underperformance, disengagement, and so on) but also in other domains. It can cause underperformance and risky decision-making, and increases in aggression levels, indulgence, and loss of self-control in domains that are completely unrelated to mathematics (Beilock, Rydell, and McConnell, 2007; Inzlicht and Kang, 2010; Carr and Steele, 2010). I refer to these as "cognitive spillover," because the primary mechanism causing the spillover is presumed to be a cognitive one—specifically one that governs executive resources, willpower, and self-control. I want to expand this notion though to also talk about a kind of epistemic spillover. Instead of a cognitive mechanism being the primary culprit, our networks of belief and knowledge are. So, if a doubt influences our beliefs about not just the specific domain it pertains to, but also other domains as well, then it causes epistemic spillover. For example, if someone doubts their ability to succeed in mathematics, and that doubt in turn affects how certain they are about succeeding in college more generally, or succeeding in a related domain such as computer science, then that doubt has epistemic spillover. Or again, if we find ourselves sincerely doubting the existence of some of our limbs, that doubt will very likely spillover into our beliefs about our perception's reliability.

Most beliefs and uncertainties cause epistemic spillover of some sort, since ideas usually imply or entail other ideas. Many of these implications and entailments can be trivial in the degree to which they impact a person's life on the whole. So not all spillover is interesting spillover. But, whether or not spillover is

---

[12] Inzlicht and Kang (2010) coined the phrase "stereotype threat spillover," arguing that, "stereotype threat has lingering effects that continue to influence people after they leave threatening environments, such that it has residual effects on behavior even in areas unrelated to the impugning stereotype" (467).

epistemologically interesting may be heavily influenced by the context in which it happens. For instance, doubting whether you locked the front door is not likely to cause that much (important) epistemic spillover. However, if you recently learned that you were at risk for developing Alzheimer's disease, that same doubt about the front door may gain additional spillover, since now it may function as a piece of evidence for an important fact about you. Similarly, a doubt about one's ability or potential to succeed in a given sport, hobby, or intellectual endeavor could be trivial for one person, but contain completely destabilizing epistemic spillover for another person. As we shall see, stereotypes can be a moderator of such spillover. So it is this sort of destabilizing doubt that I will explore, because of the potential strength of its impact on our lives.

4 Stereotype Threat, Stigma, and Epistemic Injustice

We already know that stereotype threat causes self-doubt.[13] I argue further that we have reasons to suspect that stereotype threat causes instances of self-doubt whose epistemic spillover can deeply affect our lives—particularly its epistemic aspects, including our self-identity. At its worst via self-doubt, stereotype threat can potentially undermine our sense of our own humanity and our sense of ourselves as rational, reliable knowers. There is a lot to explore in the relationships between stereotypes, self-doubt, and our epistemic lives. Here I use the framework of epistemic injustice, which includes the lens of focusing on social stigma, to trace out a few threads in these complicated relationships.

Scientific research on stereotype threat and stigmatized social groups has already implied some ways that stereotype threat can have significant epistemic spillover. Claude Steele traced out the general contours of such spillover even before he helped identify the phenomenon of stereotype threat as such. In the opening epigraph of this chapter, Steele observes that for members of a stigmatized group, a simple mistake on a test can imply much more than just incompetency in that moment, and also more than incompetency in just that specific domain. The very humanity of such students is suddenly put on the table, all because of "a mistaken stroke of the pen" (Steele, 1992). The situation Steele describes in this quotation is very likely an instance of stereotype threat. The "broader, racial inferiority they are suspected of" is another way of saying "the broader stereotype that is attached to their social identity." Furthermore, this

---

[13] For reports of uncertainty and self-doubt as an effect of stereotype threat, see Steele and Aronson (1995); Stangor, Can, and Kiang (1998); Stone (2002); Steele, Spencer, and Aronson (2002); Aronson and Inzlicht (2004); Derks, Inzlicht, and Kang (2008).

situation fits the expanded definition of stereotype threat, which is any situation where a person reacts to the possibility of devaluation that is triggered by the potential salience of a negative stereotype. So in this quotation from a researcher we have a vivid example of worrisome epistemic spillover from something that is most likely an instance of stereotype threat.

Next, we have reasons to think that the significant instances of epistemic spillover from stereotype threat can be, or likely are, instigated by self-doubt. Although Steele himself attempts to decouple stereotype threat from self-doubt, he does this to decouple self-doubt as a potential *cause* of stereotype threat. He does not contest that it is an *effect* of the phenomenon (Gates and Steele, 2009: 252). Moreover, research by other psychologists has shown how self-doubt with significant epistemic spillover can be triggered by social identity threat—and thus potentially by stereotype threat more specifically. Walton and Cohen (2007) argue that in some settings, "members of socially stigmatized groups are more uncertain of the quality of their social bonds and thus more sensitive to issues of social belonging" (82).[14] They find that a negative characterization of a group (i.e. a threat of devaluation) in a specific domain can exacerbate this global uncertainty. Forms of social identity threat can increase a global "belonging uncertainty" that extends far beyond the domain of the initial threat.

Here is a picture of what that could look like. Consider individuals who are mathematics majors and experience stereotype threat in a college mathematics course. Experiencing belonging uncertainty in mathematics—feeling unsure of the social bonds with mathematics professors and fellow mathematics majors—could unsettle them greatly. It can shake their confidence to the point that they wonder whether any of their social bonds in college, or in life, are certain, reliable, or stable. For, if they were a bad judge of the social bonds they had in the field that they love and are passionate about, then why think they are a good judge of any of their social bonds? The specific uncertainty they have in the domain of mathematics spills over and spreads into the domain of their social life more generally.

Notice, in this picture, the more global uncertainty is triggered by an uncertainty about their ability to judge or accurately perceive the strength of their social bonds. So, these instances of spillover from social identity threat may also affect our epistemic agency—that is, our capacity to reliably undertake directed action as a knower, and our sense of ourselves as such. It affects our ability to act in the world as potential knowers. An example of what it looks like when someone has their epistemic agency undermined by self-doubt comes from the television show *Scandal*. The character Abby Wheelen explains how an abusive

---

[14] See also Inzlicht and Good (2006).

marriage undermined her general capacity to interact with the world as a reliable knower. She says: "If someone [. . .] tells you that you're worthless, if the man that's supposed to love you, your husband, does that enough, you stop thinking you can be right about anything."[15] This consequence, the doubt that you can be right about anything, is what it is like to have your epistemic agency undermined.[16] Moreover, this example shows the kind of epistemic spillover that I think stereotype threat is capable of. Wheelan is epistemically destabilized by the dissonance between what she expects herself to be able to know about her husband (that as her husband, he loves her) and what her experience indicates about him (that he engages in incredibly unloving behavior). This particular epistemic upset is so great that she wonders whether she can have secure knowledge in "anything."

Miranda Fricker's work on epistemic injustice provides a useful framework for thinking about this experience of Wheelan's, and for thinking about how stereotype threat can cause similar experiences, such as the example with global belonging uncertainty. Fricker argues that what she calls "hermeneutical injustice" is any situation where someone is not able to understand, interpret, or render intelligible a significant experience. Often, this is because our society lacks the requisite vocabulary, as was the case in historical examples of women trying to understand and talk about sexual harassment and postpartum depression before we had the terms "sexual harassment" and "postpartum depression." However, this hermeneutical failure can occur for other reasons, such as a person's speaking or testimonial style not being acknowledged as credible. In Wheelan's case, the hermeneutical injustice she experiences stems from the dissonance between her cultural knowledge (i.e. that someone who becomes your spouse loves you greatly) and her personal experience that her husband acted in a grossly unloving manner. The existence of the cultural knowledge (or, really, presumption) made it hard for her to render her experience intelligible, to the extent that she started questioning whether she really knew anything at all. For, if her husband did not actually love her, how could she have missed that? Similar to Wittgenstein's observation about the connection between our beliefs about our hands and our certainty about our perception, Wheelen reckons that if it is possible that the man she thought was her loving husband is really abusive and unloving, then she is unsure why she should trust her judgment about anything.

An important factor that exacerbates Wheelan's uncertainty is social stigma and marginalization—the very things that make an epistemic injustice an

---

[15] Season 2, episode 19: "Another Chance."
[16] For further examples and discussion of agency being undermined, see Haslanger (2014).

injustice, and not just a tragedy. Even though women are not a numerical minority in our society, their experiences have often been marginalized through gendered social hierarchies. The result is that, for example with the historical cases, even though many women experienced the phenomena of sexual harassment and postpartum depression, for a very long time women could not render these experiences fully intelligible to themselves and to others. (In fact, this still may be the case to some degree.) It is not just that they did not have a name for the phenomena, but that their own experience of the phenomena clashed with what their culture presumed to know. Their culture "knew" that people like receiving compliments about their appearance, but women found themselves not liking it when their coworkers repeatedly told them how nice an ass they had. And their culture "knew" that women felt a certain way about their newborn babies and the experience of being mothers, but new mothers found themselves having experiences of paranoia, detachment, sadness, depression, and so on, that were unacknowledged and even presumed impossible. This dissonance, maintained by women's marginalization, exacerbates the epistemic spillover of the doubts some of them developed. They doubted whether they were overreacting to a coworker's remark, and that in turn made some of them doubt whether they were reliable knowers at all. As Fricker (2007) observes: "When you [...] seem to be the only one to feel the dissonance between received understanding and your own intimated sense of a given experience, it tends to knock your faith in your own ability to make sense of the world" (163). This is the reason why Wheelan's faith in her ability to make sense of the world is shaken. So, this is a way that social stigma can exacerbate or catalyze serious epistemic spillover effects via self-doubt. It undermines your epistemic self-trust.

It is very plausible that stigma in the form of stereotypes will do the same thing. As we saw in the opening epigraph, Steele describes how Black students face severe epistemic spillover stemming from what I argued previously can be framed as a racial stereotype. Steele's observation is useful because we can compare his report on Black students to what we know about White students who experience stereotype threat. While just about every student may at some point feel stupid or consider themselves an academic failure if they perform poorly enough, there is an additional dimension to feeling stupid when experienced in conjunction with something like racism. Not only must Black students contend with the fear that they will be seen through the lens of an unflattering suspicion (i.e. of academic inferiority), but this suspicion can raise the specter of a more fundamental inferiority: that their race simply blocks off or stunts certain avenues of human achievement and potential.

White students can also experience stereotype threat, for instance, in relation to the stereotypes that they are less athletic than Black students (Stone et al., 1999) or less mathematically inclined than Asian students (Aronson et al., 1999). But they are not likely to experience the same degree of epistemic spillover described in the epigraph. White students must contend with the possibility of being seen as less than top-notch mathematics students or athletes, which is a real threat of devaluation, but the stereotype they face does not suggest a "broader [...] inferiority." It does not insinuate that those failings could be signs of a deeper, more fundamental flaw. Not all devaluations are created equal. Individual White students could experience the threat of a more universal inferiority, but that would stem either from another aspect of their social identity (their gender, class, and so on)[17] or from a more individualized aspect of their identity, such as a local stereotype that applies within a close circle of friends. But for White students as a racial group, there are no cultural suspicions of subhuman status to be aroused. Thus, they will not likely experience damaging epistemic spillover of the sort that Black students experience.

Therefore, when members of stigmatized social groups experience stereotype threat, they face the possibility of also experiencing self-doubt of the sort that can undermine their very humanity. This may occur by having their agency as reliable knowers challenged, or perhaps by some other mechanism as well. This is an important potential effect of stereotype threat that neither psychologists nor philosophers have spent much time looking at. Stereotype threat may be capable of serious damage to our epistemic lives by way of the self-doubt it can give rise to, if that self-doubt spills over into broader concerns about one's agency and humanity. Furthermore, it seems that some of the effects of stereotype threat can constitute an epistemic injustice—a relationship that deserves further study. In Section 5 I examine a potential catalyst for this spillover—that is, a factor that may amplify the tendency or degree to which self-doubt from stereotype threat can spillover in this way. The catalyst is certain cultural ideals of rationality.

5 Stereotype Threat and Rationality

Ideals of personhood and humanity are often bound up with ideals of rationality. Whatever rationality is, it is often taken to be important, and perhaps necessary,

---

[17] For instance, White men who underperform on certain tasks might worry that such under-performance undermines their masculinity, which in turn undermines their humanity by threatening them with the stigmatized, sometimes-taken-to-be-not-quite-fully-human identity of non-masculinity, i.e. femininity.

for being a full human person—especially in many philosophical discussions. Along with this connection comes the implicit suggestion that if one's rationality or humanity is under suspicion, then the other one could be, or should be, as well. Fricker makes a similar observation in her work on epistemic injustice, arguing that such injustice can challenge a person's very humanity when it undermines their rationality—insofar as rationality is taken to be "essential to human value" (Fricker, 2007: 136). Fricker does not flesh out this argument, but she provides possible examples of how such a connection might play out.

For instance, one way that epistemic injustice can undermine a person's rationality is by making it more likely that they "are not heard as rational" when they give testimony or recount an experience (Fricker, 2007: 6). But, could this apply to the cases of self-doubt that I have discussed? I think so, since Fricker notes that epistemic injustice can lead to members of marginalized groups having experiences "left inadequately conceptualized and [...] ill-understood, perhaps even by the subjects themselves." This suggests that we may not even be able to hear ourselves as rational at times, if we are unable to make sense of an important experience. That is, in some instances of epistemic injustice we may doubt our own rationality.

In fact, W. E. B. Du Bois has already articulated an instance of such an experience. In *The Souls of Black Folk* he describes how systematic and structural racism can cause a member of a stigmatized racial group to doubt their own humanity and rationality. He calls this specific uncertainty "the temptation of doubt," suggesting that it is one of the greatest psychological and spiritual challenges faced by those who experience unrelenting structures of oppression. He illustrates this doubt as the following thought: " ... suppose, after all, the World is right and we are less than men? Suppose this mad impulse within [for liberty and equality] is all wrong, some mock mirage from the untrue?" (Du Bois, 1903: 49). This voice expresses the doubt that perhaps the racist hierarchies are the correct ordering of the world. If those hierarchies are correct and proper, then Black Americans' demands for equality and dignity are inappropriate and mis-taken. This creates such a dissonance that the doubting voice posits that the desire for equality is crazy and delusional—a "mad impulse" or a "mirage." The voice could be contemplating whether the desire for equal rights is a symptom of a mental illness; but more likely, these words are being used as stand-ins for irrationality—which is an all too common conflation. Thus, not only could we be subhuman, says the voice of doubt, but this further implies that we fail at being rational and reliable processors of information and perceivers of reality. Instead, we are stuck with a "mad impulse" or "mirage from the untrue." Thus, the temptation of doubt not only undercuts a person's social and political bonds, but it also undercuts their faith in themselves as knowers. So when a person's humanity or sociopolitical personhood falls into doubt, one's rationality and epistemic status may not be far behind.

This worry of irrationality can be very damaging because it makes a person's doubts susceptible to ever greater spillover. Rationality undergirds many of our intellectual and social endeavors, so by a person entertaining the possibility that they may be deficient in their rational capacity, that opens them up to wondering whether they are deficient in dozens if not hundreds of specific domains from mathematics and philosophy to even perhaps being a good friend or a good citizen.

Regarding the question of whether stereotype threat can have the sort of epistemic spillover that is fueled by suspicions of irrationality, it seems highly plausible because there are countless stereotypes concerning stigmatized social groups and their supposed lack of rational capacity. Women are called flat-out irrational, as well as crazy and bad at rigorously analytic subjects such as mathematics and philosophy, which can imply a lack of rationality. Many people of color face stereotypes of irrationality, ranging from Black people being accused of having out-of-control emotions (which are often presumed to be in contrast to rational thinking) to certain groups of indigenous people being presumed to have access to forms of wisdom that are contrasted with more rational, scientific forms of knowledge. The interplay between stereotype threat and ideals of rationality deserves more detailed study. I have laid out a preliminary account of how cultural suspicions of irrationality can be a catalyst for epistemic spillover from stereotype threat, resulting in the undermining of personhood and epistemic agency.

6 Conclusion

What I have discussed here is but one of many lines of inquiry we can take up from an expanded account of stereotype threat. To recap, stereotype threat's effects on performance are important, but they are also importantly not the whole picture. Stereotype threat has many other effects, such as anxiety, disengagement, domain avoidance, and self-doubt. These effects play just as central a role in constituting the phenomenon as the underperformance effect does, and so they deserve more attention from psychologists and philosophers than what they have received thus far. I focused here on fleshing out the epistemic ramifications of self-doubt and ideals of rationality, as played out through stereotype threat, and more widely, social identity threat. In short, self-doubt and suspicions of irrationality can undermine a person's sense of self in ways that damage and stunt their epistemic life.

Although stereotype threat's ability to influence our performance has far-reaching consequences of its own, our lives extend far beyond the reach of the tests that we take. Since stereotype threat affects aspirations and motivations as well as performance, then it might be playing a bigger role in the dearth of certain social groups within philosophy, for example. This suggests that we should consider shifting some of our premises and questions regarding underrepresentation. For instance, instead of accepting as a given that fields like philosophy simply do not seem desirable career choices for many women, we can investigate whether stereotype threat plays a role in the degree to which philosophy comes off desirable or as stressful and potentially threatening to women's self-worth. This may demystify some of the patterns we are seeing. It can seem a mystery why women, as a group, seem to not be interested in philosophy, mathematics, or engineering as much as are men. However, it should be no surprise that individuals tend to avoid domains where they experience increased levels of stress, lower motivation, and greater potential for feeling worthless. If women are more likely than men to experience stress and implicit threats to their self-worth in domains like philosophy, this can go a long way towards explaining the dearth of women there. The hypothesis that women are innately uninterested in philosophy is not needed.

A further implication is that the epistemological damage stereotype threat seems capable of suggests a further kind of "metaphysical" damage. If stereotype threat can undermine our sense—and others' sense—of our humanity, then it might also affect our social ontology in some way. Along these lines, Jenkins has argued that social oppression can affect what kind of beings we are seen as, and thus in a way what kind we are. She calls this phenomenon "ontic injustice" (Jenkins, 2014)—modeling it after epistemic injustice. Stereotype threat and social identity threat more widely are very good candidates for being potential sources of this possible ontic injustice.

There is also room to flesh out the exact relationship between social identity threat (including stereotype threat) and epistemic injustice. It would be fruitful to follow up on McKinnon's (2014) and Haslanger's (2014) work, which suggest ways (besides those involving self-doubt) that disengagement and domain avoidance can damage a person's epistemic agency. There is likely a whole web of connections between epistemic injustice and these phenomena of psychological threat—one that deserves to be fleshed out more fully than what I have been able to sketch here.

Lastly, and perhaps most pertinent for this volume, the category of social identity threat gives us a new way to conceive of the relationship between stereotype threat and implicit bias. Strictly speaking, stereotype threat is not a form of implicit bias.[18] Both, however, can involve implicit forms of cognition,[19] and both are involved in issues of social injustice. But by recognizing the broader effects of stereotype threat, and the broader category to which it belongs, we can grasp another, more specific connection between these two phenomena. Social identity threat and implicit bias are two sides of the same coin—the coin itself being stigma. Social identity threat describes devaluation of a social group from the perspective of the target of that devaluation. Implicit bias describes that devaluation from the perspective of the actor of that devaluation. Since stereotype threat always involves a target but often not an actor (unless the environment counts as one), it is an instance of social identity threat, but clearly not one of implicit bias. However, social identity threat in general can be exacerbated by implicit bias. That is, one of the main harms of implicit bias—one of the reasons why we care about it so much—is because it causes instances of social identity threat. And if those instances involve a stereotype, then it will be an instance of stereotype threat. Therefore, implicit bias and stereotype threat are connected together by social identity threat.

There is a fine line to walk with these connections. On the one hand, we do not want to conflate implicit bias and social identity threat. They are not the same thing, but they are often both present in interactions between actors and targets. On the other hand, we also do not want to research and theorize about these phenomena in complete isolation of one another. Doing so can isolate the target's perspective (in social identity threat) from the actor's perspective (in implicit bias) when often, both are occurring simultaneously in a given event. We might avoid these two pitfalls by focusing on the interactions of actors, environments, and targets as the locus of bias and threat.

Furthermore, using the concept of social identity threat in work on implicit bias can help us avoid collective navel-gazing. For instance, when we talk about a "chilly climate" as an instance of implicit bias, we prime ourselves to think about whose bias it is, and who is responsible for creating said chilly climate. That can be an important question, but in a field where demographically there are more potential actors of bias than there are targets of it, we should make sure we do not collectively overemphasize the importance of this question. In many circumstances, who is at fault is less pressing than what sort of damage is being done to

---

[18] For a discussion of the heterogeneity of phenomena that philosophers have discussed under "implicit bias," including stereotype threat, as well as some working definitions of implicit bias, see Holroyd and Sweetman (this volume).

[19] For instance, a group of individuals under stereotype threat might not consciously report the stress that their elevated cortisol levels are almost certainly causing them (Townsend, Major, Gangi, and Mendes, 2011).

the target and what we can do to mitigate it. So, if we instead talk about a chilly climate as a social identity threat, then we prime ourselves to think about whom the climate is a threat to, and how it is being experienced as chilly and unwelcoming to them. This framing forefronts the impacts on the targets of threat and bias. Just who exactly is to blame, and in what degree, is pushed to the background—where in some cases, it should be.

What we end up with are very wide-ranging implications that stem from a fairly simple matter of acknowledging that it is worth talking about all the recorded effects of stereotype threat. By taking seriously an expanded account of the phenomenon, we gain the broader category of social identity threat, which in turn offers a framework that complements work on implicit bias. It gives us a tool to distinguish when we are more concerned with the bias itself, and when we are actually concerned with the threat that the bias causes. Therefore, if this chapter has convinced you of one thing, I hope it is that stereotype threat is a phenomenon of great philosophical import, and one where we have only scratched the surface with regards to mapping out how it, and similar phenomena, can affect our lives.

References

Antony, Louise (2012). "Different voices or a perfect storm: Why are there so few women in philosophy?" *Journal of Social Philosophy* 43(3): 227–55.

Aronson, Joshua, and Michael Inzlicht (2004). "The ups and downs of attributional ambiguity: Stereotype vulnerability and the academic self-knowledge of African American college students." *Psychological Science* 15(12): 829–36.

Aronson, Joshua, Michael J. Lustina, Catherine Good, and Kelli Keough (1999). "When white men can't do math: Necessary and sufficient factors in stereotype threat." *Journal of Experimental Social Psychology* 35: 29–46.

Beilock, Sian, Robert Rydell, and Allen McConnell (2007). "Stereotype threat and working memory: Mechanisms, alleviations, and spillover." *Journal of Experimental Psychology: General* 136: 256–76.

Ben-Zeev, Talia, Steven Fein, and Michael Inzlicht (2005). "Arousal and stereotype threat." *Journal of Experimental Social Psychology* 41: 174–81.

Blascovich, Jim, Steven Spencer, Diane Quinn, and Claude Steele (2001). "African Americans and high blood pressure: The role of stereotype threat." *Psychological Science* 12(3): 225–9.

Bosson, Jennifer, Ethan Haymovitz, and Elizabeth Pinel (2004). "When saying and doing diverge: The effects of stereotype threat of self-reported versus non-verbal anxiety." *Journal of Experimental Social Psychology* 40: 247–55.

Carr, Priyanka and Clause Steele (2010). "Stereotype threat affects financial decision making." *Psychological Science* 21(10): 1411–16.

Crocker, Jennifer, Brenda Major, and Claude Steele (1998). "Social stigma." In Daniel Gilbert, Susan Fiske, and Gardner Lindzey (eds.), *The Handbook of Social Psychology*, vol. 2, 4th edn. Boston, MA: McGraw-Hill: 504–53.

Davies, Paul, Steven Spencer, Diane Quinn, and Rebecca Gerhardstein (2002). "Consuming images: How television commercials that elicit stereotype threat can restrain women academically and professionally." *Personality and Social Psychology Bulletin* 28(12): 1615–28.

Davies, Paul, Steven Spencer, and Claude Steele (2005). "Clearing the air: Identity safety moderates the effects of stereotype threat on women's leadership aspirations." *Journal of Personality and Social Psychology* 88(2): 276–87.

Derks, Belle, Michael Inzlicht, and Sonia Kang (2008). "The neuroscience of stigma and stereotype threat." *Group Processes and Intergroup Relations* 11(2): 163–81.

Du Bois, W. E. B. (1903/2009). *The Souls of Black Folk*. eBook available from *Journal of Pan African Studies*: <http://www.jpanafrican.com/ebooks.htm>. (Retrieved November 2013.)

Fogliati, Vincent, and Kay Bussey (2013). "Stereotype threat reduces motivation to improve: effects of stereotype threat and feedback on women's intentions to improve mathematical ability." *Psychology of Women Quarterly* 37(3): 310–24.

Forbes, Chad, Toni Schmader, and John Allen (2008). "The role of devaluing and discounting in performance monitoring: A neurophysiological study of minorities under threat." *Social Cognitive Affective Neuroscience* 3: 253–61.

Fricker, Miranda (2007). *Epistemic Injustice: Power and the Ethics of Knowing*. Oxford: Oxford University Press.

Gendler, Tamar (2011). "On the epistemic costs of implicit bias." *Philosophical Studies* 156: 33–63.

Gates, Henry Louis Jr. and Claude Steele (2009). "A converation with Claude Steele: Stereotype threat and black achievement." *Du Bois Review* 6(2): 251–71.

Gupta, Vishal, and Nachiket Bhawe (2007). "The influence of proactive personality and stereotype threat on women's entrepreneurial intentions." *Journal of Leadership and Organizational Studies* 13: 73–85.

Haslanger, Sally (2014). "Studying while black: Trust, opportunity, and sisrespect." *Du Bois Review* 11(1): 109–36.

Inzlicht, Michael and Catherine Good (2006). "How environments threaten academic performance, self-knowledge, and sense of belonging." In Shana Levin and Colette van Laar (eds.), *Stigma and Group Inequality: Social Psychological Approaches*. Mahwah, NJ: Erlbaum: 129–50.

Inzlicht, Michael and Sonia Kang (2010). "Stereotype threat spillover: How coping with threats to social identity affects aggression, Eating, decision making, and attention." *Journal of Personality and Social Psychology* 99(3): 467–81.

Inzlicht, Michael, and Toni Schmader (eds.) (2011). *Stereotype Threat: Theory, Process, and Application*. New York: Oxford University Press.

Jamieson, Jeremy, and Stephen Harkins (2007). "Mere effort and stereotype threat performance effects." *Journal of Personality and Social Psychology* 93(4): 544–64.

Jenkins, Katharine (2014). "Ontic injustice." Association of Legal and Social Philosophers, Annual Conference, University of Leeds.

Keller, Johannes, and Dirk Dauenheimer (2003). "Stereotype threat in the classroom: Dejection mediates the disrupting threat effect on women's math performance." *Personality and Social Psychology Bulletin* 29(3): 371–81.

Major, Brenda, Stephen Spencer, Toni Schmader, C. T. Wolfe, and Jennifer Crocker (1998). "Coping with negative stereotypes about intellectual performance: The role of psychological disengagement." *Personality and Social Psychology Bulletin* 24: 34–50.

McKinnon, Rachel (2014). "Stereotype threat and attributional ambiguity for trans women." *Hypatia* 29(4): 857–72.

Murphy, Mary, Claude Steele, and James Gross (2007). "Signaling threat: How situational cues affect women in math, science, and engineering settings." *Psychological Science* 18(10): 879–85.

Nussbaum, A. David, and Claude Steele (2007). "Situational disengagement and persistence in the face of adversity." *Journal of Experimental Social Psychology* 43: 127–34.

Osborne, Jason, and Walker, Christopher (2006). "Stereotype threat, identification with academics, and withdrawal from school: Why the most successful students of colour might be the most likely to withdraw." *Educational Psychology* 26: 563–77.

Oswald, Debra, and Richard Harvey (2000/2001). "Hostile environments, stereotype threat, and math performance among undergraduate women." *Current Psychology* 19(4): 338–56.

Saul, Jennifer (2013). "Implicit bias, stereotype threat and women in philosophy." In Fiona Jenkins and Katrina Hutchinson (eds.), *Women in Philosophy: What Needs to Change?* New York, NY: Oxford University Press: 39–60.

Shapiro, Jenessa, and Joshua Aronson (2013). "Stereotype threat." In Stangor and Crandall (2013): 95–117.

Smith, Jessi, Carol Sansone, and Paul White (2007). "The stereotyped task engagement process: The role of interest and achievement motivation." *Journal of Educational Psychology* 99(1): 99–114.

Stangor, Charles, and Christian Crandall (eds.) (2013). *Stereotyping and Prejudice.* New York: Psychology Press.

Stangor, Charles, Christine Can, and Lisa Kiang (1998). "Activating stereotypes undermines task performance expectations." *Journal of Personality and Social Psychology* 75: 1191–7.

Steele, Claude (1992). "Race and the schooling of black Americans." *The Atlantic Monthly* (April 1992). *The Atlantic Online*: <http://www.theatlantic.com/past/docs/unbound/flashbks/blacked/steele.htm> (Retrieved March 2012.)

Steele, Claude (1997). "A threat in the air: How stereotypes shape intellectual identity and performance." *American Psychologist* 52(6): 613–29.

Steele, Claude, and Joshua Aronson (1995). "Stereotype threat and the intellectual test performance of African Americans." *Journal of Personality and Social Psychology* 69(5): 797–811.

Steele, Claude, Stephen Spencer, and Joshua Aronson (2002). "Contending with images of one's group: the psychology of stereotype and social identity threat." In Mark P. Zanna (ed.), *Advances in Experimental Social Psychology*, vol. 34. San Diego, CA: Academic Press: 379–440.

Steele, Jennifer, Jacquelyn James, and Rosalind Barnett (2002). "Learning in a man's world: Examining the perceptions of undergraduate women in male-dominated academic areas." *Psychology of Women Quarterly* 26: 46–50.

Stone, Jeff (2002). "Battling doubt by avoiding practice: The effects of stereotype threat on self-handicapping in white athletes." *Personality and Social Psychology Bulletin,* 28(12): 1667–78.

Stone, Jeff, Christian Lynch, Mike Sjomeling, and John M. Darley (1999). "Stereotype threat effects on black and white athletic performance." *Journal of Personality and Social Psychology* 77: 1213–27.

Thoman, Dustin, Jessi Smith, Elizabeth Brown, Justin Chase, and Joo Young Lee (2013). "Beyond performance: A motivational experiences model of stereotype threat." *Educational Psychology Review* 25(2): 211–43.

Townsend, Sarah, Brenda Major, Crynthia Gangi, and Wendy Mendes (2011). "From 'in the air' to 'under the skin': Cortisol responses to social identity threat." *Personality and Social Psychology Bulletin* 37(2): 151–64.

von Hippel, William, Courtney von Hippel, Leanne Conway, Kristopher Preacher, Jonathan Schooler, and Gabriel Radvansky (2005). "Coping with stereotype threat: Denial as an impression management strategy." *Journal of Personality and Social Psychology* 89(1): 22–35.

Walton, Gregory, and Geoffrey Cohen (2007). "A question of belonging: Race, social fit, and achievement." *Journal of Personality and Social Psychology* 92(1): 82–96.

Wittgenstein, Ludwig (1951/1972). *On Certainty, ed. Elizabeth Anscombe and Georg von Wright*. New York, NY: Harper and Row.

2.4

The Status Quo Fallacy
Implicit Bias and Fallacies of Argumentation

Catherine E. Hundleby

Implicit biases are not sexism or racism in the usual sense. They are often unconscious, and as a result many of us have unrecognized cognitive dispositions that we do not want. For instance, my scores on the Implicit Association Test (<https://implicit.harvard.edu>; hereafter IAT) show a moderate to strong tendency to associate men more than women with careers. This conflicts with my long-standing and deeply explored feminist views, and suggests that the implicit bias operates as an "aversive bias"—one that persists despite my desires and best intentions.[1] Its conflict with my identity as a professional woman indicates too that I may hold a "false consciousness"—an aversive bias regarding myself.[2] Thinking such as this that reflects social stereotypes can be not only unjust but also erroneous, as my own case shows. Errors like these may result from a psychological need to justify the social system (as a person perceives it, largely unconsciously). This system justification motive includes social and psychological requirements to grant legitimacy to the status quo, "whatever form the current regime takes" (Kay and Zanna, 2009: 165), and to see it as "good, fair, natural, desirable, and even inevitable" (Jost, Banaji, and Nosek 2004: 887).

People's general tendency to believe in the justness of the social system or to sanction the status quo can affect how we perceive groups of people and

---

[1] The gender bias that I show operates in much the same way as bias described as aversive racism and earns the description "aversive sexism" (Ramirez-Melgoza and Cox, 2006; Dovidio and Gaertner, 2004).

[2] This notion of "false consciousness" differs from the philosophical (Marxist or existential) notions of false consciousness, and is defined as "holding beliefs that are contrary to one's personal or group interest and which thereby contribute to the maintenance of the disadvantaged position of the self or the group" (Jost and Banaji, 1994: 3). While the IAT is not designed to be a measure of individual bias, the effect of taking it can be deeply humbling nonetheless.

individuals. It often includes a tendency to unconsciously grant higher value to men, to males, and to qualities associated with masculinity, as well as adopting a masculine standard, altogether described as "androcentrism" (Lem, 1993).[3] Male stereotypes have been found cross-culturally to be generally more positive than female stereotypes (Williams et al., 1999: 523),[4] and these stereotypes capture how people view men and women, boys and girls, and perhaps even how we conceive ourselves (524). Describing such biases as *status quo biases* helps to distinguish them from other fundamental social dispositions, which include preference for those like ourselves or with whom we identify ("in-group justification"), and prioritizing our personal interests over the interests of others, based on self-esteem ("self-justification").[5]

Status quo biases such as the one exhibited by my IAT result have been shown by psychologists to affect almost everyone (Jost et al., 2009), as we view each other along lines of gender, age, and often race, among other dimensions of social difference. While all people as we reason may need to interpret our experiences using social categories, reliance on those categories can undermine even the knowledge that we value especially for its objectivity. Scientific findings can systematically exhibit androcentrism, treating men, males, or masculinity as standard (for sampling, setting goals, or establishing research problems, for instance), in a way that suggests problems with the popular conception that objectivity is a quality that an individual person can possess.

I begin by explaining the nature of status quo bias, as identified by system justification theory, describing how its implicit operation distinguishes it from other social biases, and considering its effects on what we take ourselves to know. I then explore the remedies for errors arising from that bias that the fallacies approach to argument evaluation might provide, through Douglas Walton's account of fallacies. He maintains that fallacies arise from excessive discursive pressure on presumptive schemes of reasoning. I show how that understanding of fallacies can helpfully diagnose some of the epistemological (and ultimately political) problems posed by status quo bias, and address the foundation of status

---

[3] The article originally proposing system justification theory, Jost and Banaji (1994), does not specify that the stereotypes underpinning status quo bias involve hierarchies, but in practice stereotypes reflect hierarchical relationships among groups of people, which in later formulations the second tenet of system justification theory makes explicit (Jost, Banaji, and Nosek, 2004: 889).

[4] The results show high scores for males in four out of five evaluative factors for self-esteem.

[5] Sometimes "status quo bias" refers in the literature to the not specifically social bias toward the default choice, rather than new options (e.g. Suri et al., 2013). However, the same language has been used (more accurately in my view, given the social connotations of "status quo") to refer specifically to the implicit social biases that reflect social hierarchies; and that name captures well both the contingent and political qualities of the basic dispositions described by system justification theory.

quo bias and the motivation for system justification, which is the psychological need for stability and control. The fallacies approach to addressing errors in argumentation has a historical and philosophical pedigree tracing back to Aristotle that lends it authority. Identifying the source of error as a fallacy also stresses that other reasoners share in this bias, and that the resulting mistakes do not entail a personal moral or epistemic culpability (at least to the extent that reasoners have been ignorant of how to address that bias). Thinking about fallacies provides tools for shared discourse and a more social and effective approach to objectivity that can help reasoners to grapple with the influence of status quo bias.

1 Androcentrism, Implicit Bias, and Biased Knowledge

Androcentrism may be understood as a form of "centrism" more generally: the presumption that those with social privilege are standard, in the sense of average or exemplary. Centrism takes the forms of racism or ethnocentrism, heterosexism, and ableism, as well as other types of discrimination (Plumwood, 1996), and it operates by way of stereotypes.[6] In androcentric (and so patriarchal) cultures and thought, masculinity brings privilege. The androcentric dimension of status quo bias entails the employment of androcentric stereotypes, the association of men, males, and masculinity with valued characteristics, which supports the treatment of those subjects or those types of features as standard. Such stereotypes orient people to the social realities where we make predictions and moral decisions, and yet stereotypes may have little basis in fact. They also often override biases that provide self-esteem and social identity, as I will explain, which provides the critical evidence of their implicit operation. So, implicit biases, such as the status quo bias accounted for by system justification theory, may have profound effects on people's judgment and decisions.

1.1 System justification motive and status quo bias

System justification theory developed historically out of the earlier "just world hypothesis" and the theory of cognitive dissonance (Jost and Banaji, 1994: 13–14; Lerner, 1980). It recognizes like the just world hypothesis people's psychological motivation to believe in the steadiness and justness of the current social system. According to system justification theory, trust that the world is and will continue

---

[6] Treating androcentrism as part of the web of centrism to which system justification appeals helps to address some of the problems with critiques of androcentrism discussed by Hegarty et al. (2013).

to be somewhat fair serves three needs: epistemic, existential, and relational. Epistemically, it provides a sense of predictability that reduces the uncertainty people feel and creates a steady worldview. Likewise, if the social system appears just then many sorts of threats seem more manageable, stable, and predictable, which psychologists describe as existential needs. Finally, sharing a perception of reality improves how people can relate to each other, and so it "may be easier to establish common ground concerning system-justifying (vs. system-challenging) beliefs" (Jost et al., 2012: 322–3). Social stereotypes provide a framework for shared understanding, and can bias reasoning toward the political status quo that includes male social dominance.

People's implicit motivation to justify the status quo makes it likely that a person's impressions and evaluations of others reflect social stereotypes in ways that evade that person's self-reflection. Some influential stereotypes include the association of white men with ambitious careers rather than "mere" jobs or the traditional home-making that tends to be associated with women, and broadly negative associations for people of color. The structure of the social order, or how we perceive it to be structured—for instance, with white men labouring in the prestigious public sphere and people of color having low status—affects how reasoners view people according to membership in those social categories. Some of these impressions have no evidential basis and amount to cultural myths; they may even conflict with our experience of real individuals. A physician friend of mine had a toddler who knew well that his mother was a "girl" and a "doctor" but was also convinced that only boys and not girls could be doctors. The use of such stereotypes becomes complicated as each person we perceive belongs to multiple categories and the stereotypes used to interpret them interact in novel ways. For instance, some men may not work in the public sphere, and this may hold for most older men; or a person's ethnic identity may be perceived in opposite ways to gender identity, as is the case for ethnically Asian[7] women regarding their skill at quantitative reasoning (Shih, Pittinsky, and Ambady, 1999). Exactly how forms of marginalization intersect, such that stereotypes take more specific forms—for gay men, perhaps, or working-class women—has received little attention. The quite large body of available evidence indicates that stereotypes—"schemas" in Virginia Valian's preferred terminology (1998) and "frames" for Cecilia Ridgeway (2011)— quite universally and often unconsciously influence how we perceive people.

Status quo social predictions generally seem justified—the "justification" in "system justification theory"—as well as probable. Cognitive stereotypes based on

---

[7] While "Asian" is not an ethnicity in any traditional sense, it nevertheless marks out a social category perceived to be distinctively strong in quantitative reasoning.

our past impressions of social difference influence our perceptions and thus our predictions. The first tenet of system justification theory holds that people view what we consider likely to happen as also desirable. "People will rationalize the (anticipated) status quo by judging likely events to be more desirable than unlikely events..." (Jost, Banaji, and Nosek, 2004: 889). The second tenet of system justification theory explains that "people will use stereotypes to rationalize social and economic status differences between groups, so that the same target group will be stereotyped differently depending on whether it is perceived to be high or low in status" (889).

Status quo bias regularly overrides group identity and personal interest. People tend to hold biases favouring members of our own social groups: "partisanship" and "ethnocentrism" both fall under "group justification" which has long been recognized (Jost, Banaji, and Nosek 2004: 882). This bias receives attention in Howard Kahane's classic textbook on reasoning and argumentation, when he posits the fallacy of "provincialism" as showing preference for members of one's own group (Kahane, 1971; Kahane and Cavender, 2005). A historical bias towards one's own time, such as treating late-twentieth-century fertility rates as representing humans historically (Lloyd, 2005: 91), would be an example. In addition, people hold biases that favour our own individual interests over the interests of others. Both these other forms of social bias can be overwhelmed by the status quo bias favouring members of more advantaged groups, such as men and white people, and marginalizing members of less advantaged groups, such as women and people of color. A case in point is that women regularly author accounts of the female orgasm that employ a male standard (Lloyd, 2005).

1.2 The implicit operation of status quo bias

The key evidence for status quo bias that distinguishes its operation from social identity bias is studies showing that people belonging to disadvantaged groups hold a distinct and otherwise inexplicable "out-group bias" (Jost, 2001). This preference for people in the more privileged group demonstrates the operation of a social motive that conflicts with social identity (and self-esteem) to the extent that it has been described as creating a "false consciousness" (Jost and Banaji, 1994). It may also conflict with explicit political commitments, operating as an "aversive bias," such that even feminists may exhibit bias against women. Both conflicts persist because status quo bias tends to operate implicitly through the broad associations of stereotypes and so mostly unconsciously, rather than being readily or clearly present to people's minds. A heightened sense of personal objectivity, such as scientists may have, actually makes reasoners more vulnerable to status quo bias.

The implicit nature of the status quo or system justification motive makes it possible for people in low-status groups (e.g. women and people of color) to exhibit out-group favoritism (e.g. for men and white people)—a phenomenon described by the sixth hypothesis of system justification theory (Jost, Banaji, and Nosek, 2004: 892–99). Social stereotypes, such as that men have careers or African Americans are lazy, can affect our thinking even when we are women or African American—members of the disadvantaged groups, and when we have contrary conscious beliefs (Dovidio and Gaertner, 2004). Members of disadvantaged groups sometimes exhibit status quo bias most strongly. "If there is a motive to justify the system in order to reduce ideological dissonance and defend against threats to the system's legitimacy, it follows that those who suffer the most from the system are also those who have the most to explain, justify, and rationalize" (Jost, Banaji, and Nosek, 2004: 909). This phenomenon reveals how system justification helps reasoners to deal with cognitive dissonance: a powerful mechanism for neutralizing the appearance of threat turns out to be the endorsement of stereotypes. The stereotypes become internalized and grant favour to the privileged group. While confidence in the social order may be quite contrary to one's own individual self-esteem and group identity, it encourages positive feelings and discourages negative feelings. For instance, in at least some racial groups (European Americans but not African Americans), low-income people who score high for system justification motive also have heightened senses of well-being, security, and mastery (Rankin, Jost, and Wakslak, 2009).

Status quo bias operates more strongly on implicit than on explicit measures (Jost, Banaji, and Nosek, 2004), which helps to explain why people's results on the IAT can surprise and alarm them. Many people taking the test experience personal epiphanies, though not a happy "eureka moment" that we might enjoy and more like the disillusioned recognition that "the emperor has no clothes." The discomfort people feel when confronted with the evidence for implicit bias marks the power of that bias, Jost et al. (2009) argue. Many people find the evidence difficult to accept, though the idea has a long history and the results of the IAT are merely the latest addition to decades of research into unconscious social biases.

The main operation of status quo motives being unconscious also distinguishes them from people's avowed commitments and our social identities. People tend to exaggerate their self-interest and group solidarity because of peer pressure to affirm those biases (Jost, Banaji, and Nosek, 2004: 893; Ratner and Miller, 2001). We regularly hear advice to "believe in yourself," "root for the home team," and "take pride in your country" even from those appalled by the notion of "white pride." The public nature of such encouragement seems to make it easier to observe those biases in ourselves. Such appeals for self-esteem and group affiliation can also mask implicit commitments to the status quo.

Given the substantially implicit operation of status quo bias, we should expect to have trouble finding explicit examples of it. Plus, social dimensions such as race and gender are socially sensitive: people do not want to be seen as socially biased. Furthermore, people may wish to directly eliminate bias in their own thinking and to "treat people as people"—for instance, to be "color-blind" or "gender-blind." Thus, both social pressure and explicit personal values can motivate people to control the expression of prejudice so that explicit expressions and behaviour do not exhibit implicit biases (Jost et al., 2009: 44–5; Greenwald et al., 2009; Uhlmann and Cohen, 2007: 208). So we may easily underestimate how status quo thinking affects our reasoning.

Psychological studies indicate that people define merit in ways that reflect the qualities of members of privileged groups (Uhlmann and Cohen, 2005). Participants high in self-perceived objectivity are especially likely to favour men over women, independently of their conscious biases (Uhlmann and Cohen, 2005: 475–6).

Participants were primed with a sense of personal objectivity by asking them to complete (ostensibly as part of a separate study) four self-perceived objectivity questionnaire items. These items were "In most situations, I try to do what seems reasonable and logical," "When forming an opinion, I try to objectively consider all of the facts I have access to," "My judgments are based on a logical analysis of the facts," and "My decision making is rational and objective."   (Uhlmann and Cohen, 2007: 209)

Scientists may be especially subject to contextual cues about personal objectivity that can license the expression of personal biases. Organizational contexts may enhance one's sense of personal objectivity, and the popular perception that scientists should be more objective than other people may undermine itself, as may the positions of power and titles that scientists hold (Uhlmann and Cohen, 2007: 218–20).

The practice of wearing lab coats in laboratory settings may make people feel that they are dispassionately rational, leading them to act on stereotypic beliefs and thoughts that they might have. And the use of certain formal titles in professional and organizational contexts (e.g. sir, director, professor) may implicitly instigate a sense that one's judgmental tendencies are above reproach. Simply advancing in the corporate hierarchy may further give rise to a sense of objectivity.   (Uhlmann and Cohen, 2007: 219)

Scientists may come to perceive objectivity as a personal quality gained through their own rigorous training, which may make them more vulnerable than others to implicit biases. Certainly, studies show faculty members in the biological and physical sciences to be no less biased than the students who are more typical research subjects, and the bias appears to be unintentional because it operates independently of scientists' gender, discipline, age, or tenure status (Moss-Racusin et al., 2012: 16477). The masculine associations of science may also increase the operation of such biases, and it does with gender priming (Uhlmann and Cohen, 2007). As Uhlmann and Cohen note, heightened confidence in one's intuitions may be advisable when those intuitions are tested and true, but a significant danger remains that such confidence become overextended and generalized.

1.3 Androcentric 'knowledge'

System justification theory builds on decades of research that indicates many different ways in which people's behaviour and reasoning reflect status quo assumptions. Classic examples include the effect that the gender or ethnicity of a name can have on the grade given for a school assignment (Harari and McDavid, 1973), and whether a person receives a tenancy, a job, a promotion, or retains a position (Moss-Racusin, Molenda, and Cramer, in press; Moss-Racusin et al., 2012; Uhlmann and Cohen, 2005; Uhlmann and Cohen, 2007; Lee, 2005). More subtly, recent research shows that people will expend more effort in a task that supports the status quo than one that seems neutral (Jost et al., 2012: 323; Ledgerwood et al., 2011). The success of personal relationships—friendships and dating—that cross racial boundaries also seems to depend more on implicit bias than conscious political views (Jost et al., 2009: 44–5), and even our interaction with robots reflects gender stereotypes (Eyssel and Hegel, 2012). Gender-based thinking has broad cultural presence, near universality, and provides a basic framework for organizing and understanding social environments (Ridgeway, 2011; Williams, Satterwhite, and Best, 1999). We can find androcentric reasoning in all sorts of ordinary contexts, from playgrounds and parking lots to dinner tables, boardrooms, and editorial pages. One of the central insights of feminist theory has been the ubiquity of androcentric views (Little, 1996), and much of the history of feminism involves weeding out androcentrism (Hegarty et al., 2013).

A range of compelling examples showing how androcentric assumptions impede people's attempts to gain knowledge have emerged from the biological sciences, medicine, and psychology.[8] An androcentric norm entails the treatment

---

[8] Kathleen Okruhlik explains why these examples have special importance: "Feminist critiques of biology have been especially important in the political struggle for gender equality because biologically determinist arguments are so often cited to 'explain' women's oppression. They explain why it is

of women and feminine behaviours as requiring explanation (Miller, Taylor, and Buck 1991). Many articles and books from the feminist critiques of science reveal androcentrism operating in forms of reasoning that we consider most true and reliable. Science tends to be upheld as the highest, most value-neutral and objective, or most sophisticated form of understanding, in part because it is most practically powerful and heavily scrutinized. The power to explain and guide can however be corrupted by the tacit presence of sociopolitical biases. The operation of gendered stereotypes in science may be reasonably attributed to status quo bias so long as we have no evidence of another source for it.

Androcentric assumptions can also take the form of treating women in the same way as men. The recommendation to diagnose women's inability to have orgasm in the same terms as men's can be found in (at least in the third edition of) *The Diagnostic and Statistical Manual* of the American Psychiatric Association, Carol Tavris notes. That treatment neglects relevant features common to women's lives, including relative lack of sexual freedom or encouragement to experiment, poorer physical self-image, low status in intimate relationships with men, likelihood of past sexual exploitation, insecure reproductive rights, and a limited window of conventional sexual attractiveness (1992: 231). In addition, women's physiology entails much less stimulation and, as mentioned above, radically lower likelihood of orgasm than men experience in the sexual activity that receives the most attention, i.e. penis in vagina. Scientists have treated women in men's terms also by assuming women fall asleep after orgasm or reach orgasm reliably from sexual intercourse (Lloyd, 2005).

Androcentric assumptions entail that any difference in women, girls, or femininity stands to be explained. The normative slide from different to deviant may account for some of the obstacles women face in the discipline of philosophy (Beebee, 2013: 69–70). Also, the designation of 'pre-menstrual syndrome' or 'PMS' entails that women have a 'normal disorder' which may seem to validate women's experience but also stigmatizes them. The "woman problem" designation obscures difficulties that deserve attention such as irregular cycles and depression, along with personal and professional grievances; it also deflects attention from normal feelings of grumpiness and weariness that both women

'natural' for women to function in a socially subordinate role, why men are smarter and more aggressive than women, why women are destined to be homebodies, and why men rape. Genes, hormones, and evolutionary processes are cited as determinants of this natural order and ultimately as evidence that interventions to bring about a more egalitarian and just society are either useless or counterproductive" (1994, "Gender and the biological sciences," *Canadian Journal of Philosophy* Supplementary Volume 20: 21).

and men may have. For these reasons, Tavris argues against treating women as abnormal without also questioning the masculine norm (1992: 144–57).

Reasoners evaluate females and femininity according to a model that privileges males and masculinity whenever we advise that women and girls change their behaviour to accommodate men and boys. For instance, notoriously, in 2011 a representative of the Toronto Police stated 'women should avoid dressing like sluts in order not to be victimized' (SlutWalk Toronto, 2013). Such arguments tend to assume that men's and boys' behaviour cannot and should not be questioned or criticized, never mind reformed; masculinity sets the standard around which everyone must operate. Many well-placed editorials (e.g. Yoffe, 2013, discussed further below) have taken such a stance recently by raising panic about women's alcohol consumption (Hess, 2013), and seem to show the force of implicit androcentrism.

How androcentric bias operates in science and can become perpetuated by virtue of science's authority can be seen in a popular form of health education. Human reproduction, as many of us were instructed in 'sex-education' classes,[9] involves the active sperm charging up and fighting off competitors to conquer or (alternatively) animate the passive ovum. Further dimensions of male stereotypes come into play: militarism, competitiveness, aggression, invigoration, and other valued traits describe the contribution of the sperm to fertilization. Such metaphors long dominated how people understood fertilization, and prevented the observation of activity that does not accord with gender stereotypes. Whatever accuracy the androcentric model may hold, it remains quite incomplete in neglecting activity on the part of the ovum and the participation of the surrounding reproductive organs (Biology and Gender Study Group, 1988; Martin, 1991). Another classic case pertains to the anthropological theory of "man the hunter." That androcentric account was rejected in the 1970s and 1980s through the advance of an alternative "woman the gatherer" theory, and paved the way for more complex and intersectional accounts of gender (Longino and Doell, 1983; Liesen, 1998; Sterling, 2014).

Suppressing or counteracting status quo bias demands more effective strategies than broad social pressure and good intentions may provide. Consider, for instance, that people viewing research evidence consider it to be stronger and more valid when it suggests that economic rewards come from effort. Tacit faith in meritocracy plays out even in people who have contrary commitments, explicitly maintaining that their society fails to be adequately meritocratic

---

[9] Confusing reproduction with sexuality also displays androcentrism: reproduction does not require female orgasm as it does the male orgasm.

(Ledgerwood et al., 2011). Ordinary exposure to evidence about how inequality operates in our society may do little to undermine androcentric thinking; status quo bias may even prevent us from recognizing the evidence. Other biases, such as in-group bias, might compound that difficulty, as men tend to have greater difficulty recognizing evidence of bias against women (Moss-Racusin, Molenda, and Cramer, in press). Practices that do not work to remedy status quo bias include personal reflection and self-evaluation of the sort that have been central to awareness training that aims to sensitize people to their own biases, as Valian explains (1998: 315).

Sexism and social injustice in science, as elsewhere, consists of more than androcentrism and other forms of centrism (Bem, 1993), and the ultimate, permanent solution to the effects of hierarchical stereotypes probably lies in how we raise children to view the social world (Ridgeway, 2011; Valian, 1998: 331–2)—a line of reform that can be traced back via the notion of socialization at least to Simone de Beauvoir (1989/1949). Changing children's upbringing involves many obstacles, and at best provides only a long-term strategy. In the meantime we need to negotiate contexts in which status quo bias infects our reasoning with sexist (and other unjust) stereotypes. We can draw inspiration from some successes, such as the now regular practice of using a screen for auditions to hide a musician's identity which has allowed women to get much more orchestra work (Goldin and Rouse, 1997). Techniques for other situations and more general strategies need development.

2 Resources in the Fallacies Approach to Argument Evaluation

Among the possible strategies remaining to be explored we must consider techniques of argumentation.[10] The fallacies approach to argument evaluation constitutes the most traditional technique for criticizing reasoning, though it has often lacked coherence and argumentation theorists have contested its value (Hamblin, 1970; Hundleby, 2010; Woods, 2013). The identification of fallacies has described errors in reasoning since ancient times, beginning with Aristotle's *On Sophistical Refutations*. The technique grew and developed over time, and it became standard to learn a list of fallacy names to describe patterns of error,

---

[10] Virginia Valian begins *Why So Slow? The Advancement of Women* (1998) with several examples of how small differences in credibility can affect women's progress, including those in contexts of argumentation.

especially for students in logic and critical thinking courses (at least in philosophy, and where such courses are offered—primarily in North America) and also for law students. In this way, fallacy names such as "begging the question" and "*ad hominem*" can even serve as a shorthand and *lingua franca* among educated professionals when we criticize each other's reasoning.[11]

Some appeals to the status quo might be analyzed with the established fallacy of *ad verecundiam,* which addresses arguments that appeal to authority. Deference to a person holding high social status receives the description *ad verecundiam* reasoning in John Locke's *Essay Concerning Human Understanding.* Prior to Locke, the problematic effect of social status on reasoning received attention from Antoine Arnauld and Pierre Nicole in "The Port-Royal Logic," formally titled *Logic, or the Art of Thinking.* These precursors to the fallacy now known as "inappropriate appeal to authority" directed reasoners to pay attention to what people say and to what expertise they may have, instead of to social status. That contemporary fallacy label helps to reveal some occasions when testimonial bias operates, when we are more likely to believe a claim because of the person who utters it. When we listen to a physician rather than a midwife, it may be a case of inappropriate appeal to expertise, if the physician is not an obstetrician, say. "Inappropriate appeal to authority" stands among many other kinds of fallacy that figure commonly in textbooks and classes in critical thinking. It may serve to help reasoners identify the more relevant matter—expertise—that ought to guide our reasoning instead of the social authority that status quo bias encourages us to prioritize. The seventeenth–eighteenth-century advice seems to have become so accepted in contemporary liberal democracies that current textbooks often neglect to address social authority as a distraction from the proper sources of persuasion; instead, they focus on mistaken appeals to expertise (Hansen, 2006; Goodwin, 1998).

Even with the direction to attend to appropriate expertise rather than social status, a man's testimony may gain unwarranted credibility due to androcentric bias. The influence of social authority has not been neutralized by meritocratic ideals. People unsatisfied with the level of meritocracy in their society still implicitly assume that reward follows merit and that people gain positions of authority due to demonstrated merit (Ledgerwood et al., 2011). So, we might listen better to the male nurse even if we have consciously learned that his female "peer" works harder and is more qualified for the job. The effects of such bias on credibility and the acceptance of testimony are beginning to receive attention

---

[11] The classic texts and central articles from the late twentieth century can be found in Hansen and Pinto, 1995.

from argumentation theorists (Bondy, 2010; Linker, 2014; Linker, 2011; Rooney, 2012; Yap, 2013). Although the traditionally recognized fallacy of appeal to authority provides some assistance with the effects of status quo bias on the acceptance of testimony, that bias has further effects, and the fallacies approach to argument evaluation can offer further resources.

Identification of fallacies provides rather unique resources for debiasing because they are inherently dialectical or discursive, operating in a verbal exchange between people. They were originally, for Aristotle, tactics in a dialectical exercise, and the scholars who have been most seriously concerned with a unified account of fallacies—Hamblin (1970) and Walton (1995)—have directed us to treat them as tools for argumentative discourse. Fallacy allegations are meant to engage the speaker who allegedly stands in error, and provide a debiasing strategy that people work through together.

3 Fallacies as Serious Mistakes in Inference Schemes

Walton provides the most advanced account of fallacies of argumentation, analyzing them as serious types of error in argumentation, often associated with typical *schemes* of inference constituted by structures involving characteristic presumptions.[12] Walton agrees with other argumentation theorists, such as Johnson (1987), who stress that errors must be serious to count as fallacies. Attributing a fallacy to a piece of reasoning constitutes a strong charge, more than pointing out a misstep or fumble. Status quo bias may not always entail serious error; however, the serious errors that may be reasonably attributed to status quo bias might become easier to discern if reasoners would scout argumentation for fallacies characterized by status quo bias. One form we can identify assumes centrism, that one group of people or their qualities are the norm, such as men providing the standard in androcentrism.

Inference schemes involve characteristic assumptions described as *presumptions* to mark their pivotal role in the structure or scheme of the inference. A presumption lends an argument greater strength than a mere assumption

---

[12] Following J. Anthony Blair, I refer to *inference* schemes rather than *argumentation* schemes, changing Walton's language that seems too restrictive. Also, based on Walton's description of schemes as acceptable, I take it to be a normative concept, though we might choose to use the word in a more descriptive fashion especially given the dependence of a scheme's value on its proper employment in dialectical context (Blair, 2001: 368). It is important to note too that Walton (1995) recognizes a range of fallacies that do not correspond to any particular scheme, such as appeals to force. What goes wrong in such cases must be diagnosed at the larger level of argumentation *themes* and the purpose served by the discourse in which the argument occurs. I will not be dealing with those sorts of error, in order to simplify the discussion.

(though it is a type of assumption) because it suggests that the assumption or line of reasoning is broadly acceptable (Walton, 2010). Presumptive schemes of inference have characteristic strengths, may be supported by additional premises, and remain vulnerable to related questions. For instance, *ad hominem* arguments presume that personal characteristics may undermine the truth of a speaker's claim: person x's undesirable quality z provides reason to doubt x's claim about y. That presumption should remain open for question or support, regarding whether personal qualities have any relevance to the line of reasoning, and more specifically how a generally undesirable quality z relates particularly to claims regarding subject matter y. So long as that presumption stands, it helps to define and direct the burden of proof for the argument as a whole. Accepting the presumption in an argument commits the speaker and the audience to employing specific patterns of defeasible reasoning. By contrast, ordinary assumptions may play more incidental roles and not influence the importance of each other, or assumptions may play stronger roles when taken to be independently relevant facts, rather than aspects of an integrated and defeasible pattern of reasoning (Walton, 1995).

Other presumptions that establish the nature of a scheme might include that a certain sample allows a type of generalization, or that a person's expertise or authority warrants what he or she says (*ad verecundiam*). Each type of presumption gains force from supporting premises that contribute in ways specific to that particular scheme of presumption. For instance, the *ad hominem* form becomes acceptable when supported by a demonstration that the qualities of the person in question have relevance to the person's claims. People's honesty, say, may have some general relevance to the acceptability of their claims, but their political affiliations may not. Other premises may play supporting roles according to the type of presumption, and together they constitute the scheme of inference.

Supporting premises in presumptive inferences address characteristic vulnerabilities of a sort not found with inductive or deductive inferences. Just as the proper use of *ad hominem* depends on establishing a connection between generally undesirable qualities of the speaker and the type of subject matter addressed by the speaker, the inference scheme of an appeal to expertise depends on supporting assumptions and admits certain exceptions regarding the presumed expertise. The assumptions may include that the supposed expert has (relevant) knowledge (premise 1) and that he or she has knowledge in the specific field (premise 2).

1. *p is an expert in q.*
2. *r is a matter in field q.*
3. *p asserts that r.*
4. *r is true.* (Walton, 2010: 170)

The exceptions include evidence that the purported expert is personally unreliable:

5. *p has committed research fraud before.* (170)

Such qualifying reasons may be considered by a skilled reasoner, and may be filled out discursively with critical questions specific to the scheme. For instance, among scientists we would not need to question the expertise of a speaker regarding science in general, but more specific critical questions might become relevant. Supporting premises may be added as a result of the questioning process. So Walton's "pragmatic approach" to fallacies has been described also as the "critical questions approach."[13]

These full-fledged schemes provide ideals and do not represent universal or even common practice. Many people, and everyone some of the time, may neglect some components of a scheme and rely only on the more basic version, the parascheme:

6. *p is an expert.*
3. *p asserts that r.*
4. *r is true.* (Walton, 2010: 170)

Proposition 6, *p is an expert*, or in the full scheme propositions 1 and 3, provide the presumption(s) characteristic of appeals to expertise. Employing it in an attenuated version of the scheme need not always be a problem, such as when the audience understands well the scope of the expertise and finds uncontroversial its relevance to the topic at hand.

However, when reasoners neglect—as we often do—the dependence of an inference's strength on its characteristic presumptions and fail to consider the necessary context by way of adding assumptions or addressing critical questions, we can fall into error. According to Walton (2010), reasoners often lack awareness of the defeasible nature of the premises in an inference scheme. That ignorance arises because we hear others use and find that others accept shorter "paraschemes" consisting in the core inference of a scheme. When reasoners depend too heavily on paraschemes and fail to recognize the robust implication of background considerations, then errors arise. Fallacies result from a particular use of an inference scheme becoming irretrievably mucked up in the discursive processes in which argumentation operates, Walton argues; some applications of inference schemes cannot be adequately filled out with acceptable supporting premises.

---

[13] A textbook adaptation of Walton's approach can be found in Tindale (2007).

A presumptive scheme of inference can be undermined in ways quite local to a particular inference scheme, when speakers violate the rules that govern particular presumptions. Consider an argument that appeals to expertise from a physicist in order to account for the origin of a biological species—an area not part of a physicist's expertise. Such mistakes—sometimes made on creationist websites—can be prevented by attention to premise (1) or by asking critical questions about the nature of the expertise in (6).

Disruption of an inference scheme also may arise from complications that have no characteristic role in that scheme. For instance, linguistic ambiguity can make a generalization too hasty (a fallacy of sampling) or distort a character-based argument (suggesting *ad hominem* and *ad verecundiam*), which are forms of argumentation governed by distinct presumptive schemes.

The discursive norms identified by Grice (1991) explain the central stumbling blocks that give rise to fallacies, according to Walton (1995). Grice's cooperative principle of conversation requires that one "make . . . conversational contribution such as is required, at the stage at which it occurs, by the accepted purpose or direction of the talk exchange . . ." (Grice, 1991: 26). This principle gives rise to four maxims demanding: (1) an appropriate *quantity* of information; (2) adherence to norms of *truth*; (3) *relevance*; and (4) efficient *manner*. Violation of these norms may be quite commonplace, and norm (4) demanding efficient manner may sometimes be served by employing paraschemes as a shorthand. Yet the violation of the norms may also lead to serious errors in presumptive reasoning that render an argument impossible to repair, thus constituting a fallacy, according to Walton.

Larger-scale illicit shifts in discourse may work their way down into specific lines of reasoning. Some serious types of mistake involving the broadest aspects of argumentative discourse can muddle any number of particular schemes of inference all at once. Argumentation tortured by intertwining falsehoods and fallacies is the stock in trade of sensationalist journalists. Such tangles arise more generally when a discussion switches from one form of dialogue to another without that change being agreed upon by the discussants. For instance, *ad baculum* reasoning, or appeal to force, has no proper role in what tends to be considered the most important form of argumentative dialogue, persuasion, in which speakers aim to resolve a disagreement. Purposes for argumentation besides persuasion—and which may conflict with that goal—include venting emotions in a quarrel dialogue or a verbal 'fight,' and reaching the terms for a material exchange, such as in a negotiation dialogue or bartering. Forceful tactics can be quite appropriate for quarrels and even negotiations, but not for persuasion or inquiry, discursive contexts in which they constitute the *ad baculum* fallacy (Walton, 1995, 1998). These tactics only have merit if the discussants agree to participate in a form of discussion in which force can properly belong; otherwise, they constitute serious violations of Grice's cooperative principle.

4 The Status Quo Presumption and Parascheme

Identifying the inference scheme that characteristically manifests status quo bias demands some reverse engineering, starting with the presumption, and short parascheme, working back to consider what conditions might make it reasonable, and noting omissions that can be problematic. Unequivocal examples of any fallacy can be difficult to find, which provides part of the reason that textbook authors manufacture examples or draw them from conversation and on-line discussion. Examples of androcentric argumentation occur whenever one person criticizes another for being like a girl or a woman, or being a "wuss" or a "sissy." They include assuming that people will only relate to characters in books and movies that are men or boys, and taking masculine pronouns as neutral; sometimes they seriously interfere with the reasoning, but not all androcentric errors in argumentation will amount to fallacies. While interesting and substantial examples may not often make it to official publication venues, even science provides examples of reasoning seriously disrupted by status quo or centrist assumptions. Violations of all of Grice's conversational maxims can be found entwined with androcentric bias that Elisabeth Lloyd (2006) finds to be ubiquitous to the evolutionary accounts of the female orgasm.

First, all evolutionary accounts of the female orgasm (at the time of Lloyd's analysis) assume that female sexuality is like male sexuality (Lloyd, 2005: 225). Failing to address the quantity of available evidence about female sexuality violates Grice's first maxim. Neglect of evidence becomes especially apparent in the assumption that women orgasm only in intercourse—an act that is highly conducive to male orgasm (224). That assumption can be found in every available evolutionary account of female orgasm. Another common assumption based on male patterns of orgasm, found in twelve of the original eighteen theories analyzed by Lloyd, is that orgasm reliably occurs with intercourse. To top it off, ten accounts ignore how their hypotheses conflict directly with the available research on female sexuality, such as in the famous studies by Alfred Kinsey and Shere Hite.

Second, androcentrism in the study of the evolution of the female orgasm flouts norms of truth, violating Grice's second maxim. Even when evolutionary biologists cite the sexology research, they bypass the overwhelming evidence that it provides that women are unlikely to orgasm during "unassisted" intercourse[14]—a fact that Lloyd describes as "the orgasm–intercourse discrepancy" (2, 59). Their use of evidence runs contrary to accepted norms of research—norms that these scientists themselves otherwise employ (241).

When accounts of the female orgasm do draw on the sex research, they use it selectively, and they misinterpret it especially by presenting evidence that comes exclusively from men as applying generally to humans; they misinterpret the word "men" as including women (43, 224–6). In this way, violations of both Grice's third maxim of relevance and fourth maxim of efficient expression, that would demand consistent use of language, interfere with the progress of the discourse. The violation of multiple discursive maxims need not indicate that different fallacies come into play. Many fallacies break more than one rule (Walton, 1995: 228–9) as holds for androcentrism. However, the various faces of the problem revealed by the ways available for categorizing errors suggest that the forms of diagnosis we have do not suffice to characterize the general pattern.

Some androcentric argumentation in science can be identified as adherence to a form of androcentric inference:

x is true of men, males, or masculinity.
Therefore, x.

The more general inference pattern can be expressed in the following parascheme:

1. x is true of subjects that are y.
2. Therefore, x.

(I speak of subjects rather than people because social categories sometimes influence people's views of non-humans topics, including biological components such as gametes, and activities such as childcare.) The questions remain of what sort of inference scheme gets mucked up, and what gets left out in the parascheme just identified. Because in many environments reasoners would not assent to such an inference, we need to consider what circumstances might make it acceptable. For Walton (2010), the warranted practice explains the attraction of the parascheme.

Psychology shows that implicit social biases significantly influence how people evaluate others as job applicants and students. While we might hope that science would be immune from these sorts of biases, the evidence indicates the contrary:

---

[14] The idea that anything going on at the same time as intercourse (notably clitoral stimulation) "assists" intercourse assumes the centrality of intercourse and men's orgasm, but not women's orgasm, to sexuality. Androcentrism operates in that background consideration too, though may not undermine discursive reasoning the way the violations of Grice's maxims can.

the ideal of the objective scientist may make scientists more vulnerable to implicit biases such as sexist stereotypes.

More commonplace manifestations of this bias, and cases where there are few alternative explanations, can be found in decisions about hiring, promotion, and awards. When these judgments rest on shared deliberation, argumentation comes into play. In all these cases, the crucial missing presumption that would discharge the burden of proof is the following:

1.1   Subjects that are *y* are standard.

Premise (1.1) indicates the background presumption with a complexity and contestability that demand qualification. Further premises and critical questions addressing it will flesh out the full inference scheme.

This presumption resembles errors in generalization from samples, including hasty generalization, *secundum quid*, unrepresentative sample, and accident. That is how Walton (1999: 103) diagnoses social stereotypes, but it fails to address the political dimension and social force behind the error. After all, there exists no tendency corresponding to androcentrism to assume gynocentrism. Hierarchy plays a central role in status quo bias.

In certain cases, androcentric standards may be appropriate: if the research concerns males exclusively or almost exclusively, for instance addressing prostate cancer, a male standard makes sense. Even in the case of prostate cancer, androcentrism may problematically exclude trans-, intersex, and gender fluid people with prostates, an intersectional complication of cissexism and gender binarism. We must be wary of when generalizations reinscribe social marginalization, although no standard will ever be wholly representative. When we presume a standard, the critical questions turn out to be, is *y* standard? Is *y* average? Is *y* ideal?

Sometimes there may be a kernel of truth in stereotypes, but if we allow that automatic presumption we neglect the possibility for change and exception. Furthermore, the predictive accuracy of stereotypes tends to be minimal compared with how heavily we employ them, so that it causes substantial cognitive dissonance for members of subordinate groups (Jost, Banaji, and Nosek, 2004). The stereotype conflicts with their own experience of themselves and other members of the same marginalized group. Moreover, social stereotypes may have no basis in fact at all, not even in personal experience, but derive from cultural tropes, the images of people that we grow up with, as much as real people in our past. A masculine standard is part of many cultural traditions; it is a common, almost universal assumption, as psychology shows, regardless of how many of us consciously reject it.

5 Fallacy Analysis as a Strategy for Status Quo Bias

Fallacies address argumentation, an explicit means of reasoning, and so fallacy analysis might seem to be an unlikely resource for dealing with implicit bias. The hiddenness of appeals to the status quo may be why logicians mostly have ignored them, with the most recent exception being Locke's eighteenth-century recognition of the problem posed by *ad verecundiam* reasoning. Also, status quo biases are often aversive; many of us already try to eliminate them from explicit reasoning, and they conflict with explicit beliefs in ways that can be upsetting. In a deep sense, reasoners do not want any more attention to our own biases. Yet I suggest that fallacy analysis might be trusted for a few different reasons where other approaches might fail. First, the identification of fallacies has a venerable history that makes it seem trustworthy. Second, fallacies are a shared problem, and analyzing errors in those terms may destigmatize them. People also share in the processes of assessing whether a fallacy has been committed such that, third, reasoners can benefit from the perspectives of others. These three conditions may help the technique of fallacy allegation to unearth hidden and unwanted biases and to make them explicit and recognized.

Fallacy analysis holds an established place in "critical thinking" education—a mostly North American practice and ideal, and outside North America logic education regularly includes fallacies too. That cultural entrenchment may allow the fallacies approach to undermine the resistance which people have in accepting the possibility for social change, including accepting that their own psychology may be influenced by unjust stereotypes. It may help assuage people's anxiety, whether conscious or not. Jost et al. (2009: 40) note that "resistance is all the more likely when social scientific discoveries seem to challenge long-cherished personal or cultural assumptions, such as the relatively hopeful messages that (a) human thought and behavior are largely under the control of individual will and consciousness, and (b) racial prejudice in Western societies. .. is a thing of the past." While approaching status quo bias as a fallacy flies in the face of beliefs that social biases are under personal control, it also promises control in a way that may be more palatable than alternatives. Its appeal lies in reassuring reasoners of their individual agency through a technique already established in Western culture. Addressing status quo reasoning alongside *ad verecundiam* and *ad hominem* reasoning makes the questioning seem—to a degree—controllable.

The employment of the fallacies approach suggests also that the bias does not constitute a personal moral failing but a *shared* cognitive difficulty. *Everyone commits fallacies* and ought to learn to avoid them (even if those people never gain the understanding that the problems they avoid have been known by others as "fallacies"). Awareness of that commonality may reassure us about our ability to operate effectively in the world—the same existential need that underlies status quo bias. Alleging that a fallacy has been committed suggests that the error is not personal, and that it is quite predictable. Johnson's (1987) view that an error deserving to be called a fallacy must be frequent underpins much contemporary scholarship on fallacies.

Walton adds that fallacies must be distinguished from arguments that simply have false or questionable premises. Fallacies, on his pragmatic account, are problems because they seriously impede discussion from achieving its goals. Charging someone with committing a fallacy amounts to engaging the other person in a critical discussion—a disagreement in which each person tries to persuade the other regarding the value of a piece of reasoning. Fallacy allegation turns the discussion—or keeps it—in that direction rather than categorically dismissing the reasoning, and stopping the discussion. This employment of critical discussion has a side benefit of contributing to knowledge, according to Walton, helping us to unearth and reflect on background considerations, which he calls a *maieutic effect*, in reference to Socratic epistemic "skill in midwifery."

The maieutic function of a dialogue is the enabling of a participant to express her previously unarticulated but deeply felt commitments in a much more explicit and carefully qualified way through testing them out and trying to defend them in a reasoned discussion with another party who may be skeptical about them or not so inclined to accept them initially.   (1995: 103)

Although a fallacy allegation constitutes a sort of challenge, it also provides an opportunity to reflect on what has been said and to consider it more deeply. When the listener or an audience-member alleges that a fallacy has been committed, that allegation serves as a short-hand to request information, a gesture toward critical questions. The arguer's response must address the sorts of considerations demanded by the full inference scheme in order to fulfill the resulting burden of proof.

One educational challenge will be to ensure that instructors use the right approach in teaching fallacies: most textbooks written by argumentation scholars provide a dialectical context that allows for argumentation repair as part of shared practices of reasoning. When a person alleges that an arguer has committed a fallacy, then that interlocutor takes on an obligation to show how the inference errs. Thus the fallacies approach can be less confrontational than it appears in textbooks which tend to be simplistic and outdated (Hundleby, 2010). When criticizing a piece of writing from an absent author, that author's potential to respond to the criticism must be considered. For example, consider Yoffe's (2013) argument that young women should limit their alcohol consumption because that will lower risks of sexual assault; that position may appeal to androcentric assumptions. Accepting men's behaviour as standard, as we do when we only demand women to reform, can be justified only in very particular circumstances, outlined by a full argumentation scheme. So, to assess the worth of the claim, we look at the supporting reasons. Look first at the reporter who made the claim, then perhaps at the study she cites.[15] The larger social context may be worth addressing too, as a person always speaks against a backdrop—in this case a context in which people often blame the victims of sexual assault and demand sexual responsibility from women to a much greater extent than from men. It may be important that the author offers her point against her questionable background assumption that people generally resist making women accountable for sexual assault. Although that consideration remains doubtworthy, if true (or acceptable) it would explain her minimal criticism of men. The status quo inference scheme might not be in play, and rather some other form of argument. But if we do not accept the premise, then Yoffe remains accountable to the critical questions for appeal to the status quo and seems unlikely to fare well against them.

The *dialectical* context of argumentation, involving different points of view, may be crucial in effectively exhibiting the operation of status quo bias. Even though I may not be able to directly observe my own bias at work, fallacy discourse allows others to suggest its role in my reasoning; it demands that we consider whether the evidence justifies the reasoning and assists by suggesting critical questions. The second-person engagement can take over from the implicit mechanisms we use to resolve cognitive dissonance (Walton, 1995: 248); it can relieve the pressure that encourages reasoners to employ intuitions. Admittedly, shared biases, as status quo biases must regularly be, will limit the contrast provided by the second-person perspective. Yet the differences of one person's biases from another's and the fact that conscious reasoning can sometimes override implicit cognition provide windows for scrutinizing implicit biases that fallacy analysis exploits.

6 Conclusion: The Status Quo Fallacy and Objectivity

The fallacies approach to argument evaluation provides a framework that encourages reasoners to question our own reasoning and also to question each other's. Such a social approach to the status quo bias may help to bring to light

---

[15] Yoffe cites Krebs et al. (2009).

the bias's effects. The critical questions required to suss out fallacies may help us to account for the patterns in our reasoning that we prefer to deny, whether because they are not conscious or because they conflict with our social identities and values. The operation of status quo bias primarily at the implicit level allows it to have significant and far-ranging effects. Its impact may be especially difficult to control, and its effects may extend so far as the content of science. A problem of such a scope demands careful innovation, but that can include the retooling of the classical techniques and ideals. Fallacy analysis helps to diagnose errors in reasoning, especially if treated as a discursive tool; and although the valuing of objectivity can exacerbate status quo bias, objectivity has other dimensions with greater promise.

Critical questions may provide helpfully independent standards, and committing to criteria for evaluation before making decisions reduces discrimination (Uhlmann and Cohen, 2005: 478). Given latitude, reasoners will retrospectively invent criteria to rationalize a preference for male candidates over female (Uhlmann and Cohen, 2005). Just as reasoning about job candidates can be inoculated against the influence of implicit gender bias by structuring an interview according to previously developed questions (Uhlmann and Cohen, 2005: 479; Bragger et al., 2002), so if we make arguers answerable to the critical questions surrounding appeals to the status quo we may help them resist when those appeals are unwarranted.

People often see themselves as not susceptible to bias, but education about the influence of nonconscious processes helps people accept that they might themselves be influenced (Pronin and Kugler, 2007). So might education about fallacies when connected with the psychological literature.

We can also educate against the view of objectivity as a personal quality, which emerged quite recently in the history of the concept of objectivity (Daston, 1992; Daston and Galison, 2007), and encourage alternatives. "Aperspectival objectivity became a scientific value when science came to consist in large part of communications that crossed boundaries of nationality, training and skill." (Daston, 1992: 600). Other meanings are tied to mechanical practices and perceived qualities, and the term is still sometimes used that way. Consider how Uhlmann and Cohen speak of "objective contexts" as those in which "considerable and non-conflicting information is available" (2007, 2008) as those that limit the influence of bias. The information provided by attention to the critical questions fills out the inference scheme and makes clear if there is considerable non-conflicting information to support the presumptive inference. In that sense of objectivity, the fallacies approach provides a significant improvement.

Acknowledgments

Work on this project began during a Visiting Fellowship at Stanford University's Michele R. Clayman Institute for Gender Research in 2011, and was supported by a Social Sciences and Humanities Research Grant from the University of Windsor in 2012–13. This chapter benefits from discussions at a number of meetings: discussion of a poster version at the Implicit Bias and Philosophy Project at the University of Sheffield in July 2013, the Canadian Philosophical Association at the University of Waterloo in 2012, the Joint Session at Stirling University in 2012, Psychology, Emotion and the Human Sciences at the University of Windsor in April 2012, the Feminist Philosophy and Bias conference at Humboldt University in 2011, at Argumentation: Cognition and Community at the University of Windsor in 2011 (and on the CD proceedings), and initially at Oregon State University in April 2011. Advice and questions from Margaret Hundleby, Tim Kenyon, Jennifer Saul, Michael Brownstein, and suggestions from anonymous reviewers helped develop my reasoning, and Brian Nosek pointed me to the key sources in psychology on status quo bias.

References

Beauvoir, S. de (1989/1949). *The Second Sex.* New York: Vintage.

Beebee, H. (2013). "Women and deviance in philosophy." In Hutchison, K. and Jenkins, F. (eds.) *Women in Philosophy: What Needs to Change?* Oxford: Oxford University Press: 61–80.

Bem, S. L. (1993). *The Lenses of Gender: Transforming the Debate on Sexual Inequality.* New Haven, CT: Yale University Press.

Biology and Gender Study Group (1988). "The importance of feminist critique for contemporary cell biology." *Hypatia* 3(1): 172–87.

Blair, J. A. (2001). "Walton's argumentation schemes for presumptive reasoning: A critique and development." *Argumentation* 15: 365–79.

Bragger, J. D., Kutcher, E., Morgan, J., and Firth, P. (2002). "The effects of the structured interview on reducing bias against pregnant job applicants." *Sex Roles* 46(7): 215–26.

Bondy, P. (2010). "Argumentative injustice." *Informal Logic* 30(3): 263–78.

Daston, L. (1992). "Objectivity and the escape from perspective." *Social Studies of Science* 22(4): 597–618.

Daston, L. and Galison, P. (2007). *Objectivity.* New York, NY: Zone Books.

Dovidio, J. F. and Gaertner, S. L. (2004). "Aversive racism." *Advances in Experimental Social Psychology* 36: 1–52.

Eyssel, F. and Hegel, F. (2012). "(S)he's got the look: Gender stereotyping of robots." *Journal of Applied Social Psychology* 42(9): 2213–30.

Goldin, C. and Rouse, C. (1997). "Orchestrating impartiality: The impact of 'blind' auditions on female musicians." *National Bureau of Economic Research Working Paper Series* 5903. Cambridge, MA.

Goodwin, J. (1998). "Forms of authority and the real *ad verecundiam*." *Argumentation* 12: 267–80.

Greenwald, A. G., Poehlman, T. A., Uhlmann, E. L., and Banaji, M. R. (2009). "Understanding and using the Implicit Association Test: III. Meta-analysis of predictive validity." *Journal of Personality and Social Psychology* 97(1): 17–41.

Grice, P. (1991). *Studies in the Way of Words*. Cambridge, MA: Harvard University Press.

Hamblin, C. L. (1970). *Fallacies*. London: Methuen.

Hansen, H. V. (2006). "Whately on arguments involving authority." *Informal Logic* 26(3): 319–40.

Hansen, H. V. and Pinto, R. C. (eds.) (1995). *Fallacies: Classic and Contemporary Readings*. New York: Cambridge University Press.

Harari, H. and McDavid, J. W. (1973). "Name stereotypes and teachers' expectations." *Journal of Educational Psychology* 65(2): 222–5.

Hegarty, P. Parslow, O., Ansara, Y. G., and Quick, F. (2013). "Androcentrism: Changing the landscape without leveling the playing field?" In Ryan, M. K. and Branscombe, N. R. (eds.) *The SAGE Handbook of Gender and Psychology*. New York, NY: Sage: 29–41.

Hess, A. (2013). "The year of the wasted woman." <http://www.slate.com/blogs/xx_factor/2013/12/23/binge_drinking_among_women_trend_stories_blame_feminism_for_a_dubious_increase.html>.

Hundleby, C. E. (2010). "The authority of the fallacies approach to argument evaluation." *Informal Logic* 30(3): 279–308.

Johnson, R. H. (1987). "The blaze of her splendors: Suggestions about revitalizing fallacy theory." *Argumentation* 1(3): 239–53.

Jost, J. T. (2001). "Outgroup favoritism and the theory of system justification: A paradigm for investigating the effects of socioeconomic success on stereotype content." In Moskowitz, G. (ed.), *Cognitive Social Psychology: The Princeton Symposium on the Legacy and Future of Social Cognition*. Mahwah, NJ: Erlbaum: 89–102.

Jost, J. T. and Banaji, M. R. (1994). "The role of stereotyping in system-justification and the production of false consciousness." *British Journal of Social Psychology* 33: 1–27.

Jost, J. T., Banaji, M. R., and Nosek, B. A. (2004). "A decade of system justification theory: Accumulated evidence of conscious and unconscious bolstering of the status quo." *Political Psychology* 25(6): 881–919.

Jost, J. T., Liviatan, I., van der Toorn, J., Ledgerwood, A., Madisodza, A., and Nosek, B. (2012). "System justification: A motivational process with implications for social conflict." In Kals E. and Maes, J. (eds.), *Justice and Conflicts*. Berlin: Springer-Verlag.

Jost, J. T., Rudman, L. A., Blair, I. V., Carney, D. R., Dasgupta, N., Glaser, J., and Hardin, D. C. (2009). "The existence of implicit bias is beyond a reasonable doubt: A refutation of ideological objections and executive summary of ten studies that no manager should ignore." *Research in Organizational Behaviour* 29: 39–69.

Kahane, H. (1971). *Logic and Contemporary Rhetoric*. Belmont, CA: Wadsworth.

Kahane, H. and Cavender, N. (2005). *Logic and Contemporary Rhetoric: The Use of Reason in Everyday Life*, 9th edn. Belmont, CA: Wadsworth.

Kay, A. C. and Zanna, M. P. (2009). "A contextual analysisof the system justification motive and its societal consequences." In Jost, J. Y., Kay, A. C., and Thorisdottir, H. (eds.), *Social and Psychological Bases of Ideology and System Justification*. New York: Oxford University Press: 158–81.

Krebs, C. P., Lindquist, C. H., Warner, T. D., Fisher, B. S., and Martin, S. L. (2009). "College women's experiences with physically forced, alcohol- or other drug-enabled, and drug-facilitated sexual assault before and since entering college." *Journal of American College Health* 57(6): 639–49.

Ledgerwood, A., Mandisodza, A. N., Jost, J. T., and Pohl, M. J. (2011). "Working for the system: Motivated defense of meritocratic beliefs." *Social Cognition* 29(2): 322–40.

Lee, A. J. (2005). "Unconscious bias theory in employment discrimination ligitation." *Harvard Civil Rights–Civil Liberties Law Review* 40: 481–503.

Leisen, L. (1998). "The legacy of woman the gatherer: The emergence of evolutionary feminism." *Evolutionary Anthropology* 7(3): 105–13.

Lem, S. L. (1993). *The Lenses of Gender: Transforming the Debate on Sexual Inequality*. New Haven, CT: Yale University Press.

Lerner, M. J. (1980). *The Belief in a Just World: A Fundamental Delusion*. New York: Plenum Press.

Linker, M. (2011). "Do squirrels eat hamburgers? Intellectual empathy as a remedy for residual prejudice." *Informal Logic* 31(2): 110–38.

Linker, M. (2014). "Epistemic privilege and expertise in the context of meta-debate." *Argumentation* 28(1): 67–84.

Little, M. O. (1996). "Why a feminist approach to bioethics?" *Kennedy Institute of Ethics Journal* 6(1): 1–18.

Lloyd, E. A. (2005). *The Case of the Female Orgasm: Bias in the Science of Evolution*. Cambridge, MA: Harvard University Press.

Longino, H. and Doell, R. (1983). "Body, bias, and behavior: A comparative analysis of reasoning in two areas of biological science." *Signs* 9(2): 206–27.

Martin, E. (1991). "The egg and the sperm: How science has constructed a romance based on stereotypical male–female roles." *Signs: Journal of Women in Culture and Society* 16(3): 485–501.

Miller, D. T., Taylor, B., and Buck, M. L. (1991). "Gender gaps: Who needs to be explained?" *Journal of Personality and Social Psychology* 61(1): 5–12.

Moss-Racusin, C. A., Dovidio, J. F., Brescoll, V. L., Graham, M. J., and Handelsman, J. (2012). "Science faculty's subtle gender biases favor male students." *Proceedings of the National Academy of the Sciences* 109(41): 16474–9.

Moss-Racusin, C. A., Molenda, A. K., and Cramer, C. R. (in press). "Can evidence impact attitudes? Public reactions to evidence of gender bias in STEM fields." *Psychology of Women Quarterly*.

Plumwood, V. (1996). "Androcentrism and anthrocentrism: Parallels and politics." *Ethics and Environment* 1(2): 119–52.

Pronin, E. and Kugler, M. B. (2007). "Valuing thoughts, ignoring behavior: The introspection illusion as a source of the bias blind spot." *Journal of Experimental Social Psychology* 43: 565–78.

Ramirez-Melgoza, A. and Cox, J. W. (2006). "Aversive sexism and emotion regulation in a masculine organization." *Academy of Management Annual Meeting Proceedings*.

Rankin, L. E., Jost, J. T., and Wakslak, C. J. (2009). "System justification and the meaning of life: Are the existential benefits of ideology distributed unequally across racial groups?" *Social Justice Research* 22(2–3): 312–33.

Ratner, R. K. and Miller, D. T. (2001). "The norm of self-interest and its effects on social action." *Journal of Personality and Social Psychology* 81: 5–16.

Ridgeway, C. L. (2011). *Framed by Gender: How Gender Inequality Persists in the Modern World.* New York: Oxford University Press.

Rooney, P. (2012). "When philosophical argumentation impedes social and political progress." *Journal of Social Philosophy* 43(3): 317–33.

Shih, M., Pittinsky, T. L., and Ambady, N. (1999). "Stereotype susceptibility: Identity salience and shifts in quantitative performance." *Psychological Science* 10: 80–3.

Suri, G., Sheppes, G., Schwartz, C., and Gross, J. J. (2013). "Patient inertia and the status quo bias: When an inferior option is preferred." *Psychological Science* 24(9): 1763–9.

SlutWalk Toronto (2013). "Why." <http://www.slutwalktoronto.com/about/why>.

Sterling, K. (2014). "Man the hunter, woman the gatherer? The impact of gender studies on hunter-gatherer research (a retrospective)." In Cummings, V., Jordan, P., Zvelebil, M. (eds.), *The Oxford Handbook of the Archaeology and Anthropology of Hunter-Gatherers.* New York: Oxford University Press: 151–73.

Tavris, C. (1992). *This Mismeasure of Women: Why Women are Not the Better Sex, the Inferior Sex, or the Opposite Sex.* New York: Simon and Schuster.

Tindale, C. (2007). *Fallacies and Argument Appraisal.* Cambridge: Cambridge University Press.

Uhlmann, E. and Cohen, G. (2005). "Constructued criteria: Redefining merit to justify discrimination." *Psychological Science* 16(6): 474–80.

Uhlmann, E. and Cohen, G. (2007). "'I think, therefore it's true': Effect of self-perceived objectivity on hiring discrimination." *Organizational Behavior and Human Decision Processes* 104: 207–23.

Valian, V. (1998). *Why So Slow? The Advancement of Women.* Cambridge, MA: MIT Press.

Walton, D. (1995). *A Pragmatic Approach to Fallacies.* Toronto: University of Toronto Press.

Walton, D. (1998). *The New Dialectic: Conversation Context of Argumentation.* Toronto: University of Toronto Press.

Walton, D. (1999). *One-Sided Arguments: A Dialectical Analysis of Bias.* Albany, NY: State University of New York Press.

Walton, D. (2010). "Why fallacies appear to be better arguments than they are." *Informal Logic* 30(2): 159–84.

Williams, J. E., Satterwhite, R. C., and Best, D. L. (1999). "Pancultural gender stereotypes revisited: The five factor model." *Sex Roles* 40(7/8): 513–25.

Woods, J. (2013). *Errors of Reasoning: Naturalizing the Logic of Inference.* London: College Publications.

Yap, A. (2013). "Ad hominem fallacies, bias, and testimony." *Argumentation* 27: 97–109.

Yoffe, E. (2013). "College women: Stop getting drunk." Slate, October 15. <http://www.slate.com/articles/double_x/doublex/2013/10/sexual_assault_and_drinking_teach_women_the_connection.html>.

2.5

Revisiting Current Causes of Women's Underrepresentation in Science

Carole J. Lee

What explains the continued underrepresentation of women in Science, Technology, Engineering, and Mathematics (STEM) disciplines? In a recent article in the *Proceedings of the National Academy of Sciences*, Stephen Ceci and Wendy Williams argue that claims of gender discrimination in journal review, grant funding, and hiring are "no longer valid" (Ceci and Williams, 2011). They conclude that

the ongoing focus on sex discrimination in reviewing, interviewing, and hiring represents costly, misplaced effort: Society is engaged in the present in solving problems of the past rather than in addressing meaningful limitations deterring women's participation... today (Ceci and Williams, 2011).

The basis for this conclusion is what they deem a "more recent and robust empiricism" (Ceci and Williams, 2011) in particular, very large correlation studies of actual publication, grant award, and hiring outcomes that demonstrate no gender effect.

From the perspective of the robust social psychological literature on gender bias, this result may seem surprising. Experimental studies have added credence to the ecological validity and generalizability of implicit gender bias studies to STEM contexts by demonstrating that faculty in psychology (Steinpreis et al., 1999), biology, chemistry, and physics (Moss-Racusin et al., 2012) are susceptible to gender bias in hiring decisions. Furthermore, large meta-analyses measuring the predictive validity of Implicit Association Test measures on behavioral, judgment, and physiological test scores found small-to-moderate effect sizes, with correlation sizes ranging from 0.148 to 0.274 (Greenwald et al., 2009;

Oswald et al., 2013). Even when dealing with small effect sizes, we should expect to see differential outcomes (in this case, for women versus men) in the context of large samples/populations (Greenwald et al., 2015).

How do we reconcile the substantial experimental evidence (which demonstrates implicit *gender bias*) with the large-scale correlational studies (which demonstrate no *gender effect*)?[1] How we answer this question has important social and institutional consequences. Rhetorically, Ceci and Williams's appeal to large empirical studies demonstrating no gender effect has the potential to be very damaging to the credibility of programs designed to recruit and retain women in STEM disciplines. After all, marshaling empirical evidence for gender bias played a central role in persuading faculty, administrators, and grant institutions about the need to undertake institutional changes.[2]

In this chapter I will try to reconcile these two literatures by motivating alternative (and not mutually exclusive) interpretations of the correlational studies that are consistent with the continued presence of implicit gender bias alongside women's reliance on strategies for counterbalancing such bias and the effectiveness of gender-equity programs to moderate its effects. In Section 1 I will argue that, despite their laudable efforts to control for quality indirectly through proxy, the correlational studies cited by Ceci and Williams cannot rule out the possibility that a quality confound is responsible for cancelling out the impact of ongoing implicit gender bias in journal review, grant funding, and hiring. Nor can the correlational studies rule out the possibility of a quality-related sample bias in the sample of women and men—a worry aggravated by the systematic underrepresentation of women among those submitting manuscripts (Lane and Linden, 2009), grant proposals (Grant et al., 1997; RAND, 2005; Marsh et al., 2008), and job applications (Committee on Gender Differences in the Careers of

---

[1] For the sake of clarity I will distinguish questions about gender bias from questions about gender effects. By convention, I will refer to "gender bias" as a psychological disposition/tendency, underwritten by cognitive representations and processes, that is studied experimentally. In contrast, I will refer to "gender effects" as differential outcomes for men versus women in "natural" settings, where possible confounds are controlled for by proxy rather than through direct experimental means (Bornmann et al., 2007). I will distinguish "effects" (i.e. the outcomes of causal processes) *simpliciter* from "gender effects" in particular by marking *gender* effects as such.
[2] Virginia Valian's classic (1998) compellingly synthesized psychological work on cognitive schemas and evaluation bias and helped to catalyze the creation of the National Science Foundation's ADVANCE initiative (Stewart et al., 2007a; LaVaque-Manty, 2007). MIT's 1999 Report on Women in Science (Massachusetts Institute of Technology, 1999), which revealed unequivocal gender differences in resource allocation among faculty, also reverberated throughout academe, leading to national media attention as well as internal (Hopkins, 2006) and external (Ginther, 2003) examinations of hiring, tenure, and resource allocation at other institutions.

Science et al., 2010). Studies in experimental psychology, by contrast, use stricter methods for controlling for quality and demonstrate clear gender bias.

In Section 2 I will identify how moderator variables present in STEM contexts may have contributed to the null results cited by Ceci and Williams by diminishing the influence of implicit gender bias in hiring. To motivate this possibility I will identify moderating factors that have been experimentally demonstrated to diminish the impact of implicit bias and whose presence in STEM contexts have been promoted by ADVANCE and other resource-intensive gender-equity efforts.

Please note that this chapter does not question Ceci and Williams's positive claims about additional causes of women's underrepresentation in STEM disciplines or about the relative strength of those other causes. Instead, my goal is to challenge their negative claim that gender discrimination is no longer a problem facing women scientists—that gender discrimination is a "historical rather than current" problem (Ceci and Williams, 2011)—by explaining how gender discrimination qua implicit gender bias can persist alongside counterbalancing and moderating factors.

1 Controlling for Quality in Correlational Studies

In the correlational studies, gender effects are discovered when the rate with which women garner successful outcomes is not proportionate to their representation in submission/application rates (Lee et al., 2013). Ceci and Williams rightly take the best studies to be those that control for quality-impacting factors such as author institution type (Xie and Shauman, 1998), experience (RAND, 2005), rank (Ley and Hamilton, 2008), discipline (RAND, 2005), and number of publications (Committee on Gender Differences in the Careers of Science et al., 2010). However, inferring lack of gender bias, as a causal claim, on the basis of these analyses requires adopting an important simplifying assumption: we must assume that, in the aggregate, women and men—with similar institutional resources, experience, rank, disciplines, and number of publications—submit manuscripts, grant applications, and job dossiers of comparable quality (Lee et al., 2013).

1.1 The sociality of peer review

However, the peer evaluation process is social in a very basic Weberian sense (Weber, 1947): actors make decisions (about, for example, the content or quality of work to submit) that are conditioned on beliefs about what others (e.g. reviewers and search committees) implicitly and explicitly believe and value (Lee et al., 2013). We can see this kind of social decision-making by manuscript authors and grant proposal writers across the sciences. Among published studies across the physical, social, and human sciences, "positive" results favoring the experimental hypothesis are disproportionately valued and published (Fanelli, 2010). As a result, it should not be surprising that authors choose not to write up and submit studies reporting null results in preemptive anticipation of their perceived unimportance (Easterbrook et al., 1991) and likely rejection (Dickersin et al., 1992; Ioannidis, 1998). Authors also engage in research practices aimed at crafting positive results (Lee, 2013): a meta-analysis suggests that 33.7% of scientific researchers admit to using at least one questionable research practice in order to achieve a positive result (Fanelli, 2009), though estimates have surpassed 90% for specific disciplines (John et al., 2012). Analogous findings can be found in the literature on grant review. Applicants to the National Institutes of Health and National Science Foundation perceive the grant review process to be biased against highly innovative research (Gillespie et al., 1985; McCullough, 1989; National Research Council, 2007). Not surprisingly, then, grant applicants report downplaying the more transformative aspects of their research proposals (McCullough, 1989; Travis and Collins, 1991). It is "normal practice" for scientists to tune the content of their publication and grant submissions to forestall or defuse anticipated reviewer biases.

If women in STEM contexts anticipate gender bias in the evaluation of their manuscripts, grant proposals, and job applications, then we should expect that they try to offset this discrimination by submitting higher-quality work to counterbalance it (Gopnik, 2011; Budden et al., 2008b). Surveys support the idea that women believe that gender bias is a problem for them as individuals and as a group. A large survey of STEM researchers sponsored by the American Association for the Advancement of Science found that 62% of women scientists believed that gender biases were barriers faced by individuals working in the sciences (Cell Associates, 2010). 52% of women scientists reported having personally experienced gender bias (Cell Associates, 2010). A survey of female STEM faculty at the University of Michigan found that 42% of white women and 48% of women of color reported experiencing gender discrimination (UM ADVANCE Program, 2008). Surveys also suggest ways in which women strategize around anticipated gender bias. Even though single-anonymous journal review is the norm across the sciences (Ware, 2008), women prefer double-anonymous over single-anonymous journals (Budden et al., 2008a, Ware, 2008). A survey of women in physics revealed that women felt the need "to work twice as hard, do twice as much just to be considered half as qualified" (Ivie and Guo, 2006).

Even if women do not believe in the existence of gender bias (and do not strategically try to counterbalance it), they may have, through their education, training, and professional experiences (Lee and Schunn, 2011), internalized stricter standards for what counts as quality work—a possibility indirectly evidenced by the relatively consistent and robust finding that female reviewers and editors are tougher than male ones in the evaluation of manuscripts (Wing et al., 2010; Lane and Linden, 2009; Gilbert et al., 1994) and grant proposals (Broder, 1993; Jayasinghe et al., 2003) authored by women or men.

1.2 Some of the fine print

The fine print of some of the large-scale studies cited by Ceci and Williams acknowledge the quality-related methodological limitations that qualify their results. The Faculty Committee on Women in Science, Engineering, and Medicine as well as NSF's report on *Gender Differences in the Careers of Academic Scientists and Engineers* acknowledged that using "simple numerical counts" as measures for publishing success and productivity is problematic insofar as it accounts for "neither [the] quality nor the importance of scholarship" (Committee on Gender Differences in the Careers of Science et al., 2010; Bentley and Adamson, 2003). The large-scale study on grant review at NIH, NSF, and USDA made clear that "[i]f women are in fact less likely to apply for funding" as discovered across a range of large-scale studies on grant review (Grant et al., 1997; RAND, 2005; Marsh et al., 2008), then "female and male applicants for federal research grants likely differ in ways not observed in the data sets" (RAND, 2005). The Committee on Gender Differences in the Careers of Science notes that the slightly "higher rates of success" for female job candidates "may be explained by the possibility that only the strongest female candidates applied for Research I positions" (Committee on Gender Differences in the Careers of Science et al., 2010). So long as the correlational studies control for quality through proxy, this leaves open the possibility of a quality confound, where implicit gender bias coexists alongside the submission of higher-quality work by women who anticipate and/or have been socialized to find strategies for overcoming implicit (or explicit) gender bias.

1.3 Controlling for quality in experimental studies

In light of the sociality of peer review, it is critical to control for the quality of submissions directly before drawing conclusions about the influence of gender on outcomes. The most convincing studies do this by submitting for evaluation work that is *identical with the exception of the gender of the author/applicant*. This is effectively what Steinpreis and her colleagues famously did: their study discovered that academic psychologists deemed a female job candidate as having less adequate teaching, research, and service than a male candidate with an identical CV (Steinpreis et al., 1999). This result is reinforced by a more recent study showing that biology, chemistry, and physics faculty at research institutions deemed a female student less competent and hirable for a lab manager position than a male one with identical application materials, and offered the female applicant a 12% lower starting salary than the male applicant (Moss-Racusin et al., 2012).[3]

As Ceci and Williams note, ecologists sought to replicate this style of experimental research by having graduate students and postdocs review a paper that was identical save for the gender of the author (faculty were invited but failed to participate, making this study less generalizable to the STEM faculty population than the studies mentioned above). They discovered no gender effect (Borsuk et al., 2009). However, it is important to note that from a methodological point of view, this study used as their test manuscript a paper that had already been published (Borsuk et al., 2009) in a field that (at the time) enjoyed a rather generous 35–40% acceptance rate (Wardle, 2012). As I will explain, this choice of target manuscript runs the risk of being too clearly over the threshold for publishability to serve as a challenge to the experimental work on gender bias.

Within social psychology, the "convention established in classic experimental studies" is to use target materials for which it is ambiguous whether that target lies above or below the threshold for a particular attribute, such as publishability or hirability (Heilman et al., 2004; Biernat and Kobrynowicz, 1997). So, for example, Moss-Racusin and her colleagues elicited gender bias by crafting application materials for a student sufficiently "qualified to succeed in academic science" while not being "irrefutably excellent" (Moss-Racusin et al., 2012). Steinpreis and her colleagues' widely cited work elicited gender bias for an ordinary job applicant (Steinpreis et al., 1999).

We need not expect implicit gender bias in judgments about whether a target lies above some threshold in less ambiguous cases where the target clearly lies above the threshold, either because the target is exceptional or because the threshold is sufficiently low. So, for example, Steinpreis and her colleagues did not discover gender bias in judgments about the hirability of job candidates

---

[3] A note about STEM salaries: Ceci and Williams cite work by Ginther and Hayes to support their claim that salary disparities by gender are fully attributable to other factors. However, the cited author's work suggests a more complex picture in which there is no statistically significant gender gap except among full professors in science: men earned 12% more than female full professors, where a third of the salary gap is not explained by observable, non-gender factors (Ginther, 2004; Ginther and Kahn, 2009). The cited authors go on to suggest that gender factors—in particular, the accumulation of disadvantage by women versus men—may be to blame for this discrepancy.

whose credentials were exceptional and merited early tenure (Steinpreis et al., 1999).

1.4 Possible implications for interpreting the correlational studies

I propose that Borsuk and her colleagues did not find gender bias in the evaluation of the ecology manuscript because rejection rates at the time were sufficiently low for the already published manuscript to be well above the threshold for publishability. Contrast Borsuk's result with that of the classic Peters and Ceci study which found that an already published paper covertly resubmitted for review was more likely to be accepted for publication when the fictional author was affiliated with a prestigious institution than a non-prestigious one (Peters and Ceci, 1982). In this study, determining whether a strong manuscript exceeded the threshold for publishability was more difficult than in the Borsuk case, since the psychology journals under study had lower acceptance rates (about 20%, compared to Borsuk et al.'s 35–40%). Borsuk et al.'s result—what should be the most convincing result cited by Ceci and Williams with respect to journal reviewing because of its ability to control for quality directly rather than by proxy—is not inconsistent with the robust literature on gender bias in social psychology or with methodologically similar studies on stereotype-based evaluation bias.

A similar problem may afflict a correlational study that is frequently cited. Rebecca Blank randomly assigned manuscripts at *The American Economic Review* to single-anonymous and double-anonymous review conditions and discovered no statistically significant gender effects after controlling for author's institutional rank (Blank, 1991). However, Blank notes that double-anonymous review did not impact acceptance rates for authors at the highest and lowest ranking institutions and that the vast majority of submitting female authors were at lower-ranked universities. If we expect gender bias to play a larger role in ambiguous cases where a manuscript is not clearly above or below the threshold for publication, then the results of this study are not inconsistent with qualified psychological claims about seeing the disproportional effects of gender bias in near-threshold cases.

This observation animates yet another possible explanation for the null results cited by Ceci and Williams. It may be that in STEM contexts the distribution of quality among women's submissions is such that there are too few near-threshold cases for implicit gender bias to impact overall outcome measures; implicit gender bias persists, but impacts too few cases to skew the overall outcome.

Ideally, we would be able to compare all the above hypotheses (including Ceci and Williams's) by finding gender-independent ways of measuring the quality of submissions and individuals and identifying their distribution across the

272 CAROLE J. LEE

population of women versus men in STEM disciplines.[4] In the absence of such techniques, we are left to control for quality through institutional/structural proxy (as the correlational studies do) or through stricter experimental means (as psychological studies do). Because of the inescapable sociality of peer review and the methodological advantage experimental studies have when controlling for quality, I give preferential weight to their results. However, I do not take the experimental results to be fully decisive, since the process of generalizing to STEM disciplines (and the distribution of quality found among women versus men there) requires its own set of inductive and interpretive inferences.

2 Moderators for Implicit Gender Bias

So far, my critiques have identified weaknesses in the correlational studies that may have systematically skewed the observed association between gender and outcomes towards the null result. This analysis motivated the possibility of an *unimpeded* psychological process between perceived gender (of author/applicant by evaluators) and outcomes, whose negative effects are not observed because they are cancelled out by counterbalancing gender differences in the quality of submitted work/applications. In contrast, this section will be dedicated to identifying moderating variables that reduce and even eliminate the influence of implicit gender bias by *impinging directly upon* the psychological process between (perceived) gender and outcomes.[5]

Psychologists have long recognized that moderating variables and competing processes present in real-life contexts may diminish or even eliminate a behavioral effect otherwise elicited in controlled laboratory conditions (Aronson et al., 1998). This appreciation has given rise to a crucial shift in questions about which properties from the laboratory are most important to project to the target context when evaluating the external validity of psychological studies: the primary object of generalization is no longer the stimulus–behavior pair (Campbell, 1957), but the *process* mediating the link between them and explaining their covariation in laboratory conditions (Mook, 1983). This means that failing to observe the expected behavior in the target context does not rule out the possibility that the cognitive process was triggered, carried out, and contributed causally toward

---

[4] Controlling for quality via number of publications or citations is not, for example, gender independent, since women publish fewer articles and are cited less frequently than men (Larivière et al., 2013).

[5] Moderator variables diminish or enhance the degree of the final effect in the presence of the cause (Baron and Kenny, 1986). Unlike mediator variables, moderator variables are not thought to be necessary to complete the process connecting the cause to the effect (Brewer, 2000).

the behavior even in cases where moderating variables and competing processes tempered or even eliminated its effect. A null result in the target context does not imply the lack of a causal relationship in that context.

Since implicit biases are triggered automatically even in the absence of explicit attention being drawn to the stereotype-relevance of perceptual cues across a range of different perceptual modalities (Rudman and Lee, 2002, Dasgupta and Greenwald, 2001, Dasgupta and Asgari, 2004), I take the present question not to be whether the cognitive processes underwriting implicit gender bias play a causal role in STEM contexts, but what moderators may diminish their effect. In what follows, I will identify some of the moderating factors that have been found to diminish implicit bias's behavioral impact, and identify ways that resource-intensive gender-equity efforts and institutions have contributed to the presence of such moderators in the context of hiring.

2.1 Motivation

Motivation to avoid behaving with prejudice attenuates implicit bias (Maddux et al., 2005) and the influence of implicit bias on explicit social judgment tasks (Payne, 2005). Motivation to be similar to one's peers can decrease implicit bias and discriminatory behavior in contexts where one's peers are thought to be more egalitarian than one's self (Stewart et al., 2007b). And, for aversive racists (those with low explicit prejudice but high implicit bias), being reminded of one's previous discriminatory behavior can increase motivation to control prejudice and decrease prejudiced behavior (Son Hing et al., 2002).

How can institutions increase motivation and diminish implicit gender bias and prejudiced behavior in STEM contexts? Programs like ADVANCE can inspire and foster such motivation. If we infer that the institutionalization and endorsement of gender-equity programs such as ADVANCE change faculty perceptions about what their peers believe about women—especially by selecting highly credible senior male and female faculty to lead evaluation bias training programs (Stewart et al., 2007b)—then we have psychological reasons for thinking that this helps motivate faculty to control for implicit bias and decrease discriminatory behavior (Sechrist and Stangor, 2001). And, if ADVANCE-organized training about evaluation bias and reporting past hiring decisions reminds faculty with low explicit prejudice but high implicit bias about previous prejudicial behavior (such as gendered patterns of hiring in their department), we have psychological reason to think this will increase motivation to control prejudice and decrease discriminatory behavior (Son Hing et al., 2002).

Deans provide an additional source of motivation: the large hiring study cited by Ceci and Williams reported a "dean effect" in which women were more likely to be offered a faculty position when the institution's dean reviewed and approved job offers as opposed to cases where the dean played no role (Committee on Gender Differences in the Careers of Science et al., 2010). The beneficial influence of upper administration has been noted at MIT (Hopkins, 2006), the University of Michigan (Stewart et al., 2007b), Georgia Tech (Fox et al., 2007), and Case Western Reserve University (Bilmoria et al., 2007).

As a locus of sustained change, diversity-dedicated programs such as ADVANCE may be more consistent over time than the dean effect. The dean effect is sensitive to the commitment of individual deans to gender equity and is, therefore, subject to variation across deans: for example, at MIT the number of women faculty hired in the School of Science increased sharply as a function of Dean Birgeneau's response to the 1996 Report on Women Faculty in Science but decreased when he left (Hopkins, 2006).[6] In contrast, we have reason to think that programs like ADVANCE and MIT's Gender Equity Committee (Hopkins, 2006) enjoy more stability over time by providing an ongoing organizational structure responsible for monitoring and improving the representation of female faculty in STEM disciplines.[7]

2.2 Cognitive capacity

When cognitive capacity has been hampered, due to the spontaneity of judgment (Hofmann et al., 2005), limited executive control (Payne, 2005), or low need for cognition (Florack et al., 2001), implicit bias proceeds along unhampered by the influence of more deliberate and careful processing. However, when attention and effort is increased, so is the moderating influence of explicit processing (Hofmann et al., 2005; Payne, 2005; Florack et al., 2001; Smith and DeCoster, 2000; Strack and Deutsch, 2004).

In an effort to increase attention and effort in hiring deliberations, ADVANCE programs have evaluation tools that focus on "specific and individuating evidence" and "emphasized clarity and completeness of candidates' contributions, mentoring and faculty development" (Fox et al., 2007). Twenty-one unique institutions have uploaded their best practices (including check lists) for search

---

[6] The increase in female hires in the sciences happened despite no change in the percentage of women completing PhDs at MIT, where the institution has the unusual practice of hiring its own graduates (Hopkins, 2006).

[7] Along these lines, a large-scale correlational study found that when it comes to improving diversity among managers employed in the private sector, the presence of organizational structures responsible for increasing diversity (such as diversity officers, committees, departments, and task forces) is more effective than diversity training, evaluation, mentoring, or networking. The same study found that the presence of diversity-related organizational structures enhances the effectiveness of the other initiatives (Kalev et al., 2006).

committees on the ADVANCE web portal (ADVANCE). Since the institution of ADVANCE programs, the relative rate with which women have been hired has improved at the University of Michigan (Stewart et al., 2007b), Georgia Tech (Fox et al., 2007), New Mexico State University, and the University of California at Riverside, San Diego, and Irvine (ADVANCE, 2006). According to Beth Mitchneck, the program director for ADVANCE at the National Science Foundation, they hope to publish a more complete portfolio analysis in the future (Email, October 29, 2014). Note that reviving the institutional knowledge embodied by hiring evaluation tools with regular, systematic training/education requires sustained investment in institutional structures charged with implementing and enforcing these best practices.

2.3 Context effects

Experimental studies have demonstrated that contextual cues can attenuate implicit bias, as measured by decreased IAT scores (Barden et al., 2004; Wittenbrink et al., 2001): participants primed with violent, misogynist rap music showed more implicit bias against black men compared to those in the control group (Rudman and Lee, 2002); exposing participants to exemplars of famous women in leadership positions increased implicit associations between leadership qualities and women (Dasgupta and Asgari, 2004); and, exposure to admired black and disliked white individuals attenuates implicit bias against blacks while exposure to disliked black and admired white individuals increases it (Dasgupta and Greenwald, 2001).[8]

In light of this research, we would expect the presence of counterstereotypical female faculty on search committees to attenuate implicit gender bias. The large-scale hiring study cited by Ceci and Williams found that the odds that female job candidates get interviewed for a position improves with an increase in the percentage of female faculty on the search committee and when the search committee is chaired by a woman (Committee on Gender Differences in the Careers of Science et al., 2010). Note that putting women in leadership positions is a central goal of ADVANCE (National Science Foundation).

Ceci and Williams are right that gender-equity efforts focused on high-stakes gate-keeping moments are resource-intensive.[9] They are also right to worry

---

[8] Contexts are thought to moderate IAT scores through the temporary activation of select characteristics/properties associated with the concept in question (Barden et al., 2004, Barsalou, 1982, 1987, Wittenbrink et al., 2001, Gawronski and Bodenhausen, 2006).

[9] The National Science Foundation's ADVANCE initiative has invested more than $130 million in more than a hundred institutions of higher education since 2001 to support the hiring, retention, and advancement of women in STEM disciplines (National Science Foundation, 2013); and

about *comparative* questions about the strongest factors responsible for the underrepresentation of women in STEM disciplines and to think about how equity-supporting resources should be allocated accordingly. However, if my analysis is correct, then taking away resources from current gender-equity efforts and institutions may erode the "fragility of progress" (Hopkins, 2006) achieved thus far.

3 Conclusion

Ceci and Williams argue that claims of gender discrimination in journal review, grant funding, and hiring are "no longer valid"—that worries about gender discrimination target "historical rather than current problems facing women scientists" (Ceci and Williams, 2011). I challenged this conclusion, arguing that null results in correlation studies may be consistent with the continued presence of implicit gender bias alongside women's reliance on strategies for counterbalancing such bias and the effectiveness of gender-equity programs to moderate its effects. I have not challenged Ceci and Williams's positive claims about other causes of women's underrepresentation or the relative strength of those other causes. It is likely that there are multiple factors responsible for the underrepresentation of women in STEM disciplines, including the need to change disciplinary cultures and environments to increase women's feelings of belonging (Cheryan et al., 2009), the fact of women's underrepresentation itself which leads to women's lower self-identification with and motivation to pursue STEM careers (Murphy et al., 2007; Stout et al., 2011), as well as "gendered expectations, lifestyle choices, and career preferences" and "factors surrounding family formation and childrearing" (Ceci and Williams, 2011). However, if gender discrimination qua implicit gender bias persists, then withdrawing resources and institutions dedicated to monitoring and preventing gender discrimination in high-stakes gatekeeping moments may erode hard-earned progress.

Acknowledgments

I am grateful for the Career Enhancement Fellowship (funded by the Mellon Foundation and administered by the Woodrow Wilson Foundation) and Royalty Research Fund grant #A79071 (University of Washington) for the research time to complete this article. I would also like to thank Diana Bilimoria, Michael Brownstein, Sapna Cheryan,

---

individual institutions and investigators have invested additional resources dedicated to assessing gender differences in resource allocation and outcomes (Massachusetts Institute of Technology, 1999; Ginther, 2003).

Catherine Elgin, Jennifer Saul, Miriam Solomon, Abigail Stewart, Joyce Wen, and the anonymous reviewers for comments and/or references that helped to sharpen this chapter.

References

ADVANCE (online). "Search Committees." <http://www.portal.advance.vt.edu/index. php/tags/Search-Committees> (Accessed October 29, 2014).

ADVANCE (2006, online). "Using program evaluation to ensure the success of your advance program." <http://www.advance.vt.edu/documents/other/advance_evalu ation_toolkit.pdf> (Accessed October 29, 2014).

Aronson, E., Wilson, T. D., and Brewer, M. B. (1998). "Experimentation in social psychology." In Gilbert, D., Fiske, S. and Lindzey, G. (eds.), *The Handbook of Social Psychology*. Boston, MA: McGraw-Hill.

Barden, J., Maddux, W. W., Petty, R. E., and Brewer, M. B. (2004). "Contextual moderation of racial bias: The impact of social roles on controlled and automatically activated attitudes." *Journal of Personality and Social Psychology* 87: 5–22.

Baron, R. M. and Kenny, D. A. (1986). "The moderator–mediator variable distinction in social psychological research: Conceptual, strategic, and statistical considerations." *Journal of Personality and Social Psychology* 51: 1173–82.

Barsalou, L. W. (1982). Context-independent and context-dependent information in concepts." *Memory and Cognition* 10: 82–93.

Baesalou, L. W. (1987). "The instability of graded structure: Implications for the nature of concepts." In Neisser, U. (ed.), *Concepts and Conceptual Development: Ecological and Intellectual Factors in Categorization*. New York, NY: Cambridge University Press.

Bentley, J. T. and Adamson, R. (2003). *Gender Differences in the Careers of Academic Scientists and Engineers: A Literature Review*. Arlington: National Science Foundation.

Biernat, M. and Kobrynowicz, D. (1997). "Gender- and race-based standards of competence: Lower minimum standards but higher ability standards for devalued groups." *Journal of Personality and Social Psychology* 72: 544–57.

Bilmoria, D., Hopkins, M. M., O'Neil, D. A., and Perry, S. R. (2007). "Executive coaching: An effective strategy for faculty development." In Stewart, A. J., Malley, J. E., and LaVaque-Manty, D. (eds.), *Transforming Science and Engineering: Advancing Academic Women*. Ann Arbor, MI: University of Michigan Press.

Blank, R. M. (1991). "The effects of double-blind versus single-blind reviewing: Experimental evidence from *The American Economic Review*." *The American Economic Review* 81: 1041–68.

Bornmann, L., Mutz, R., and Daniel, H.-D. (2007). "Gender differences in grant peer review." *Journal of Informetrics* 1: 226–38.

Borsuk, R. M., Aarssen, L. W., Budden, A. E., Koricheva, J., Leimu, R., Tregenza, T., and Lortie, C. J. (2009). "To name or not to name: The effect of changing author gender on peer review." *BioScience* 59: 985–9.

Brewer, M. B. (2000). "Research design and issues of validity." In Reis, H. T. and Judd, C. M. (eds.), *Handbook of Research Methods in Social and Personality Psychology*. New York, NY: Cambridge University Press.

Broder, I. E. (1993). "Review of NSF economics proposals: Gender and institutional patterns." *The American Economic Review* 83: 964–70.

Budden, A. E., Aarssen, L. W., Koricheva, J., Leimu, R., Lortie, C. J., and Tregenza, T. (2008a). Does double-blind review favor female authors? Reply." *Frontiers in Ecology and the Environment* 6: 356–7.

Budden, A. E., Aarssen, L. W., Koricheva, J., Leimu, R., Lortie, C. J., and Tregenza, T. (2008b). "Response to Whittaker: Challenges in testing for gender bias." *Trends in Ecology and Evolution* 23: 480–1.

Campbell, D. T. (1957). "Factors relevant to the validity of experiments in social settings." *Psychological Bulletin* 54: 297–312.

Ceci, S. J. and Willliams, W. M. (2011). "Understanding current causes of women's underrepresentation in science." *Proceedings of the National Academy of Sciences* 108: 3157–62.

Cell Associates (2010). *Barriers for Women Scientists Survey Report.* American Association for the Advancement of Science.

Cheryan, S., Plaut, V. C., Davies, P. G., and Steele, C. M. (2009). "Ambient belonging: How stereotypical cues impact gender participation in computer science." *Journal of Personality and Social Psychology* 97: 1045–60.

Committee on Gender Differences in the Careers of Science, Engineering, and Mathematics Faculty; Committee on Women in Science, Engineering, and Medicine; Committee on National Statistics; National Research Council (2010). *Gender Differences at Critical Transitions in the Careers of Science, Engineering, and Mathematics Faculty.* Washington: National Academies Press.

Dasgupta, N. and Asgari, S. (2004). "Seeing is believing: Exposure to counterstereotypic women leaders and its effect on the malleability of automatic gender stereotyping." *Journal of Experimental Social Psychology* 40: 642–58.

Dasgupta, N. and Greenwals, A. G. (2001). "On the malleability of automatic attitudes: Combating automatic prejudice with images of admired and disliked individuals." *Journal of Personality and Social Psychology* 81: 800–14.

Dickersin, K., Min, Y.-I., and Meinert, C. L. (1992). "Factors influencing publication of research results: Follow-up of applications submitted to two institutional review boards." *Journal of the American Medical Association* 267: 374–9.

Easterbrook, P. J., Berlin, J. A., Gopalan, R., and Matthews, D. R. (1991). "Publication bias in clinical research." *The Lancet* 337: 867–72.

Fanelli, D. (2009). "How many scientists fabricate and falsify research? A systematic review and meta-analysis of survey data." *PLoS One* 4: 1–11.

Fanelli, D. (2010). "'Positive' results increase down the hierarchy of the sciences." *PLoS One* 5: 1–10.

Florack, A., Scarabis, M., and Bless, H. (2001). "When do associations matter? The use of automatic associations toward ethnic groups in person judgments." *Journal of Experimental Social Psychology* 37: 518–24.

Fox, M. F., Colatrella, C., McDowell, D., and Realff, M. L. (2007). "Equity in tenure and promotion: An integrated institutional approach." In Stewart, A. J., Malley, J. E., and LaVaque-Manty, D. (eds.), *Transforming Science and Engineering: Advancing Academic Women.* Ann Arbor, MI: University of Michigan Press.

Gawronski, B. and Bodenhausen, G. V. (2006). "Associative and propositional processes in evaluation: An integrative review of implicit and explicit attitude change." *Psychological Bulletin* 132: 692–731.

Gilbert, J. R., Williams, E. S., and Lundbert, G. D. (1994). "Is there gender bias in JAMA's peer review process?" *Journal of the American Medical Association* 272: 139–42.

Gillespie, G. W., Chubin, D. E., and Kurzon, G. M. (1985). "Experience with NIH peer review: Researchers' cynicism and desire for change." *Science, Technology, and Human Values* 10: 44–54.

Ginther, D. K. (2003). "Is MIT an exception? Gender pay differences in academic science." *Bulletin of Science, Technology and Society* 23: 21–6.

Ginther, D. K. (2004). "Why women earn less: Economic explanations for the gender salary gap in science." *AWIS Magazine* 33: 1–5.

Ginther, D. K. and Kahn, S. (2009). "Does science promote women? Evidence from academia 1973–2001." In Freeman, R. B. and Gorgoff, D. L. (eds.), *Science and Engineering Careers in the United States: An Analysis of Markets and Employment.* Chicago, IL: University of Chicago Press.

Gopnik, A. (2011, online). "What John Tierney gets wrong about women scientists: Understanding a new study about discrimination." <http://www.slate.com/id/2285355/>.

Grant, J., Burden, S., and Breen, G. (1997). "No evidence of sexism in peer review." *Nature* 390: 438.

Greenwald, A. G., Banaji, M. R., and Nosek, B. A. (2015). "Statistically small effects of the Implicit Association Test can have societally large effects." *Journal of Personality and Social Psychology* 108: 553–61.

Greenwald, A. G., Poehlman, T. A., Uhlmann, E. L., and Banaji, M. R. (2009). "Understanding and using the Implicit Association Test: III. Meta-analysis of predictive validity." *Journal of Personality and Social Psychology* 97(1): 17–41.

Heilman, M. E., Wallen, A. S., Fuchs, D., and Tamkins, M. M. (2004). "Penalties for success: Reactions to women who succeed at male gender-typed tasks." *Journal of Applied Psychology* 89: 416–27.

Hofmann, W., Gawronski, B., Gschwendner, T., Le, H., and Schmitt, M. (2005). "A meta-analysis on the correlation between the Implicit Association Test and explicit self-report measure." *Personality and Social Psychology Bulletin* 31: 1369–85.

Hopkins, N. (2006). "Diversification of a university faculty: Observations on hiring women faculty in the schools of science and engineering at MIT." *MIT Faculty Newsletter* XVIII(1): 16–23.

Ioannidis, J. P. A. (1998). "Effect of the statistical signifcance of results on the time to completion and publication of randomized efficacy trials." *Journal of the American Medical Association* 279: 281–6.

Ivie, R. and Guo, S. (2006). "Women physicists speak again." American Institute of Physics, Pub. Number R-441.

Jayasinghe, U. W., Marsh, H. W., and Bond, N. (2003). "A multilevel cross-classified modelling approach to peer review of grant proposals: The effects of assessor and researcher attributes on assessor ratings." *Journal of the Royal Statistical Society (A)* 166: 279–300.

John, L. K., Loewenstein, G., and Prelec, D. (2012). "Measuring the prevalence of questionable research practices with incentives for truth telling." *Perspectives on Psychological Science* 23: 524–32.

Kalev, A., Dobbin, F., and Kelly, E. (2006). "Best practices or best guesses? Assessing the efficacy of corporate affirmative action and diversity policies." *American Sociological Review* 71: 589–617.

Lane, J. A. and Linden, D. J. (2009). "Is there gender bias in the peer review process at *Journal of Neurophysiology*?" *Journal of Neurophysiology* 101: 2195–6.

Larivière, V., Ni, C., Gingras, Y., Cronin, B., and Sugimoto, C. (2013). "Bibliometrics: Global gender disparities in science." *Nature* 504: 211–13.

LaVaque-Manty, D. (2007). "Transforming the Scientific Enterprise: An interview with Alice Hogan." In Steward, A. J., Malley, J. E., and LaVaque-Manty, D. (eds.), *Transforming Science and Engineering: Advancing Academic Women*. Ann Arbor, MI: University of Michigan Press.

Lee, C. J. (2013). "The limited effectiveness of prestige as an intervention on the health of medical journal publications." *Episteme* 10: 387–402.

Lee, C. J. and Schunn, C. D. (2011). "Social biases and solutions for procedural objectivity." *Hypatia* 26: 352–73.

Lee, C. J., Sugimoto, C. R., Zhang, G., and Ceonin, B. (2013). "Bias in peer review." *Journal of the American Society for Information Science* 64: 2–17.

Ley, T. J. and Hamilton, B. H. (2008). "The gender gap in NIH grant applications." *Science* 322: 1472–4.

Maddux, W. W., Jamie, B., Brewer, M. B., and Petty, R. E. (2005). "Saying no to negativity: The effects of context and motivation to control prejudice on automatic evaluative responses." *Journal of Experimental Social Psychology* 41: 19–35.

Marsh, H. W., Jayasinghe, U. W., and Bond, N. W. (2008). "Improving the peer-review process for grant applications: Reliability, validity, bias, and generalizability." *American Psychologist* 63: 160–8.

Massachusetts Institute of Technology (1999). "A Study on the status of women faculty in science at MIT." *The MIT Faculty Newsletter*. Cambridge, MA: Massachusetts Institute of Technology.

McCullough, J. (1989). "First comprehensive survey of NSF applicants focuses on their concerns about proposal review." *Science, Technology, and Human Values* 14: 78–88.

Mitchneck, B. (2014). Email, October 29, 2014.

Mook, D. G. (1983). "In defense of external validity." *American Psychologist* 38: 379–87.

Moss-Racusin, C. A., Dovidio, J. F., Brescoll, V. L., Graham, M. J., and Handelsman, J. (2012). "Science faculty's subtle gender biases favor male students." *Proceedings of the National Academy of Sciences* 109: 16474–9.

Murphy, M. C., Steele, C. M., and Gross, J. J. (2007). "Signaling threat: How situational cues affect women in math, science, and engineering settings." *Psychological Science* 18: 879–85.

National Research Council (2007). *Rising Above the Gathering Storm: Energizing and Employing America for a Brighter Economic Future*. Washington: National Academies Press.

National Science Foundation (online). "ADVANCE at a glance." <http://www.nsf.gov/crssprgm/advance/> (Accessed August 29, 2013).

Oswald, F. L., Mitchell, G., Blanton, H., Jaccard, J., and Tetlock, P. E. (2013). "Predicting ethnic and racial discrimination: A meta-analysis of IAT criterion studies." *Journal of Personality and Social Psychology* 105: 171–92.

Payne, B. K. (2005). "Conceptualizing control in social cognition: How executive functioning modulates the expression of automatic stereotyping." *Journal of Personality and Social Psychology* 89: 488–503.

Peters, D. P. and Ceci, S. J. (1982). "Peer-review practices of psychological journals: The fate of published articles, submitted again." *Behavioral and Brain Sciences* 5: 187–255.

RAND Corporation (2005). "Is there gender bias in federal grant programs?" Santa Monica: RAND Corporation.

Rudman, L. A. and Lee, M. R. (2002). "Implicit and explicit consequences of exposure to violent and misogynous rap music." *Group Processes and Intergroup Relations* 5: 133–50.

Sechrist, G. B. and Stangor, C. (2001). "Perceived consensus influences intergroup behavior and stereotype accessibility." *Journal of Personality and Social Psychology* 80: 645–54.

Smith, E. R. and Decoster, J. (2000). "Dual-process models in social and cognitive psychology: Conceptual integration and links to underlying memory systems. *Personality and Social Psychology Review* 4: 108–31.

Son Hing, L. S., Li, W., and Zanna, M. P. (2002). "Inducing hypocrisy to reduce prejudicial response among aversive racists." *Journal of Experimental Social Psychology* 38: 71–7.

Steinpreis, R. E., Anders, K. A., and Ritzke, D. (1999). "The impact of gender on the review of the curricula vitae of job applicants and tenure candidates: A national empirical study." *Sex Roles* 41: 509–28.

Stewart, A. J., Malley, J. E., and LaVaque-Manty, D. (2007a). "Analyzing the problem of women in science and engineering: Why do we need institutional transformation?" In Stewart, A. J., Malley, J. E., and LaVaque-Manty, D. (eds.), *Transforming Science and Engineering: Advancing Academic Women*. Ann Arbor, MI: University of Michigan Press.

Stewart, A. J., Malley, J. E., and LaVaque-Manty, D. (2007b). "Faculty recruitment: Mobilizing science and engineering faculty." In Stewart, A. J., Malley, J. E., and LaVaque-Manty, D. (eds.), *Transforming Science and Engineering: Advancing Academic Women*. Ann Arbor, MI: University of Michigan Press.

Stout, J. G., Dasgupta, N., Hunsinger, M., and McManus, M. A. (2011). "STEMing the tide: Using ingroup experts to inoculate women's self-concept in science, technology, engineering, and mathematics (STEM)." *Journal of Personality and Social Psychology* 100: 255–70.

Strack, F. and Deutsch, R. (2004). "Reflective and impulsive determinants of social behavior." *Personality and Social Psychology Review* 8: 220–47.

Travis, G. D. L. and Collins, H. M. (1991). "New light on old boys: Cognitive and institutional particularism in the peer review system." *Science, Technology, and Human Values* 16: 322–41.

UM ADVANCE Program (2008). "Assessing the academic work environment for science and engineering and social science faculty at the University of Michigan in 2006: Gender, race, and discipline in department- and university-related climate factors." <http://advance.umich.edu/resources/ADVANCE-2006-R2-FullReport.pdf> (accessed September 28, 2015).

Valian, V. (1998). *Why So Slow? The Advancement of Women*. Cambridge, MA: MIT Press.

Wardle, D. A. (2012). "On plummeting manuscript acceptance rates by the main ecological journals and the progress of ecology." *Ideas in Ecology and Evolution* 5: 13–15.

Ware, M. (2008). "Peer review in scholarly journals." *PRC Summary Papers* 4. London: Publishing Research Consortium.

Weber, M. (1947). *The Theory of Social and Economic Organization*, New York: Oxford University Press.

Wing, D. A., Benner, R. S., Petersen, R., Newcomb, R., and Scott, J. R. (2010). "Differences in editorial board reviewer behavior based on gender." *Journal of Women's Health* 19: 1919–23.

Wittenbrink, B., Judd, C. M., and Paek, B. (2001). "Spontaneous prejudice in context: Variability in automatically activated attitudes." *Journal of Personality and Social Psychology* 81: 815–27.

Xie, Y. and Shauman, K. A. (1998). "Sex differences in research productivity: New evidence about an old puzzle." *American Sociological Review* 63: 847–70.

2.6

Philosophers Explicitly Associate Philosophy with Maleness

An Examination of Implicit and Explicit Gender Stereotypes in Philosophy

Laura Di Bella, Eleanor Miles, and Jennifer Saul

1 Background

Philosophy is, like mathematics and the physical sciences, overwhelmingly male. For simplicity, we shall just look at US and UK data.[1] In the US, women hold only 17% of full-time permanent philosophy positions, according to the latest figures available (Norlock, 2011). In the UK, women hold 24% of such positions (Beebee and Saul, 2011). These figures are lower than those for many of the STEM subjects that have been the subject of much concern. Recent studies of progression through careers in philosophy show a steady pattern of drop-off from undergraduate to professional level. What initially seem to be very different pictures in the US and UK in fact hide a commonality. In the UK, women constitute 46% of undergraduate students enrolled on philosophy degrees. This drops to 37% of MA students, 31% of PhD students, and 24% of permanent staff (Beebee and Saul, 2011). In the US, women consitute only about 35% of those majoring in philosophy at undergraduate level (Paxton et al., 2012). One might initially wonder why so many more undergraduate women do philosophy degrees in the UK. The answer to this is likely to be a structural one. In the US, one declares a major only after spending around two years sampling various subjects. In the UK, one is accepted directly onto a degree course, and it is quite difficult to change degrees after arriving. Once we reflect on this, we can see a

---

[1] But for a fuller international picture, see Bishop et al. (2013).

similarity rather than a difference: in both countries, the percentage of women exposing themselves to university-level philosophy is between 40% and 50% (42% in introductory classes in the US, according to Paxton et al.). At the point of first easy exit—MA level in the UK, major declaration in the US—this percentage drops precipitously. It seems, then, that something puts women off *at university*, once they have sampled philosophy as taught to them at university.[2]

It is almost certainly true that the underrepresentation of women is due to a variety of factors.[3] This chapter explores the possible role of stereotypes by examining the stereotypes that philosophers at various levels hold about philosophy and philosophers. The claim that philosophers hold these stereotypes is commonly taken to underlie two very popular lines of explanation for the underrepresentation of women in philosophy: those involving implicit bias and stereotype threat—which are hypothesized to play a significant role in the underrepresentation of women in STEM subjects.[4] For example, Sally Haslanger (2008) and Jennifer Saul (2013a) have suggested that there is likely to be an association between maleness and philosophy, much like that which has been shown to exist between maleness and STEM subjects (e.g. Cvencek, Meltzoff, and Greenwald, 2011; Nosek, Banaji, and Greenwald, 2002). The presence of this association is likely, they have argued, to give rise to stereotype threat and implicit biases against women in philosophy. (By 'implicit bias' we mean a largely unconscious, automatic association of the sort that is the subject of much discussion in this volume. Of course, a part of that discussion concerns how to define the notion, so this characterization is merely a rough and imperfect one.)

In cases of stereotype threat, members of groups that are stereotyped as not very good at some activity underperform in high-stakes situations in which the stereotype is made salient. Crucially, this seems to be due to members of stereotyped groups being aware of the stereotype about them, whether or not they accept it. Steele hypothesizes that this is due to fear of confirming the stereotype (which may be implicitly or explicitly held, or both), though others have offered

---

[2] A recent article by Dougherty et al. (2015) contests this, arguing for the importance of pre-university causes.

[3] In addition to the explanations discussed in this chapter, other hypothesized explanations include sexual harassment (Saul, 2013b), micro-inequities (Brennan, 2013), undergraduate curricula (Friedman, 2013), and methodology (Jenkins 2013; Buckwalter and Stich, 2011; but see also Antony (2012), Adleberg, Thompson, and Nahmias (2014) on Buckwalter and Stich), combative discussion styles and metaphors (Beebee, 2013; Moulton 1983), and the value placed on innate genius (Leslie et al., 2015). Our focus here on implicit bias and stereotype threat should by no means be taken to be an attack of any of these explanations. We are quite confident that something like Louise Antony's (2012) 'perfect storm' metaphor is correct, and that a great many of these forces contribute to the problem.

[4] See Hill, Corbett, and St Rose (2010).

other explanations (Steele, 2010). This has been shown to occur for women in STEM subjects (Spencer et al. 1999; Appel, Kronberger, and Aronson, 2011; Good, Aronson, and Harder, 2008), so Haslanger and Saul hypothesize that it is likely to happen to women in philosophy as well. In addition to the underperformance effect, it has been suggested that stereotype threat may also lead to avoidance of stereotype threat-provoking situations (McKinnon 2014; Goguen, this volume). This can give rise to a self-perpetuating underrepresentation.

In cases of implicit bias, those from stereotyped groups may be wrongly judged in a negative manner—due to largely automatic, largely unconscious biases. We know these judgments are *wrong* because e.g. the very same paper is judged as less good with a less prestigious institutional affiliation (Peters and Ceci, 1982), or the very same CV is judged as less good with a female rather than male name (Steinpreis et al., 1999; Moss-Racusin et al., 2012). Again, Haslanger and Saul hypothesize that actions based on these unconscious associations—refereeing decisions, non-anonymous grading, reference writing, hiring—are likely to play a role in the underrepresentation of women in philosophy.[5]

Underlying both of these explanations, as they have been put forward by Haslanger and Saul, is the thought that philosophers are likely to associate philosophy with maleness. The pattern of women's progression through the profession shows a steady drop-off from undergraduate to postgraduate to employment.[6] Because of this we hypothesized that both men and women would come increasingly to associate philosophy with maleness as they progress in the profession. We conducted several studies, which showed that men associate philosophy with maleness, both implicitly and explicitly. Women also associate philosophy with maleness, explicitly. Implicitly, however, women tend to associate philosophy with femaleness. This result is an exciting one for those who want to change the demographics of the profession, as it suggests quite a hopeful situation: other work has shown that women who implicitly associate mathematics with femaleness are more affected by interventions to reduce stereotype threat. The findings of this chapter indicate that women in philosophy who suffer from stereotype threat should be susceptible to threat-reducing interventions.

---

[5] This has not yet been tested directly. However, a study by Forgas (2011) examines the interaction between mood and 'halo effects', assuming that a middle-aged male philosopher's work will be assessed as better than a young woman philosopher's work. After inducing either a happy or a sad mood, they had subjects evaluate a single philosophy essay, with a photograph of the 'author' at the top. They found that the bias (which they assumed would be present) in favour of the middle-aged male author was stronger when subjects were in a happy mood. Their goal was not one of testing for bias, as they thought it was simply obvious that it would be there (and it was). But the experiment was not designed to separate effects of gender and age.

[6] See, for example, Beebee and Saul (2011).

2 Study 1 (Pilot)

We began by testing the claim that students would come increasingly to associate philosophy with maleness via a gender–philosophy Implicit Association Test. (See the Introduction to this volume for a description of the Implicit Association Test.)

First we created a single-category gender–philosophy IAT, planning to have students take this test at various points in their undergraduate career. We initially planned to recruit undergraduate students at the University of Sheffield's Philosophy Department as participants. However, we had trouble securing participation in the study and we found that students who were interested in the study were eagerly forwarding it to interested parties elsewhere. Because the sample was already so different from our intended one, we decided to treat this study as a pilot and to recruit yet more participants by circulating a link on widely read philosophy blogs, deliberately not using the widely read feminist blog Feminist Philosophers, as we suspected that feminist philosophers would be likely to display very different patterns from other philosophers (in part due to much higher numbers of prominent women in this area of philosophy, so many more counterstereotypical exemplars).

In total we recruited 732 participants, of whom 77.5% were male. The majority of participants were from the United States (50%), Canada (8%), the UK (7%), and continental Europe (13%). In terms of age, the sample aged between 15 and 70+ years old, and the most represented groups were participants aged between 21 and 30 (48%) and between 30 and 40 (27%). Only a minority of participants had no familiarity with philosophy (7%), while approximately 19% of the sample had taken some philosophy classes and 36% had a degree/MA in philosophy or were studying to obtain one. Finally, 39% of the sample had a PhD in philosophy or were studying to obtain one.

The study was conducted online via SurveyMonkey (Palo Alto, California). After giving informed consent, participants were asked to take the IAT and to provide some demographic information (e.g. age, gender, level of exposure to philosophy). Because feminist philosophy contains far more women authors than other areas, we also asked participants about their level of exposure to feminist philosophy. Exposure to counterstereotypical exemplars (members of the stereotyped group that do not fit the stereotype) is known to reduce the manifestation of bias (Blair 2002; Power, Murphy, and Coover, 1996). Indeed, this has been used to suggest that one might make a case for affirmative action on the basis of hiring counterstereotypical exemplars as debiasing agents (Kang and Banaji, 2006).

2.1 Measures

2.1.1 IAT

Implicit associations between gender and philosophy were assessed using a Single Category Implicit Association Test (SC-IAT; Karpinski and Steinman, 2006). The concept *philosophy* and the concept gender (*female* or *male*) were used as targets. On each trial of the SC-IAT, participants were required to categorize a stimulus (i.e. a picture) into its corresponding category by pressing one of two response keys ('E' or 'I'). On each trial, a stimulus picture from the target concept *philosophy* (signs of philosophy departments, or philosophy journal covers, in black and white) or from the *male* or *female* categories (pictures of men and women in their 50s and 60s, taken from the normed faces database from Kennedy, Hope, and Raz, 2009) was presented at the centre of the screen and remained on screen until a response was made. In a first block of trials, participants were instructed to categorize *philosophy* and *female* stimuli with the same response key, and male with the other. In the second block of trials, participants were instructed to categorize *philosophy* and *male* stimuli with the same response key, and *female* with the other. Each block consisted of thirty-six practice trials and seventy-four experimental trials (the order of the two blocks being counterbalanced across participants). Faster response latencies to the *philosophy–male* pairing than to the *philosophy–female* pairing indicated stronger associations between philosophy and male gender. The SC-IAT was scored using the methods described by Karpinski and Steinman (2006), based on the established algorithm devised by Greenwald, Nosek, and Banaji (2003), giving a bias (D) score in which a negative value represents a male bias (i.e. associating philosophy more strongly with the male gender) and a positive value represents a female bias (i.e. associating philosophy more strongly with the female gender).

2.2 Other measures

On completion of the IAT, participants were also asked to provide us with information about age, gender, country, academic experience with philosophy, and amount of time spent reading feminist philosophy.

2.3 Results

2.3.1 OVERVIEW

Looking only at results across all participants, we (misleadingly, it turns out) did not see any tendency to implicitly associate philosophy with gender. But, as we will see, this overall result concealed some very interesting differences among groups of participants. Very much to our surprise, all participants showed an almost significant tendency to implicitly associate philosophy with their own gender. We also found that amount of reading of feminist philosophy was a strong predictor of both level and kind of bias. Those (male or female) who read no feminist philosophy had a trend for male bias, and those (male or female) who read feminist philosophy as much as or more than other kinds of philosophy had a significant female bias. In fact, reading (or not reading) feminist philosophy turned out be a far better predictor of bias than gender was. Overall, we found that the groups with the highest bias levels were men who do not read any feminist philosophy (male bias), men aged 50–60 (male bias), and women who read feminist philosophy (female bias).

2.4 Overall gender bias

Table 1 contains the bias score details for the sample. The overall bias score of the sample was -0.01 ($SD = 0.32$), which does not differ significantly from the gender-neutral reference of 0 ($t(731) = -0.94$, $p = 0.349$), thus indicating no gender bias. Comparison between male and female participants revealed a marginally significant difference ($t(725) = 2.49$, $p = 0.052$), indicating that males tend toward a male bias ($M = -0.02$, $SD = 0.32$), whereas females tend toward a female bias ($M = 0.03$, $SD = 0.28$). However, neither group was significantly different from the gender-neutral reference point ($t(567) = -1.65$, $p = 0.100$, and $t(159) = 1.45$, $p = 0.150$, respectively).

2.5 Academic experience

We also explored the impact of academic experience, comparing participants with little formal experience with philosophy (i.e. no formal training or some undergraduate classes), participants with a completed undergraduate or MA degree in philosophy, and participants who had begun or completed PhD

Table 1. Means and Standard Deviations of bias for men and women, across age groups.

Age group	Women			Men		
	N	M	SD	N	M	SD
15–20	16	−0.02	0.27	40	−0.04	0.23
21–30	72	−0.2	0.24	273	−0.03	0.32
31–40	39	0.04	0.30	151	0.01	0.33
41–50	10	0.12	0.30	47	0.09	0.24
51–60	10	0.13	0.32	24	−0.15	0.44
61+	6	0.21	0.40	18	−0.02	0.32

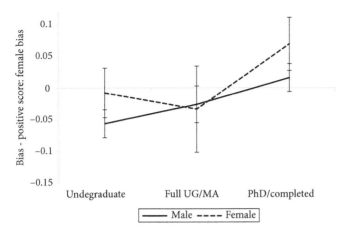

Figure 1. Interaction between gender and academic experience on gender bias. The more academic experience with philosophy, the less male bias participants display. Error bars indicate standard errors.

study. To do this, we ran a 2 (gender: male vs. female) x 3 (academic experience: undergraduate student vs. completed undergraduate/MA vs. doing or completed a PhD degree) ANOVA. When controlling for amount of academic experience the gender effect is non-significant: $F(1, 668) = 0.91$, $p = 0.341$. In other words, when controlling for academic experience with philosophy, men and women do not differ on their gender bias. However, when controlling for gender the effect of academic experience was marginally significant, $F(2, 668) = 2.92$, $p = 0.055$. In other words, learning more about philosophy appears to affect the type of bias that participants have: overall, more academic experience is associated with less male bias (see Figure 1). Post hoc analyses with Hochberg correction revealed a significant difference in bias between undergraduate participants and participants who were studying for, or had already obtained, a PhD ($p = 0.027$; all other pairwise comparisons between groups were non-significant, $ps > 0.274$). Comparison of these two groups with the gender-neutral reference point revealed that undergraduate students display a significant male bias ($t(364) = -2.42$, $p = 0.016$), whereas participants with a PhD reveal no gender bias ($t(262) = 1.27$, $p = 0.204$). Finally, there was no interaction between academic experience and gender, $F(2, 668) = 0.03$, $p = 0.770$, which implies that the effect of academic experience on bias is similar for men and women.[7]

---

[7] It is worth noting that age and academic experience with philosophy do not perfectly co-vary. Some of the older participants in this study actually had low levels of academic experience with philosophy.

2.6 Engagement with feminist philosophy

Finally, we also explored the impact of engaging with feminist philosophy literature. Feminist philosophy reading habits were significantly and positively correlated with gender bias (r = 0.094, p = 0.011). Further exploration of this effect revealed that those who read feminist philosophy as much as, or more than, other types had a female bias ($t(91)$ = 2.26, p = 0.026), while those who read no feminist philosophy had a trend for a male bias ($t(299)$ = −1.86, p = 0.064).

Since females tend to read more feminist philosophy ($t(202.19)$ = 5.65, p < 0.001), we also explored interactions between gender and engagement with feminist philosophy. As such, we run a 2 (gender: male vs. female) x 3 (reading: none vs. a little vs. some/a lot) ANOVA. When controlling for amount of feminist reading the gender effect becomes non-significant: F (1, 719) = 0.94, p = 0.333. In other words, the overall gender effect actually seems to reflect differences in reading habits. However, the effect of feminist philosophy is significant even when controlling for gender: F (2, 719) = 3.64, p = 0.027. In other words, people who read feminist philosophy do not just have a female bias because they themselves are female. Finally, there was no interaction between reading habits and gender: F (2, 719) = 0.34, p = 0.711. In other words, reading more feminist philosophy leads to more of a female bias, no matter what gender you are (see Figure 2). Finally, 59% of our sample spent at least some time reading feminist philosophy.

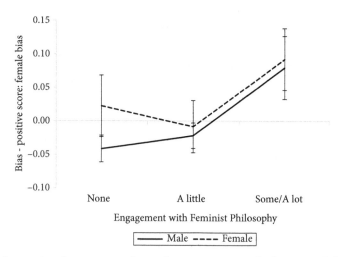

Figure 2. Interaction between gender and engagement with feminist philosophy on gender bias. The more engagement with feminist philosophy, the less male bias participants display. Error bars indicate standard errors.

3 Discussion

The findings of this study were initially startling. Since philosophy is 76–83% male, it is very surprising to see results indicating that the more time one spends in philosophy, the less one associates it with maleness. However, a closer look suggested that this was very likely due to the demographic oddness of our sample.

The sample we ended up with was quite an unusual one, and unrepresentative of the profession in some obvious ways. First, it was young (both chronologically and professionally): 76% of participants were between 21 and 40 years old, and only 18% of them had PhDs. This is probably due to the means by which we ended up recruiting—blog-followers may well tend to be younger than typical philosophers. Second, there were a lot of readers of feminist philosophy. While we cannot know this for sure, we strongly suspect that it is not the case that 59% of philosophers spend time reading feminist philosophy. As noted in Results (Section 4.3), time spent reading feminist philosophy was correlated with less-ened levels of male bias. It is in fact no surprise for time in the profession to reduce one's level of male bias, if that time is spent reading feminist philosophy. For our sample, this was unusually often the case.

Despite these limitations, the results we obtained were suggestive. A high level of male bias was found in 50–60-year old men. Since such people are likely to be in positions of power, if these biases influence their decisions (as they are likely to), this could certainly have a negative effect on the career prospects of women in philosophy. Moreover, the high levels of male bias in undergraduates could well contribute to the exodus of women from philosophy at early stages. We also learned that reading feminist philosophy has a strong effect on unconscious associations: men who do not read feminist philosophy show male bias, and women who do read feminist philosophy show female bias (especially once they reach PhD level). This is wholly consistent with the well-established thought that exposure to counterstereotypical exemplars can affect bias levels (Blair, 2002).

4 Study 2

This study was designed to more systematically explore the changes in gendered associations with philosophy through the course of an undergraduate career, and specifically relationships between gendered associations with philosophy and retention of women in philosophy. We also carefully recruited what we hoped would be a broader spectrum of participants by asking a wide range of philoso-phy lecturers to invite their students to take the IAT. We still expected to see a pattern of increasing male bias during progression through a philosophy degree, reasoning that our failure to find this in the previous study had been due to our unusual sample's devotion to reading feminist philosophy.

4.1 Participants and procedure

Participants were recruited online among undergraduate students taking philosophy classes at fourteen UK and US universities. In total, 659 participants were recruited, of whom 45.98% were male. Almost half of the participants (48%) were taking their first philosophy class, whereas 20.5% had already taken one or two classes, 12.3% had taken between three and five classes, and finally, 18.2% had already taken six or more classes in philosophy. In order to compensate participants for their time, respondents were offered the opportunity to opt into a prize draw to win an iPad.

The study was again conducted online via SurveyMonkey. After giving informed consent, participants were asked to take the IAT, and to provide some demographic information.

4.2 Measures

4.2.1 IAT

In this study the implicit associations between gender and philosophy were assessed using a standard Implicit Association Test (Greenwald et al., 1998). This version of the IAT presents participants with a control category (e.g. furniture) in addition to the main category target. On each trial of the test a stimulus picture from the categories *philosophy* (signs of philosophy departments, or philosophy journal covers) or *furniture* (pictures of furniture magazines and stores), or from the concept gender (*female* or *male* names), were used as targets. In the first set of pairings participants classify stimuli related to *male* or *philosophy* with one response key, and *female* or *furniture* with the other response key. In the second set of pairings, participants classify items related to *male* or *furniture* with one response key, and *female* or *philosophy* with the other key. For each set of pairings, participants completed a set of sixty practice trials (twenty with only gender targets, twenty with only philosophy and furniture targets, and twenty with both types of target), followed by forty experimental trials. The order of presentation of the two pairings was counterbalanced across participants. Again, faster response latencies to *philosophy–male* pairing than to *philosophy–female* pairing indicated stronger associations between philosophy and male gender. Responses were scored using the established algorithm devised by Greenwald et al. (2003), giving a bias (*D*) score in which a negative value represents a male bias and a positive value represents a female bias. As part of this algorithm, participants whose reaction times were too fast were excluded from the analyses (n = 9).

4.3 Results

To our surprise, we once again found that women had a significant tendency to implicity associate philosophy with femaleness, and men had a significant tendency to implicity associate philosophy with maleness.

4.4 Gender bias

The overall bias score of the sample was −0.05 (SD = 0.41), which differs significantly from the gender-neutral reference of 0 ($t(655)$ = −2.79, p = 0.005), thus indicating a significant male bias. Comparison between male and female participants also revealed a significant difference ($t(649)$ = 6.49, p < 0.001), indicating that men tend toward a male bias (M = −0.16, SD = 0.40), whereas women tend toward a female bias (M = 0.04, SD = 0.40). These biases were significant both for men ($t(296)$ = −6.92, p < 0.001) and for women ($t(353)$ = 2.09, p = 0.037).

4.5 Academic experience

We explored again the impact of academic experience, this time operationalized as how many previous philosophy classes participants had already taken (none, one or two, three to five, or six or more), and also its interaction with gender. To do this, we ran a 2 (gender: male vs. female) x 4 (academic experience: none vs. a little vs. medium vs. a lot) ANOVA. When controlling for amount of academic experience, the gender effect is still significant:, $F (1, 638)$ = 53.43, p < 0.001. In other words, regardless of academic experience with philosophy, females display a female bias, and males display a male bias. At the same time, when controlling for gender the effect of academic experience was non-significant: $F (3, 638)$ = 2.08, p = 0.101. In other words, learning more about philosophy was not associated with an overall increase or decrease in the average level of bias across all participants. However, this effect was qualified by an interaction between academic experience and gender: $F (3, 638)$ = 4.48, p = 0.004. As can be seen in Figure 3, more academic experience leads to more of a female bias for women, and to more male bias for men.

The relationship between philosophy experience and bias depended upon the participant's gender (interaction between gender and experience, p < 0.05). In female participants, more experience was associated with more female bias; in male participants, more experience was associated with more male bias.

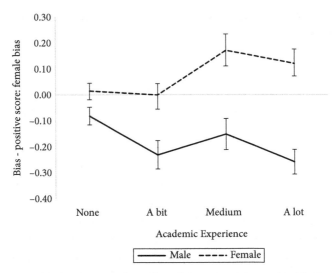

Figure 3. Interaction between gender and academic experience on gender bias. The more academic experience with philosophy, the greater the in-group bias becomes. Error bars indicate standard errors.

Female participants had non-significant levels of bias if they were taking their first class (bias score = 0.04), or if they had taken up to five classes (bias score = 0.06), but had a significant female bias when they had taken six or more classes (bias score = 0.13, $p < 0.05$). Male participants had a significant male bias at all levels, and this bias increased in significance as the level of experience increased.

5 Discussion

The results obtained were broadly consistent with our first, pilot study, but were nonetheless puzzling. Once more, there was a significant implicit tendency for men to associate philosophy with maleness, which could well lead to biases impeding women's progression.

The increasing tendency for women to implicity associate philosophy with femaleness was puzzling. To some extent, this might seem to fit with Nosek and Smyth's (2011) work showing that those women who remain in mathematics have lower tendency to implicity associate mathematics with maleness. This lessened tendency may make them more comfortable remaining in the subject. An increasing tendency for women to implicitly associate philosophy with femaleness is perfectly consistent with this. But it nonetheless raises some difficulties. Unlike the case with mathematics, there is no initial tendency for women philosophy students to associate philosophy with maleness. This fits well with the fact that women and men enroll in their first philosophy classes in fairly close to even numbers. Perhaps our broader culture lacks gendered stereotypes of philosophers, leading to roughly equal enrolment, and those women who come to identify with the field most strongly are those who stay.

We realized, however, that it was premature for us to accept the result that the women who continue in philosophy lacked a tendency to implicitly associate philosophy with maleness. After obtaining the results, correspondence with the lecturers who administered the IAT revealed that many of these had gone to great lengths to include women on their syllabi, even though their classes were not feminist philosophy classes. This means that the syllabi were likely to be atypical for philosophy.[8]

For the next study we sought out two UK departments with more traditional syllabi. These universities were selected for their traditional curriculum after consultation with contacts at various philosophy departments. While many philosophy departments have made an effort to add women to syllabi in recent years, these departments have not done so. They also lack feminist philosophy modules. This, we thought, would minimize exposure to counterstereotypical exemplars, thus allowing us to see if such exposure had been the explanation for the implicit association between philosophy and femaleness displayed by women students in previous studies. Since transferring from one department to another is difficult at a UK university, this study also allowed us to control for a drop-out rate effect, and thus test the viability of the thought that the women who stay in philosophy are those who associate it with femaleness. (The previous study had included US, Canadian, and UK participants, and a relatively small number of the latter.)

6 Study 3

For this study we used the same IAT as for Study 2, and sent it to all philosophy undergraduates at two UK universities selected for their traditional curriculum.

6.1 Participants and procedure

A total of 228 participants were recruited online among undergraduate students taking philosophy courses at two British universities, with 56.6% male

---

[8] Indeed, one appealing line of thought might be that the women on these syllabi served as counterstereotypical exemplars, combating a male–philosophy association that would otherwise be present, and giving rise to a female–philosophy association. However, this would not explain why women more than men tended to associate philosophy with femaleness.

participation. Participants were recruited among first-year (29.8%), second-year (30.7%), third-year (29.8%), and fourth-year (8.3%) students. (British undergraduate degrees are normally three years in duration.)

Measures and procedures were the same as those employed in Study 2. In order to compensate participants for their time, respondents were offered the opportunity to opt into a prize draw to win an iPad.

6.2 Results

6.2.1 GENDER BIAS

The overall bias score of the sample was −0.04 (SD = 0.42), which does not differ significantly from the gender-neutral reference of 0 ($t(227)$ = −1.50, p = 0.136), thus indicating no gender bias. Comparison between male and female participants revealed a significant difference ($t(225)$ = −5.25, $p < 0.001$), indicating that males tend toward a male bias (M = −0.16, SD = 0.39), whereas females tend toward a female bias (M = 0.12, SD = 0.41). These biases were significant both for men ($t(128)$ = −4.73, $p < 0.001$) and for women ($t(97)$ = 2.86, p = 0.005).

This sample was very different from that in Study 2. There had been no particular effort to expose these students to women philosophers. Nonetheless, results were much the same. Males exhibited a significant male bias, and females a significant female bias.

6.3 Academic Experience

We explored again the impact of academic experience, and also its interaction with gender. We ran a 2 (gender: male vs. female) x 4 (academic year: first vs. second vs. third vs. fourth) ANOVA. When controlling for academic year the gender effect is still significant: F (1, 216) = 34.20, $p < 0.001$. In other words, regardless of academic experience with philosophy, women display a female bias, and men display a male bias. At the same time, when controlling for gender the effect of academic experience is also significant, F (3, 216) = 2.98, p = 0.032, and the interaction with gender is marginally significant, F (3, 216) = 2.42, p = 0.067. Post hoc test with Hochberg correction reveal that students in their fourth year of study tend toward a female bias as compared to students in their first or second year (p = 0.034, and 0.039; all other $ps > 0.181$). Moreover, pairwise comparisons on the interaction with gender show that men display the same male bias across all years (all ps = 1.000), whereas women display a much more pronounced female bias in their fourth year of studies as compared to the other years ($ps <$ 0.008; all other ps = 1.000). These effects are better understood by observing Figure 4, which clearly shows how the effect of academic experience is strongest

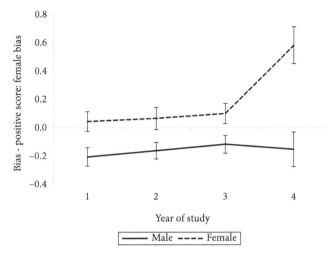

Figure 4. Interaction between gender and academic experience on gender bias. The more academic experience with philosophy, the greater in-group bias women display. Error bars indicate standard errors.

in women in their fourth year of study. However, as this group of participants was quite small (n = 9), we believe this result should be interpreted cautiously.

7 Discussion

The results of Study 3 pose two problems for the hypothesis based on Nosek and Smyth (2011)—that women who associate philosophy less strongly with female-ness drop out, leaving upper level women who associate philosophy more strongly with femaleness. The first problem is that in this study the level of association remained constant, not changing at all across years of study. The second problem is that in UK universities, dropping out is not an option in the same way that it is in the US. An undergraduate student is accepted *into a particular department*, and transferring to a different one is very difficult. Even students who want to change departments will often find that they cannot. In the US, by contrast, decisions about what subject to major in are not made until after two years of study, sampling different departments and seeking a place where one feels comfortable.

This study, then, provides yet more confirmation for a result that has held constant across all the studies undertaken: a tendency for men to associate philosophy with maleness and for women to associate it with femaleness. The levels of male bias found are certainly consistent with the thought that implicit bias against women philosophers might impede women's progress. But it is nonetheless surprising that women lack the tendency to display this bias. This is at odds with findings from STEM subjects (Cvencek et al., 2011; Nosek et al., 2002). Still, given the demographics of the field and the likelihood that important gatekeepers (teachers, editors, those hiring) will be male, it is plausible to suspect that implicit bias is a factor in women's underrepresentation.

Turning to stereotype threat, however, an overhasty but appealing thought might be that our results show it to be unlikely that women in philosophy suffer from stereotype threat: if women do not implicitly stereotype philosophy as male, why would it give rise to any stereotype threat for women? This worry, however, is misguided. Kiefer and Sekaquaptewa's (2007) study of women and mathematics examined the relationship between implicit stereotyping and stereotype threat. Stereotype threat was present for all subjects when tests were described as diagnostic of mathematics ability—a description known to provoke stereotype threat in women. It was only in situations designed to reduce stereotype threat (by describing the test as not diagnostic of mathematics ability) that level of implicit stereotyping bore a relationship to level of stereotype threat. Labelling the test as non-diagnostic only helped those women with weak or absent implicit stereotyping of mathematics as male. Moreover, they found that 'The performance of women who do not implicitly stereotype, i.e. who associate women with math, was most benefited by the reduction of stereotype threat' (Kiefer and Sekaquaptewa: 6). Crucially, the women who implicitly associated women with mathematics *did* suffer from stereotype threat—otherwise reducing stereotype threat would not have helped them. The fact that women in philosophy implicitly associate philosophy with femaleness, then, does not indicate that they will not suffer from stereotype threat (assuming that gender–mathematics implicit associations function similarly in these respects to gender–philosophy implicit associations). However, it does indicate that *if they do* it should be easier to reduce this than it might otherwise have been.

However, there is no room for stereotype threat without an awareness of a stereotype. Our next question, then, is whether women in philosophy explicitly associate it with maleness.

8 Study 4

In order to investigate the stereotype content of philosophers that students held, we adopted a two-step method (similar to Edwards, 1992; Madon, 1997; Rosenkrantz, Vogel, Bee, Broverman, and Broverman, 1968). The first step consisted of the free response procedure, whereby participants were invited to list as many traits as possible that describe the *typical* philosopher. This list of traits is then screened for synonyms and idiosyncratic responses, and in the second step of the procedure—the rating scale—the list is presented to a second sample of participants who evaluate how typical these traits are for philosophers. Details of the experimental procedures and results are described as follows.

8.1 Procedures

8.1.1 PHASE 1: FREE RESPONSE PROCEDURE

Participants were recruited among undergraduate philosophy students ($N = 71$,[9] F = 44.6%), and data were collected online using Qualtrics (Qualtrics Labs Inc, Provo, Utah). As a compensation for their participation, participants had the opportunity to opt into a prize raffle to win an Amazon Kindle.

After having collected informed consent, participants were presented with the following instructions:

> Please list all the traits and adjectives that come to mind when you think about the typical philosopher. You do not necessarily need to endorse these descriptors, or to think that they are accurate descriptions. We simply would like you to write down *any trait that comes to mind when thinking of the typical philosopher*, regardless of accuracy. Try to *include personality descriptors, behavioural descriptors, and also physical descriptors*, if you can. Please use adjectives and avoid sentences.

Participants were then asked to provide demographic data, and following that they were thanked for their time and fully debriefed.

The traits generated by participants were screened for synonyms (e.g. disorganized and unorganized, free thinker and free thinking) and idiosyncratic responses, as in Rosenkrantz et al. (1968). This procedure generated a final list of seventy-one traits.

8.1.2 PHASE 2: RATING SCALE

Participants were recruited among philosophy students ($N = 150$,[10] F = 48.0%), and data were collected online using Qualtrics (Provo, Utah). As a compensation for their participation, participants had the opportunity to opt into a prize raffle to win an Amazon Kindle.

Participants were presented with the list of traits generated in Phase 1, and were asked to rate their typicality for philosophers on a numerical scale (1 = very atypical; 7 = very typical). The traits were presented in random order to avoid presentation-order confounds.

---

[9] A total of eighty-eight people accessed the survey, but only seventy-one completed it.
[10] A total of 240 people accessed the survey, but only 150 completed it. Five of these participants submitted their responses, but did not provide demographic information, i.e. gender.

Table 2. List of traits that describe the typical philosopher. Ratings indicate the percentage of participants that evaluated the trait as fairly or very typical of philosophers, and the percentage of participants that evaluated the trait as fairly or very atypical of philosophers.

Trait	Atypical rating (%)	Typical rating (%)	Trait	Atypical rating (%)	Typical rating (%)
Questioning	1.33	78.00	Sceptical	2.04	60.54
Intellectual	2.67	76.67	Abstract	2.04	60.86
Curious	2.04	76.87	Argumentative	4.83	59.31
Educated	2.67	75.33	Logical	3.45	59.31
Opinionated	2.76	71.03	Observational	2.07	58.62
Intelligent	1.38	71.03	Insightful	3.40	57.14
Passionate	4.08	68.03	Deep	2.72	56.46
Contemplative	2.00	65.33	Dedicated	2.76	53.10
Analytical	1.36	63.27	Rational	4.08	50.34
Thoughtful	3.45	62.76	Wise	2.04	46.94
Studious	4.08	61.22	Male	2.76	46.21
Critical	1.38	60.69	Interesting	3.45	44.14
			Serious	1.36	40.14

Similarly to Madon (1997), we considered a trait to be part of the stereotype if they were believed to be fairly or very typical by more than 40% of the sample, and if at the same time they were believed to be fairly or very atypical by less than 5% of the sample.[11] This procedure generated a final list of twenty-five traits, which constitute the core of the stereotype of philosophers (see Table 2 for the list and the typicality ratings expressed by participants). A series of t-tests comparing typicality ratings for men and women detected no gender differences (all $ps >$ 0.100), with the exception of the trait 'rational', which elicited a marginally significant statistical difference ($t(143) = 1.81$, $p = 0.073$). This indicated that men rate the trait 'rational' typical of philosophers to a higher extent ($M = 5.40$, $SD = 1.37$) as compared to women ($M = 4.99$, $SD = 1.37$).

Of particular interest to this investigation is the presence of the trait 'male' in the stereotype, which suggests that when students think of a philosopher, they automatically think of a man. This was true of both male and female subjects. Also, it is relevant to point out that prior research has associated some of the other traits with men. Indeed, being analytical, along with being good at

---

[11] In the original procedure, Madon (1997) adopted a 10% cut-off point for atypicality rating (accepting traits which were considered atypical by up to 10% of subjects), whereas we adopted a more conservative approach in order to obtain a shorter list of core traits.

Table 3. List of traits that describe the typical philosopher; female participants only. Ratings indicate the percentage of participants that evaluated the trait as fairly or very typical of philosophers, and the percentage of participants that evaluated the trait as fairly or very atypical of philosophers.

Trait	Atypical rating (%)	Typical rating (%)	Trait	Atypical rating (%)	Typical rating (%)
Questioning	1.39	84.72	Passionate	4.17	62.50
Intellectual	2.78	81.94	Dedicated	4.17	55.56
Educated	1.39	76.39	Sceptical	1.39	55.56
Curious	2.78	75.00	Independent	2.78	52.78
Reader	1.39	73.61	Logical	1.39	51.39
Intelligent	1.38	72.22	Intense	4.17	48.61
Contemplative	4.17	68.06	Male	4.17	47.22
Analytical	1.39	68.06	Serious	0.00	41.67
Observational	2.78	66.66			

reasoning and at problem solving, are part of the cognitive traits that are perceived to more likely to be found in men rather than in women (Cejka, and Eagly, 1999; Diekman, and Eagly, 2000). Moreover, there is empirical evidence that being clever, rational, and intelligent is more desirable for men than for women, and that being rational is more typically thought to be a male trait. 'Intelligent' is the only term on the list that is typically associated with women, but it is worth bearing in mind that it is also thought to be less *desirable* in women than in men (Prentice and Carranza, 2002). There were very few interesting differences between women's and men's stereotypes of 'philosopher'. However, women did not have 'rational' as part of their stereotype, and men (but not women) had 'white' as part of theirs (see Tables 3 and 4).

It turned out that maleness is a part of the stereotype content of *philosopher* for both male and female philosophy students, as are several traits known to be associated with maleness—despite our earlier findings on implicit bias.

9 Concluding Discussion

The studies described here reveal a fascinating yet puzzling picture—and many directions for future study. These studies were motivated initially by a desire to explore the underpinnings for the implicit bias and stereotype threat explanations that have been suggested with respect to the underrepresentation of women in philosophy. In this section, then, we will review the implications of our findings for these explanations, identifying areas that merit future study.

Table 4. List of traits that describe the typical philosopher; male participants only. Ratings indicate the percentage of participants that evaluated the trait as fairly or very typical of philosophers, and the percentage of participants that evaluated the trait as fairly or very atypical of philosophers.

Trait	Atypical rating (%)	Typical rating (%)	Trait	Atypical rating (%)	Typical rating (%)
Curious	1.40	75.34	Argumentative	2.74	60.27
Educated	0.00	75.34	Contemplative	1.37	60.27
Reader	0.00	73.97	Thoughtful	1.37	60.27
Intellectual	1.37	72.60	Rational	2.74	58.90
Questioning	1.37	72.60	Insightful	2.74	54.79
Intelligent	1.37	69.86	Liberal	2.74	53.42
Critical	1.37	67.12	Dedicated	1.37	50.68
Logical	1.37	67.12	Deep	0.00	50.68
Opinionated	4.11	64.38	Independent	2.74	49.32
Sceptical	2.74	64.38	Male	1.37	46.57
Passionate	2.74	61.64	Wise	4.17	40.28
Abstract	0.00	61.64	Interesting	1.37	45.21
			White	4.11	41.10

We predicted that we would find a tendency on the part of both women and men to implicitly associate philosophy with maleness. We also expected that the degree to which philosophy is associated with maleness would increase with exposure to the subject at university level. This is precisely what we found—for men. It is very different from what we found for women. Both genders implicitly associate philosophy more strongly with femaleness if they spend a substantial amount of time reading feminist philosophy—an activity that would expose them to large numbers of female philosophers as counterstereotypical exemplars. Women, it seems, implicitly associate philosophy increasingly with femaleness. However, women are like men in *explicitly* associating philosophy with maleness.

We turn now to the issue of what these findings mean for the oft-discussed implicit bias and stereotype threat explanations for the underrepresentation of women in philosophy.

10 Implicit Bias

Men (other than those who read a lot of feminist philosophy) show a significant tendency to implicitly associate philosophy with maleness. This association, while significant, is small. But small levels of bias are known to have very significant effects, especially cumulatively (Kang et al., 2012; Valian, 1999). This by no means *demonstrates* that these men are manifesting these biases in their marking, hiring, mentoring, discussion-running, and reference-writing behavior. But there is a substantial body of literature showing the predictive validity of implicit bias scores (Greenwald et al., 2009). It would be very surprising if these biases were not having these sorts of real-world effects. Further studies would be needed to establish whether or not this is taking place. However, the presence of this implicit bias is a necessary condition for its manifestation. The studies discussed here demonstrate that this condition is met.

Women, surprisingly, do not have an implicit tendency to associate philosophy with maleness. Indeed, as they spend more time in philosophy they seem to implicitly associate it increasingly with femaleness. This means that women in philosophy are not likely to manifest one specific sort of implicit bias in their assessment of other women in philosophy—implicit biases which stem from associating *male* with *philosophy*. One should not, however, leap to the conclusion that women in philosophy will not be prone to implicit biases *tout court* in their assessments of other women's work. They are still quite likely to share the sorts of implicit biases that are widely shared in the culture—those that in general lead to women's work being assessed as less impressive than men's (Valian, 1999). And they may well have other relevant philosophy-specific biases, as discussed in more detail at the end of this chapter. All that these results show is that women may not be so prone to implicitly associate maleness with *philosophy*. One should also note, of course, that our findings show women philosophers to implicitly associate philosophy with femaleness. It is possible, then, that women philosophers may display implicit biases against *men in philosophy*. Importantly, this suggests yet another reason why one should take action such as instituting anonymous marking and CV review—not just to correct for possible biases against women in philosophy, but also for possible biases against men in philosophy.

11 Stereotype Threat

This investigation began with the thought that women in philosophy were likely to suffer stereotype threat, which could lead to both underperformance and departure from the subject. We expected to find that women implicitly associated philosophy with maleness, but instead we found that women studying philosophy increasingly implicitly associated philosophy with femaleness—an in-group bias that we did not expect to find. Our UK study allowed us to rule out drop-out rate as an explanation for this. However, we also found that male (and related items) are common components of the explicit stereotype for *philosopher*, which could plausibly serve to underpin stereotype threat amongst women in philosophy.[12] Interestingly, Sarah-Jane Leslie and colleagues have found that philosophers are some of the most likely to agree with the claim that women are less well suited than men to high-level work in their discipline. (The only fields with higher levels of agreement are mathematics, physics, computer science, engineering and Middle Eastern studies.) While none of this proves that women in philosophy are subject to stereotype threat (direct experiments to test this hypothesis need to be done), our work does suggest that some of the preconditions for stereotype threat are in place. Moreover, and very promisingly, it suggests that if women in philosophy do suffer from stereotype threat it should be easier to carry out threat-reducing interventions than it would have been if they had held the stereotype implicitly as well as explicitly.

Importantly, however, the findings of this chapter also indicate a need for revisions in some aspects of how philosophers think about gender and stereotype threat in philosophy. If these findings hold up, it is a mistake to suggest (as did Saul, 2013a) that stereotype threat for women in philosophy might be underpinned by an *implicit* association between philosophy and maleness—that association is explicit, but seems not to be implicit (though there might, as noted in the following, be an implicit association between logic or aggressive argumentation and maleness, which could also give rise to stereotype threat).

We now suggest several promising lines of inquiry for further investigation.

1. Why do women in philosophy increasingly implicitly associate philosophy with femaleness as they progress in the subject? This cannot be due to the departure of women who associate philosophy less strongly with femaleness, as the final sample was of a group for whom dropping out was not a viable option. Further studies need to be done to better understand this finding and what it means. It could simply be in-group bias, but this would leave unexplained why (a) the same does not happen in other fields, and (b) why the association increases with exposure to the overwhelmingly male profession. An alternative explanation might cast it as some sort of self-protective measure. Perhaps women react to the overwhelming maleness of the profession by seeking out writings by women authors, or female role models, which helps them to associate philosopher with femaleness.

2. If our findings here hold up in future work (see the following for some ways in which they may not), then it appears that women are more likely to explicitly stereotype philosophy as male than to implicitly do so. This is an

---

[12] We have not yet tested for the presence of stereotype threat among women in philosophy.

interesting fact, which raises many questions. A key question to explore is why this pattern holds in philosophy.

3. It is worth investigating whether there is an implicit association between *philosopher* and gender. The studies discussed in this chapter only tested for implicit associations with the subject *philosophy*, rather than with the role *philosopher*. If a mechanism could be found which would allow us to test the role rather than the subject, we might well find very different results.

4. It is possible that even if philosophy is not implicitly associated with maleness, certain things commonly found in philosophy may be. Possibilities include logic (likely to be stereotyped as male, due to spillover from mathematics), and (as argued by Beebee, 2013) aggressive discussion styles. These possibilities need to be investigated.

5. It remains possible that our findings on the Implicit Association Tests were due to choice of items. All cues used were visual cues, featuring philosophy journals and departments. It is possible that a different set of cues would produce different results. We plan to study this in future experiments.

6. We need to fully explore manifestations of implicit bias and stereotype threat in philosophy. We now know that the associations required to support these explanations for the underrepresentation of women are in place. But we do not know the extent to which these phenomena manifest themselves in behavior within philosophy. We need to conduct studies of each of these.

7. The pilot study showed what seemed to be a significant correlation between time spent reading feminist philosophy and gendered associations with philosophy (those who read more feminist philosophy associate philosophy more with femaleness and less with maleness). Several questions are raised by this.

   • What is the causal relationship? Most likely, reading feminist philosophy is affecting the associations that subjects have with philosophy. But we need to rule out the thought that those who already associate philosophy less with maleness have a tendency to seek out feminist philosophy.

   • What is doing the work, if the relationship is as suggested above? Is it the subject matter, or the fact that a much higher percentage of authors in this area are female than in other areas of the subject?

Acknowledgements

We are very grateful to many people for discussions of this material—so many, that we fear we have left some out: participants at the Implicit Bias and Philosophy workshops; the Intergroup Relations Lab at the University of Sheffield; Louise Antony, Elizabeth Barnes, Irene Blair, Michael Brownstein, Shannon Dea, Ray Drainville, Sally Haslanger,

Jules Holroyd, Tim Kenyon, Matthew Kopec, Carole Lee, Olivia Levinson, Neil Levy, Rachel McKinnon, Denise Sekaquaptewa, Paschal Sheeran, and Virginia Valian.

References

Adleberg, T., Thompson, M., and Nahmias, E. (2014). 'Do men and women have different philosophical intuitions? Further data'. *Philosophical Psychology* 28(5): 615–41.

Antony, L. (2012). 'Different voices or perfect storm: Why are there so few women in philosophy?' *Journal of Social Philosophy* 43(3): 227–55.

Appel, M., Kronberger, N., and Aronson, J. (2011). 'Stereotype threat impairs ability building: Effects on test preparation among women in science and technology'. *European Journal of Social Psychology*, 41(7): 904–13. doi:10.1002/ejsp.835.

Beebee, H. (2013). 'Women and Deviance in Philosophy'. In Hutchison, K. and Jenkins, F. (eds.), *Women in Philosophy: What Needs to Change?* Oxford: Oxford University Press: 61–80.

Beebee, H. and Saul, J. (2011). 'Women in philosophy in the UK: A report by the British Philosophical Association and the Society for Women in Philosophy in the UK'.

Bishop, G., Beebee, H., Goddard, E., and Rini, A. (2013). 'Seeing the Trends in the Data'. In Hutchison, K. and Jenkins, F. (eds.), *Women in Philosophy: What Needs to Change?* Oxford: Oxford University Press: 231–52.

Blair, I. (2002). 'The malleability of automatic stereotypes and prejudices'. *Personality and Social Psychology Review* 6: 242–61.

Brennan, S. (2013). 'Rethinking the moral significance of micro-inequities: The case of women in philosophy'. In Jenkins, F. and Hutchison, F. (eds.), *Women in Philosophy: What Needs to Change?* Oxford: Oxford University Press: 180–96.

Buckwalter, W. and Stich, S. (2011). 'Gender and philosophical intuition (final draft)'. In Knobe, J. and Nichols, S. (eds.), *Experimental Philosophy*, vol. 2. Oxford: Oxford University Press. Available at <http://ssrn.com/abstract=1966324>.

Cejka, M. A. and Eagly, A. H. (1999). 'Gender-stereotypic images of occupations correspond to the sex segregation of employment'. *Personality and Social Psychology Bulletin* 25(4): 413–23. doi:10.1177/0146167299025004002.

Cvencek, D., Meltzoff, A. N., and Greenwald, A. G. (2011). 'Math-gender stereotypes in elementary school children'. *Child Development* 82: 766–79. doi:10.1111/j.1467-8624.2010.01529.x.

Diekman, A. B. and Eagly, A. H. (2000). 'Stereotypes as dynamic constructs: Women and men of the past, present, and future'. *Personality and Social Psychology Bulletin* 26(10): 1171–88. doi:10.1177/0146167200262001.

Dougherty, T., Baron, S., and Miller, K. (2015). 'Female under-representation among philosophy majors: A map of the hypotheses and a survey of the evidence.' *Feminist Philosophy Quarterly* 1(1): Article 4.

Edwards, G. H. (1992). 'The structure and content of the male gender role stereotype: An exploration of subtypes'. *Sex Roles* 27(9–10): 533–51. doi:10.1007/BF00290008.

Forgas, J. P. (2011). 'She just doesn't look like a philosopher...? Affective influences on the halo effect in impression formation'. *European Journal of Social Psychology* 41: 812–17.

Friedman, M. (2013). 'Women in philosophy: Why should we care?' In Jenkins, F. and Hutchison, J. (eds.), *Women in Philosophy: What Needs to Change?* Oxford: Oxford University Press: 21–38.

Good, C., Aronson, J., and Harder, J. A. (2008). 'Problems in the pipeline: Stereotype threat and women's achievement in high-level math courses'. *Journal of Applied Developmental Psychology* 29(1): 17–28. doi:10.1016/j.appdev.2007.10.004.

Greenwald, A. G., McGhee, D. E., and Schwartz, J. L. K. (1998). 'Measuring individual differences in implicit cognition: The implicit association test'. *Journal of Personality and Social Psychology* 74(6). 1464–80. doi:10.1037/0022-3514.74.6.1464.

Greenwald, A. G., Nosek, B. A., and Banaji, M. R. (2003). 'Understanding and using the Implicit Association Test: I. An improved scoring algorithm'. *Journal of Personality and Social Psychology*, 85: 197–216. doi:10.1037/0022-3514.85.2.197

Greenwald, A. G., Poehlman, T. A., Uhlmann, E. L., and Banaji, M. R. (2009). 'Understanding and using the Implicit Association Test: III. Meta-analysis of predictive validity.' *Journal of Personality and Social Psychology* 97(1): 17–41.

Haslanger, S. (2008). 'Changing the ideology and culture of philosophy: Not by reason (alone)'. *Hypatia* 23(2): 210–23.

Hill, C., Corbett, C., and St Rose, A. (2010). *Why So Few? Women in Science, Technology, Engineering, and Mathematics. Association of University Women*: 134. <http://eric.ed. gov/ERICWebPortal/recordDetail?accno=ED509653>.

Jenkins, F. (2013). 'Singing the post-discrimination blues: Notes for a critique of academic meritocracy'. In Jenkins, F. and Hutchison, J. (eds.), *Women in Philosophy: What Needs to Change?* Oxford: Oxford University Press: 81–102.

Kang, J. et al. (2012). 'Implicit bias in the courtroom'. *UCLA Law Review* vol. 59, no. 5.

Kang, J. and Banaji, M. R. (2006). 'Fair measures: A behavioral realist revision of 'affirmative action'. *California Law Review* 94: 1063–118; University of California, Los Angeles, School of Law Research Paper No. 06-08.

Karpinski, A., and Steinman, R. B. (2006). 'The single category implicit association test as a measure of implicit social cognition'. *Journal of Personality and Social Psychology*, 91: 16–32. doi:10.1037/0022-3514.91.1.16.

Kennedy, K. M., Hope, K., and Raz, N. (2009). 'Life span adult faces: norms for age, familiarity, memorability, mood, and picture quality'. *Experimental Aging Research* 35(2): 268–75. doi: 10.1080/03610730902720638.

Kiefer, A. K. and Sekaquaptewa, D. (2007). 'Implicit stereotypes and women's math performance: How implicit gender-math stereotypes influence women's susceptibility to stereotype threat'. *Journal of Experimental Social Psychology* 43: 825–32. doi:10.1016/ j.jesp.2006.08.004.

Leslie, S., Cimpian, A., Meyer, M., and Freedland, E. (2015). 'Expectations of brilliance underlie gender distributions across academic disciplines'. *Science* 347(6219): 262–5.

Madon, S. (1997). 'What do people believe about gay males? A study of stereotype content and strength'. *Sex Roles* 37(9–10): 3–85. doi: 10.1007/BF02936334.

McKinnon, R. (2014). 'Stereotype threat and attributional ambiguity for trans women'. *Hypatia* 19(4): 857–72.

Moss-Racusin, C. et al. (2012). 'Science faculty's subtle gender biases favor male students'. *Proceedings of the National Academy of Sciences* 109(41): 16395–6.

Moulton, J. (1983). 'A paradigm of philosophy: The adversary method.' In Harding, S. and Hintikka, M. (eds.), *Discovering Reality*. New York, NY: Springer: 149–64.

Norlock, K. (2011). 'Women in the profession: 2011 update'. <http://www.apaonlinecsw.org/data-on-women-in-philosophy>.

Nosek, B. A., Banaji, M. R., and Greenwald, A. G. (2002). 'Math = male, me = female, therefore math not = me'. *Journal of Personality and Social Psychology* 83: 44–59. doi:10.1037/0022-3514.83.1.44.

Nosek, B. A. and Smyth, F. (2011). 'Implicit social cognitions predict sex differences in math engagement and achievement'. *American Educational Research Journal* 48(5): 1125–56.

Paxton, M., Figdor, C., and Tiberius, V. (2012). 'Quantifying the gender gap: An empirical study of the underrepresentation of women in philosophy'. *Hypatia* 27(4): 949–57.

Peters, D. P. and Ceci, S. J. (1982). 'Peer-review practices of psychological journals: The fate of published articles, submitted again'. *Behavioral and Brain Sciences* 5: 187–255.

Power, J. G., Murphy, S. T., and Coover, G. E. (1996). 'Priming prejudice: How stereotypes and counter-stereotypes influence attribution of responsibility and credibility among ingroups and outgroup'. *Human Communication Research* 23: 36–58. doi:10.1111/j.1468-2958.1996.tb00386.

Prentice, D. A. and Carranza, E. (2002). 'What women and men should be, shouldn't be, are allowed to be, and don't have to be: the contents of prescriptive gender stereotypes'. *Psychology of Women Quarterly*, 26(4): 269–81. doi:10.1111/1471-6402.t01-1-00066.

Rosenkrantz, P., Vogel, S., Bee, H., Broverman, I., and Broverman, D. M. (1968). 'Sex-role stereotypes and self-concepts in college students'. *Journal of Consulting and Clinical Psychology* 32(3): 287–95. doi:10.1037/h0025909.

Saul, J. (2013a). 'Implicit bias, stereotype threat and women in philosophy'. In Jenkins, F. and Hutchison, J. (eds.), *Women in Philosophy: What Needs to Change?* Oxford: Oxford University Press: 39–60.

Saul, J. (2013b). 'Philosophy has a sexual harassment problem'. *Salon*, 15 August 2013. <http://www.salon.com/2013/08/15/philosophy_has_a_sexual_harassment_problem/>.

Spencer, S. J., Steele, C. M., and Quinn, D. M. (1999). Stereotype threat and women's math performance. *Journal of Experimental Social Psychology*, 35, 4–28.

Steele, C. (2010). *Whistling Vivaldi: And Other Clues to How Stereotypes Affect Us*. New York: W. W. Norton.

Steinpreis, R., Anders, K., and Ritzke, D. (1999). 'The impact of gender on the review of the curricula vitae of job applicants and tenure candidates: A national empirical study'. *Sex Roles* 41(7–8): 509–28.

Valian, V. (1999). *Why So Slow? The Advancement of Women*. Cambridge, MA: MIT Press.

Index of Names

Alcoff, L. 168n16
Ambady, N. 118, 134
Amodio, D. M. 9, 11, 84–6, 90–1, 92n10, 93–4, 99
Anderson, E. 157n1, 169n18
Antony, L. M. 12–13, 191n1, 206, 284n3
Appiah, K. A. 142
Aristotle 240, 248, 250
Arnauld, A. 249
Aronson, J. 133–4, 137–9, 144–5, 148, 217–20

Banaji, M. R. 7–8, 88, 116, 238, 238n2, 239n3, 242–3, 287
Bargh, J. 65, 68, 106, 137–8, 147
Bayer, C. 206
Beeghly, E. 191n1
Bem, D. J. 114
Berkeley, G. 164
Bishop, M. 182–3
Blair, I. V. 118
Blair, J. A. 250n12
Blank, R. M. 271
Bodenhausen, G. V. 69
Bordo, S. 165
Borsuk, R. M. 271
Brownstein, M. S. 50n2, 60n6, 85
Burrows, L. 137

Cadinu, M. 143, 145
Carey, S. 180
Carnap, R. 160, 174
Carruthers, P. 31–2, 34, 39n14
Ceci, S. J. 14, 265–7, 269–71, 270n3, 273, 275–6
Cesario, J. 147
Chamberlain, W. 99
Chen, M. 137
Chomsky, N. 179–80
Cohen, G. 145, 226, 244–5, 260
Correll, J. 193
Crandall, C. S. 134, 148
Crockett, M. 56, 65n8
Cunningham., W. A. 116–17

Danaher, K. 134, 148
Darley, J. 134
Dasgupta, N. 48–9, 69, 71–2, 118
Daston, L. 260
Davies, P. 218
de Beauvoir, S. 248

De Houwer, J. 4n13, 105n2
Descartes, R. 26
Devine, P. G. 86, 88, 90–1, 92n10, 94–5, 99
Di Bella, L. 12, 14
Doyen, S. 137
Du Bois, W. E. B. 230
Dweck, C. 140

Eberhardt, J. L. 210
Egan, A. 13, 191–4, 194n5, 199n11, 209
Einstein, A. 178
Eitam, B. 203, 204n19
Epstein, S. 121
Erman, S. 167

Fazio, R. H. 7, 87, 105n2, 109, 117, 119
Fodor, J. 132
Forbes, C. 139
Fordham, S. 140
Forgas, J. P. 285n5
Fox, M. F. 274
Frankish, K. 10–11
Freud, S. 104, 109–10, 109n10
Fricker, M. 159n5, 227–8, 230
Fryer, R. 141

Gawronski, B. 69, 118
Gelman, S. A. 187
Gendler, T. S. 12–13, 82, 108–10, 137n6, 191–4, 195n7, 197, 199n11, 209, 222–3
Gigerenzer, G. 181–2
Ginther, D. K. 270n3
Goguen, S. 12–14
Gollwitzer, P. M. 206, 208
Good, C. 145
Grafman, J. 65
Greenwald, A. G. 7–8, 69, 108, 118–20, 287, 292
Grice, P. 253–5
Guo, S. 268

Hacking, I. 141–2
Hamblin, C. L. 250
Han, H. A. 202n16
Harder, J. A. 145
Hardin, C. 88, 118
Haslanger, S. 93–4, 222, 232, 284–5
Hempel, C. G. 177, 179
Henderson, D. 181

Hicks, D. 169n20
Higgins, E. T. 203, 204n19
Holcomb, J. E. 210
Holroyd, J. 10–11, 67
Horgan, T. 181
Huebner, B. 10–11
Hume, D. 164, 176
Hundleby, C. 12, 14

Inzlicht, M. 219n6, 224n12
Ivie, R. 268

James, W. 28
Jenkins, K. 232
Johns, M. 139, 145–7
Johnson, D. 70
Johnson, R. H. 250, 258
Jordan, M. 69, 99
Jost, J. T. 238, 238n2, 240–5, 257

Kahane, H. 242
Kahneman, D. 181, 192, 203
Kang, S. 224n12
Karpinski, A. 287
Kawakami, K. 99
Kay, A. C. 238
Kiefer, A. K. 298
Kim, B. 195n8
Kleinberg, F. 187
Kriegel, U. 108–9
Kuhn, T. 177–9
Kunda, Z. 204n19

Lee, C. J. 12, 14
Lee, M. R. 118
Lenton, A. P. 118
Leslie, A. 180
Leslie, S.-J. 186–7, 304
Lindsey, S. 108
Lloyd, E. 254–5
Locke, J. 163, 249, 257
Longino, H. 157n1, 168–70, 178
Lowery, B. S. 118
Luther King, M., Jr. 69–70
Lynch, C. I. 134

Ma, J. E. 118
McConahay, J. 7n14
Machery, E. 10–11, 67
McKinnon, R. 217, 221–2, 232
Macrae, C. 61, 92n10
Madon, S. 300
Madva, A. M. 12–13, 91n9, 99
Mallon, R. 10–12, 222
Mandelbaum, E. 50
Mendoza, S. A. 206
Miles, E. 12, 14

Mill, J. S. 164
Mills, C. W. 196n9
Milne, E. 65
Morewedge, C. K. 192, 203
Moskowitz, G. B. 204–5
Moss-Racusin, C. A. 172, 270
Mueller, A. 118

Nagel, T. 166
Nicole, P. 249
Niv, Y. 57
Nosek, B. A. 87–8, 95, 116, 238, 242–3, 287, 294, 297

Obama, B. 106
Ogbu, J. U. 140
Okruhlik, K. 245n8
Olson, M. A. 87, 117
Oswald, F. L. 120

Park, J. H. 118
Pashler, H. 137
Pavlov, I. 52
Payne, B. K. 206
Peck, T. C. 118
Peters, D. P. 271
Pittinsky, T. L. 134
Plato 110, 199
Potter, E. 168n16
Preacher, K. J. 116
Putnam, H. 186

Quadflieg, S. 61
Quine, W. V. 160, 165n14, 174–9

Rescorla, R. 52
Richeson, J. A. 118
Ridgeway, C. L. 241
Rosenkrantz, P. 299
Ross, L. D. 145
Rudman, L. A. 118
Rydell, R. J. 118
Ryle, G. 122–3

Sartre, J.-P. 211
Sassenberg, K. 204–5
Saul, J. 12–14, 81–3, 81n1, 141n9, 157–63, 166, 171–2, 183, 185, 188, 284–5
Schaller, M. 118
Schmader, T. 137n5, 139, 144n10, 148, 219n6
Schooler, T. Y. 108
Schwitzgebel, E. 24–7, 29–30, 122–3
Sekaquaptewa, D. 298
Sheeran, P. 205, 208
Sherman, S. J. 116
Shih, M. 134, 136–8, 147–8, 201n15
Sinclair, S. 118

Sjomerling, M. 134
Skinner, B. F. 164, 164n12
Smyth, F. 294, 297
Socrates 110
Soon, W.-H. 173n29
Spelke, E. 180
Spencer, S. 167, 204n19, 217–20
Staples, B. 133, 142
Steele, C. 133–4, 137–9, 143–5, 148, 216–20, 225–6, 228, 284
Steinman, R. B. 287
Stewart, B. D. 206
Stone, J. 134, 137, 142
Stricker, L. J. 134, 148
Sweetman, J. 10–11, 67

Tavris, C. 246–7
Tetlock, P. E. 209–10
Torelli, P. 141
Townsend, S. 220
Twain, M. 30

Uhlmann, E. L. 244–5, 260

Valian, V. 94, 191n1, 193, 199, 241, 248, 248n10, 266n2

Walton, D. 14, 239, 250–3, 250n12, 255–6, 258
Walton, G. 167, 172, 226
Ward, W. C. 134, 148
Ware, E. A. 187
Webb, T. L. 205
Williams, J. E. 239
Williams, M. R. 210
Williams, W. 14, 265–7, 269–71, 270n3, 273, 275–6
Wilson, T. D. 108–9
Wittgenstein, L. 224, 227

Yeager, D. S. 145
Yoffe, E. 258–9

Zanna, M. P. 238

Index of Subjects

absentmindedness 29–30
acceptance 33, 37
acting white theory 140–1
akrasia 30
approach/avoidance behavior 10, 60, 62, 92, 98–9
association
  action-outcome 51–68
  affective 11, 86–100
  encoded 49–50, 59–63
  extrapersonal 202n16
  implicit 11, 15, 64, 80, 87, 91, 95, 98–100, 284–5
  mechanisms of 51
  non-propositional 113
  philosophy and gender association 286–305
  propositional 112
  semantic 11, 86–100
  valence 93–4
associative functions
  associative learning 51–2, 69
  associative processes 8, 36, 49–51, 56–7, 66–7, 69, 86, 93, 135n4
  associative states 29, 35
  associative systems 50–62, 67–71
attitude 28
  abstract 49
  accessibility 8, 13, 50, 67, 192, 195, 200–8
    hyperaccessibility 199n12
  alief 108, 137n6
  ambivalent 124
  contextual variance 50–1, 56, 119
  explicit 104
  formal object of 105
  implicit 7, 104
  intensity 28
  introspective (un)availability 8, 25, 31, 106, 159
  malleability 8n15
  non-propositional 29
  propositional 8–9, 27–42, 105, 122n15, 131–42
  social 7, 49
  valence 28, 105, 114, 123–4
  unconscious 25, 104
automaticity 7–11, 35, 49–51, 68–70, 82–3, 106–20, 131–49, 160, 193–5, 202–4, 219n6, 256–73, 284–5, 300
awareness of bias 2n6, 26, 68, 81, 82n2, 248

beliefs
  ascription 32
  avowal 32–3, 157, 243
  background 27–8, 147, 210
  commitment 12, 23, 32–43, 143, 195, 242–7
  dispositional 108–11, 122
  explicit 23, 31–42, 96, 144
  false 32, 158
  implicit 25–43
  self-ascription 32
  Spinozist fixation 41
bias content 87–96, 162
  androcentrism 14, 239–56
  aversive: *see* difference in explicit and implicit states
  competence evaluation 91–9, 216
  gender 12–14, 172, 183–5, 238n1, 260, 265–76, 288–305
  in-group preference 6, 248, 294–304
  out-group 197, 242
  racial 24–36, 63–71, 99, 183, 192n2, 193, 206
  status quo 14, 239–60
bias functions 87–96, 105–10
brain networks 54–60, 63–4, 70

case studies of implicit bias
  capital punishment 210
  conversations 157
  CV/resume evaluation 2, 80, 85, 97, 269–70, 285, 303
  forbidden base rates case 209–11
  grading of student work 24–6, 32, 42, 157, 285
  journal acceptance 157
  orchestra auditions 166, 184, 248
  shooter bias study 2, 48, 65, 70, 85, 206
  standardized tests 130, 167
climate 233–4
cognitive behavioral theory 140
cognitive dissonance 240–60
cognitive load 42, 65–8, 130, 138–49, 195, 220, 274–5
cognitive mechanisms 219–23
cognitive structure 88, *see also* theory of mind models
cognitivist revolution 179
computational accounts 10, 36, 47–71, 162–82, 203

difference in explicit and implicit states 24,
    29–30, 88, 104, 144, 273–4
diversity 167–72, 274n7

effects of bias 2, 25, 31, 41–3, 48, 83–4, 89,
    98–100, 158–9, 240, 249–50, 259–60,
    272–3
egalitarian ideals 1, 47, 49, 68, 70–3, 114, 191,
    200, 204, 207–8, 273–4
empiricism
    behaviorism 164, 179
    conception of mind 163–4
    logical positivism 163, 174
epistemology
    arguments to the best explanation 115
    communities of knowers 168
    epistemic agency 12–13, 259–60, 183, 222,
        226–32, 257
    epistemic cost 195–206, 222–5
    epistemic injustice 12, 216, 225–31
    epistemic integrity 163
    epistemic norms 161–2, 166n15, 198
    epistemic self-esteem 159, 228
    epistemic value 167–8
    epistemic virtue 168–9, 208
    individualist conception of epistemic
        subject 168
    justification 177
    naturalistic 160–1, 175
    objectivity 163–74, 239, 256–60
    philosophical thought experiments 158, 180,
        223
    reliability 158, 181
    safe epistemology 181
    self-deception 25
    situatedness 180–1
    skepticism 12–13, 157–63, 166, 171, 183,
        185, 188
    testimony 37, 164, 182, 230, 249–50
    underdetermination 162, 165, 168, 175
    warrant 158, 161, 176
equal opportunity 186
evolutionary explanations 197
    conservative hypotheses 176
    'folk' psychology 23, 131, 150, 180
    Law of Effect 53
    niche construction 47, 71–3
explicit cognition 37

fallacies 239–60
fear conditioning 9, 60
female orgasm 246–60
feminist critique 168, 238
Feminist Philosophers (blog) 286
fixed vs. growth mindsets 140–2
frames: see stereotypes

generic expressions 186–8
grammatical categories 180–1

heterogeneity of bias 80–100
heuristics 36, 158, 180–1, 184, 207–8

institutional change 192, 266, 273
interracial relationships 245

just world hypothesis 240
justice 185

knowledge
    a priori 159–63, 172
    accessibility 192, 200–4
    of stereotypes 194–210
    scientific 173
    self 31, 114
    social 191

language acquisition 164n12, 179
linguistic ambiguity 253

measures of implicit bias
    Affect Misattribution Procedure 6,
        108, 113
    Affective Priming Task 85, 108, 117
    dream interpretation 110
    Extrinsic Affective Simon Task 108
    Implicit Association Test 2, 4, 24n2, 43n16,
        49, 85, 108, 112, 116–20, 159, 238, 265,
        286–92
    Implicit Association Test correlations 90,
        116–20
    Implicit Association Test manipulations 60
    Go/No-go Association Task 6, 49, 108
    multinominal (formal process) model 6
    predictive value 119, 303
    Quadruple Process Model 7
    Rorschach test 110
    Semantic Priming Task 6, 108
    verbal slip interpretation 110
mental architecture 181
    domain-general mechanism 164
    domain-specific mechanism 179
    innate mental structure 165
    mental shortcut 181–3
    modules 180
    natural cognitive kind 162n9
    nativism 174–6
mental disorder
    dissociative identity disorder 141
    multiple personality disorder 123, 141
    postpartum depression 227–8
    symptom "scripts" 141–2
mitigation strategies 11, 132, 159–60

active control of reasoning 40, 139
anonymity 15, 166, 248
belief eradication 37
belief override 10, 29, 32, 37–44, 108,
    240–2, 259
counter-stereotypical thoughts 206–8
counterstereotypical exemplars 286–302
creativity 204–11
critiques of 81, 84, 98–100
design-stance 160
diversity-dedicated programs 274
environmental modification 68
gender-equity programs 266
if-then plans, see implementation intentions
imagination 68–73
implementation intentions 70–1, 205–7
institutional structures 275
linguistic reform 188
narrative engagement 70
positive contact 72
self-control 36–43
social decision-making 276–8
value-driven aversions 63
moral-epistemic dilemma 192–211
    Sartrian unresolvable conflicts 211
motivation 54–6, 65–8, 94, 136, 140, 147, 218,
        221, 232, 240–1, 273, 276
    metacognitive 10, 40–3
    rational 48
    reflexive 48

naïve inductivism 177
naturalistic philosophy 15
non-reductive materialism 107
norms 30, 36, 63–4, 73, 82, 254–5
    discursive 253
    fairness 24
    social 37, 41, 54, 62–3, 72
    see also epistemic norms

OCEAN model 111
ontological status 107, 232
ontic injustice 232

pavlovian systems 10, 51–3, 56–68, 71
performative utterances 32
poverty of the stimulus 189, 196–7
philosophy (the discipline) 3, 232, 246
practical reasoning 26–9, 135
privilege 240–8

rational choice theory 140
rational reconstruction 174
reason-based explanation 131
reproduction 247
"reverse discrimination" 171

schema: see stereotypes
scientific reasoning 173–80
    conservatism 178
    dogmatism 178
    paradigm 177
self-reported attitudes 2, 88–9, 193
sincerity 32–3
skepticism 12–13, 157–63, 166, 171, 183,
        185, 188
social group membership 1, 58–9, 85,
        141–2, 157
    in-group 6, 196, 239, 248, 294–304
    looping effect of human kinds 141
    out-group 6, 49, 60–4, 70, 196–7,
        242–3
    racial categories 48–9, 48n1, 86–7, 93–4, 185,
        217n2
social-institutional forces 192
speech act 34, 114–15
STEM fields 265–76, 284
stereotypes 93, 146, 158, 266
    accuracy 200, 256, 299
    gendered 12–15, 24, 92, 130, 134, 145–8,
        192, 228–9, 239, 245–6, 271–4,
        294–304
    hierarchical 239n3, 239n5, 248
    irrational 216, 229–31
    philosopher 298–301
    racial 2, 24–9, 48–51, 61–3, 71–3, 82, 90–4,
        98–9, 125, 206, 228–9, 243–5, 257
    subhuman status 229–30
    suppression 82, 160n6, 194–207
stereotype threat 9, 130–50, 167, 216–34,
        284, 298
    belonging uncertainty 226
    devaluation 221
    domain avoidance 220–34, 285
    false consciousness 238–44
    global uncertainty 226–7
    priming 130–51, 245
    psychological disengagement 220–34
    self-doubt 216, 223, 230
    self-worth 220
    sense of self 216, 225
    spillover 224–5
    stereotype activation 137
    stereotype threat reducing intervention
        285, 304
    underperformance 133–5, 217–23, 285
structure-sensitive grammar rules 179–80
system justification motive 238–60

theory of mind models
    Descartes/transparency model 26
    dual-process model 8–10, 23, 34–6,
        130–50, 158

theory of mind models (*cont.*)
    Personal/Subpersonal 11, 33–7, 130–1, 162
    System 1/System 2 83n3, 130–50, 158–9,
       162n9
  Freudian model 105–10
  Memory Systems Model 9
  Meta-Cognitive Model 8
  model-based systems 57–67
  model-free systems 58–67
  single-process model 8

traits/multitrack dispositions 11, 28, 67, 105,
   110–25

underrepresentation 222
  women 3, 24, 265–6, 276, 284–5, 298, 301–5
  people of color 3
upshots for empirical psychology research 100,
   124, 304–5

working memory 31, 35, 42, 57, 64–5, 70, 139